C0-AGZ-102

The Dictionary
of
Historical and Comparative
Linguistics

For Jan,
"just like two schoolkids"

The Dictionary
of
Historical and Comparative
Linguistics

R. L. Trask

FITZROY DEARBORN PUBLISHERS
CHICAGO • LONDON

© R. L. Trask, 2000

Published in the United Kingdom by
Edinburgh University Press Ltd
22 George Square, Edinburgh

Published in the United States of America by
Fitzroy Dearborn Publishers
919 North Michigan Avenue,
Chicago, Illinois 60611

Typeset in Ehrhardt
by Bibliocraft Ltd, Dundee, and
printed and bound in Great Britain
by The University Press, Cambridge

A Cataloging-in-Publication
record for this book is available from
the Library of Congress

ISBN 1-57958-218-4 Fitzroy Dearborn

All rights reserved, including the
right of reproduction in whole or in
part or in any form

Contents

Preface

Historical linguistics was the first branch of linguistics to be placed on a firm scholarly footing, around the beginning of the nineteenth century, and for most of that century the study of language was virtually synonymous with its historical study. Like any discipline, historical linguistics has generated a sizeable number of specialist terms, and it continues to generate new terms today. Yet, in spite of all this, our venerable discipline has never received a dictionary devoted to its terminology. This book is an attempt to put that right.

It provides thorough coverage of the terminology of classical historical linguistics, including particularly Indo-European studies: **umlaut, palatalization, transferred sense,** *Schwebeablaut,* **lenition,** *sandhi, visarga,* **loss of the conditioning environment** and hundreds of other traditional terms are entered and explained. Also included are older terms which are now little encountered in the literature, like **proethnic, media aspirata, agglutination theory, crasis** and **grammatical change.**

Techniques of comparison and reconstruction, and the pitfalls they present, are well covered: **internal reconstruction, top-down reconstruction, indeterminacy, beech-tree problem, semantics control problem, overlapping correspondences, total accountability principle, portmanteau reconstruction** and many others. Particular attention is given to instances of faulty methodology: **"reaching down", edited evidence, neglect of known history, false segmentation** and others.

All the named 'laws' and processes I have been able to track down are entered: **Verner's Law, Bartholomae's Law, Saussure's Law, Dahl's Law,** *rendaku,* **Caland's Law, Whorf's Law, Dorsey's Law, Caldwell's Law,** the **Great Vowel Shift,** the **Great Tone Split,** the **First Palatalization** and many others.

Our companion discipline of dialectology is well represented: **dialect geography, dialect mixing, relic area, peripheral-region criterion, discontinuous spread, buffer zone** and others.

Also entered are named processes of word-formation: **clipped form, acronym, stump compound,** *bahuvrīhi,* **back-formation, calque** and others.

Specifically philological terms are well represented: **diplomatic, codex, by-name, lacuna,** *lectio difficilior,* **stemma, gloss** and others.

Treatment is provided equally, however, for the blizzard of new terms which have been coined, or have become prominent, only in recent years: **metatypy, exaptation, Traugott progression, rule inversion, esoteric language, entrenchment, multilateral comparison, phonogenesis, panchrony, Northern Cities Shift** and hundreds of others.

The vastly illuminating sociolinguistic study of language change has produced a sizeable number of new terms, among them **Bill Peters effect, lexical diffusion, actuation, speaker-oriented framework, variable rule, vernacularization, lower-middle-class crossover, historicization,** all included here together with many others.

Pidgin and creole studies, and contact and convergence phenomena generally, are covered in some detail: **non-genetic language, recreolization, abrupt creolization, post-creole continuum, mixed language, portmanteau language** and others.

The most prominent language families are entered, together with the names of the chief branches of the largest ones: **Indo-European, Uralic, Dravidian, Sino-Tibetan, Athabaskan, Pama-Nyungan, Afro-Asiatic, Celtic, Samoyed, Burmese-Lolo, Benue-Congo** and others. Also entered are the names of proposed larger groupings which are not generally accepted at present, together with assessments of their degree of acceptance: **Nostratic, Khoisan, Indo-Pacific, Aztec-Tanoan, Na-Dene, Penutian** and all the others which I have found in the literature.

Names of individual languages are entered only when the named language is an isolate, is the sole member of one branch of a large family, is extinct, or is of surpassing importance: **Basque, Yuchi, Greek, Armenian, Sumerian, Lepontic, Sicel, French, Arabic, Hebrew** and many others.

I have devoted particular attention to very recent work which has so far not made it into the standard textbooks, at least not prominently: notably, population typology (**accretion zone, genetic marker**), mathematical and computational methods (**probabilistic approach, Oswalt shift test, Monte Carlo test, best-tree approach**), models of linguistic descent (**crystallization model, rake model, social-network model, punctuated-equilibrium model**) and grammaticalization (**actualization, emergent grammar, grammaticalization chain, unidirectionality**).

Moreover, I have carefully entered the various Latin phrases and abbreviations used in historical and philological work, including a few which are not peculiar to us: *vel sim.*, *cf.*, *qq.v.*, *v. infra*, *apud*, *pace*, *err.*, *id.*, *ms.*, *om.*, *sc.*, *s.v.*, *passim*, among others. Under their names, I have also entered a number of symbols and notational conventions which occur in our work with special functions: **question mark, square brackets, capital letters, pipe, swung dash, equal sign, slash, hyphen, asterisk** and many others. A list of these can be found on the next page.

Finally, I have been careful to enter certain everyday historical terms which are commonplace in our field but often exasperatingly difficult for beginning students to look up, such as **mediation, comparandum, secondary, economy, reflex,** and the proper use of **common, Pre-** and **Proto-** preceding the names of languages or of families.

Wherever it seemed helpful to do so, I have provided both real linguistic examples of the term entered and references to the original literature.

I hope that colleagues and students everywhere will find this dictionary a valuable resource.

List of Symbols Entered

angle brackets	< >
asterisk	*
capital letter	N, R, V etc.
dagger (obelos)	†
dash	—
division sign	÷
equal sign	=
exclamation mark	!
hyphen	-
parentheses	( )
pipe	|
plus sign	+
question mark	?
shaftless arrow	> , <
slash	/
square brackets	[ ]
square-root sign	$\sqrt{}$
swung dash (tilde)	~

List of Abbreviations

abl.	ablative
AUX	auxiliary
C	consonant
Eng	English
Fr	French
gen.	genitive
Ger	German
Gk	Greek
Go	Gothic
IE	Indo-European
It	Italian
Lat	Latin
ME	Middle English
N	nasal
nom.	nominative
NP	noun phrase
O	object
OE	Old English
OFr	Old French
OHG	Old High German
OIc	Old Icelandic
ON	Old Norse
p.c.	personal communication
PIE	Proto-Indo-European
pl.	plural
R	resonant
RP	received pronunciation
Russ	Russian
S	subject
sg.	singular
Skt	Sanskrit
V	vowel; verb
VP	verb phrase

List of Tables

Acknowledgements

In the writing of this dictionary, I have received advice and assistance of various kinds from dozens of colleagues: answers to queries, advice on vexed points, references to the literature, copies of published and unpublished work, and more. Most of this assistance came via the HISTLING electronic list, maintained by Dorothy Disterheft. All of the following have provided assistance: Rich Alderson, Phil Baldi, Jacob Baltuch, E. Bashir, Alan Bomhard, Lars Borin, Vit Bubenik, Lyle Campbell, Miguel Carrasquer Vidal, Richard Coates, John Costello, Peter Daniels, Scott Delancey, Guy Deutscher, Aharon Dolgopolsky, Isidore Dyen, Chris Ehret, Hans-Olav Engel, Alice Faber, Suzanne Fleischmann, Stefan Georg, Mark Robert Hale, Leonard Herzenberg, John Hewson, Richard Hogg, Martin Huld, Ernst Håkon Jahr, Richard Janda, Carol Justus, Harold Koch, Bh. Krishnamurti, Paul Lloyd, Marisa Lohr, Alexis Manaster Ramer, Witold Mańczak, Sam Martin, Lars Mathieson, April McMahon, Peter Michalove, Gary Miller, Donka Minkova, Marianne Mithun, David Nash, Johanna Nichols, Derek Nurse, Marc Picard, Jim Rader, Robert Rankin, Colin Renfrew, Don Ringe, Gonzalo Rubio, Steven Schaufele, Eric Schiller, Vitalij Shevoroshkin, Sergei Starostin, Sally Thomason, Theo Vennemann, Sasha Vovin, Benji Wald, Max Wheeler, Robert Whiting, Laura Wright and Roger Wright – and probably a few more whom I have embarrassingly overlooked. To all of them I am deeply grateful; the book is much better than it could have been without their help. Further, I am profoundly indebted to Dorothy Disterheft, who commented extensively, and very valuably, on a draft of the whole book. Naturally, these people do not necessarily share the views expressed in the book and any shortcomings remain my own responsibility.

The Dictionary of Historical and Comparative Linguistics

A

abduction A type of reasoning in which we observe a result, invoke a general law which could derive that result from a given starting point, and conclude that that starting point must be true. Example: 'Communists want to ban handguns; Susie wants to ban handguns; therefore Susie must be a Communist.' Such reasoning is invalid but it appears to be important in human affairs. The linguist Henning Andersen has particularly stressed the importance of abductive reasoning in accounting for certain types of linguistic change, such as **reanalysis**. Andersen distinguishes between an *abductive mode of innovation*, in which elements of grammar are inferred from speech, and a *deductive mode of innovation*, in which elements of speech are derived from a grammar. In the abductive mode, a speaker reasons as follows: 'I have heard someone utter U; utterance U could be produced by a rule R; therefore R must be a rule of the grammar.' In the deductive mode, the reasoning is different: 'My grammar has a rule R; if I apply R in the present case I will get U; therefore I will say U.' An example of the first: 'I have heard people saying things like *books* and *trees*; therefore there must be a rule of English that nouns are pluralized by adding *-s*.' An example of the second: 'I have a rule that nouns are pluralized by adding *-s*; I have just encountered the new noun *CD-ROM*; therefore its plural must be *CD-ROMs*.' When one of these processes leads to a change in the language, we speak of *abductive change* or of *deductive change*, respectively. See Andersen (1973) for the original account, Andersen (1980) for further discussion and Anttila (1989: 196–203) for a survey.

aberrant formation A new lexical item constructed in an anomalous manner which is at variance with ordinary patterns of word-formation, or the process of forming a word in such a manner. Examples include English *typist* (for expected **typer*), the Turkish Language Academy's proposed *inerçıkar* 'lift, elevator' (literally, 'it-goes-down-it-goes-up') and Basque *aurrehistoria* 'prehistory' (literally, 'front-history'), which competes with the regular formation *historiaurre* (literally, 'history-front').

1

aberrant language A language which clearly belongs to an established family but which has undergone such complex changes that its prehistory cannot be worked out in any detail, and hence its precise location within the family cannot be determined with confidence. Such a language may fail to exhibit regular systematic correspondences with other members of the family, it may be typologically highly divergent within its family, recognizable cognates may be few, and the language may be of minimal assistance in reconstructing its proto-language. The term has been particularly applied by Grace (1981, 1990, 1996) to certain problematic Austronesian languages, especially to some of those in New Caledonia. The opposite is an **exemplary language**.

Abkhaz-Adyge (also **Northwest Caucasian**) A family of five languages spoken in and near the Caucasus to the east of the Black Sea. There are three subgroups: *Abkhazan* (*Abkhaz* and *Abaza*), *Circassian* (*Adyge* and *Kabardian*) and the single language *Ubykh* (now extinct).

ablaut (also **apophony, vowel gradation**) In IE languages, variation in the vowel of a root for grammatical purposes, as in English *sing/sang/sung*, when this derives from PIE and not from more recent assimilations, as in **umlaut**. Ablaut is prominent in the older IE languages and was apparently a central morphological feature of PIE; it may well have been conditioned by the word-accent at some early stage, but its occurrence is completely morphologized in the older IE languages, and the absence of any clear phonological conditioning factor is commonly taken as part of the definition. In PIE, a root could appear in any of five forms, with any one of the nuclei /e/, /o/, /ē/, /ō/ or Ø (zero), though few if any roots are attested in all five, and the original system was largely disrupted in most of the daughter languages, with various forms being preserved. For example, PIE **ped-* 'foot' appears as *ped-* in Latin, as *pod-* in Greek, as **pōd-* in Germanic **fōt-*, and as *pd-* (among others) in Sanskrit. English *sing/sang/sung* continues PIE **sengwh-* / **songwh-* / **sn̥gwh-*. A series of such forms distinguished by ablaut is an **ablaut series** (Ger *Ablautsreihe*).

The variant with /e/ is called the *e-grade*, while that with /o/ is the *o-grade*, formerly also called the *deflected grade* or *Abtönung*.

The contrast between /e/ and /o/, and also between /ē/ and /ō/, is *qualitative ablaut*, while that between /Ø/, /e/ and /ē/, and between /Ø/, /o/ and /ō/, is *quantitative ablaut*. The nuclei /e/ and /o/ are called the *full grade* (German *Vollstufe, Normalstufe* or

Hochstufe, French *degré plein*, Sanskrit *guṇa*); the nuclei /ē/ and /ō/ represent the *lengthened grade* (German *Dehnstufe*, French *degré long*, Sanskrit *vṛddhi*); and Ø is the *zero grade* (German *Nullstufe* or *Schwundstufe*, French *degré zéro*; the Sanskrit grammarians took this grade as basic and had no name for it). A *reduced grade* (German *Reduktionsstufe*), or *schwa secundum*, proposed by Hirt and notated as /ₑ/, is no longer generally recognized, since the forms supporting it are more economically explained by the introduction of **laryngeals** and the action of **Sievers's Law** (sense 1).

For discussion, see Beekes (1995: 164–167), from which this account is largely taken, Watkins (1998: 51–53) or another handbook of IE, and see Anttila (1989: ch. 12) for an example. See **Schwebeablaut** and *samprasāraṇa*, and compare **umlaut**. See also **accent in PIE**.

The term *ablaut* is also applied to similar phenomena in languages outside IE, such as Kartvelian. Coates (1994) recommends restricting *ablaut* to the historical change which brings such an alternation about and using **apophony** for the resulting alternation.

abnatural development The term applied by Bailey (1996 and elsewhere) to any linguistic change best interpreted as resulting from socio-communicative pressures, such as a shift from synthetic to analytic structures. Compare **connatural development**.

abnormal change Another term for **unnatural change**.

abnormal transmission A label sometimes applied to the development of a **non-genetic language**.

Abnutzung (Ger 'abrasion') The phonological reduction of grammatical morphemes of high frequency, which is typically greater than the degree of reduction suffered by other elements. For example, English *going to* is often reduced to *gonna* when serving as a grammatical marker, as in *I'm going to do it*, but the same sequence cannot be so reduced when *going* represents a lexical verb, as in *I'm going to the beach*.

aboriginal language Another term for **indigenous language**, now little used.

abrupt creolization The process in which a **creole**, instead of developing normally from an earlier **pidgin**, is constructed directly from existing mother tongues in a single generation; the result is an **early-creolized creole**. It is not clear how often this happens, or even if it happens, but there are a few plausible candidates, such as Pitcairnese, which derived from the English and Tahitian of a handful of settlers. See Thomason and Kaufman (1988: 48, 147–166) for discussion; these authors suggest that abrupt creolization should be understood as resulting from 'extreme unsuccessful acquisition of a target language'. See also **semi-creole**.

abruptness of change See the discussion under **gradualness of change**.

absolute chronology The assignment of linguistic changes to specific dates in the past, as when we conclude that **Anglo-Frisian Brightening** probably occurred in the early fifth century AD. Compare **relative chronology**.

absorption Another term for **demorphologization**.

Abstand Linguistic distance – the presence of a clear distinction between two or more closely related language varieties. In **language planning**, speakers are often eager to distance their language from a related language whose speakers may be inclined to see only a dialect of their own language; this is the case, for example, for Macedonian with respect to Bulgarian and for Belarusian with respect to Russian.

abstraction (rarely also **abstractification**) The process in which a word or morpheme of highly specific and concrete meaning loses that meaning in favour of broader and more abstract meanings and possibly further in favour of purely grammatical functions, as in **grammaticalization**. Abstraction was identified by Sapir (1921a); a recent summary is given in Heine *et al.* (1991a: 41–45). These authors cite the case of Ewe *ta'* 'head', which has acquired a number of extended senses including 'intellectual ability', 'main issue', 'division, part' and 'kind, class' (called *structure-preserving abstraction* by the authors), and further some grammatical functions as a postposition and clause subordinator, with such senses as 'over', 'in', 'on', 'in order to' and 'because'. (This is *structure-changing abstraction*.)

Abtönung [*rare*] See under **ablaut**.

accent in PIE The nature and placement of the word-accent in PIE. This issue has long been debated, and no resolution is currently in sight. The presence of a pitch accent in both Sanskrit and ancient Greek leads many scholars to posit a similar system for at least late PIE but not everyone agrees, and in any case some specialists would prefer to recognize a different sort of accent for earlier PIE, often a stress accent, occasionally even a system of tones. It is widely suspected that **ablaut** phenomena derived originally from accentual variations, but it is clear that, at least by late PIE, the ablaut variants had already become dissociated from the accent. Perhaps the single most influential view of the PIE accent is that of the German/Austrian school, as presented for example in Schindler (1975). This recognizes four basic types of accent, in terms of the usual Root-Suffix-Ending structure of PIE word-forms: *acrostatic* (*akrostatic*, *static*) Ŕ-S-E (nom. *$wód$-r*, gen. *$wéd$-n-s* 'water'), *proterokinetic* Ŕ-Ś-E (nom. *$H_1órgh$-i-s*, gen. *H_1rgh-éi-s* 'testicle'), *hysterokinetic* R-Ś-Ě (nom. *pH_2-tēr*, gen. *pH_2-tr-és* 'father') and *holokinetic* (*amphikinetic*) Ŕ-S-É (nom. *$H_2éws$-ōs*, gen. *H_2us-s-és* 'dawn'). See Beekes (1995: 148–155) for a brief survey of the word-accent in PIE and the early IE languages.

accidental resemblance Another term for **chance resemblance**.

accommodation 1. (also **coarticulation**) Modification in the articulation of a segment for the purpose of easing a transition to a following segment, as when English /k/ is fronted before a front vowel or glide (*key*, *cute*), or when /t/ shifts from alveolar to dental before a dental fricative (*eighth*). 2. The behaviour of a speaker who (consciously or unconsciously) adjusts his/her speech towards the speech of an interlocutor or of a surrounding social group. 3. The process in which, in a bilingual or multilingual community with no dominant language, the languages converge towards each other, becoming more similar than formerly, possibly to the point at which sentences in the different languages are morpheme-by-morpheme glosses of each other. A celebrated case is Kupwar in India, where Urdu, Marathi and Kannada have converged to exactly this degree (Gumperz and Wilson 1971). Compare **metatypy**.

accretion The addition to a word or word-form of additional morphological material, thus increasing its length. See the examples under **phonogenesis**. The opposite is **reduction** (sense 2) or **attrition** (sense 1).

accretion zone (also residual zone) A geographical area containing a
   sizeable number of languages which are genetically and typologically
   diverse and in which such diversity tends to increase over time. Such
   an area is a kind of 'sink' which traps and preserves a growing
   number of languages without significant extinction. Examples include the Caucasus, the Himalayas, the Ethiopian highlands, Amazonia, northern Australia and New Guinea. The concept has been
   developed by Johanna Nichols in a series of publications, beginning
   with Nichols (1992). Compare **spread zone**.

acculturation The transfer of features of culture from one population to
   a neighbouring population. This is one way in which a language may
   spread into new territory: one group of speakers adopts the language
   of its neighbours. This is **language shift**, and exactly this is
   proposed for the spread of the IE languages in the **Renfrew
   hypothesis**. Compare **demic diffusion**.

achronological restatement In a synchronic description of a language,
   particularly within a generative framework, an analysis which simply
   recapitulates the history of the language. Chomsky and Halle (1968)
   is an outstanding example: it presents many of the historical developments in English phonology, including the **Great Vowel Shift**, as
   synchronic rules of English.

acoustically motivated sound change Another term for **perceptually
   motivated sound change**.

acoustic assimilation A type of **assimilation** in which acoustic characteristics are assimilated, rather than (as more usually) articulatory
   ones. Lass (1984: 176) cites the example of certain varieties of
   Austrian German in which front vowels are rounded before a
   velarized lateral. There is no articulatory basis for this, but there is
   an acoustic one: both velarization and lip-rounding produce 'low
   tonality' – specifically, lowering of the second and third formants –
   and it is these formants that are being assimilated. Ohala (1989: 183)
   cites a number of instances of shifts of palatalized labials to acoustically similar coronals, such as Czech *m'ɛstɔ* 'town' > regional *nɛstɔ*,
   Proto-Romance **ampju* 'large' > Spanish *antʃo*, and Italian *bjaŋko*
   'white' > Genoese *dʒaŋku*.

acquisition explanation of change Any attempt at accounting for
   language change in terms of the behaviour of children acquiring

their first language. Particularly prominent here are Locke (1983) for phonology and Lightfoot (1998 and elsewhere) for syntax, and see Bybee and Slobin (1982) for counter-arguments. See McMahon (1994: *passim*) for references to the possible importance of acquisition elsewhere, and see **abduction**.

acquisition model A label applied by Heine *et al.* (1991a: 37, 116) to the process by which the sense of 'have' is expressed by a verb or a construction which etymologically means 'hold', 'take' or 'seize'. English *have* derives from the PIE root **kap-* 'grasp, seize'; western Basque *eduki* 'have' formerly meant 'hold on to' (and still does in the north); Waata Oromo *k'awa* 'have' is etymologically 'seize'.

acrolect See under **post-creole continuum**.

acronym A word constructed, in the canonical case, by combining the initial letters of the significant words in a phrase, yielding a result which has the same meaning as the phrase and which can be pronounced as a word. Classic examples are *laser*, from *light amplification by the stimulated emission of radiation*, and *scuba*, from *self-contained underwater breathing apparatus*. Not all acronyms are quite so neat: *radar*, from *radio detection and ranging*, departs from the canonical pattern in two respects (a non-initial letter and an initial letter from a minor word). A similarly formed coinage which cannot be pronounced as a word is an **initialism**, though some linguists apply the term *acronym* indiscriminately to both cases.

acrostatic See under **accent in PIE**.

act of identity A decision by speakers in a speech community to embrace and use certain linguistic forms on the ground that those forms are typical of the speech of 'their' group. In some cases, such as in *creolization* (see under **creole**), such acts of identity may lead to greater homogenization of a speech community. In others, the result may be fragmentation, as when the speakers in a tiny speech community embrace an accidentally generated innovation and make it an **emblematic feature** of their speech. The second case can lead to rapid differentiation of originally closely related language varieties, as has occurred, for example, with the languages of the Pacific. See Le Page and Tabouret-Keller (1985) for the first and M. Ross (1997: 232–236) for the second.

actualization (also **extension**) The changes in surface forms which are the consequence of a **reanalysis** (sense 2) and which demonstrate that the reanalysis has taken place. For example, when Latin *habeo scriptos libros* 'I possess written books', with verb *habeo* and a participle *scriptos* agreeing with *libros* (the object of *habeo*), was reanalysed in Romance as a compound verb-form meaning 'I have written (some) books', the former participle, now analysed as part of the verb, ceased agreeing with the noun phrase which was now the object of the entire compound verb, as in Spanish *he escrito unos libros* (not **escritos*). This is one form of **deductive change** (see under **abduction**). See Timberlake (1977).

actuation The first appearance of a change in a language.

actuation problem The problem of explaining why a **language change** appears at all, and why it appears at the time and in the place it appears. This is generally regarded as the single most refractory problem in the study of language change, and the one which we have made least progress in solving. See the **WLH model of language change** and see **speaker-innovation**.

Adamawa-Ubangi (or **Adamawa-Eastern**) One of the primary branches of **Niger-Congo**, containing around 180 mostly little-known languages spoken in north-central Africa.

adaptation (also **nativization, naturalization**) The borrowing of a word from a foreign language in such a way as to replace its foreign phonological characteristics with native ones, as when English takes over German *Muesli* as /mjuːzli/, or French *croissant* as /kwæsɑːnt/ or something similar. Compare **adoption**.

adaptive innovation In the terminology of Andersen (1980), any innovation which arises as a purposeful modification of a grammar, under communicative pressure, often arising from contact. An example is the replacement of the inherited imperative in Slavic by the optative, presumably originally as a device for obtaining the addressee's cooperation. Compare **evolutive innovation**.

adaptive rule (also **patch-up rule**) A rule which is more or less consciously introduced by a speaker who finds that his or her pronunciation or grammar is at odds with that of the surrounding community, in the hope of conforming to the surrounding pronunciation. For example, a speaker who pronounces *dew* and *new* as /du:/ and /nu:/ and who finds himself surrounded by others who say /dju:/ and /nju:/ may introduce a patch-up rule converting /u:/ to /ju:/ after a coronal consonant. Such a rule may, however, lead to **hypercorrection**, since it tends to convert *do* and *noon* (wrongly) to /dju:/ and /nju:n/. See Andersen (1973), Anttila (1989: 200), Disterheft (1990).

additive compound An uncommon type of **compound** in which the meaning of the compound is the sum of the meanings of the constituent elements, as in English *fourteen*, historically *four* plus *ten*.

adjustment A term introduced by Heine and Reh (1984: 98 *ff.*) to denote the final stage in a **grammaticalization chain**, in which the morphosyntactic marking is altered to represent the new structure directly. An example comes from the Ugandan language So, whose locative copula *nɛkɛ* requires a locative complement marked with the ablative case. To express 'S/he is behind the mountain', So has the conservative form *nɛkɛ íca cú-o sóg* 'be s/he back-abl mountain', with case-marking on the head noun *cú* 'back'; the intermediate version *nɛkɛ íca cú-o sóg-o* takes double case-marking; and the third form, *nɛkɛ íca cú sóg-o*, transfers the case-marking solely to the new head noun, *sóg* 'mountain', with the former head noun, *cú*, now reduced to a preposition. This last stage is adjustment.

adoption The borrowing of a word from a foreign language complete with its foreign phonological characteristics, as when French *genre* and *croissant* are taken into English with nasal vowels and uvular /r/. Compare **adaptation**.

adstrate (also **adstratum**) 1. A language which influences another language through *contact* (see **language contact**), but is neither more nor less prestigious than the affected language. For example, Shina has significantly influenced Burushaski, even though neither language appears to be more prestigious than the other. 2. [*rare*] A superordinate term for **adstrate** (sense 1), **substrate** and **superstrate**.

advanced In phonological change, denoting a pronunciation which appears to be **innovating** with respect to a competing and more **conservative** pronunciation. For example, in the RP accent of England, the words *tar*, *tire* and *tower* are all traditionally pronounced with different vocalic nuclei but, in a more advanced style of pronunciation, all three are homophones: /tɑ:/.

Aequian An extinct language recorded in a single brief text in east-central Italy. It seems to have been **Italic** and probably a dialect of Oscan or Umbrian.

affection The name given to various historical developments in the **Celtic** languages in which a vowel was partly assimilated to ('affected by') a vowel in the following syllable. Welsh, for example, exhibits both *i*-affection (raising before /i/) and *a*-affection (lowering before /a/); the conditioning vowel often disappeared later. Examples: **bardī* > *beirdd* 'bards'; Latin *pāpilio* > *pebyll* 'tent'; **butā* > *bod* 'be'; Latin *grammatica* > *gramadeg* 'grammar'. Affection is comparable to **umlaut** in Germanic, but involves height rather than backness.

affective change A **sporadic change** in the form of a particular word which appears to result from an attempt at adding some kind of affective meaning to it, as in the development of English *no* into *nope*. Particularly frequent is **expressive gemination**.

affective form A linguistic form which has undergone some kind of deliberate phonological modification (very often **palatalization**) for the purpose of expressing some particular attitude on the part of speakers, most commonly one of warmth or affection. For example, Basque *zoko* 'corner' (/soko/) has an affective form *xoko* (/ʃoko/) or *txoko* (/tʃoko/), roughly 'cosy little place'.

affective symbolism (also **expressive symbolism**) The systematic use in a language of phonological characteristics to express emotions, attitudes, intensity, size and other such characteristics. For example, in the Algonquian language Mandan, many roots exist in three forms: a variant with /s/, expressing a smaller or less intense version of the basic meaning; a variant with /ʃ/, expressing a medium-sized or medium-intensity version; and a variant with /x/, expressing a large or more intense version. An example is /sí/ 'yellow', /ʃí/ 'tawny', /xí/ 'brown'. For discussion, see Campbell (1996), from which this example is taken; Campbell stresses the possible importance of such phenomena in disturbing regular phonological correspondences among languages.

affinity A rather vague term used to denote some kind of (often unspecified) historical connection between languages or families.

affixation Another term for **derivation**.

affix borrowing The transfer of an affix from one language to another. This almost always happens as a result of the borrowing of both unaffixed and affixed forms. For example, the English borrowing from Latin and French of pairs like *move* and *movable* has led to the introduction of *-able* into English as a productive suffix which can be attached to native words, as in *drinkable* and *washable*. Basque borrowed so many pairs from Latin like *merkatu* 'market' (< *merca-tu(m)*) and *merkatari* 'merchant' (< *mercatariu(m)*) that *-ari* has become the ordinary professional suffix in Basque.

affix compounding The combination of two independent affixes of similar function into a single affix. For example, Old High German had two diminutive suffixes *-il* and *-īn*; in modern German, these have combined into a single diminutive suffix *-lein*, as in *Kind-lein* 'little child'.

affixization 1. The conversion of an independent word to an affix, as when Latin *mente* 'in mind', in phrases like *clara mente* 'with a clear mind' (i.e. 'clear-headedly'), was reduced to an adverb-forming suffix, as in Spanish *claramente* and French *clairement* 'clearly'. The opposite is **deaffixization**. 2. The reduction of one element of a compound to an affix, as when Old English *manlic* 'man-like' developed into *manly*, with reduction of the second element to a suffix. Both of these are varieties of **morphologization**.

affrication The development of another segment into an affricate, as when earlier /p/, /t/ and /k/ developed into /pf/, /ts/ and /kx/ in certain circumstances in High German: compare German *Pflaume* with English *plum*, and German *zehn* /tse:n/ with English *ten*. (Standard High German does not exhibit the third change.) See the **Second Germanic Consonant Shift**. The development of classical Greek /pʰ/, /tʰ/ and /kʰ/ into modern Greek /f/, /θ/ and /x/ is thought by some to have proceeded via /pf/, /tθ/ and /kx/, another instance of affrication (Horrocks 1997: 113). A more contemporary example is the development of [tʰ] into [tˢ] in the English of London. The opposite is **deaffrication**.

Afrasian Another term for **Afro-Asiatic**.

African languages The indigenous languages of Africa, excluding Madagascar. Greenberg (1963b) famously classified all of them into just four proposed families: **Afro-Asiatic, Niger-Congo** (or **Niger-Kordofanian**), **Nilo-Saharan** and **Khoisan**. Of these the first two are generally regarded as secure, the third is controversial, and the fourth is regarded with great suspicion.

Afro-Asiatic (also **Afrasian**) A large language family occupying most of northern and eastern Africa and most of the Middle East. At least five major branches are commonly recognized: **Egyptian, Semitic, Berber, Chadic** and **Cushitic**. A sixth branch, **Omotic**, is now often split off from Cushitic, and some specialists prefer to break up the remainder of Cushitic further. The proto-language is thought to have been spoken in north Africa around 8000–13,000 years ago; it has not yet been reconstructed in any detail, and recent attempts at reconstruction (Orel and Stolbova 1995, Ehret 1995) have not as yet won general acceptance. The family is commonly included in the **Nostratic** hypothesis.

age-area hypothesis (also **centre-of-gravity principle, genetic diversity principle, Sapir's principle**) A certain principle often invoked in addressing the **homeland problem**. It says this: the homeland lies in the region in which the family exhibits the highest degree of diversity – specifically, the largest number of high-level branches. Proposed by Latham (1851, 1862) and embraced by Sapir (1916), this is essentially an economy principle: it picks out a homeland which requires the fewest migrations away from it, and it forms the basis of **migration theory**. The principle has been widely invoked in identifying homelands, but Mallory (1997: 95–97) queries its utility, and Nichols (1997a) argues that the principle is only valid in certain circumstances: with families still spoken close to their ancient homelands, such as Austronesian (Taiwan) and Uralic (east of the Urals).

age-grading A type of **language change** in which individuals steadily change their speech as they grow older, while the speech of the community as a whole remains unchanged. In other words, in such a community, there is a type of speech typical of twenty-year-olds, a different type typical of forty-year-olds, yet another type typical of sixty-year-olds, and so on, and individuals modify their speech over time accordingly, but the type of speech heard from each age group remains constant over time. No clear case of such pure age-grading is known, and it may not exist, but it is beyond dispute that a measure of age-grading can be observed in some communities with respect to certain variables operating at a high level of social awareness. The phenomenon was named by William Labov and has been discussed by him in several works; see Labov (1994: *passim*) for examples. Compare **generational change, communal change**.

agglutination theory (also **coalescence theory**) A particular version of **stadialism** which holds that languages start off as purely isolating types, then become agglutinating by the reduction of some words to grammatical markers, and finally become inflecting by phonological coalescence of agglutinated morphemes. Such proposals were expressly defended in the nineteenth century by Friedrich von Schlegel and Wilhelm von Humboldt, and Franz Bopp defended them for the inflectional affixes of the early IE languages. See Heine *et al.* (1991a: 5–11) for a summary.

Agnean See under **Tocharian**.

Ainu An **isolated language** formerly spoken on and near Hokkaido in northern Japan. It has for years been on the brink of extinction and may now be actually extinct. Attempts at linking Ainu genetically to various other languages have received no support.

Aitken's Law (also **Scottish vowel-length rule**) A pair of statements intended to capture the historical reorganization of vowel-length in Scots varieties of English, as follows: (1) all long vowels and diphthongs shorten except before one of /r v z d/ or a morpheme boundary, and (2) all non-high short vowels lengthen when followed by one of /r v z d/ or a morpheme boundary. The combined effect is to make vowel length almost totally predictable from the phonological and morphological environment. This analysis was published in final form by A. J. Aitken (1981). See Collinge (1985: 3–6) for a critical survey with references.

Akkadian An eastern **Semitic** language, long extinct but widely used in Mesopotamia and Syria in ancient times. It was spoken there from no later than the early third millennium BC, though only recorded in writing from 2350 BC, and apparently only died out in the late first millennium BC, though it continued to be written until the first century AD. There were two main dialects, *Assyrian* and *Babylonian*, used by the empires of the same names. The language is classified into three periods: *Old* (before 1500 BC), *Middle* (1500–1000 BC) and *Neo-* (after 1000 BC). The Akkadian cuneiform writing system was adapted from that of the earlier **Sumerian**, which itself was displaced as a spoken language by Akkadian. See Buccelati (1997).

akrostatic See under **accent in PIE**.

Akzentumsprung Literally, 'accent shift', but the term is commonly applied to a development in which a diminuendo ('falling') diphthong changes to a crescendo ('rising') diphthong, or vice versa – that is, the syllabic nucleus moves from one element of the diphthong to the other – as when [ew] changes to [ju]. Such developments are frequent in some regional varieties of English.

Alanic The extinct **Iranian** language of the Alans, who briefly conquered much of Spain and Portugal in AD 409 but were then expelled by the Visigoths.

Albanian The principal language of Albania, also spoken in neighbouring areas, constituting a single branch of IE all by itself. There are two main dialect groupings, *Geg* and *Tosk*. Due to some dramatic internal developments and some unusually heavy layers of loan words, Albanian was only finally recognized as an IE language in 1854. Its connections with ancient European languages are debated, though a favourite conjecture is that it is descended from the little-known **Illyrian** language, spoken in roughly the same area in classical times. See Demiraj (1998) for a historical survey.

algebraism (also **formulaism, symbolic reconstruction**) In comparative reconstruction, the belief that a reconstructed segment, such as PIE */p/ or */bh/, is nothing but a piece of algebra summarizing the **systematic correspondences** identified in the daughter languages, and that no degree of phonetic reality can or should be assigned to the symbol, since ancient phonetic reality is beyond recovery. This position, which automatically excludes any possibility of introducing typological factors into reconstruction, is very much a minority view among linguists. Compare **realism**.

Algic A language family linking **Algonquian** to two languages of California, *Yurok* and *Wiyot* (sometimes called the *Ritwan* languages). Put forward by Sapir (1913), this proposal is now universally accepted. Attempts at finding further relatives for Algic have not won general acceptance. See **Almosan**.

Algonquian (also **Algonkian**) A major language family of North America, covering the larger part of southern Canada and much of the northern and northeastern USA, with one outlier in Mexico. Among its better-known members are *Arapaho*, *Blackfoot*, *Cheyenne*, *Cree*, *Shawnee* and *Kickapoo*. The largely extinct Algonquian languages of the northeast, such as *Massachusett*, were the first indigenous American languages encountered by English-speaking settlers, who took from them a number of words and place names. Algonquian is part of a larger **Algic** grouping.

Algonquian-Gulf A speculative grouping of **Algic** with the dubious **Gulf** grouping, proposed by Mary Haas in several publications but today generally abandoned.

alignment Any one of several grammatical systems for classifying NP arguments in the sentences of a language. Among the most prominent are the *nominative-accusative* system the *absolutive-ergative* system, and the *active-stative* system. A number of linguists have argued either that alignment tends to develop over time in languages according to a fixed sequence (this is one form of **stadialism**), or that alignment tends to remain stable in a language family over time. Johanna Nichols has recently been counting alignment as one kind of **genetic marker**.

alignment change Any change in the **alignment** of a language, such as from accusative to ergative. The mechanisms by which this happens are at present poorly understood, though progress is being made; see Harris and Campbell (1995: 243–251) for a survey.

allegro form An irregularly, and often heavily, reduced form of an item which is of very high frequency in discourse. Examples include English *ma'am* for *madam*, English [tʃədu:ən] for *What are you doing?*, German [mo(ə)ŋ] for *Guten Morgen* 'Good morning', and Basque [stait] for *Ez dakit* 'I don't know'. An allegro form may completely displace its longer original, as has happened with Spanish *usted* 'you', from earlier *vuestra merced* 'your grace'.

allomorphic change Any kind of change in the formal realization of a morpheme. Koch (1996: 224–237) distinguishes five types: development of allomorphy, change in relation between underlying and derived allomorphs (this is **rule inversion**), change in conditioning of allomorphy, loss of allomorphy, and redistribution of allomorphs. See Koch (1996) for examples.

allonymic dissimilation A certain tendency observable in languages, as follows: when, as a result of phonological change, two words fall together in pronunciation and one of them is replaced by a different word. For example, in French, Latin *sūtōrem* 'shoemaker' and *sūdōrem* 'sweat' would both have yielded modern *sueur*, but this word means only 'sweat', while 'shoemaker' is *cordonnier*. The name was coined by Hagège (1993: 11–12). Compare **homonymic assimilation**.

allophonic change Another term for **phonetic change**.

Almosan A proposal, by Sapir in the 1920s, to link his doubtful **Mosan** construct with **Algic**. This proposal enjoys little support.

Almosan–Keresiouan A proposed linking into a larger group of the two speculative constructs **Almosan** and **Keresiouan**, put forward by Greenberg (1987). This has found no acceptance.

Altaic A proposed language family of Asia, with about forty languages and three main branches: **Turkic, Mongolian** and **Tungusic**. The reality of the Altaic family has long been contentious, and support for it has waxed and waned. On the one hand, Poppe (1960, 1965) has presented a substantial reconstruction; on the other, critics have pointed out that the Mongolian grouping in the centre has obvious links with the two peripheral groupings of Turkic and Tungusic, while these last two have few links with each other, suggesting contact rather than common origin. Many people have tried to relate **Japanese, Korean** and **Ainu** to Altaic; at present there is growing support for the inclusion of the first two, though not for Ainu, but no consensus has been achieved. Altaic is commonly included in the **Nostratic** hypothesis. See **Ural-Altaic**.

alteration An unsystematic change in the form of a word, as in the development of Scots *sculduddery* into standard *skulduggery*. Note that the term *corruption* is never used in linguistics for such alterations.

alternation Variation in the form of a single morpheme in different linguistic environments in a single language or speech variety. An example is the alternation between intervocalic /r/ and non-intervocalic /l/ in Basque, in numerous cases like *euskara* 'Basque language' and its combining form *euskal-*, as in *euskaldun* 'Basque-speaker'; this results from the change of intervocalic **/l/ to /r/ in the early medieval period. Alternations are often of great importance in **internal reconstruction**, and shared alternations may be of great value in establishing a **genetic relationship**. Note, however, that a mere regional variation in form, such as that between eastern Basque *tipi* and western Basque *tiki*, both 'small', does *not* represent an alternation, and applying the term *alternation* to such cases is a misuse of it. Moreover, treating either a true alternation or a case of regional variation as a licence to interchange the relevant segments at will in seeking etymologies and cognates, as is sometimes done by linguistic amateurs, is a positive outrage. Compare **variant**.

amalgamation 1. The fusion of two or more words into a single word, as in English *all ways* > *always*, *never the less* > *nevertheless*, and Spanish *tan bien* 'as well' > *también* 'also'. 2. [*rare*] Another term for *blending*; see under **blend**.

amelioration (also **melioration, elevation**) Any change in meaning in which a word comes to denote something grander or more elevated than formerly, as when Old English *cwēn* 'woman' and *cniht* 'boy, servant' developed into *queen* and *knight*. The opposite is **pejoration**.

American languages The indigenous languages of the Americas. The number of living American languages is variously estimated at between 600 and 1000; in addition, an unknown number of these languages have become extinct since the European settlement, and most of the surviving ones are in grave danger of extinction now. The number of **language families** in the Americas is about 150; this figure includes a large number of isolates. More than most areas of the world, the Americas have been plagued by ambitious attempts at grouping established families into hopeful larger groupings, some of them very large, on the basis of little or no evidence, and the names of these speculative groupings have often entered the general literature as though they were secure families. See Campbell (1997a) for a detailed account, and Campbell and Mithun (1979) for a historical assessment.

Amerind A proposed vast language family joining all the languages of North and South America *except* **Eskimo–Aleut** and **Na-Dene**. Proposed by Greenberg (1987), the Amerind hypothesis is deeply controversial, and it is rejected as unfounded by the great majority of specialists. The languages assigned to Amerind constitute, in the view of most Americanists, at least 150 distinct genetic families. See Greenberg *et al.* (1987) for a presentation and critical discussion,

Goddard (1987), Campbell (1988), Adelaar (1989) and Matisoff (1990) for critical reviews, and Greenberg (1989) for a reply to Campbell. Greenberg and Ruhlen (1992) is a brief popular presentation. The Amerind idea was hinted at by Sapir (1916), more than hinted at by Swadesh (1954) and expressly endorsed by Lamb (1959), who called it *Macro-American*. The putative family was, according to Greenberg, set up on the basis of **multilateral comparison**, but see Campbell (1997a: 210–211) for a case that in fact Greenberg reached his conclusions before he had examined any evidence at all.

Amorite A sparsely recorded **Semitic** language spoken in northern Syria about 2000–1500 BC. See Gordon (1997).

amphikinetic See under **accent in PIE**.

analogia, principle of [*obsolete*] An early term for the statement that **systematic correspondences** are required to establish **genetic relationships**.

analogical adaptation The process in which, for historical reasons, a language borrowing words from a neighbouring language regularly renders some sound or sound-sequence in the lending language by a different, and seemingly unexpected, sound or sound-sequence. A good example involves Basque, in which Spanish words ending in *-ón* are regularly borrowed with final *-oi*, as in *kamioi* 'lorry, truck' from Spanish *camión* and *abioi* 'aeroplane' from *avión* – in spite of the fact that final *-on* is perfectly normal in Basque, as in *gizon* 'man'. The reason for this is that the frequent ending *-one(m)* in Latin and early Romance was borrowed into Basque as *-*one*, which in the medieval period underwent the categorical Basque loss of intervocalic /n/, yielding first *-*oe* and then *-oi*, while the same Romance ending was merely reduced to *-ón* in Spanish. As a result, Basque-speakers noticed the existence of many pairs like Spanish *ratón* and Basque *arratoi* 'rat', from Latin *ratone(m)*, and seemingly concluded that Basque *-oi* was the normal equivalent of Spanish *-ón*.

analogical change See **analogy**.

analogical creation 1. The creation of a new lexical item by the extension of an established pattern of word-formation. English examples include *kissable* and *unkillable*, by extension of the productive suffix *-able*. 2. The creation of a new inflected form by **analogy**, such as *octopi* and *syllabi*, non-historical plurals constructed on the model of forms like *radii*.

analogical extension The spread of a linguistic form or pattern, by **analogy**, to items which formerly were not subject to it. For example, in early Romance, the inflectional paradigms of the two large classes of *o*-stems and *a*-stems were extended to the nouns in the much smaller classes of *u*-stems and *e*-stems, respectively, and, in English, the plural in -*s* has been extended to many nouns which formerly did not accept it. See also **analogical transfer**.

analogical levelling The elimination of alternations in the inflected forms of a lexical item. For example, the regular development of Latin stressed /a/ to /ai/ in Old French left alternations in the paradigms of certain verbs; levelling then removed the alternations by generalizing one stem-alternant. See Table 1. See **analogical restructuring** and **reversion**.

analogical maintenance (also **analogical preservation**, **preventive analogy**) The state of affairs in which the operation of a regular phonological change is blocked exactly in those cases in which its application would introduce **alternations** into a paradigm. For example, the regular English loss of /w/ before /o/, as in *sword*, should also have applied to *swore* to produce **sore*, but no such form is recorded, and it is possible (though not certain) that the analogical influence of *swear*, which retained its /w/, may have blocked the loss of /w/ in *swore*. In the absence of textual evidence, it is impossible to distinguish analogical maintenance from **analogical restoration**, and Hock (1986: 4647) is sceptical that analogical maintenance ever occurs at all.

analogical pressure The tendency of an existing pattern in a language to be extended to new cases.

Latin	Old French	French
ámo	*aim*	*aime*
ámo	*aimes*	*aimes*
ámat	*aimet*	*aime*
amámus	*amons*	*aimons*
amátis	*amez*	*aimez*
ámant	*aiment*	*aiment*

Table 1

analogical reformation Another term for **folk etymology**.

analogical restoration The state of affairs in which a segment which has been lost or altered by regular phonological change, in such a way as to produce **alternations** in a paradigm, is restored to its original form in order to eliminate the alternations. For example, the Pre-Latin loss of /w/ before /o/ should have applied to *parwos* 'little', genitive *parwī*, to produce *parus, parvī*, but in fact the classical form is *parvus, parvī*. It is possible that the regular change did in fact produce *parus*, just as in the related adverb *parum* 'too little' (< *parwom*), and that the resulting alternation was later eliminated by the analogical restoration of the /w/ (orthographic) in the nominative. Without textual evidence, it is usually impossible to distinguish analogical restoration from **analogical maintenance**. However, Schindler (1974: 5) presents a good example. In PIE, there is good evidence that final *-n* was categorically lost. In Pre-Greek, however, after subsequent changes had reintroduced final *-n* after a long vowel in other circumstances, alternating nouns like *khiō* 'snow', genitive *khión-os*, had their final *-n* analogically restored in the nominative, producing Homeric and classical *khiōn, khiónos*.

analogical restructuring A name sometimes given to instances of **analogical levelling** in which the change applies to the most central form in a paradigm. An example is provided by the Latin word for 'honour': Pre-Latin *honōs*, genitive *honōsis* developed regularly to *honōs, honōris* by the usual Latin **rhotacism**, and analogical restructuring then converted the nominative singular to classical *honor*.

analogical transfer A kind of **analogical extension** involving metaphor. Heine *et al.* (1991a: 79–86) cite the case of Ewe *vi'* 'child', which has become a productive word-forming suffix. In a formation of the form *X-vi'*, if *X* denotes a type of human, *X-vi'* denotes a child of that type; if *X* denotes an animal, *X-vi'* denotes a young of that animal; and, if *X* denotes a social group, *X-vi'* denotes a member of that group. This last is analogical transfer.

analogy (also **analogical change**) Any linguistic change which results from an attempt to make some linguistic forms more similar to other linguistic forms. See the entries preceding this one for the various types of analogy which are distinguished, and see also **four-part analogy, intraparadigmatic analogy**. See Anttila (1977) for a study.

analogy, laws of Any of various putative principles governing the direction in which **analogy** usually works. These principles are not really 'laws' but only tendencies. The first such principles to be proposed were the six in Kuryłowicz (1947); also well known are the nine 'tendencies' given in Mańczak (1958). For a summary with examples, see Collinge (1985: 249–253), Hock (1986: ch. 10) or Trask (1996: 112–115).

anaphonesis The phenomenon, in some Tuscan varieties of Italian, in which Latin /e:/ and /i/ yield /i/ instead of the regular /e/, and Latin /o:/ and /u/ yield /u/ instead of the regular /o/, as in *lingua* 'tongue' for expected **lengua*, from Latin *linguam*. See Maiden (1995: 41–42) for a discussion with references.

anaptyxis (also *svarabhakti*) The insertion of a vowel into the middle of a word, as when early Latin *faclis* 'easy' became classical *facilis*. This is one type of **epenthesis**. The vowel inserted is called an *anaptyctic vowel*, a *svarabhakti vowel* or a *parasite vowel*; when identical to a neighbouring vowel, it is an **echo vowel**.

anastrophe In early Greek, the use of a preposition as a postposition, as in *ommátōn ápo* 'from the eyes'. Since Vedic cognates like *ápa* are also postpositions, and since Hittite is solidly postpositional, W. P. Lehmann (1974) concludes that PIE was postpositional..

Anatolian A major branch of **Indo-European**, all of whose members are long dead. The best-attested Anatolian language is **Hittite**, abundantly recorded in the second millennium BC; more sparsely recorded are **Lydian**, **Palaic**, **Lycian**, **Milyan**, two varieties of **Luwian**, and possibly also **Carian**. The Anatolian languages are strikingly divergent from the rest of IE, a fact which has led to the **Indo-Hittite hypothesis** and to the two views called the *Herkunfthypothese* and the *Schwundhypothese*. Hittite famously preserves some of the PIE **laryngeal** consonants. See Luraghi (1998).

ancestor language (also **ancestral language**) With respect to a given language, an earlier language from which the later one is directly descended by the ordinary processes of **language change**. For example, PIE is an ancestor of English.

ancestral disparity Another term for **neglect of known history**.

ancestral language Another term for **ancestor language**.

Andamanese A family of about a dozen languages spoken in the Andaman Islands, almost all of them now extinct. The Andamanese languages are usually considered to have no known relatives, but see **Indo-Pacific**.

angle brackets The notation '< >'. 1. These are used in an **edition** of a text to mark off one or more characters absent from the text, or clearly erroneous in the text, and inserted by the editor as an emendation. See the example under **square brackets** (sense 2). 2. They are used to set off a purely orthographic representation, as with English <phlegm> /flem/.

anglicization The process of modifying the pronunciation of a foreign word or name so as to produce a version which is more or less compatible with the ordinary phonology of English, as when French *détente* [detãt] and *déjà vu* [deʒa vy] are rendered as /deɪtɑ:nt/ and /deɪʒɑ v(j)u:/. This is one variety of **adaptation**.

Anglo-French Another term for **Anglo-Norman**.

Anglo-Frisian brightening (also **first fronting**) A change, applying to the Germanic dialects ancestral to English and Frisian, by which the back vowel [ɑ] was fronted to [æ] in most circumstances except before a nasal. Compare, for example, OE *daeg*, OFr *deg* 'day' with Go *dags*, OIc *dagr*, OHG *tag*. The change is usually dated to the early fifth century AD; the name is a literal translation of German *Aufhellung*. See Lass (1994: 42–44).

Anglo-Norman (also **Anglo-French**) The somewhat distinctive variety of **French** spoken by the Norman conquerors of England. See Price (1998: 8–10).

Anglo-Saxon Another term for **Old English**.

anit-**root** In Sanskrit, a root which is not a *set-root*: an ordinary root.

Anklang An unsystematic resemblance in form between words in different languages, typically resulting from chance or from sound-symbolic factors. The enthusiastic or assiduous accumulation of mere *Anklänge* among selected languages, so typical of linguistic amateurs, is of no value in comparative linguistics.

anlaut The beginning of a word, or a segment in this position. Compare **inlaut, auslaut**.

anthropological dialectology An approach to **linguistic geography** developed by J. H. Hill in work as yet unpublished. Hill interprets the spread of languages and linguistic features in terms of differing 'stances', called *localist* and *distributed*. People with secure claims on essential resources tend to adopt a localist stance, involving loyalty to their language, which hinders spread; but people in precarious economic circumstances tend towards a distributed stance, involving little language loyalty, which favours spread.

anthropomorphic model (also **body-part model, case anthropology**) In the writings of Bernd Heine (e.g. 1989), the use of human (not animal) body-part names (based on an upright human body) to construct adverbs and adpositions of location, such as Maasai *ol-kurum* 'anus' for 'back' and *ɛndʋkʋya* 'head' for 'front'. Compare **zoomorphic model**.

anticipation The phenomenon in which a speaker produces a segment or a feature earlier in an utterance than is necessary or appropriate. The term is applied both to instances of *anticipatory assimilation* (see under **assimilation**) and to slips of the tongue such as *blake fluid* for *brake fluid* and *bread and breakfast* for *bed and breakfast*.

anticipatory assimilation See under **assimilation**.

anudātta In Sanskrit, a low pitch, or a syllable bearing this; an unaccented syllable. See *udātta*, **svarita**.

anusvāra In Sanskrit, the **nasalization** of a vowel, or the raised dot used to indicate this in the most familiar orthography.

aoristic drift principle A putative principle of language change, proposed by Hagège (1993: 155), by which verb-forms referring to observed events tend constantly to acquire an evocatory content. An example is the French simple present, now often used as a narrative past.

aphaeresis (also **aphesis**) The loss of a word-initial vowel, as when *opossum* is reduced to *possum*, or when early Italian *istoria* 'history' was reduced to *storia*. The opposite is **prothesis**.

apocope 1. Narrowly, the loss of a word-final vowel, as in the development of Old Spanish *mercede* and *pane* into modern Spanish *merced* 'mercy' and *pan* 'bread'. 2. Broadly, the loss of any word-final segment or sequence of segments, such as the loss of many word-final consonants in French: *lit* 'bed' /li/, *gros* 'big' /gro/, *soûl* 'drunk' /su/ and so on. The opposite in this sense is **excrescence** (sense 1).

apomorphy A technical term for **innovation**, borrowed by Lass (1997) from biological cladistics.

apophony Another term for **ablaut**, though Coates (1994) recommends reserving this term for the alternations, rather than for the changes leading to them.

apparatus criticus The Latin for **critical apparatus**.

apparent time The distribution of linguistic forms across age groups in a speech community. If we assume that a speaker normally acquires his or her language early in life and then does not change it thereafter, the differences observed between age groups may be taken as representing the differences in the language learned by successive generations, and hence as a representation of the changes which have taken place over time in that community. Compare **real time**.

appellativization The conversion of a proper name into a common noun. The English nouns *escalator* and *aspirin* began life as trade names, and other trade names, such as *Kleenex* and *Hoover*, are now frequently used as common nouns, to the dismay of the manufacturers. This process is especially frequent with trade names, but other cases exist: English *scrooge, harlequin, vandal, maverick, yahoo, cannibal, dunce* and *slave* all derive from the names of (real or fictional) persons or peoples, while *utopia, denim, jeans* and *canary* derive from the names of (real or fictional) places.

approximation See under **merger**.

apud Preceding a person's name, an indication that you are citing that person's opinion about something. For example, if you cite an etymology and follow it with '*apud* Pokorny', you are citing Pokorny as your source for the etymology. This does not necessarily indicate that you are accepting the cited view, but only that you are not disputing it (at least not for the moment); otherwise you would use *pace* or *contra*. You can also write 'Yakhontov *apud* Starostin' to indicate that you are citing Yakhontov's work as it is presented by Starostin, when you have not seen Yakhontov's work yourself. Latin *apud* means 'in the opinion (of)'.

Aquitanian A language spoken in Roman times in southwestern Gaul, in the Pyrenees, and in a small part of Spain. Though recorded only in the form of some 470 personal and divine names, it is now accepted by specialists as an ancestral form of **Basque**.

Arabic One of the world's major languages, a **Semitic** language. Arabic was originally only the language of Arabia, where a literary version of it was used in writing the Holy Koran in the eighth century AD. As a result of the great Arab expansion involved in building the Arab Empire, Arabic largely displaced the indigenous languages in a vast area of the Near East and of north Africa, and it has also become the **liturgical language** of Islam everywhere. The Arabic-speaking countries have long been the locus of a striking case of **diglossia**, involving the prestigious *classical Arabic*, a modified and elaborated version of the language of the Koran, and a number of rather diverse regional spoken varieties collectively known as *colloquial Arabic*; these varieties are often mutually unintelligible. The Arabic spoken in Malta became disconnected from the Arab world and has evolved into an entirely distinct language, *Maltese*. See Fischer (1997), Versteegh (1997).

Aramaic A northwestern **Semitic** language which became a widespread *lingua franca* in the Near East in the first millennium BC and which displaced **Hebrew** as the mother tongue in Palestine in the third century BC; it is thought to have been the mother tongue of Jesus Christ and of the Apostles. Aramaic itself was largely displaced as a mother tongue by **Arabic** after the Arab expansion, but four rather distinct modern varieties of it are still the first language today in parts of Iran and Iraq (where it is often confusingly called 'Assyrian' or 'Chaldean') and in other small scattered areas of the Near East. A written variety called *Syriac*, recorded since the first century AD, was long important in Syria, and is still today the **liturgical language** of the Syrian Jacobite Church. See S. Kaufman (1997).

Arawakan Another term for **Maipurean**; see that entry.

archaeolinguistics A label proposed for the investigation of possible **genetic relationships** on the basis of **reconstructions** which are themselves performed at the level of **palaeolinguistics**: in other words, of possible genetic links *two* linguistic levels earlier than the securely established families like Indo-European. Décsy (1983) estimates this as corresponding to a time about 20,000–30,000 BC, while Hegedűs (1997) suggests 25,000–40,000 BC, but the label is intended to reflect linguistic depth, not absolute **time depth**. It remains to be established that any linguistic work is even possible at such depths. Compare **proto-linguistics**.

archaeological plausibility principle A proposed principle in investigating the **homeland problem**. It says this: the movements of languages, and hence perhaps of peoples, required by some posited homeland should be supported by at least some archaeological evidence. See Mallory (1997: 106).

archaic 1. Of a linguistic form, exhibiting characteristics which are retained from an earlier state of affairs but which were later lost. For example, Mycenaean Green /k^w/, continuing PIE */k^w/, is an archaism lost from all later varieties of Greek. 2. Of a language, exhibiting a number of such features. For example, Mycenaean Greek is an archaic form of Greek, being more similar to its ancestor PIE than is any later for of Greek. 3. [*often capitalized*] Preceding a language name, a conventional label for the earliest recorded variety of that language, as in Archaic Chinese.

archaic heterogeneity, principle of Either of two different principles often invoked in **reconstruction**. Version 1: anomalies shared by related languages must be reconstructed for the ancestral language. Version 2 (also **Hetzron's principle, simplification preference**): in the absence of any conditioning factors, the most heterogeneous system of several related systems in related languages is the closest to that of the ancestral language, and the more homogeneous systems result from simplification.

archaic residue Another term for **retention** (sense 1).

archaism 1. (also **retention, plesiomorphy, relic**) A linguistic form which is directly inherited by a language from its ancestor but which has been lost in related languages or which was later lost in that same language. For example, English is the only IE language which retains

PIE */w/ unchanged today, and our /w/ is therefore an archaism. The PIE labiovelar */k^w/ was still retained in Mycenean Greek but had disappeared by the time of classical Greek; it is therefore an archaism in Mycenean Greek. 2. An isolated linguistic form which retains a form or pattern which has otherwise generally been lost from the language: a **fossilized form**. 3. A linguistic form which has dropped out of regular use in a language but which is still used on occasion for special effect, such as English *hath*, now replaced by *has* in all ordinary speech and writing but used in some religious contexts and in Marconi's first radio message across the Atlantic, *What hath God wrought?* 4. An obsolete linguistic form which is self-consciously reintroduced into the language and becomes established; a **borrowing** from an earlier stage of the same language.

areal classification Classifying languages into **geographical groupings**, with or without attention to shared typological features but with no attention to ancestry.

areal consistency The degree of typological similarity among the languages of a geographical area, either in general or in respect of some particular feature(s) of interest.

areal convergence The phenomenon in which a number of neighbouring languages which are unrelated or only distantly related come to acquire numerous and striking structural features in common, leading to the formation of a **linguistic area**.

areal feature A structural feature which is prominent in a number of unrelated or only distantly related languages in some geographical area. Examples are tones in east Asia, the absence of fricatives in Australia, object–initial word order in Amazonia, the presence of a verb *have* in Europe, and front rounded vowels in northern Eurasia.

areal linguistics The study of **linguistic areas**. Sometimes the term is used more broadly to denote the examination of individual linguistic features across language boundaries – as, for example, the curious distribution of front rounded vowels in a continuous broad belt across northern and western Eurasia.

argot (also **cant**) The distinctive slang or jargon used by a particular social group, often one of questionable standing in the community, such as homosexuals, gypsies or thieves. Not infrequently, argot words pass into general usage, as has happened with English *bilk* 'cheat', *moniker* 'name', *gay* 'homosexual' and *hit* 'kill'.

Armenian The principal language of Armenia, also spoken elsewhere, abundantly recorded since the fifth century AD, though the modern forms are greatly changed. There are two main dialect groupings: *Eastern* (mainly in Armenia) and *Western* (mainly in Turkey and in the diaspora). Armenian forms a single branch of **Indo-European** all by itself. Its connections with ancient languages are debated, though a favourite conjecture links it closely to **Thracian** (in the Balkans) and **Phrygian** (in western Anatolia). Attempts at linking it closely to **Greek** have been inconclusive at best; see Clackson (1994). Armenian exhibits a greatly modified phonological system, a radically transformed verbal system and a rather conservative nominal system (though only in the earlier varieties), and it may preserve overt reflexes of some of the PIE **laryngeals**. See Ajello (1998) for a historical survey.

artificial language A language which is deliberately constructed by a single adult human being, or rarely by a committee, according to whatever principles seem good to the inventor(s), and normally intended to be used either as an auxiliary language among people with no language in common or as a vehicle of scientific or philosophical discourse. Over the past several centuries, hundreds of artificial languages have been proposed, some of them mere sketches, others equipped with large vocabularies and complete grammars. The earlier ones were mainly *a priori* languages, having no connection with existing languages and usually bearing no resemblance to them; these were often intended to be 'logical' or 'philosophical' languages with universalist pretensions, but not one of them proved to be practical. The more recent attempts have mostly been *a posteriori* in nature: derived from one or more existing languages and almost always with a much higher degree of regularity and predictability than natural languages. The most successful artificial language to date is *Esperanto*, invented by L. L. Zamenhof and published in 1887; this mixture of European languages with typical European grammatical features claims over a million speakers worldwide, and a few proponents have reportedly taught Esperanto to their children as a first language. However, no case is known of an artificial language developing into a new natural language on any scale beyond this. A few artificial languages have been invented purely for entertainment, such as the several invented by the fantasy

writer J. R. R. Tolkien and the Klingon language invented for the
Star Trek films. A rare case of an artificial language invented for
serious linguistic purposes is *Epun*, deliberately designed to have
seemingly impossible features and taught to the linguistic savant
Christopher; see Smith and Tsimpli (1995: 137–154). See **non-
genetic language** and compare **invented language**.

Aryan 1. An obsolete term for **Indo-European**, derived from a name
given to themselves by the early speakers of the **Indo-Iranian**
languages. 2. [*rare*] Another term for **Indo-Iranian**. See also
Indo-Aryan.

aspectogenesis Any process by which a language acquires new formal
distinctions of aspect which it formerly lacked.

aspirata (also **aspirate**) (plural **aspiratae**) In IE studies, a label applied
indifferently both to fricatives and to voiced aspirates (**mediae
aspiratae**). Compare **media**, **tenuis** and see *Kreislauf*.

aspiration 1. Any phonological change in which aspiration is added to a
segment which formerly lacked it. The opposite is **deaspiration**. 2.
(in Romance linguistics, often **glottalization**) The conversion of
another segment into [h], as in the change of /s/ to /h/ in Greek,
Hawaiian and some varieties of Spanish. 3. In Irish, a **mutation** in
which /p t k/ become /f θ x/, /b d g/ become /v ð ɣ/, /m/
becomes /v/, /f/ becomes /Ø/ and /s/ becomes /h/ (or in certain
circumstances /ç/).

Aspiration Throwback The name given by Collinge (1985: 47) to the
putative process, in Greek and Indic, by which, when a root-final
aspirated plosive loses its aspiration for any reason, the aspiration is
transferred to the initial plosive of the root, as when the Greek root
trikh- 'hair' forms a nominative *thriks*, in which the velar loses its
aspiration because of the following /s/ and the initial coronal
acquires it. This was originally proposed by Grassmann (1863:
110–111) as the first clause of a two-part law, but only the second
clause has come to be known as **Grassmann's Law**.

assibilation Any phonological change in which another segment is
converted to a sibilant. An example is the change of [t] to [s] before
[i] in a number of Pacific languages, in certain circumstances in early
Greek and in certain circumstances in Finnish.

assimilated loan A **loan word** which has been completely adapted to the phonological system of the borrowing language. English examples include *music* (all speakers and styles), from French *musique* [myzik], *beret* (when homophonous with *berry*), from French *beret* [bɛʀe], and *tsetse* (when pronounced /tetsi/), from Tswana *tsetse* ['tsɛtsɛ].

assimilation Any **syntagmatic change** in which some segment becomes more similar in nature to another segment in the same sequence, usually within a single phonological word or phrase. A right-to-left assimilation is *anticipatory* (or *regressive*); a left-to-right assimilation is *perseverative* (or *progressive*). (Note: some linguists use the terms *progressive* and *regressive* exactly the other way round, and these terms are therefore best avoided.) Assimilation in both directions at the same time is **mutual assimilation**. Assimilation between adjacent segments is **contact assimilation**, while that between non-adjacent segments is **distant assimilation**. Assimilation in some phonetic features only is **partial assimilation**; assimilation in all phonetic features (producing identical segments) is **total assimilation**. For example, the pronunciation of *ten pence* as *te*[m]*pence* is partial anticipatory contact assimilation (in place); that of *bacon* as /beɪkŋ/ is partial perseverative contact assimilation (in place). The change of earlier Basque *alte* 'side' into *alde* in most dialects is partial perseverative contact assimilation (in voicing), while the change of Pre-Basque **bini* 'tongue' to later **mini* is partial anticipatory distant assimilation (in nasality). The development of Latin *eclipse(m)* 'eclipse' into Italian *eclisse* is total anticipatory contact assimilation (in place and manner), while the development of Proto-Germanic **muːsiz* 'mice' to Old English *myːs* is partial anticipatory distant assimilation (in backness) (followed by loss of the final syllable). The development of common Basque *iduri* 'seem' to Zuberoan *üdürü* (where *ü* represents a front rounded vowel) is mutual distant assimilation (in backness and rounding). Particular sorts of assimilation occurring historically in particular languages are sometimes given special names, as with **umlaut** and **affection**. Some analysts regard **coalescence** as a kind of assimilation. The opposite is **dissimilation**. See **harmonic change** and see also **acoustic assimilation**.

asterisk The symbol '*', prefixed to a linguistic form for any of several purposes but always indicating 'unattested', 'non-existent' or 'impossible'. 1. The asterisk marks a form which is nowhere recorded but which has been reconstructed by linguists, as when English *head* is traced back to an unrecorded Proto-Germanic **haubudam*, or when Basque *dekuma* 'tithe' is traced back (by borrowing) to an unrecorded late Latin form **decuma* (classical *decima*). Such a form is a **starred form**. (Some European linguists use a superscript **plus sign** for this purpose instead of an asterisk: hence *+haubadam*.) This use of the asterisk was introduced by August Schleicher in the mid-nineteenth century; previously it had been common practice to represent an etymon, not by a starred form, but by the form recorded in the single language regarded as most archaic within a family, such as Gothic for Germanic and Sanskrit for Indo-European. 2. The asterisk marks a form that might have been expected to occur in a language but does not, as when we note that Latin *cattum* 'cat' should regularly have yielded Spanish **cato* rather than the actual *gato*, or that Latin *colum* 'distaff' would have yielded Spanish **colo* if it had survived in Spanish (it did not), or that Basque *bilo* '(a) hair' cannot derive from Latin *pilum* because this would have yielded a Basque **biro*, or that common Basque *golde* 'plough' cannot derive from Latin *culter* 'ploughshare' because this would have yielded **golte* in the eastern dialects, which in fact also have *golde*. 3. The asterisk marks a form as impossible, as when we note that roots of the forms **bed-*, **bhet-* and **tebh-* are impossible in PIE because of morpheme-structure constraints. The context usually makes it clear which use is intended. Some linguists prefer to use a double asterisk for certain purposes: to indicate that a proposed form has been reconstructed on the basis of other forms which are themselves reconstructed, to mark a suggested reconstruction as doubtful, to mark a form as genuinely non-existent rather than as merely unattested, or to distinguish a form as actually impossible rather then as merely non-existent or unrecorded. Campbell (1998) uses a script x for senses 2 and 3.

Athabaskan (also **Athapaskan**) A major language family of western North America containing about thirty-six languages, a few of them extinct, and divided into *northern* and *southern* branches. Among its best-known members are *Slave*, *Chipewyan*, *Navajo* and the several varieties of *Apache*. The languages are distinguished by their extraordinarily elaborate prefixing verbal morphology. See **Na-Dene**.

athematic Of a lexical item in an inflecting language, inflected by adding suffixes directly to the stem, without the intervention of a **thematic vowel**. For example, the Latin verb-stems *es-* 'be' and *fer-* 'carry' are athematic, taking the Old Latin infinitive suffix -*se* to form infinitives *es-se* and **fer-se* (classical *ferre* by assimilation). Compare **thematic**.

atonic Of a vowel or a syllable, unstressed or unaccented. Compare **tonic**.

atrophy (also **attrition**) The gradual disuse and hence disappearance of some part of a linguistic system. For example, the historical sub-junctive has atrophied in western varieties of Basque, being now confined to a few frozen expressions and to very formal styles and otherwise replaced by non-finite constructions; in early Romance, the inherited Latin case-system atrophied and fell out of use, even though phonological change alone would not have eliminated all the case-endings. In the case of **language death**, the *entire* linguistic system may atrophy as the language sinks into disuse; see the remarks under **linguistic obsolescence**.

attestation Another term for **documentation**.

attested form A linguistic form which is securely recorded in writing or in recordings of speech. Compare **unattested form**.

attitudinal factors The various social factors which are important in determining the linguistic consequences of **contact** between lan-guages (see **language contact**). See Thomason and Kaufman (1988: *passim*) for discussion.

attrition (also **erosion**) 1. Any phonological change, or any sequence of changes, which has the effect of removing segments or syllables from word-forms and hence of reducing their phonological bulk, or the resulting loss of phonological material. For example, Old English *singan* /singan/ has undergone attrition to modern *sing* /sɪŋ/; Latin *consobrinum* 'cousin' has developed to French *cousin* /kuzɛ̃/; and Latin *augustum* 'August' has undergone attrition all the way to French *août* /u/. 2. Another term for **atrophy**.

augment A verbal prefix, apparently of the form **H₁e-*, used for constructing certain verb-forms in Greek, Indo-Iranian and Arme-nian. A Greek example is *pémpō* 'send', imperfect *épempon*, aorist *épempsa*. The PIE status of the augment is debatable.

aureate word Another term for **inkhornism**.

auslaut The end of a word, or a segment in this position. Compare **anlaut**, **inlaut**.

Auslautsverhärtung The German for **final devoicing**.

Ausnahmslosigkeit Exceptionlessness: the German label for the 'exceptionless sound laws' advocated by the **Neogrammarians**.

Australian languages The indigenous languages of Australia, numbering perhaps 250 at the time of the European settlement. Most Australian languages transparently belong to the large **Pama-Nyungan** family, but the northwest coast is occupied by a further twenty-odd families which are typologically very different from Pama-Nyungan. The extinct **Tasmanian languages** are sparsely recorded and difficult to classify. See Dixon (1980) for a survey.

Austric A proposed language family linking **Austro-Asiatic** and **Austronesian**, and possibly others. W. Schmidt (1906) proposed to link these two and coined the name. Benedict (1942) included Austronesian in his **Austro-Tai** proposal, and united this with Austro-Asiatic and **Miao-Yao** (Hmong-Mien) in a larger Austric family. The proposed family is deeply controversial and far from generally accepted. See Ruhlen (1991: 151–157) for a survey.

Austro-Asiatic A large language family of southeast Asia, with over 100 languages. It consists of two branches: **Munda** (in India) and **Mon-Khmer**. Some specialists regard the tiny **Nicobarese** group as forming a third coordinate branch of the family, while others group Nicobarese with Mon-Khmer. The disperse distribution of the languages suggests that the family is ancient in southeast Asia and has lost territory to later arrivals.

Austronesian A vast language family, with nearly 1000 languages, extending from the western Indian Ocean to the eastern Pacific. There are three small Formosan branches, all on Taiwan (*Atayalic*, *Paiwanic* and *Tsouic*, though these groupings are debated), plus a vast *Malayo-Polynesian* branch including all the languages outside Taiwan. The family includes virtually all the languages of Madagascar, Malaysia, Indonesia, Sarawak, Brunei, the Philippines, Taiwan, New Zealand and the islands of the Pacific, plus some coastal languages of New Guinea. Among the better-known languages are *Malagasy*, *Malay-Indonesian*, *Javanese*, *Tagalog*, *Maori*, *Samoan*, *Fijian* and

Hawaiian, plus the extinct *Rapanui* of Easter Island. The most divergent languages are those on Taiwan, which is often thought to have been the Austronesian homeland. The family was formerly called *Malayo-Polynesian*, but this label is now reserved for the major branch of the family. See Ruhlen (1991: 160–172) for a historical survey of the family.

Austro-Tai A proposed language family linking **Austronesian** with **Tai** and **Kadai** and possibly also **Miao-Yao** (Hmong-Mien). Put forward by Benedict (1942 and especially 1975), the proposal is highly controversial but has won some support. See Ruhlen (1991: 152–158) for a survey.

automatization The term used by Haiman (1994) for the accumulation of linguistic habits leading to the establishment of a (possibly innovating) linguistic pattern.

autonomy The status of a language variety which is regarded as constituting an independent language, and not as a version of anything else. Compare **heteronomy**.

auxiliarization The conversion of a lexical verb into an auxiliary.

Avar The unknown language of a mysterious people who invaded Europe, apparently from Asia, in the sixth century AD and then effectively disappeared at the end of the tenth century. There is no connection with the modern *Avar* language, a **Nakh-Dagestan** language.

Avestan (formerly also **Zend**) The earliest recorded **Iranian** language, the language of the Zoroastrian scriptures. An earlier version, called *Gathic* or *Old Avestan*, is attested in some songs and short passages variously dated between the eleventh and sixth centuries BC. A later version, called *Later Avestan* or *Younger Avestan*, is far more copiously attested, though the texts were transmitted only orally for centuries and were finally written down only in the third to seventh centuries AD, in a specially invented and extremely elaborate alphabetic script which includes a great deal of redundant phonetic detail. Compare **Old Persian**.

avoidance of homophony Any of several putative principles sometimes invoked to account for developments in which homophony is either avoided or eliminated. 1. Irregular phonological developments occur in cases in which the regular developments would have led to homophony between semantically distinct words. 2. Homophony resulting from phonological change is eliminated by replacing one of the homophonous words with a synonym of different form. The celebrated is example is Latin *cattus* 'cat' and *gallus* 'rooster', both of which would have developed regularly to *gat* in Gascon – but the word for 'rooster' was everywhere replaced by a different word. 3. A homophone of an obscene or offensive word is replaced by a different item, as in the replacement of *cock* by *rooster* in American English. See **isomorphy**, **Humboldt's Universal** (under **isomorphy**).

avoidance of merger A putative functional principle by which phoneme systems undergoing change tend to resist **mergers**, either in general or in particular cases, in order to maintain lexical distinctions and prevent homophony. Though plausible in motivation, and supported by such data as **chain shifts**, the principle has not so far been sufficiently constrained to account for the numerous mergers which have indisputably occurred – for example, in English, Greek and Mandarin Chinese.

Aymaran (also **Jaqi**) A family of three languages spoken in the Andes, including the enormously important *Aymara*. See **Quechumaran**.

Aztec-Tanoan A proposed grouping of the **Uto-Aztecan** and **Kiowa-Tanoan** families into a single family. Put forward by Sapir (1921b) and by Whorf and Trager (1937), this hypothesis is often presented as fact, but the evidence for it is slender indeed. See Campbell (1997a: 269–273) for a critical survey with references.

B

babbling word See under **nursery word**.

back-formation (rarely also **retrograde formation**) A type of **word-formation**, or a word formed in this way, in which a new word is obtained by removing from a longer word a morph which appears to be a familiar affix but historically is not. English examples include the formation of *edit* and *sculpt* from the Latin loans *editor* and *sculptor*, and of *burgle* and *letch* from the French loans *burglar* and *lecher* (all interpreted as containing the English agent suffix *-er*), of *pea* and *cherry* from the French loans *pease* and *cherries* (originally uncountable), and of *televise* from the Graeco-Latin neologism *television*. Compare **metanalysis, reanalysis** (sense 1).

background noise In the **comparison** of languages in the hope of finding **genetic links**, the meaningless but potentially misleading presence of **chance resemblances, nursery words, onomato-poeias** and possibly ancient and unidentifiable **loan words**. In the case of languages which may or may not be remotely related, it is a critical matter to eliminate such background noise from consideration, but this is not always easy. See the **search problem**.

backing (also **retraction**) Any phonological change in which the articulation of a segment is moved backwards in the oral cavity, such as the retraction of /ɪ/ to [ə] in New Zealand, the backing of /e/ to [ʌ] in several American cities, and the retraction of /ʃ/ to [x] or [χ] in Castilian Spanish. The opposite is **fronting**.

back mutation (also **back umlaut**) One type of **umlaut**; see that entry.

back slang A type of word play in which a word is pronounced as though spelled backwards. British English has *yob* from *boy*, while the French style called *verlan* provides numerous examples, such as *meuf* for *femme* 'woman' and *keus* for *sac* 'handbag'.

back spelling (Ger *Rückschreibung*) The writing of a word with a segment which is not etymologically appropriate, particularly by a speaker who has lost a contrast retained by other speakers. An example is the writing of English *oak* as *hoke* and of Basque *ume* 'child' as *hume* by speakers who have lost the contrast between /h/ and zero retained by other speakers. Such speakers apparently know that the extra segment is required in the spelling of some words, but are not sure which words those are.

back umlaut Another term for **back mutation**.

backward projection The tendency of linguists to assume that what they perceive as the 'normal' state of affairs today was also the normal state of affairs centuries ago. Milroy and Milroy (1985a) and Milroy (1992) argue that many linguists have inappropriately projected the concept of standard English centuries back into the past while ignoring major variation, whereas sociolinguists prefer to project variation into the past. See **historicization**.

bahuvrīhi (also **exocentric compound**) A type of **compound** word in which one element modifies or restricts the other and the whole denotes an entity which is a hyponym of an unexpressed semantic head: *highbrow, redskin, heavy-handed*. The term derives from Sanskrit, in which such formations are extremely numerous but always adjectival, like English *barefoot*; the Sanskrit word itself is an example meaning 'much rice' (i.e. 'well-to-do').

Bai An **isolated language** spoken by over a million people in northern Yunnan province in southern China. Some people suspect it of being a non-Chinese **Sinitic** language.

Baltic A branch of **Indo-European** including *Latvian* and *Lithuanian*, plus the extinct *Old Prussian, Galindian, Jatvingian (Sudovian), Curonian, Zemgalian* and *Selonian*. Though fragments are recorded earlier, the first connected texts in Baltic languages date only from the fourteenth century, and most of the extinct ones are poorly recorded. The Baltic languages are exceptionally conservative, and Lithuanian is regarded as the most conservative of all living IE languages. Baltic is generally believed to be closely related to **Slavic** in a larger **Balto-Slavic** grouping. See Schmalstieg (1998) for a historical summary.

Balto-Slavic A major branch of **Indo-European**, consisting of two sub-branches, **Baltic** and **Slavic**. The validity of this grouping was debated in the past, but it is widely accepted today, though some critics prefer to see the obvious links between the two groups as resulting only from **language contact**. The prehistory of Balto-Slavic is characterized by almost numbingly complex developments in the word-accent, leading to more named 'laws' than any other single domain in all of IE; see Collinge (1985: 271–277) for a critical survey.

Bantu A single sub-branch of the **Niger-Congo** family of languages. Though Bantu forms only a low-ranking sub-branch of the **Benue-Congo** branch, the Bantu languages occupy a huge area of central, eastern and southern Africa, and many are among the most important languages on the continent: *KiKongo, Luganda, Ndebele, Shona, Chimweni, Swahili, Tsotho, Zulu, Xhosa* and many others. The Bantu languages are distinguished by their rich gender systems, their unusually elaborate agreement, and their overwhelmingly prefixing morphology. The Bantu languages seem to have spread out from the vicinity of Cameroon around 3000 years ago and to have displaced a large number of earlier languages.

Barbacoan A family of about six languages in Colombia and Ecuador, often thought to be related to **Paezan**.

Bartholomae's Law The statement, put forward by Bartholomae (1883: 48), that, either in PIE or only in Indo-Iranian (opinion is divided), a cluster consisting of a voiced aspirated plosive followed by a voiceless plosive was assimilated to a voiced plosive followed by a voiced aspirated plosive: schematically, $D^h + T > DD^h$. Examples from Sanskrit, with the verbal-adjective suffix *-ta*: *budh-* 'wake' + *-ta* > *buddha-* 'awakened'; *labh-* 'seize' + *-ta* > *labdha-*; *dah-* 'burn' (< **dagh-*) + *-ta* > *dagdha-*. The rule also applied if the second consonant was *s*: **awgh-* + 2Sg middle *-sa* > Indo-Iranian **augz^ha*. The only clear cases are found in Indo-Iranian; other languages generally show the different development illustrated by **legh-* 'lie' (as in Greek *lékhos*), but Greek *léktron*, Latin *lectus*. Consequently, some prefer to see this process as strictly Indo-Iranian, but the existence in PIE of suffix doublets like **-tro-/*-dhro-* and **-tlo-/ *-dhlo-* (continued by Latin *-trum/-brum* and *-culum/-bulum*) seems rather to point to a PIE process which has been generally obliterated by analogy outside Indo-Iranian. See Collinge (1985: 7–11) for critical discussion with references.

Barth's Law (also **Barth-Ginsberg Law**) The statement that, in certain Semitic languages, the vowel sequence /a/.../a/ shifts to /i/.../a/, so that, for example, **yaktab* becomes *yiktab*.

Bàrtoli's Law A putative change in early Greek by which the word-accent was shifted from a word-final syllable to the preceding syllable in certain circumstances. Invoked by Bàrtoli (1930) to account for correspondences like Greek *thygátēr* 'daughter' versus Sanskrit *duhitá*, this law is much debated. See Collinge (1985: 229–230) for critical discussion with references.

Bartsch's Law The statement that /ε/ diphthongizes to /jε/ in French when preceded by a palatal consonant. An example is the development of earlier **chen* 'dog' to *chien* /ʃjɛ̃/.

barytone Especially in ancient Greek, a word whose word-accent or stress does not fall upon the final syllable. Compare **oxytone**.

basic vocabulary (also **core vocabulary**) (Ger *Kernwortschatz*) Those words in a language which are of very high frequency, which are learned early by children, and which are supposedly more resistant to **lexical replacement** than other words. Among these are personal pronouns, the lower numerals, body-part names, kinship terms like *mother* and *child*, names of natural phenomena like *sun* and *rain*, names of common substances like *water* and *stone*, common verbs like *go*, *come*, *sleep* and *die*, common adjectives like *red*, *new*, *dark* and *long*, and grammatical items like *in*, *and* and *here*. Basic vocabulary is the basis of the **Swadesh word list** and of various statistical approaches to detecting remote relationships between languages, but there are linguists who doubt whether a meaningful and universally valid list of such words can ever be compiled, and also those who doubt that such words are as resistant to replacement as is sometimes assumed. In Australian languages, for instance, there seems to be little evidence that basic vocabulary is particularly resistant to replacement. Compare **peripheral vocabulary**.

basilect See under **post-creole continuum**.

Basque A language spoken at the western end of the Pyrenees, mostly in northern Spain but partly in southwestern France. Basque is the most famous **isolated language** on earth; the most strenuous attempts at finding a relative for it have been conspicuous failures and suggestions to the contrary may be safely disregarded. Note in particular that there is no evidence to relate Basque to **Iberian**, to **Berber**, or to any of the **Caucasian** languages. An ancestral form of Basque called **Aquitanian** is sparsely attested in Gaul in Roman times, and Basque is unquestionably the last surviving pre-Indo-European language in western Europe. See Trask (1997) for a historical survey and Michelena (1977) for the reconstruction of the phonological prehistory of Basque. Agud and Tovar (1988–) is the standard etymological dictionary.

becanism A fanciful guess at the etymology of a word or name, based upon nothing more than a vague resemblance in sound, as when Spanish *España* 'Spain' is derived from Basque *ezpaña* 'the lip', or when Mexican Spanish *gringo* 'foreigner' is derived from the English song-title *Green Grow the Lilacs*. The term derives from the name of

the Dutch scholar Goropius Becanus, who was much given to these
guesses; many other equivalent terms have been used on occasion.

beech-tree problem The observation, in reconstructing vocabulary, that
words frequently change their referents and so, even when we can
reconstruct the form of a word with confidence, we may be unable to
determine its earliest meaning. A celebrated example of this is the
PIE tree-name reconstructed as *$b^h\bar{a}wg$-. Its descendants in Latin
and Germanic mean 'beech', which has often been taken as the
original sense, but its Greek descendant means 'oak', while its Slavic
descendant means 'elder'. Consequently, we cannot be certain about
the original sense. This conclusion is important because people have
tried to argue that the presence of a PIE word for 'beech' proves that
PIE must have been spoken in an area with beech trees and hence
west of the 'beech line' running roughly from Königsberg (Kalinin-
grad) to the Crimea, east of which no beeches grow. Such people
typically argue that the word 'beech' was simply transferred to
different trees by speakers who moved into areas where there were
no beeches, but this interpretation cannot be certain. This problem is
one of the **pitfalls of comparison**.

Behaghel's Laws A series of five statements about word order put
forward by Behaghel (1932: 4–7); both the first and the third are
often just called *Behaghel's Law*. 1. When units of equal status are
conjoined, the longest comes last. 2. The differing degrees of sentence stress explain different patterns of element order between
paraphrase sentences in German. 3. What belongs together is placed
together. (See the **constituency principle**.) 4. Given information
precedes new information. 5. A differentiating element precedes the
element it differentiates. Some of these, especially the last, are controversial. See Collinge (1985: 241–242).

Bender test A statistical method proposed in Bender (1969), deriving
from earlier work by Swadesh and Cowan, for testing the likelihood
that some number of CVC matches within the **Swadesh word list**
constitutes evidence for something better than **chance resemblances**. Bender concludes that, providing the criteria used for
accepting matches are sufficiently strict, a mere two matches out
of 100 word-pairs constitute evidence that more than chance is
involved, at the 95 per cent confidence level, though such a result
does not rule out contact, rather than common ancestry, as the
explanation.

Bengali One of the world's top ten languages in speaker numbers, an **Indo-Aryan** language spoken in Bangladesh, in West Bengal and elsewhere in India, and by immigrants in Britain and elsewhere. Bengali has a major literary tradition, though the literary form of the language is very different from the spoken form.

Benue-Congo A huge primary branch of the **Niger-Congo** family, containing **Bantu** and some smaller groupings, and numbering over 700 languages. Apart from the far-flung Bantu group and its relatives contained in the *Bantoid* subgroup, these languages are mostly spoken in and near Nigeria.

Benveniste's theory of the IE root See **Indo-European root theory**.

Bequemlichkeitstrieb Striving for minimal effort in speech; indolence. This is one of the supposed driving forces behind **language change** introduced by Georg von der Gabelentz in the nineteenth century. Compare *Deutlichkeitstrieb*.

Berber A single language (or, in some treatments, several closely related languages) forming a separate branch of the **Afro-Asiatic** family by itself and spoken in several dialects scattered through northwestern Africa, principally in Morocco. The extinct **Guanche** appears to have been a variety of Berber.

Bergin's Law An archaic construction in the VSO language Old Irish, in which the verb, instead of standing sentence-initially in the ususal absolute (non-compound) form or in the deuterotonic form of the conjunct (compound) paradigm, is in final (or sometimes medial) position and is always in the prototonic form of the conjunct paradigm. This pattern, noted by Bergin (1938: 197), is interpreted as a residue of an earlier SOV order in Celtic. See Collinge (1985: 230–231) for a survey.

best-tree approach Any of various computer programs which are designed to address the problem of **subgrouping**. Given some set of properties (**characters**) from the languages in question and some criteria for evaluating possible **family trees**, the program searches among the (large) set of conceivable trees for the one which is optimal in terms of the input. For more than a very few languages, the number of potential trees becomes far too large to be searched completely, and so the program is confined to examining only a sample of trees, though devices exist for testing the robustness of the tree finally selected as optimal. Best-tree approaches figure in the **Pennsylvania model of IE** and are currently being developed at Cambridge University.

bidirectional diffusion The term applied by Wang and Lien (1993) to a case in which two **competing changes** spread out from different foci within a single speech community by **lexical diffusion** – effectively, a combination of lexical diffusion and **dialect mixing**. Their example is certain southern dialects of Chinese, in which the Middle Chinese third tone with voiced initials has split about evenly, and unpredictably, into two distinct tones.

bifurcational theory A novel hypothesis about the phonological development of **Germanic**, put forward by Vennemann (1984, 1988). Vennemann accepts the **glottalic theory of PIE**, and supposes that PIE */p t k/ (the traditional */b d g/) simultaneously developed into aspirates /p^h t^h k^h/ in northern (Low) Germanic but into affricates /pf ts kx/ in southern (High) Germanic. See Ramat (1998: 393–394) for a summary with references.

bilateral comparison (also **binary comparison**) Pairwise comparison; the practice of comparing just two languages at a time, especially in searching for evidence of a genetic link. The opposing term is now usually **n-ary comparison**, since the obvious **multilateral comparison** has come to be used in a specialized sense.

bilingue An inscription bearing the same text in two different languages.

Bill Peters effect (also **Labov-Yaeger-Steiner paradox**) The phenomenon in which an individual consistently makes a large difference between two phonemes in his or her spontaneous speech but, in self-conscious speech, loses that large difference, so that such speech is characterized by either a **merger** or a **near-merger** of those two phonemes. The phenomenon was identified in Labov *et al.* (1972) and named by Labov (1994: 363–364).

binary comparison Another term for **bilateral comparison**.

biological metaphor Any of various concepts or models taken into historical linguistics from evolutionary biology. Such metaphors as **language birth**, **language death**, linguistic **evolution**, **genetic**

relationship and family tree are very familiar, but their appropriateness has been much debated; critics argue that taking these metaphors too literally can be seriously misleading. For recent discussions, see Lass (1997), M. Ross (1997) and especially McMahon (1994: ch. 12).

bioprogram hypothesis The hypothesis, put forward by Bickerton (1981, 1984, 1988), that children are born with an innate default structure for language, and that this default will emerge automatically in the speech of children not adequately exposed to a surrounding language with a different structure. The most obvious case is the creation of creoles and Bickerton points to the worldwide similarities among creoles as evidence. The hypothesis is very controversial.

bleaching (also **semantic depletion**, **semantic fading**, **semantic weakening**) The removal of semantic content from lexical items undergoing **grammaticalization**, for example, in lexical verbs converted to auxiliaries, tense-markers or object-markers.

bleeding The state of affairs in which an earlier phonological change removes certain segments from the scope of a later change which would otherwise have affected them. For example, the Vulgar Latin palatalization of /tt/ and /kk/ before /j/ bled the later Spanish degemination of geminate plosives to simple ones, so that, for example, *bracchium* 'arm' yields Spanish *brazo* (<z> = /θ/ or /s/), whereas *saccum* 'sack' yields Spanish *saco* (with /k/). In a rule-based account of phonological change, *bleeding order* is the ordering of two changes in such a way that the first removes potential cases of the application of the second. The opposite is **feeding**.

blend 1. (also **portmanteau**) A word which is coined by extracting and combining arbitrary pieces of two or more existing words. Classic examples include *smog* (from *smoke* and *fog*), *motel* (*motor* plus *hotel*) and *brunch* (*breakfast* plus *lunch*). More recent examples include *Chunnel* (*Channel* plus *tunnel*), *skyjack* (*sky* plus *hijack*) and *pulsar* (*pulse* plus *quasar*). Note that, in some of these, one element remains intact. The process of forming a blend is *blending* (or **amalgamation**), and blending may be a forerunner to **reanalysis** (sense 1); it is possible that *cheeseburger* was originally simply a blend of *cheese* and *hamburger* before this last was reanalysed as *ham* plus *-burger*. Compare **clipped form, stump compound**. 2. See **syntactic blend**.

Bodic One of the primary subdivisions of the **Tibeto-Burman** group of languages.

body-part model Another term for the **anthropomorphic model**.

borrowability The readiness with which a linguistic feature can undergo **borrowing** from one language into another. There is considerable evidence, for example, that lexical items are more readily borrowed than grammatical morphemes, and that nouns are more readily borrowed than verbs. See the **Moravcsik universals of borrowing**.

borrowed sound change A phonological change which occurs spontaneously in one language and is then taken over *in toto* by a neighbouring language. For example, Castilian Spanish in the sixteenth century underwent the unusual change of [ʃ] to [χ]; this change has since been borrowed into the Gipuzkoan dialect of Basque, in which earlier [ʃ] has likewise changed to [χ]. See **rule borrowing**.

borrowing 1. (also **lexical copying**, sometimes also **lexical change**) Narrowly, the transfer of a word from one language into a second language, as a result of some kind of *contact* (see **language contact**) between speakers of the two. English, for example, has borrowed *face* from Norman French, *cigarette* from modern French, *hoosegow* from Mexican Spanish, *kayak* from an Eskimo language and *boomerang* from an Australian language, among countless others. See **adoption, adaptation, loanblend, loan shift, loan nativization.** 2. Broadly, the transfer of linguistic features of any kind from one language to another as a result of contact. The term is normally only applied to cases of the incorporation of foreign features into a language, and not merely to the effects of **interference**.

borrowing of morphology The transfer of morphological material (especially inflectional morphemes) from one language to another by contact (see **language contact**). This was once thought to be rare or even impossible, but a number of cases are now known, such as the use of Turkish inflectional suffixes with native Greek verbs in Anatolian Greek. See Thomason (1997c: 479) for a survey with references. Compare **metatypy**.

bottleneck In **linguistic geography**, either of two notions, but particularly the second. 1. A geographically narrow region through which peoples, and hence languages, are forced to pass in order to spread. An example is the Bering Strait land bridge between Siberia and Alaska. 2. The observation that a **language family**, of whatever size and extent, necessarily derives from a single **ancestor** with a single set of properties. Hence the **daughter languages** are not free to exhibit any properties at all with equal likelihood, but instead will tend to retain the ancestral properties with greater than chance probability. For example, most IE languages exhibit a first-singular marker /-m-/, purely because this marker was prominent in PIE. Compare **founder effect**.

bottom-up reconstruction The ordinary approach to **comparative reconstruction**, in which several related languages are compared in order to reconstruct their immediate ancestor. Compare **top-down reconstruction**.

boundary creation A type of **reanalysis** (sense 1) in which a morpheme boundary is introduced into a position in which none was previously present. For example, pre-Old High German neuter nouns ending in -es took the plural ending -a; by regular phonological change, *-es was lost word-finally, while in the plural *-es-a became -ir. As a result, *kalbes 'calf', plural *kalbes-a, became kalb, plural kalbir, and then -ir was reinterpreted as the plural ending by boundary creation (and extended to other nouns). This is one kind of **resegmentation**.

boundary loss The disappearance of a morpheme boundary which has become opaque as a consequence of other changes. For example, English shepherd and filth are no longer generally interpreted by speakers as sheep-herd and foul-th, English hussy is no longer interpreted as house-wife, and Basque itun 'agreement, pact' is no longer interpreted as *egite-une 'doing-occasion'. This is one kind of **re-segmentation**. See also **morphanization**.

boundary shift A type of **reanalysis** in which the boundary between two constituents is shifted from one position to another. An example is the development of complement clauses in the Germanic languages, in which an original construction of the form I say that: [he will come] has been reanalysed into the structure I say [that he will come]. The shift of a morpheme boundary from one place to another is called **metanalysis**. Boundary shift generally is one type of **resegmentation**.

branch (also **subfamily**) A larger or smaller part of a **family tree** consisting of a single (possibly unrecorded) language and all the descendants of that language: a **taxon** which forms part of a larger tree. For example, **Latin** and its **Romance** descendants form a branch of **Indo-European**, as do **Proto-Germanic** and its **Germanic** descendants.

branching The breakup of a single **ancestor language** into immediate **daughter languages,** or the structure of a **language family** after perhaps several periods of such breakup. See **elaboration rate**.

breakdown The collapse of some grammatical system in a language, leading either to its total disappearance or to residual **junk** which may lead to **exaptation**. An example is the breakdown of the Latin case system in most Romance languages.

breaking (also **fracture**, Ger *Brechung*) The **diphthongization** of a vowel. The term is specifically applied to certain instances of diphthongization of front vowels that took place in Pre–Old–English before a cluster of /l/ or /r/ plus another consonant or before /x/. Examples (involving Pre-OE */æ/ from WGerm */ɑ/): OE *bearn* 'child' (Go, OHG *barn*); OE *earm* 'arm' (Go *arms*, OIc *armr*); OE *eald* 'old' (Go *alþeis*, OHG *alt*); OE *eall* 'all' (Go *alls*, OIc *allr*); OE *seah* 'he saw' (OHG *sah*); OE *eahta* 'eight' (Go *ahtau*, OHG *ahto*). See Lass (1994: 48–51), from which these examples are taken. The opposite is **smoothing**. Compare *back mutation* (under **umlaut**).

breakup The process in which continuing change among the regional dialects of a language results in such substantial regional differences that we can no longer speak of dialects and are forced instead to speak of separate languages.

Brechung The German term for **breaking**.

bricolage A label applied by Posner (1996: 317–318) and by Lass (1997: 309–316) to the process in which a language assembles a new grammatical system out of bits and pieces of an old system which has collapsed. Posner cites the collapse of the Latin demonstrative system and the resulting cannibalism of the *ille* demonstrative to create a wide range of grammatical items of diverse functions in Romance. Lass cites the example of the Germanic dative case, which was assembled from a variety of forms continuing several entirely distinct case-forms in PIE, and describes the Germanic dative as 'cobbled together out of the remnants of a morphological disaster'. Compare **exaptation**.

brightening The **fronting** of a vowel, as in **Anglo-Frisian Brightening**.

British See under **Celtic**.

Brittonic See under **Celtic**.

broadening (also **generalization, widening, extension**) The extension of the meaning of a word to a wider range of referents than formerly, as when English *dog* was broadened from denoting a particular type of canine to denoting any kind of canine, or when Basque *akats* was broadened from 'nick, scratch' to meaning 'defect' (of any kind). The opposite is **narrowing**.

Brugmann's Law The statement that PIE short $*o$ becomes long $\bar{a}$ in open syllables in Indo-Iranian. For example, PIE $*doru$- 'wood' gives Greek *dóru* but Old Indic *dāru*, Avestan *dā^{u}ru*. Formulated by Brugmann (1876, 1879), this statement ran into difficulties and was eventually renounced by its author and declared 'dead' by others; nevertheless, it is still taken seriously today by some specialists, though in modified form. See Collinge (1985: 13–21) for a critical discussion with references.

Brythonic (also **Brittonic, P-Celtic**) See under **Celtic**.

buffer zone A geographical region which separates two other regions in which a single word has conflicting senses and within which the word either is absent or has only a superordinate sense. Anttila (1989: 182–183) cites the case of *Korn*, which means 'rye' in the central German-speaking region but 'spelt' in the southwest; the two are separated by a buffer zone in which the word means 'grain' in general. He also cites the case of eastern Belgium, in which the word *Opper* has several conflicting senses, all separated by buffer zones in which the word is absent.

Bugge's Canon A statement, by Bugge (1874: 400 *ff.*), about the history of the third-singular active verb-endings in the **Italic** languages. Bugge concludes that primary $*\text{-}t\text{-}i$ yields -*t* in Italic, while secondary

*-*t* yields -*d* or -*Ø*, but that Latin generalized the primary endings throughout its verbal system. See Collinge (1985: 231–232) for an account.

Bugge's Rule A proposal, by Bugge (1887), that the Germanic fricatives descending from PIE word-initial voiceless plosives regularly underwent voicing to / v ð ɣ / if the inherited word-accent fell not less than three syllables from the onset of the word. The proposal is controversial. See Collinge (1985: 232) for an account.

Bulging Hub Principle An early model of **linguistic geography**, put forward by Morris Swadesh (1971). Swadesh sees almost all the world's languages as reaching their present positions as a result of repeated waves of expansion from an epicentre located in west-central Asia.

Burgundian The extinct and little-known east **Germanic** language of a people who formerly inhabited east-central France.

Burmese-Lolo (also **Lolo-Burmese**) A major, and possibly primary, branch of the **Tibeto-Burman** grouping, including about forty-five languages, of which *Burmese* is the best known.

Burushaski An **isolated language** spoken in two neighbouring valleys in the Himalayas, in the disputed territory of Kashmir. It is suspected of being a remnant of the languages spoken in the region before the arrival of the **Indo-Aryan** languages.

by-name Especially in the era before **surnames** were established, an additional name conferred upon an adult in order to distinguish him or her from others with the same **given name**. A by-name might represent a physical characteristic (*Black*, *Small*), a personal quality (*Meek*, *Fox* for a cunning person), occupation (*Miller*, *Smith*), origin (*Bristol*, *Scott*) or almost anything else. Many surnames arose as by-names.

C

Caddoan A small family (six languages, some extinct) in the central USA; the best-known members are *Caddo*, *Wichita* and *Pawnee*. Caddoan is included in the **Macro-Siouan** and **Keresiouan**

hypotheses and other speculative groupings, but there is no compelling evidence for any external links at all.

Caland's Law The statement, put forward by Caland (1892, 1893), that, in early IE, certain adjectives with stems ending in *-ro-* replaced this ending with another (such as *-i-* or *-mo-*) when serving as the first element in a compound or when forming a comparative. An example is Greek *kydrós* 'renowned', *kydi-áneira* 'bringing renown to men'. For critical discussion with references, see Collinge (1985: 23–27) or Szemerényi (1996: 193–194). The several endings alternating here are called the *Caland system*.

Caldwell's Law The statement, by Caldwell (1856), that, in Proto-Dravidian (and also in several daughter languages, including Old Tamil), voiceless and voiced stops are in complementary distribution.

calque (also **loan translation**, rarely **semantic copying**) A word or phrase constructed by taking a word or phrase in another language as a model and translating it morpheme by morpheme. For example, ancient Greek *sympathia* 'sympathy' was calqued into Latin by translating *syn-* 'with' as *con-* 'with' and *pathia* 'suffering' as *passio* 'suffering', producing Latin *compassio*. The Latin word was then calqued into German by means of *mit* 'with' and *Leid* 'grief', producing *Mitleid* 'sympathy, compassion'. Calquing is often much favoured by advocates of **purism**.

Campbell's principle A putative principle of **borrowing**, put forward by Campbell (1976: 83, 191–192). It says this: in borrowing, segments tend not to be subject to the distributional restrictions holding in the donor language.

Camunic An extinct language of unknown affiliation, recorded in about seventy rock inscriptions in a modified Etruscan alphabet, in the Valcomonica valley in northwestern Italy and dating from the second half of the first millennium BC. It is possibly related to **Etruscan**, but this is not certain.

Canadian raising The phenomenon, occurring in most Canadian and some American accents, by which the first element of the diphthongs /ai/ and /au/ (and sometimes also /ar/) is centralized ('raised') in specified circumstances, most commonly before an underlyingly voiceless consonant in the same morpheme. In accents with this feature, there are distinct nuclei in pairs like *ride* and *write* and *loud* and *lout*, and some varieties also have different nuclei in further pairs, like *rider* and *cider*, *louder* and *chowder*, and *hard* and *heart*. The name is probably a misnomer, since the centralized pronunciation was seemingly once general in English, and hence we have not a raising but a failure to lower.

cant Another term for **argot**.

capital letter In a **reconstruction**, a notational device indicating that the phonetic quality of a segment is uncertain. Thus, 'N' denotes an unspecified nasal, 'R' an unspecified liquid and 'V' an unspecified vowel. Particular usages vary considerably from case to case.

Carian An extinct and poorly recorded language of ancient Anatolia. It is usually thought to have been an **Indo-European** language, and quite likely **Anatolian**, though these conclusions are not certain.

Cariban A language family of northern South America and the Caribbean containing about sixty languages, many of them now extinct. The Carib language *Hixkaryana* was the first language ever discovered with OVS basic word order.

case anthropology Another term for the **anthropomorphic model**, used by Hagège (1993: 108).

case vide The French for **hole in the pattern**.

catachresis A formal term for a **malapropism**.

catapult mechanism A proposed mechanism, put forward by Randall (1990), for accounting for the retreat from overgeneralization: that is, for the observation that structures like *He said his friend a funny thing* remain ungrammatical in English in spite of the obvious model provided by grammatical cases like *He told his friend a funny thing*. In this case, the proposal is that hearing things like *He said a funny thing*, compared with the absence of *He told a funny thing*, interacts with a universal principle ('an optional element cannot occur inside an obligatory element') to 'catapult' the learner into rejecting the original structure. See van der Wurff (1995), and compare the **subset principle**.

categorial borrowing The acquisition by a language of grammatical categories through *contact* (see **language contact**). For example, Chinookan appears to have acquired grammatical gender by contact, and Bengali has acquired negative verbs by contact with Dravidian.

categorial metaphor The term used by Claudi and Heine (1986) and Heine *et al.* (1991a) for any of a broad range of **metaphors** which they see as involving shifts along the following scale: person > object > activity > space > time > quality.

category change Another term for **category shift**.

category change, principle of A putative principle governing **lexical diffusion**, proposed by Labov (1994: 603). It says this: changes that affect several features of a sound simultaneously proceed by altering the category memberships of individual words – that is, by shifting words from one phonological category to another.

category shift (also **category change**) Any change in which a linguistic form is moved from one syntactic category to another, such as when a noun or a verb becomes an adposition. Category shifts are frequent in many types of **grammaticalization** and **reanalysis**; see also **restoring reanalysis**.

category stability, principle of The observation, put forward by Labov (1994: 109–111), that individuals who change their accents on moving to a different speech area tend strongly to preserve the distribution of lexical items among the phoneme categories of the system – that is, while they may change their phonetic realizations, they do not introduce **mergers**, **splits** or different distributions of phonemes, even when these are typical of their new area.

Caucasian (also **Ibero-Caucasian**) A group of about thirty-eight languages spoken in and near the Caucasus. There are three genetic families: **Abkhaz-Adyge (Northwest Caucasian)**, with five languages; **Nakh-Dagestan (Northeast Caucasian)**, with about thirty languages; and **Kartvelian (South Caucasian)**, with five languages. Counting languages is difficult, since many Caucasian languages exhibit extraordinary dialectal divergence, often involving mutual unintelligibility, and hence decisions about language boundaries are often arbitrary. A genetic link between the Nakh and Dagestan groups was formerly considered doubtful but is now widely accepted. Early and recent attempts at demonstrating a remote genetic link between the two northern groups have not been widely accepted, and no one is currently defending a link between Kartvelian and either of the northern groups. Note that linguists who accept a genetic link between the two northern groups often use *Caucasian* specifically for their putative northern grouping, excluding Kartvelian.

causation of change See under **explanation of change**.

ceceo See under *seseo*.

Celtiberian A **Celtic** language (or possibly a group of languages) spoken in much of the Iberian Peninsula (Spain) before the Roman conquest, also called *Peninsular Celtic*. Little of Celtiberian is preserved apart from personal names and place names, and its classification within Celtic is accordingly unknown. See Price (1998: 82–83).

Celtic (formerly also **Keltic**) A group of languages forming one major branch of the **Indo-European** family. In pre-Roman times Celtic languages were spoken all across Europe, including (at least) Ireland, Britain, Spain, France, the Low Countries, southern Germany, Switzerland, northern Italy, Austria, Bohemia, parts of the Balkans and later also part of Anatolia. The languages have been losing ground ever since, however, and today the surviving Celtic languages are confined to the western fringes of Europe. Best known are the *insular Celtic* languages, divided into two branches: *Goidelic* (or *Gaelic*) (*Irish*, *Scots Gaelic* and the recently extinct *Manx*) and *Brythonic* (or *Brittonic*) (*Welsh*, *Breton* and the extinct *Cornish* and *Cumbric*); the common ancestor of the Brythonic languages, called *British*, was spoken in much of Britain before the Anglo–Saxon invasion. Fragments are preserved of a few extinct Celtic languages, notably **Pictish** in Scotland, **Gaulish** in Gaul, **Celtiberian** in Spain and **Lepontic** in northern Italy, but not enough is known about them to establish their position within the Celtic family. Goidelic (and apparently Celtiberian) are *Q-Celtic* languages, in which PIE $*k^w$ survives as such or becomes k; Brythonic, Lepontic, most of Gaulish and possibly Pictish are *P-Celtic* languages, in which $*k^w$ develops to p. See P. Sims-Williams (1998) or Russell (1995) for a historical survey of the family, and Ball and Jones (1993) or MacAulay (1993) for surveys of the individual languages.

centralization Any phonological change in which a vowel becomes more central than formerly. An example is the shift of [uː] to [ʉː] in Scottish accents of English.

Central Sudanic One of the principal branches of **Nilo-Saharan**, containing 40–60 languages spoken in two widely separated areas. Greenberg (1963b) assigns it further to his **Chari-Nile** grouping.

centre of gravity In **dialect geography**, either of two related concepts. 1. The geographical region in which a **dialect continuum** exhibits the highest degree of diversity. 2. The projection of the root of a **family tree** on to the ground.

centre-of-gravity principle Another term for the **age-area hypothesis**.

centre of innovation Another term for **locus**.

centricity The point of reference for a spatial item. Heine *et al.* (1991a: 139) conclude that 'under' and 'on' (for example) are stable in a speech situation, having the same reference for speaker and hearer, and hence tend to be constructed according to the **landmark model**, whereas 'back' and 'front' have a different significance for speaker and hearer, are correspondingly more sensitive to centricity, and tend overwhelmingly to be constructed according to the **anthropomorphic model**.

centum language Any branch of **Indo-European** in which certain PIE consonants developed into velar plosives, often (but not invariably) merging with the reflexes of the PIE velars. The centum languages include **Celtic, Italic, Germanic, Greek, Anatolian** and **Tocharian**. The name derives from the IE word for '100', which began with one of the relevant consonants and which exhibits an initial velar in the centum languages: Latin *centum*, Greek *(he)katón*, Gothic *hund* (/h/ < */k/), Old Irish *cēt* and so on. In the remaining IE languages, the **satem languages**, the same consonants developed instead into palatals (and usually later into sibilants), remaining distinct from the inherited velars. These divergent developments have often been taken as evidence that PIE possessed a contrastive set of palatal plosives */kʹ gʹ ghʹ/, the **first palatal series**, distinct from the velars and serving as the source of the centum and satem developments, but the evidence is conflicting and not all specialists accept the reality of the palatal plosives.

cerebral Especially in discussions of Sanskrit, a philological term for
retroflex.

cf. The abbreviation for *compare* (Latin *confer*). 1. An instruction to consult
a cited work for a different viewpoint from that just described, as in
'This is the view advanced by Beekes (1995), but *cf.* Szemerényi
(1996)' (that is, for a different view). Note that *cf.* is *not* properly used
merely to cite a work to which the reader's attention is being directed;
a mere instruction to consult a certain work for more information is
written 'see Buck (1949)' or '*v.* Buck (1949)', but *not* '*cf.* Buck (1949)'.
2. In etymological entries, this is often used to signal **cognates** in
other languages. For example, the entry 'English *daughter*, Old
English *dohtor*; *cf.* Sanskrit *duhitar-*' means that the English word
is directly descended from the Old English one, which in turn is
cognate with the Sanskrit word. Note that *cf.* does *not* mean 'comes
from'; here the English word is not derived from the Sanskrit word.

Chadic A family of about 140 languages spoken in west Africa. By far the
most important is *Hausa*, which has more speakers than any other
sub-Saharan African language. Chadic forms one branch of the
Afro-Asiatic family.

chain shift A complex type of phonological change in which a number of
phonemes change their phonetic realizations in a systematic way.
Typically, phoneme X acquires the phonetic character formerly
possessed by phoneme Y, which in turn acquires the former phonetic
characteristics of phoneme Z and so on; at least one phoneme must
leave an unfilled 'hole' behind it, and at least one must 'get out of the
way', either by acquiring an entirely new phonetic feature or by
merging with some other phoneme. The **Great Vowel Shift** of
English was a chain shift, as is the **Northern Cities Shift**; see those
entries for details.
    Two pure types of chain shift are recognized: a *push chain*, in which
the chain starts with a phoneme moving too close to another one and
pushing it out of the way, and a *drag chain* (or *pull chain*), in which the
chain starts with a phoneme that moves into currently empty space,
thus dragging other phonemes along to fill the space left behind. A
combined pull-drag chain is also possible; in this type, one phoneme
in the middle of the group simultaneously moves towards one
neighbour, pushing it, and away from another neighbour, dragging
that. There is also a rather different type called a **solidarity chain**. A
chain shift may be *sequential*, in which one change is completed before

the next begins, or *covarying*, in which all changes are more or less simultaneous.

Chain shifts were first explicitly recognized by André Martinet, particularly in his 1955 book; they have recently been investigated in detail by William Labov (1994: chs 5–9) but see also Lass (1997: § 1.6). Most chain shifts involve vowels, but some Mayan languages exhibit the shifts */r/ > /t/, */t/ > /tʃ/, */tʃ/ > /ʈʂ/ and */ʃ/ > /ʂ/ (Campbell 1997a: 164) and this, like the **First Germanic Consonant Shift**, is an example of a chain shift affecting consonants.

Labov (1994: 116) offers four principles governing chain shifts affecting vowels, as follows. In chain shifts, (1) long vowels rise, (2) short vowels fall, (3) the nuclei of upgliding diphthongs fall, and (4) back vowels move to the front. These are not exceptionless. The first two are later (p. 176) restated as follows: (1) tense nuclei rise along a peripheral track; (2) lax nuclei fall along a non-peripheral track.

See Lichtenberk (1991: 74) for a possible case of a non-phonological (lexico-grammatical) chain shift.

chance resemblance (also **accidental resemblance**) A striking similarity in form and meaning between words or other elements in two or more different languages which results from nothing more than a chance accident. For example, English *much* and Spanish *mucho* 'much', English *day* and Spanish *día* 'day', and English *have* and Spanish *haber* 'have' all look strikingly similar in form and meaning, but nevertheless no two of them are related or connected in any way. These are chance resemblances, even though English and Spanish are remotely related.

Such examples can be multiplied at tedious length, and they are devoid of interest. Every language has thousands of meanings to provide forms for but only a small number of phonemes to build those forms, and, by the ordinary laws of probability, two or more languages will sometimes happen to hit on very similar forms to express the same or similar meanings. For example, Hawaiian and ancient Greek exhibit a startling number of impressive-looking accidental matches, such as Hawaiian *mele* 'sing' and *aeto* 'eagle', and Greek *melos* 'melody' and *aetos* 'eagle'.

Such chance resemblances, or **Anklänge**, can usually be found between any two languages whatever. Failing to realize this, linguistic amateurs and cranks are forever collecting lists of such chance resemblances between whichever languages their eye has fallen on and brandishing them as 'evidence' for something or other. Even a few professional linguists have at times fallen into this trap. Chance resemblances constitute one of the **pitfalls of comparison** which must be avoided, and their inevitable existence is the chief reason that most historical linguists pay no attention to mere lists of miscellaneous resemblances between languages. See the **search problem**.

change from above 1. A linguistic change which is introduced, deliberately and self-consciously, by the members of a high-ranking social class and which then spreads into the speech of lower-ranking classes. A good example, on a large scale, is the borrowing of Norman French words into English after the Norman Conquest. Most of the population of England remained monoglot English-speakers, but a small minority of rather high-ranking people acquired some knowledge of the then prestigious Norman French and introduced French words into their English; these words spread into the English of other speakers who knew no French and the vocabulary of English was transformed as a result. 2. Linguistic change resulting from the conscious awareness of the social significance of competing forms. Compare **change from below**.

change from below 1. A linguistic change which appears first in speech-varieties of low prestige and then spreads up the social scale, perhaps eventually becoming general. Before its spread upwards, the innovation may be strongly stigmatized or it may not even be noticed. Several centuries ago, the loss of non-prevocalic /r/ in words like *far* and *dark* was stigmatized in England as a vulgarism, but it spread up the social scale so successfully that such non-rhotic speech is now the prestige norm in England and speakers who still pronounce /r/ in these words are considered rustic. Something similar is perhaps happening now to the **glottalization** of plosives in England; long a prominent feature of several urban accents but strongly stigmatized, this 'glottalization' is becoming increasingly frequent in middle-class speech and has even been heard from some younger members of the royal family. 2. Linguistic change which occurs below the level of awareness. Compare **change from above**.

change in progress A linguistic change which has been under way for some time in a given speech community and which is still happening at the time of investigation. Scarcely thought possible before the 1960s, the study of changes in progress is now a major concern of both historical linguists and sociolinguists, and it has led to the discovery of such unexpected phenomena as **lexical diffusion**, near-mergers and the **Bill Peters effect**. See Milroy (1992), McMahon (1994) and Labov (1994) for surveys and discussion.

character Any individual linguistic feature, present in some languages in a family but absent in others, which is appealed to in order to aid in grouping those languages into a **family tree** on the basis of **shared innovations**. For examples, see Lass (1997: 143–159) for Germanic and Warnow *et al.* (1995) for IE.

Chari-Nile In the classification of Greenberg (1963b), the largest branch of the **Nilo-Saharan** family, including perhaps 100 languages, with **Central Sudanic** and **East Sudanic** as its two chief branches. Like the family itself, this branch is controversial and it has been widely rejected in more recent classifications of the family.

Chibchan A family of twenty-odd languages spoken from Nicaragua to Colombia.

Chibchan–Paezan A proposed grouping of **Chibchan** and **Paezan** with a number of other languages, one of the eleven branches assigned to **Amerind**.

Chimakuan A tiny language family (with just two languages) of the Pacific Northwest of North America. It is included in the **Mosan** hypothesis.

Chinese (also **Sinitic**) A family of about seven distinct but related languages (or better seven groups of dialects) spoken in the eastern half of China. Since all Chinese used a single written language until recently, the Chinese themselves prefer to speak of the 'dialects' of Chinese, but in fact the several Chinese languages differ from one another so substantially that they are unquestionably distinct languages by any linguistic criteria. By far the most important Chinese language is *Mandarin*; the others are *Wú* (Shanghainese), *Yuè* (Cantonese), *Gàn, Xiāng, Hakka* and *Mǐn*. For a survey, see Norman (1988) or Ramsey (1987). Chinese forms one branch of the **Sino-Tibetan** family.

Chinookan A family of four languages in Oregon and Washington. It is included in the **Penutian** hypothesis.

chreod A term proposed by Lass (1997), as follows. Just as rainwater is channelled along certain pathways by the contours of the landscape, Lass suggests that the structure of a language might be viewed as a kind of landscape through which certain pathways of change are more readily available than others, and these hypothetical pathways he calls *chreods*. This idea is intended as a contribution to the explanation of **drift** and **conspiracies**, and Lass further suggests that the mathematical concept of an *attractor* might be helpful in understanding these phenomena.

chronology See **absolute chronology, relative chronology.**

Chukchi-Kamchatkan (also **Chukotko-Kamchatkan, Luorawe-tlan**) A language family in northeastern Siberia, consisting of five languages; its most important member is *Chukchi*.

Cimbrian An extinct and unrecorded language, almost certainly **Germanic**, spoken by a people from Jutland who invaded much of western and central Europe in the first two centuries BC.

Cimmerian The extinct and unrecorded language of a people who inhabited the land north and east of the Black Sea in prehistoric times, before being driven out by the Scythians. The best guess is that it was an **Indo-European** language, possibly close to **Thracian**.

circularity problem A potential pitfall in **comparative reconstruction**. We assume that forms in different languages are cognate because they can be reconstructed with the same proto-phoneme, when the proto-phoneme itself is the result of assuming that they *are* cognate.

clade [*rare*] Another term for **taxon**.

cladistic model Another term for the **genetic model**.

classical language A highly developed literary language of the past which continues to be studied and learned and which often serves as a source of vocabulary for later languages. Examples include **Latin** and classical **Greek** in Europe, **Sanskrit** in India and classical **Arabic** in the Muslim world.

classification of languages Any of several ways of grouping languages into larger assemblies. Languages are commonly classified in at least three ways: by ancestry (in **genetic relationships**), by structural features (in a **typology**) and by geography (in **geographical groupings**). It is important not to confuse these three.

clause fusion The term used by Harris and Campbell (1995: 172–194) for a diachronic process in which a biclausal structure (main clause plus subordinate clause, each with its own verb) is converted into a single-clause structure with a lexical verb and an auxiliary verb. In their definition, it is always the originally subordinate verb which becomes the lexical verb and the originally main verb which becomes the auxiliary. They cite the example of an Old Georgian verb meaning 'want', which took a dative subject and a finite complement clause; after this verb was reduced to an auxiliary, the former complement verb became the lexical verb, and the former subject of 'want' was shifted to the subject-case required by the new lexical verb. This syntactic dominance of the former subordinate verb they call the *heir-apparent principle*.

cline 1. In **dialect geography**, a more or less steady change in the shape of a set of linguistic forms across a geographical area. For example, Latin /k/ before /a/ appears as /k/ in southern France, as /tʃ/ in central France, and as /ʃ/ in northern France. The number of contrasting tones in the Chinese languages ranges from three in the north (adjacent to the toneless Altaic languages) to nine in the south (adjacent to the tone-rich languages of southeast Asia). 2. Especially in **population typology**, a steady shift in the frequency of a typological feature across a geographical area. When such a shift can be identified for the whole planet, the result is a *global* cline.

clipped form A word which is coined by stripping away one or more syllables from an existing word, leaving a much shorter word, usually of the same meaning. Examples include *gym* from *gymnasium*, *bra* from *brassière*, *flu* from *influenza*, *phone* from *telephone*, and *cello* from *violoncello*. More complex cases exist, such as *sci-fi* from *science fiction* and *quasar* from *quasi-stellar object*. Occasionally a clipped form displaces its source word entirely, as *bus* has displaced *omnibus*. Sometimes the label is extended to cases of **form reduction** like *canary* from *canary bird*. A clipped form is a real word and not an abbreviation. The process of constructing a clipped form is *clipping* (**form reduction, compression**). Compare **blend, contraction, stump compound**.

cliticization The reduction of an independent word to a clitic. If the resulting clitic is an proclitic, the process is *procliticization*; an example is the reduction of personal pronouns to proclitics (preceding the verb) in French. If the resulting clitic is an enclitic, the process is *encliticization*; an example is the reduction of English *will* to an enclitic (following the subject) in *John'll do it*. The opposite is **decliticization**.

closed comparison A way of performing **comparison** among languages. In this approach, the investigator works only with a fixed set of words and compares only the words of those particular meanings; this is often done with the **Swadesh word list**. Compare **open-ended comparison**.

closed-syllable shortening The phenomenon by which an underlying or historical long vowel is shortened in a closed syllable, as when Old English *fīfta* became modern *fifth*.

cluster reduction The simplification of a consonant cluster by the deletion of one or more of its members. English-speakers, for example, often delete the first /n/ in *government*, the /d/ in *handbag* and the /θ/ in *sixths*.

Coahuiltecan A proposed family linking any of various isolates and tiny families in Texas and northern Mexico, all of them extinct and mostly sparsely recorded. Versions of Coahuiltecan have been defended by Sapir and others, but have won little support. Manaster Ramer (1996a) has defended a modified version called *Pakawan*; Campbell (1997a: 298–304) criticizes this severely but concludes that it looks promising.

coalescence (also **desegmentalization, fusion**) Any syntagmatic change in which a sequence of two segments is converted to a single segment bearing some features of each of the original segments. For example, the sequences /sj/ and /zj/, common in English words borrowed from French and Latin, have often coalesced to /ʃ/ and /ʒ/, respectively, as in *mission* and *pleasure*. The opposite is **unpacking**. Compare **merger**.

coalescence theory Another term for the **agglutination theory**.

coarticulation Another term for **accommodation** (sense 1).

coastal-density phenomenon The observation, made by Nichols (1990 and elsewhere), that a (non-Arctic) coastal region typically differs from an interior region in several linguistic respects. A coastal region supports a much higher density of languages; it admits stable languages with much smaller numbers of speakers; and it retains **isolated languages** better.

code-mixing and **code-switching** Terms applied to the act of changing back and forth between languages on the part of bilingual (or multi-lingual) speakers. These terms are not used by everyone in the same way. For most sociolinguists, *code-switching* denotes the practice of choosing one language for any given occasion, depending upon the circumstances or the subject matter. An example would be Basque-Spanish bilinguals who normally speak Basque at home but Spanish in the street or when discussing politics. Then *code-mixing* denotes the repeated switching back and forth between languages in a single conversation and frequently even in a single sentence, as in the Malay/English example *This morning I hantar my baby tu dekat babysitter tu lah* 'This morning I took my baby to the babysitter'. However, Hock (1986: 479–481) uses *code-switching* for this second case, and reserves *code-mixing* for the insertion of individual content words from one language into sentences or utterances otherwise constructed entirely in another language.

codex A volume containing copies of ancient manuscripts.

codification In **language planning**, the business of agreeing on, and imposing, a single set of forms and usages as standard, together with the rejection of all competing forms and usages as non-standard.

coéfficient sonantique Saussure's original term for each of the several resonants he recognized as an optional constituent of a PIE root: /y w r l m n/ and the hypothetical consonants later called **laryngeals**.

coexistent phonemic systems The presence in a single language of two rather different sets of phonemes, each of which is used to construct some sizeable part of the lexicon. The most familiar cases result from extensive borrowing. A case in point is Turkish; in native Turkish words, there are phonemes /k/, /g/ and /l/, each of which has front allophones next to front vowels and back allophones next to back vowels (a native word contains only one or the other), but in the numerous loans from Arabic, Persian and French fronted /kʲ/, /gʲ/

and /l/ contrast before back vowels with backed /k/, /g/ and /ɬ/, and so the borrowed vocabulary has three extra phonemes not present in native words. A spectacular case is the **mixed language** Michif, in which all words of French origin are constructed from a set of French phonemes, while all words of Cree origin are constructed from a very different set of Cree phonemes – and recent loans from English are often constructed with a *third* set of phonemes taken from English (Bakker and Papen 1997, Bakker 1997). The term was coined by Fries and Pike (1949).

cognacy Another term for **cognation**.

cognate 1. Narrowly, and most usually, one of two or more words or morphemes which are directly descended from a single ancestral form in the single common ancestor of the languages in which the words or morphemes are found, with no borrowing. For example, English *father* and German *Vater* 'father' are cognate, being descended from Proto-Germanic **fader*, and both are more distantly cognate with Spanish *padre*, Irish *athair* and modern Greek *patéras*, all 'father', all of these being descended from PIE **pəter*. 2. Broadly, and less usually, one of two or more words which have a single common origin but one or more of which have been borrowed. For example, English *jail*, Old French *jaiole* 'jail', Spanish *jaula* 'cage' (Old Spanish *javola*), Basque *txabola* 'hut', Occitan *cayola* 'cage' and Basque *kaiola* 'cage' are all ultimately descended from an unrecorded Latin **caveola* 'small enclosed place', but only the French, Occitan and Spanish words are narrowly cognate; the English and the two Basque words have been borrowed from Old French, Old Spanish and Occitan, respectively. Note: some linguists object to the use of the word in the second sense. 3. [*erroneous*] A label improperly applied to items of similar form and meaning in languages not known to be related, when these are presented as candidates for possible **cognation**. Common among linguistic amateurs, this objectionable usage is not unknown even among linguists, but it should be avoided; items cannot be labelled 'cognates' until a substantial case has been made that they genuinely *are* cognate. See **oblique cognates**, **partial cognates**, **root cognates**.

cognate languages [*obsolete*] Languages which are connected in a **genetic relationship**; genetically related languages.

cognate set A set of **cognate** words or morphemes from several related languages, sometimes particularly when these are being used as the basis for the **reconstruction** of an ancestral form or a set of ancestral forms.

cognation (also **cognacy**) The relationship which holds between **cognates**: descent from a common ancestor.

cohesion Especially in **grammaticalization**, the degree of independence of a linguistic form: an independent word, a clitic, an affix or an unanalysable part of a larger unit. Grammaticalization typically involves an increase in the cohesion (a reduction in independence) of the item being grammaticalized.

coinage Another term for **neologism**.

colouring In PIE, the process by which the basic root-vowel $*/e/$ was modified in character by an adjacent **laryngeal**; $*/e/$ was unaffected by H_1, lowered to $*/a/$ by H_2, and rounded to $*/o/$ by H_3.

combinatory change Another term for **conditioned change**.

combining form 1. A bound form of a lexical item used in constructing compounds and derivatives. For example, Basque *gizon* 'man, person' has the combining form *giza-*, as in *gizarte* 'society', *gizaldi* '(a) generation' and *gizakoi* 'philanthropic'. 2. In English, just such a form extracted from Greek or Latin and used in constructing technical terms, sometimes with specific senses not found in the original language. Examples are *bio-* 'life', *thermo-* 'heat', *electro-* 'electricity', *eco-* 'environment', *-phile* 'lover' and *-logy* 'science'. These are routinely combined to devise needed terms, like *thermophile* 'heat-loving organism' and *ecology* 'study of the relations between organisms and their environment'.

common 1. Used with the name of a language family, denoting a period of time when the ancestor of the family could still be regarded as a single language. The term is similar to **Proto-**, but typically used slightly differently: *Proto-Slavic* is the ancestor of the Slavic languages as reconstructed by linguists, while *common Slavic* denotes the Slavic languages at the time when the degree of dialectal diversification was still small enough that all Slavic varieties could reasonably be regarded as dialects of a single language. In the particular case of IE, *common* has replaced the earlier term **proethnic**. 2. Of a linguistic form, occurring very widely in a language, a family or a geographical region. For example, a *common Australian* form is found very widely in Australian languages.

common origin Another way of expressing a **genetic relationship**. Two or more languages which are genetically related (derived from the same ancestor) are said to have a *common origin*. Occasionally **cognates** are also said to have a common origin.

communal change A type of language change in which all or most members of the community acquire innovations simultaneously or change their frequency of competing forms in step. Common in lexical and syntactic change, communal change is rare in phonological change. Compare **generational change, age-grading**.

compacting [*rare*] Another term for **morphologization** (sense 2).

comparandum (plural **comparanda**) A word, morpheme or linguistic form in a given language which is being compared with one in one or more other languages, either in the hope of finding a genetic link or, if that is already established, in the hope of finding **cognates**. Not all linguistic forms are equally valid as comparanda: **nursery words, onomatopoeias** and (when they can be identified) **loan words** are useless as comparanda in all but a few special circumstances.

comparative linguistics (also **genetic linguistics**) That part of **historical linguistics** which seeks to identify and elucidate **genetic relationships** among languages.

comparative method The central method in **comparative linguistics**, allowing us to establish and elucidate **genetic relationships** among languages and hence to identify **language families**. The basis of the comparative method began to be understood by European linguists towards the end of the eighteenth century, particularly in connection with the **Uralic** and **Indo-European** families. During the nineteenth century the method was clarified and elaborated, and the **Neogrammarian Hypothesis** was promulgated. By the end of the century the method was being held up as a model of scientific procedure. During the first half of the twentieth century the method was successfully applied to further language families, such as **Algonquian** (by Bloomfield) and **Austronesian** (by Dempwolff).

Oddly, in spite of the great success and the universal acceptance of the method, there were hardly any attempts at characterizing it explicitly, and it is largely only within the last few years that linguists have attempted to provide detailed characterizations of the procedures involved. Even today, there are still conspicuous differences among linguists in their understanding of what the method is, how it is applied, and what it can establish. Still, a number of points command broad assent.

There are several identifiable steps in the method. First, we must satisfy ourselves by **inspection** that there exists a *prima facie* case for genetic relatedness among the languages of interest and hence cause to proceed further. When the languages are very closely related, this may be easy; for example, no one looking at several **Slavic** languages would fail to conclude quickly that they must be related. When the languages are more distantly related, this step is more difficult. Mere lists of miscellaneous resemblances do not constitute evidence, though it may be possible to extract evidence from such lists by careful statistical methods; see the **search problem**. Similarly, we can attach no weight to shared typological characteristics like word order, ergativity, tones or vowel harmony. The most persuasive diagnostic evidence of relatedness is **grammatical correspondences** (shared morphological paradigms) and **shared anomalies**, features which are almost totally inexplicable by anything other than common ancestry. Languages with little or no morphology cannot exhibit this kind of evidence, and such languages are accordingly often more difficult to work with.

Once we are satisfied that we have clear evidence of relatedness, we may proceed to the second step: the identification of **systematic correspondences** in sound between words and morphemes of similar meaning or function, and with it the identification of **cognate sets**. This step is generally only possible when the languages are moderately closely related; if a genetic link is real but distant, we may be unable to find systematic correspondences even though we have clear evidence of relationship. Such appears to be exactly the position at present with the **Afro-Asiatic** family, and possibly with other families.

If we can find enough recurrent correspondences, we can go on to the third step: setting up a proto-phoneme for each correspondence and assigning a provisional phonetic value to each proto-phoneme, as represented by the symbol chosen. (Some linguists would prefer to regard these as two separate steps.) Once we have done this, we should be able to do three further things. We can provide a **reconstruction** (sense 2) of each word and morpheme we can assign to the ancestral language as a sequence of proto-phonemes (this is

comparative reconstruction); we can lay out the system of proto-phonemes in that ancestral language; and we can identify the specific sound changes that applied in every branch of the family.

With a reasonably substantial skeleton now worked out, we should be able to identify further cognates, systematic correspondences and sound changes which eluded us at first, and we may possibly be able to bring additional languages into the family.

Naturally, in practice our work is never so orderly as is suggested here; we must work back and forth, roughing out provisional patterns and then revising them in the light of further evidence or flashes of insight, until we have something that stands up well to further scrutiny. However, the work is never done. Overlooked cognates may be lurking in our data; a few good-looking cognates may prove to be specious; a brilliant inspiration may offer an elegant solution to a previously intractable problem; our reconstructed phoneme system may be judged unnatural and in need of revision; newly discovered languages may prove to belong to the family but to exhibit evidence requiring revision of our earlier conclusions; and so on. Of course, almost any proposal, addition or revision may well also be controversial, evoking heated arguments. Finally, there are always outstanding problems still awaiting explanations. Even our greatest successes are constantly subject to revision; as one wag has remarked, 'No language has changed so much in the twentieth century as Proto-Indo-European.'

Once we have reconstructed several proto-languages in moderate detail, it is possible in principle (though very difficult in practice) to identify genetic links between some of our proto-languages and to apply the comparative method to them in turn; this has been dubbed **palaeolinguistics**, and it is the methodology espoused (in principle, at least) by the proponents of the **Nostratic** hypothesis – 'in principle', because secure reconstructions are not in fact available for some of the families included in this hypothesis. All historical linguists except the few proponents of **multilateral comparison** agree that this methodology is the only reliable way of identifying genetic links older than the well-established families, but the majority are also deeply pessimistic about the likelihood of enjoying much success in such enterprises, because of the **fadeout effect** and the unavoidably 'fuzzy' nature of our reconstructed proto-languages, which always contain less information than attested languages.

See Fox (1995: chs 2–6) for a textbook presentation of the comparative method, the papers in Durie and Ross (1996) for critical discussion of a number of aspects of the method, and a standard textbook such as Trask (1996: ch. 8), Crowley (1997: ch. 5), W. P. Lehmann (1992: ch. 7), Hock (1986: chs 18–19) or Campbell (1998: ch. 5) for illustrations of the method. Compare **internal reconstruction** and see the **pitfalls of comparison**.

comparative philology An older term for **comparative linguistics**.

comparative reconstruction That part of the **comparative method** in which the analyst, on the basis of **systematic correspondences**, sets up a system of proto-phonemes in the ancestral language being reconstructed and constructs a proto-form for each word or morpheme assignable to that language as a sequence of those proto-phonemes; where possible, morphological paradigms and other grammatical features are also reconstructed. The unrecorded language that emerges from this process is a **proto-language**, the ancestor of the languages used in performing the reconstruction. Comparative reconstruction is usually performed **bottom-up**, but may sometimes also be done **top-down**. See **algebraism, realism**.

comparison A label applied very broadly to any of various procedures in which data from two or more languages are placed side by side and scrutinized for possible connections. This may be done in the hope of finding evidence for genetic links among the languages, or, if genetic links have already been established, it may be done in order to identify **cognates** and pave the way for **reconstruction**. The simplest type of comparison is mere **inspection**; this is usually a necessary first step in any case, but some linguists would elevate inspection alone to the status of a method for identifying genetic links, as is done in **multilateral comparison**. Most historical linguists reject inspection alone as a method, and prefer to rely on more sophisticated techniques, typically involving the identification of **systematic correspondences** in vocabulary, shared morphological paradigms, **shared anomalies** and various statistical techniques (see the **search problem**). See Nichols (1997d) for a proposed classification of methods of comparison, most notably a contrast between **closed comparison** and **open-ended comparison**, and between **heuristic comparison** and **Neogrammarian comparison**. See Manaster Ramer and Hitchcock (1996) for a contrast between **wide-scope** and **narrow-scope comparison**. See also **bilateral comparison** and **n-ary comparison**, and see **Ludolf's rule** and **Hamp's principles of comparison**.

compensatory accretion Another term for **reinforcement**.

compensatory change Any linguistic change which, in some intuitive sense, cancels the effect of some other change. For example, the reduction or loss of case-endings may be compensated for by the creation of prepositions, or phonological changes leading to increased homophony among lexical items may be compensated for by the creation of new compounds. There exist linguists who take the view that, for communicative reasons, a language must always maintain a kind of dynamic equilibrium, with changes being compensated for by other changes.

compensatory lengthening The lengthening of a vowel when a following syllable-final consonant is lost, as when Pre-Latin *fasnom 'shrine' became Latin fānum, or when early Old French feste [fɛstə] 'feast' became late Old French [fɛ:tə], later spelled fête.

competing changes The state of affairs in which two linguistic changes, especially two phonological changes, are occurring in the same language at the same type, both of them trying to apply to the same forms. An example comes from early medieval Basque, in which two changes were competing for some of the same forms: (1) intervocalic /n/ was being lost, and (2) intervocalic /n/ was being assimilated to a preceding high vowel. The competition led to two different outcomes for some words. For example, *magina 'sheath' (< Latin vagina(m)) appears in modern Basque both as magia and as magiña (with a palatal nasal), and *kuna 'cradle' (< Latin cuna(m)) appears both as kua and as kuma. (In contrast, *ballena 'whale', from Latin ballaena(m), appears only as balea, since the first vowel is not high.) See Wang (1969) for an argument that competing changes may be a cause of **residue** (sense 1), and see **bidirectional diffusion**.

complementary distribution In **dialect geography**, the state of affairs in which two competing linguistic forms never occur in a single variety. For example, Basque jaugin 'come' and jin 'come' are never found in the same local variety, confirming that jin is an irregular contraction of the longer form.

completion, going to The termination of a linguistic change, because there is no remaining scope for further change. See the discussion under **gradualness of change**.

complexity principle Another term for the **iconic coding principle**.

complication Any linguistic change which, in some pretheoretical sense, causes some part of a language to become more elaborate, more irregular or more highly marked than previously. Complication is the opposite of **simplification** (sense 1), but in practice many changes involve simplification in one domain but complication in another, as stated by the **'simplification brings complication'** principle.

composite set The term used by Hoenigswald (1960: 126) for a correspondence set with overlapping segments. His example is the set English /d/ : German /t/ (as in English *sword*, *hold*, German *Schwert-*, *halten*), Eng /θ/ : Ger /d/ (as in Eng *hearth*, *mouth*, Ger *Herd-*, *Mund-*), and Eng /d/ : Ger /d/ (as in Eng *gold*, *bind*, Ger *Gold-*, *binden*). Here both English /d/ and German /d/ participate in two of the three correspondences. Some such sets may require three proto-phonemes to be posited, but this one requires only two: Proto-Germanic */θ/ develops into English /θ/ in most cases but into English /d/ after */l/, and develops into German /d/; Proto-Germanic */d/ develops into English /d/ and into German /t/ in most cases but into /d/ after */n/.

compound A word constructed by combining two (or more) existing words, such as English *girlfriend*, *blackbird*, *redneck*, *see-through*, *upend* and *forget-me-not*. The process of forming a compound is *compounding*. See **bahuvrīhi, dvandva, additive compound, endocentric compound**.

compression Another term for *clipping*; see under **clipped form**.

conceptual expansion The extension of the semantic domain of a word or morpheme by the extraction of semantic features from it. Heine *et al.* (1991a: 79–97) show how the Ewe word *ví* 'child' has become a word-forming suffix with a variety of meanings, such as 'offspring', 'young', 'small', 'typical', 'marginal', 'inexperienced', 'apprentice', 'unsuccessful', 'unimportant', 'weak' and 'harmless'.

conceptual shift In some views, the first step in **grammaticalization**, in which the item in question comes to receive a new interpretation while still exhibiting its original grammatical behaviour.

conceptual transfer Any process in which an item of concrete meaning comes to be used to express a more abstract meaning, as when a word for 'back' acquires the sense of 'behind' or a word for 'go' acquires the sense of 'future'.

condensation [*rare*] Another term for **grammaticalization**.

conditioned change (also **combinatory change**) Any phonological change which applies to a segment only in certain syntagmatic circumstances. Examples: Pre-Basque */e/ became a glide /j/ when word-initial and immediately followed by a non-high vowel, but not otherwise; Pre-Old English */k/ was palatalized to /tʃ/ when immediately followed by a front vowel, but not otherwise; Proto-Romance */a/ diphthongized to /ai/ in Old French when stressed but not otherwise; the **First Germanic Consonant Shift** changed PIE voiceless plosives to voiceless fricatives whenever the plosive was *either* word-initial *or* preceded by the accented syllable but not immediately preceded by another voiceless consonant. The majority of phonological changes are conditioned and, as the last example suggests, the conditioning factors can be rather complex. The syntagmatic circumstances which induce the change are its *conditioning* factors and their effect is *conditioning*. The opposite is an **unconditioned change**.

conditioned merger See under **merger**.

conflicting reconstructions The state of affairs in which two seemingly **cognate** items absolutely require contradictory **reconstructions** in the parent language. A classic case is that of Latin *communis* 'common', which requires PIE **k-*, and the synonymous Gothic *gamains*, which requires PIE **gh-*. Such cases, when not simply illusory, may point to instances of variation or of alternation in the parent language. For this case, Fourquet (1976) proposes an alternation **k- ~ *gh-* in PIE, with varying lexicalizations of each alternant in the daughter languages, and he suggests that Latin *hic* 'this' (< **gh-*) versus *cis* 'on this side (of)' (< **k-*) might represent another instance.

Congo-Saharan (also **Niger-Saharan**) A putative macro-family consisting of **Niger-Congo** (or **Niger-Kordofanian**) and **Nilo-Saharan**, proposed by Gregerson (1972) and Blench (1995). This proposal has found little support.

connatural development The term applied by Bailey (1996 and elsewhere) to any linguistic change best interpreted as resulting from neurobiological factors, such as **assimilation**. Compare **abnatural development**.

conservatism principle A principle sometimes invoked in connection with the **homeland problem**. It says this: the **homeland** (the centre of dispersal) is the region in which the most **conservative daughter languages** are found – that is, in the area in which there has been the least linguistic change from the **proto-language**. The rationale for this principle is that such conservative languages are the ones least affected by foreign **substrates**. Applied to IE, this principle forces the conclusion that the IE homeland was the Baltic region, since the Baltic languages are the most conservative IE languages; applied to the Scandinavian languages, it forces the absurd conclusion that Iceland is the Scandinavian homeland. The principle rests on the fallacious assumption that virtually all linguistic change results from contact.

conservative 1. Of a linguistic form, remaining more similar to an ancestral form than a cognate form recorded elsewhere or later. For example, Latin *cārum* /ka:rum/ 'dear' is the source of both Spanish *caro* /kaɾo/ and French *cher* /ʃɛʁ/, but the Spanish form is clearly more conservative than the French; northern Basque *ihintz* 'dew' is more conservative than western Basque *intz*. The opposite is **innovating** or, in certain circumstances, **advanced** or **secondary**. 2. Of a language or variety, exhibiting fewer innovations than a related language or variety, and hence remaining more similar to their common ancestor. For example, Icelandic is much more conservative than its close relatives Norwegian, Danish and Swedish, in that it is far closer in form to their common ancestor Old Norse. The opposite is **innovating**.

conspiracy, diachronic A group of formally unrelated changes which combine to produce a result not required by any one of them. An example is the series of independent changes in Slavic which conspired to make all syllables open (see the Law of **Open Syllables**). See Hock (1986: 159–164), Lass (1987, 1997: 300–303).

constituency principle The following principle: words that form a constituent are placed in adjacent positions. This is one version of **Behaghel's** (third) **Law**, and exceptions to it pose some interesting diachronic problems.

constraints on borrowing Any of various putative constraints on the ability of languages to acquire linguistic features from neighbouring languages. See Thomason and Kaufman (1988: ch. 2) for a (mostly dismissive) review of proposed constraints, and see the **Moravcsik universals of borrowing**.

constraints on linguistic change Hypothetical limitations on the changes which can possibly occur in a language. No such limitations have so far been securely identified. It is widely assumed that mutual intelligibility between successive generations must be such a limitation, but Milroy (1992: 35–36) queries even this, suggesting that very rapid social change or a desire for exclusivity may override mutual intelligibility.

constraints problem The problem of determining the general constraints on language change that determine possible and impossible changes and directions of change. See the **WLH model of language change**.

constructional iconicity principle The putative principle that **isomorphy** is the norm in language. See *Humboldt's Universal* under **isomorphy**.

contact See **language contact**.

contact assimilation See under **assimilation**.

contact-induced change Another term for **external change**.

contact language Any speech variety which arises out of an instance of intense **language contact**. Contact languages are highly variable in nature, but three types are commonly distinguished: **pidgins**, **creoles** and **mixed languages**. Only the last two are mother tongues, and these are sometimes called **non-genetic languages**. See the references under the bold entries.

contamination Any unsystematic change in which the form of a linguistic item is irregularly influenced by the form of another item associated with it. For example, the former English *femelle* /fiːməl/ became *female* under contamination with its unrelated opposite *male*; English *covert* /k ʌ vət/, a variant of *covered*, has become /kəʊˈvɜːt/ by contamination from its unrelated opposite *overt*; Latin *gravis* 'heavy' became popular *grevis* by contamination from *levis* 'light'; Basque *bigira* 'watchfulness', a loan from Latin *vigilia*, and the derived verb *bigiratu* 'look at' have become *begira* and *begiratu* by contamination from native *begi* 'eye'; the expected Russian **nevjat'* 'nine' has become instead *devjat'* by contamination from the following *desjat'* 'ten'. Mutual contamination is possible: Old French *citeien* and *denzein* have yielded English *citizen* and *denizen* by contaminating each other. Compare **cross**.

context-induced reinterpretation The term used by Heine *et al.* (1991a: ch. 3, 1991b) to label their view that changes like **grammaticalization, metaphor** and **metonymy** are largely gradual and continuous, rather than abrupt and discontinuous, in that an item used in one sense may simultaneously permit a somewhat different interpretation in a particular context, so that this new (pragmatically derived) sense becomes available as a further central sense of the item. One of their examples is the semantic development of Ewe *megbé* from 'back' (body-part) to 'back' (of object), 'space behind', 'behind', 'late' and 'mentally retarded'; the point is that many particular utterances allow at least two of these interpretations simultaneously.

contra Preceding a person's name, an indication that you are disagreeing bluntly with some view expressed by that person. For example, '*contra* Pokorny' indicates that you are rejecting some conclusion of Pokorny's in favour of a quite different view. Latin *contra* means 'against'. Compare *apud, pace*.

contraction The irregular phonological reduction of a word or a sequence of words which is of high frequency in a language, or the form resulting from this. English examples include *I'm* for *I am*, *won't* for *will not*, *she'd've* for *she would have*, and the poetic *o'er* for *over*. The term is usually applied to cases (like these) in which the reduced form continues to coexist with its longer form, but occasionally it is extended to obligatory reductions, like that of French *de le* to *du* 'of the (masculine singular)'. Compare **clipped form**.

conventionalization The first step in **grammaticalization**, in which a particular syntactic structure comes to be regularly used to do a particular job. Some writers use this term interchangeably with **idiomatization**.

convergence Any of various phenomena in which languages come to be more similar than formerly. The simplest type of convergence is the independent occurrence of identical changes in distinct languages, such as the independent change of /u:/ to /ɑʊ/ in English and High German. (This is **independent parallel innovation**.) **Language contact**, however, can lead not only to **diffusion** but to more complex and interesting types of convergence, notably in the creation of a **linguistic area**. Until recently, historical linguistics paid little attention to the possibility of any further types of convergence, and **divergence** (sense 1) was seen as the primary phenomenon under investigation. In the last few years, however, convergence has begun to be taken far more seriously; the examination of convergence phenomena is now seen as a major and growing part of the field, and some linguists are suggesting that individual languages can actually arise out of convergence. We now see intensive work on **non-genetic languages** like **pidgins** and **creoles**; the reality of **mixed languages** has been established, and the possibility of **portmanteau languages** has been mooted. Some **models of linguistic descent** are being put forward which expressly provide for language birth by convergence, such as the **rhizotic model**, the **crystallization model** and the **punctuated-equilibrium model**. Thomason and Kaufman (1988) is now seen as the seminal work introducing, or perhaps rather reintroducing, the study of convergence into the field, and it seems safe to say that convergence will be a major theme in historical linguistics in the years to come. In any case, convergence phenomena are among the principal **pitfalls of comparison**.

convergence area Another term for a **linguistic area**.

convergent lexical development The development of two words of distinct form and meaning into a single word covering all the meanings of the original two. For example, Crowley (1997: 239) reports that, in New Zealand English, the word *kete* 'Maori basket', of Maori origin, has converged with English *kit*, with the result that *kit* now means 'Maori basket' in addition to its other senses.

conversion (also **zero–derivation, functional shift**) Moving a word from one part of speech to another, with no affixation or modification. For example, the adjective *brown* becomes a verb in *Please brown the meat*; the noun *smoke* becomes a verb in *Susie smokes* and then the verb becomes a new noun in *Susie was having a smoke*; and the preposition and particle *up* becomes a verb in *She is upping the ante* and a noun in *ups and downs.*

coordinate compound Another term for *dvandva.*

coordinate languages Languages which share the same immediate ancestor and which are therefore depicted as **sister languages** in a **family tree**. For example, the Omotic languages were formerly seen as a mere sub-branch of Cushitic, but today they are commonly regarded as constituting a primary branch of Afro-Asiatic, coordinate with the other primary branches.

Coptic The name given to the later stages of the ancient **Egyptian** language, conventionally beginning about the fourth century AD, when the earlier writing systems were abandoned and the language began to be written exclusively in the Greek alphabet. Coptic died out as a spoken language in about the fourteenth century, but it is still used today as a **liturgical language** by Coptic Christians.

copulative compound Another term for **dvandva**.

copy vowel Another term for **echo vowel**.

core area 1. Another term for **focal area**. 2. [*rare*] Another term for **homeland**.

core vocabulary Another term for **basic vocabulary**.

correptio iambica A development in Latin by which a word-final long vowel was shortened in a disyllable, as in *cave* 'beware' and *bene* 'well' for earlier *cavē* and *benē.*

correption The **shortening** of an originally long vowel.

correspondence See **systematic correspondence**.

correspondence mimicry Another term for **loan nativization**.

correspondence set A group of **cognate** words or morphemes from two or more related languages which illustrates one or more **systematic correspondences**. See the example under **systematic correspondence**.

corruption 1. With reference to an ancient document, the presence in an existing copy of it of layers of errors which have been introduced and propagated by perhaps a series of copyists. Only rarely are philologists lucky enough to have the original version of a document; more often they must make do not just with copies of the original, but with copies of copies of copies, and errors in copying are almost inevitable. See **stemmatology**. 2. A view of language change embraced by early European linguists: ancient languages were seen as pristine and perfect, or nearly so, and language change was seen as nothing more than corruption of an originally unsullied state. Today we realize that those ancient languages were themselves the result of accumulated changes in still earlier languages, and the term *corruption* is never used by linguists to denote any kind of language change. See **alteration**.

covarying chain shift See under **chain shift**.

cranberry morpheme An apparent morpheme which occurs only in a single word, such as the *cran-* of *cranberry*, the *twi-* of *twilight* or the *-tril* of *nostril*. This most commonly results from the loss of what was once an independent word; for example, *nostril* continues the lost Old English *thyrel* 'hole'.

crasis The combination of two vowels across a word boundary into a single long vowel or diphthong, as in Greek *tú:noma* for *tò ónoma* 'the name'. Compare **synaeresis, synizesis**.

crazy rule [*informal*] A phonological process, or a set of phonological processes, in a language which appear superficially to be bizarre and incomprehensible. An example is the process in the Gipuzkoan dialect of Basque in which the prefix /e-/ appearing in non-finite verb-forms (as in *etorri* 'come' and *ebaki* 'cut') appears as /χ/ before /a/ or /o/, as in *jan* /χan/ 'eat' and *josi* /χośi/ 'sew'. Bach and Harms (1972) argue that crazy rules typically result from the interaction of a series of phonological changes, each of which is itself natural. In the Gipuzkoan case, it seems clear that the development has been roughly /e/ > /j/ > /ʒ/ > /ʃ/ > /χ/, with the last change borrowed from Castilian Spanish.

creative metaphor See under **metaphor**.

creole A natural language (mother tongue) which derives from an earlier **pidgin**. While the formation of creoles is still under investigation, a creole seems to arise most typically when children born into a society in which a pidgin is the only common vehicle of communication acquire that pidgin as a mother tongue and quickly elaborate its grammar and lexicon, producing a true natural language. This process is *creolization*. A creole is thus not descended from a single ancestral natural language in the ordinary way; it represents a case of a **non-genetic language**. The possibility of certain special cases has been suggested: see **abrupt creolization**, **early-creolized creole** and **semi-creole**. See Holm (1988/89), Romaine (1988) or Sebba (1997) for creoles generally and see Thomason and Kaufman (1988) for discussion of creole origins. See also **fusion creole**.

critical apparatus (also *apparatus criticus*) The comments, emendations, variant readings and other scholarly material contributed by the editor to an **edition** of a text.

critical edition See under **edition**.

cross A word which is derived, not from a single source, but from two sources which have become confused in some way. For example, Basque *bilo* '(a single) hair' cannot derive from the synonymous Latin *pilum* because the form is wrong (we would expect **biro*), while a phonologically perfect source is Latin *villum* 'tuft of hair', which, however, has the wrong meaning. It may well be, then, that the Basque word derives from a cross of the two Latin words, with the form of one but the sense of the other. Compare **contamination**.

crystallization The term used by Weinreich (1953) and others since to denote the emergence of a single stable and characterizable language, particularly a **creole**, from an earlier welter of linguistic activity.

crystallization model (also *lingua franca* model) A **model of linguistic descent** which, in its strongest form, denies the validity of the **genetic model**, by which a language descends from a single ancestor by the ordinary processes of linguistic change, and asserts instead that a language 'crystallizes' out of a welter of diverse linguistic activity, a 'pool of linguistic resources', as speakers gradually narrow down the range of options available in their community and produce a tolerably unified language as a result. Since the 1950s, ideas of this general sort have been espoused by a number of linguists, including for example

Weinreich (1953, 1958), Chew (1976, 1981), Grace (1981), Le Page (1993 and elsewhere) and Bailey (1996 and elsewhere), and a variety of terms, such as *totemization* and *reification*, have been applied to the putative process of language-building within this model. Grace (1981) draws attention to Melanesia, where speakers have access to a variety of words and forms, and may at times not care, nor even know, whether particular forms 'belong' to their own language or not. Acceptance of this model has profound consequences for such familiar notions as *language* and **language family**.

cultural borrowing The borrowing of words for objects, practices and concepts which were previously unknown to the speakers of the borrowing language. Many borrowings into Basque from Latin and early Romance were of this sort, such as *liburu* 'book', *el(e)iza* 'church', *diru* 'money' and *gaztelu* 'castle'.

culture contact The term used by M. Ross (1996: 210) for cases in which one language significantly influences another in the absence of bilingualism, such as the case of English influence on Japanese. Compare **language contact**.

Cushitic A family of languages in eastern Africa, variously numbered between thirty-five and seventy, depending upon the view of the investigator, and forming part of the larger **Afro-Asiatic** family. The original Cushitic grouping of Greenberg (1963b) recognized the larger number, but since then it has become commonplace to separate out the thirty-four **Omotic** languages as a distinct coordinate group. Since Cushitic still looks rather like a 'residue' grouping within the larger family, many specialists would go further and break up the remainder of Cushitic into three coordinate groups: *South Cushitic*, *North Cushitic* and the single language *Beja*. The best-known Cushitic language is *Somali*.

cycle See the **linguistic cycle hypothesis**.

Dacian See under **Thracian**.

dagger (also **obelos**) The symbol '†'. 1. In an etymological entry, it marks a word of unknown origin – that is, one for which the etymology can be traced back no further. 2. Attached to the name of a language or a scholar, it indicates that the language is extinct or that the scholar is deceased. 3. A mark denoting a **pseudoreconstruction**. 4. In an **edition** of a text, a mark indicating that a certain passage has undergone such severe **corruption** that it cannot be interpreted.

Dahl's Law The statement that, in Bantu, when two consecutive syllables begin with voiceless plosives, the first becomes voiced, possibly because the plosives had become aspirated, leading to dissimilation of the first. Hence the Proto-Bantu *-pota* 'twist together' becomes first *-pʰotʰa* (?) and then -botʰa. The observation was made by Edmund Dahl and named by Meinhof (1932). See Collinge (1985: 279–281) for critical discussion.

Daic A label applied sometimes to the **Kadai** family and sometimes to the speculative **Tai-Kadai** grouping.

Dalmatian A **Romance** language formerly spoken on the Adriatic coast of Croatia. It died out in the nineteenth century, but is recorded to a certain extent. See Price (1998: 121–122).

Dante classification An early attempt at classifying some of the languages of Europe, put forward by the Italian poet Dante Alighieri in the early fourteenth century. Dante classified languages exclusively by their word for 'yes', and it was this classification that led to the labels *langue d'oc* for Occitan and *langue d'oïl* for French. Compare the **Scaliger classification**.

Darden's Law The observation that, in Tubatulabal, an unstressed vowel undergoes **syncope** together with any adjacent [ʔ] or [h]. The observation was made by Bill Darden in unpublished work; the name was conferred by Manaster Ramer (1992, 1993b).

Dardic 1. A small group of languages spoken in and near the Himalayas; best known are *Kashmiri* and *Shina*. They are clearly **Indo-Iranian** and are usually classed as a distinctive branch of **Indo-Aryan**. 2. [*erroneous*] A label frequently but wrongly applied to the **Nuristani** languages.

Darwinism Any of various views which see a language as an organism subject to some or all of growth, development, advancement, perfection, degeneration or decay. The nineteenth-century German linguist August Schleicher espoused a version of linguistic Darwinism;

Henry Sweet considered that the English loss of 'illogical' grammatical gender constituted progress; and Otto Jespersen (1922) maintained that analytic languages like English were more highly evolved than synthetic languages like Latin. Nevertheless, few if any linguists take such ideas seriously today; for us, change is just change, and no value judgements are appropriate or possible. Note that this conventional term is inappropriate, since biological Darwinism does not recognize any kind of absolute improvement, perfection or degeneration. Compare **stadialism, functionality of change**.

dash The symbol '–', used in a table of **cognate sets** to indicate that a particular language exhibits no known cognate within a particular set.

daughter language (also **descendant**) With respect to a given language, another language which is directly and immediately descended from it. For example, each of the **Romance** languages is a daughter of **Proto-Romance**, itself a spoken version of **Latin**. The opposite is **parent language**.

deadjectival Of a lexical item, derived from an adjective. For example, the noun *width* and the verb *widen* are derived from the adjective *wide*.

dead language A label applied to two quite different cases. 1. (also **extinct language**) A language which was formerly spoken as a mother tongue but has now ceased to be spoken and left no living descendant, either because (usually) its last speakers abandoned it in favour of a different language or because (rarely) all of its speakers died. Dead languages in this sense include Sumerian, Hittite, Etruscan, Dalmatian, Cornish, Manx, the Tasmanian languages and the Australian language Mbabaram. 2. A language which has never ceased to be spoken, but whose modern forms are so different from it (and from one another, if several exist) that we no longer find it convenient to regard these modern forms as the same language. An example is **Latin**, whose modern forms (the **Romance** languages) are so different from one another and from the language of the Romans that we prefer not to call them 'Latin'.

deaffixization (also **degrammaticalization**) The conversion of an affix, or of a string of affixes, into an independent word. A simple example is the conversion of the English suffix *-ism* (as in *Marxism*) into a word *ism* 'creed, doctrine'. Langdon (1990: 63) reports a more complex case from the Yuman language Paipai: the sense of English 'always' can be expressed either by a series of verbal suffixes of the form Verb-*m-yu:-č* 'Verb-subject-be-Plural', or by an independent adverb *myu:č*, which must appear either before the verb or sentence-initially. Clearly the second form represents an extraction of the affix sequence from inflected verb-forms. The opposite is **affixization**.

deaffrication Any phonological change in which an affricate is converted to a plosive or a fricative, such as the change of /ts/ to /s/ in some varieties of Pipil. The opposite is **affrication**.

deaspiration Any phonological change in which aspiration is removed from a segment which formerly had it. For example, it is generally thought that the voiceless plosives /p t k/ were aspirated in Proto-Germanic, as they are in most Germanic languages today, but Dutch and some varieties of Swiss German have unaspirated /p t k/ and have apparently undergone deaspiration. The opposite is **aspiration**.

debuccalization (also **deoralization**) The conversion of an oral consonant into one involving no oral activity, as when Polynesian */k/ developed into /ʔ/ in Hawaiian, or when [x] becomes [h], as in Proto-Germanic (word-initially), or when non-prevocalic /s/ becomes [h] in some regional varieties of Spanish.

decategorialization In **grammaticalization**, the loss by a grammaticalized item of the morphosyntactic properties of its class, as when a noun being converted to an adposition loses the ability to take number-marking, modifiers, case-endings or articles. See Hopper and Traugott (1993: 103–113). See **hybrid form**, and compare **recategorialization**.

decay (also **degradation**) The loss of functionality by a morphological or syntactic system in a language, often especially when the morphological forms remain in the language but without their former functions or distinctions. Such decay may lead to **exaptation**. Note that this term carries no negative overtones; unlike the nineteenth-century proponents of **Darwinism**, modern linguists do not recognize any kind of 'deterioration' in languages, save only for the special case of **language death**.

decipherment The process of determining the relation between an extinct and unknown writing system and the language it represents. Strictly, decipherment is the the elucidation of the *script* – that is, determining the values of the written characters. Often, however, the term is extended to include the process (where necessary) of working out the structure of the language thus revealed and hence of understanding the texts. It is possible to achieve the first without the second; for example, we have successfully deciphered the script in which the **Iberian** language was written, and we now know the phonetic values of its characters, but we still can't make the slightest sense of the texts, since Iberian is neither a known language nor apparently related to any known language. See Daniels and Bright (1996: part III) and the references therein.

decliticization Any linguistic change in which a clitic is converted into an independent word. Such changes are extremely rare, but Campbell (1991) reports a development in Estonian in which an unproductive affirmative enclitic *-p* has become an independent word *ep* 'yes, indeed'. The opposite is **cliticization**.

decreolization The process in which a **creole** is heavily affected by the prestige language upon which it is largely based, leading to movement of the creole toward that prestige language and typically producing a **post-creole continuum**.

deductive change See under **abduction**.

deep family A **language family** whose members are rather distantly related and whose ancestor therefore probably dates back several thousand years or more. Compare **shallow family**.

default procedure In **reconstruction**, any of various procedures requiring us to select an obvious reconstruction in the absence of evidence to the contrary. For example, given Latin /maːter/, Doric Greek /maːtɛːr/, Sanskrit /maːtaː/ and Old High German /muoter/, all 'mother', we automatically reconstruct */m/ for the initial segment of the PIE word, since anything else would be perverse. Likewise, given Latin /ped-/, Greek /pod-/, Sanskrit /pad-/ and Gothic /foːt-/, all 'foot', we reconstruct the majority sound */p/ for the initial segment in the absence of counterevidence. However, given French /sɑ̃/, Spanish /θjento/, Italian /tʃento/ and Sardinian /kɛntu/, all '100', we do not reconstruct the majority sibilant, because a change from a sibilant to /k/ would be without parallel.

deflected grade [*rare*] See under **ablaut**.

deflection The loss of form-meaning distinctions, as when English lost most of the agreement markers in its finite verb-forms: one kind of **reduction**.

deformation See under **taboo**.

degemination Any phonological change in which a geminate segment is reduced to a simplex. Degemination of plosives is regular in the history of Spanish: Latin *lappa* 'bur', *gutta* 'drop', *bucca* 'mouth', Spanish *lapa* 'limpet', *gota* 'drop', *boca* 'mouth'. The opposite is **gemination**.

degeneralization The phenomenon in which a phonological change which applies very generally and regularly in one area becomes less general or less regular or both as it spreads into neighbouring regions. Hock (1986: 435–440) shows how the **Second Germanic Consonant Shift**, originating in Alemannic, became steadily less general and less regular as it spread out across the Germanic-speaking area.

degeneration Another term for **pejoration**.

degradation Another term for **decay**.

degrammaticalization 1. The conversion of a grammatical item into a lexical item. This process violates **unidirectionality** and it is extremely rare, if indeed it ever happens at all. See C. Lehmann (1982) for discussion. 2. Another term for **fossilization** (sense 1). 3. Another term for **deaffixization**.

Dehnstufe See under **ablaut**.

deictic erosion A label proposed by Hagège (1993: 220) for the observable tendency of deictic verbs, such as motion verbs, to lose much of their deictic value when they become markers of tense, aspect or mood. See Bybee *et al.* (1994) for an examination of this.

delabialization Any phonological change in which a segment loses a labial element which it formerly possessed. For example, PIE $*/k^w/$ usually developed into /p/ in Attic Greek, but it delabialized into

/t/ before certain front vowels: hence /pu:/ 'where?' but /tis/ 'who?', both from PIE forms with initial */k^w/. The opposite is **labialization**.

delateralization Any phonological change in which a segment loses its lateral character. A common example is the development of a velarized alveolar lateral [ɫ] ('dark *l*') into a glide [w]; this has occurred in standard Polish and in certain circumstances in English (*walk, folk, Holborn*). In much of the south of England, all syllable-final instances of /l/ have been delateralized, as in *feel, field, milk* and *ball*.

deletion Another term for **loss** (sense 1).

demic diffusion The movement of sizeable numbers of people from one place to another. This is one way in which a language may spread into new territory; an example is the introduction, by Roman soldiers and colonists, of Latin into much of the Roman Empire. We may distinguish **demographic expansion** from **migration**. Compare **acculturation**.

demographic expansion The spread of a group of people (and hence often also their language) into a larger area than formerly, but without producing any discontinuities in their territory. Compare **migration**.

demorphologization (also **absorption**, **stem-incorporation**) A type of **morphological change** in which an affix is reinterpreted as part of a stem to which it is attached. For example, English *seldom* incorporates the ancient English dative plural affix *-um* attached to the lost adjective *seld* 'rare, strange'; English *friend* and *fiend* incorporate the ancient present participle ending *-ende* attached to lost verbal roots meaning 'love' and 'hate'; Kaytetye *arlweye* 'father' incorporates the possessive suffix *-ye* 'my' (which survives in the language) attached to earlier **arlwe-* 'father'; earlier Afrikaans *kinder* 'children', with plural suffix *-er*, has been reinterpreted as a stem and given a new plural *kinders*. See **phonogenesis** and compare **incorporation, exaptation**. The term *demorphologization* was coined by Hopper (1990: 154). See Joseph and Janda (1988) for discussion.

demotic Denoting the everyday speech of ordinary people of limited education.

Dempwolff's Law The statement, based on the Austronesian language Kâte but intended more generally, that consonants articulated 'in the throat' are unstable and tend to disappear, often with accompanying velarization of adjacent consonants and/or the creation of new tonal contrasts.

denasalization Any phonological change in which nasality is lost from a segment. For example, Occitan *musti* 'moist' has been borrowed into Basque, in which the denasalized form *busti* now predominates over regional *musti*; this is denasalization of the initial segment. On a larger scale, the contrastive nasal vowels of medieval Basque have completely lost their nasality in all but the easternmost dialects and merged with the corresponding oral vowels. Several languages of the Pacific northwest of North America have categorically converted all instances of inherited */m n/ into /b d/, thereby winding up with no nasal consonants at all. The opposite is **nasalization**.

Dene-Caucasian (or **Dene-Sino-Caucasian**) A putative macro-family linking **Sino-Tibetan**, **Na-Dene**, **Yeniseian**, **Nakh-Dagestan** and **Abkhaz-Adyge**, and sometimes also additional languages. (**Burushaski, Basque, Sumerian, Hattic, Hurrian, Urartian** and **Iberian** (!) have been defended or suggested.) Chiefly proposed and developed by Russian linguists, this idea has so far won little support. See Shevoroshkin (1991) for a defence with references. An earlier version excluding Na-Dene was called **Sino-Caucasian**.

deneutralization Any change which eliminates **syncretism** in a paradigm.

denominal (rarely also **denominative**) Of a lexical item, derived from a noun. For example, *powerful* is a denominal adjective derived from the noun *power*.

density of attestation For a given linguistic form being offered as evidence in support of a proposed **genetic relationship**, the number of languages or subgroups within the proposed family in which that form is either attested or securely reconstructible. We can easily imagine varying degrees of this: the form is attested in just two languages (e.g. Welsh and Armenian within IE); it is securely reconstructible for the proto-languages ancestral to two branches of the family (e.g. Germanic and Indo-Iranian within IE); and so on. Naturally, the fewer the forms on offer as evidence, the greater the density of attestation we must demand, up to a possible maximum of requiring it to be securely reconstructible for *every single branch* of the proposed family. In practice, linguists differ widely in the density of attestation they are willing to accept, but laxness on this point is dangerous, since it can lead quickly to the acceptance of spurious 'cognates'. One reason that so many linguists are hostile to certain of the attempts at identifying **remote relationships** is their proponents' practice of adducing proposed cognates from only two or three of perhaps eight or ten major branches of a proposed family, and more particularly their practice of '**reaching down**' into individual languages and tiny groupings to retrieve possible cognates which cannot be reconstructed for the proto-languages ancestral to the larger groupings recognized within the proposed family, such as when a word found only in Avar is taken as evidence for linking Nakh-Dagestan to something else.

dentalization The conversion of a non-dental consonant to a dental consonant, as in the development of some reflex of palatalized /k/ to /θ/ in European Spanish.

deoralization Another term for **debuccalization**.

depalatalization Any phonological change in which a palatal quality is removed from a segment which formerly had it or in which a palatal segment is converted to a different place of articulation. For example, the Indo-Iranian palatal affricates */ć/ and */ǰ/ were depalatalized in common Iranian to dental */ts/ and */dz/, which later developed further to /s/ and /z/ in most Iranian languages. The opposite is **palatalization**.

deparadigmatization Any change, or set of changes, with the consequence that linguistic forms which formerly belonged to a single paradigm become separated and no longer perceived as related. For example, the former English stem-formative *-wa-*, which once united many nouns and adjectives into a single declensional paradigm, survives today only as a final segment in a miscellaneous group of words, including *callow, yellow, fallow* and *slow,* among others.

dephonologization Especially in Prague School terminology, another term for **merger**.

deregionalization Another term for **koinéization**.

derivation (also **affixation**) The type of **word-formation** in which new lexical items are created by adding affixes to existing words, as in *powerful* and *powerless* from *power*, *rewrite* and *writer* from *write*, and all the steps in *palate* > *palatal* > *palatalize* > *depalatalize* > *depalatalization*. Each such form is a **derived form**. For some languages, the term *affixation* must be interpreted rather broadly, as in Arabic, in which the root *ktb* 'write', for example, yields derivatives like *ka:tib* 'writer' and *kita:b* 'book'.

derivative A word obtained by **derivation** from another. For example, *rewrite* and *writer* are derivatives of *write*.

derived contrast A surface phonetic contrast arising from the presence of a morpheme boundary. An example is the contrast between the fricatives of German *kuchen* 'cook', with [x] arising from /ku:x-/ + /-ən/, and *Kuhchen* 'little cow', with [ç] arising from /ku:/ + /-çən/. This is the only circumstance in which [x] and [ç] contrast in German.

derived form A form obtained by **derivation**.

descendant Another term for **reflex** or for **daughter language**.

descent The ancestry of a language. For example, English descends from its ancestor **Proto-Germanic**, which in turn descends from an earlier ancestor, **Proto-Indo-European**.

descriptive form Another term for **expressive formation** (sense 2).

desegmentalization Another term for **coalescence**.

desemanticization The loss of semantic content by a word or morpheme, often particularly one undergoing **grammaticalization**.

desulcalization The loss of the /r/-constriction, as occurs in non-prevocalic position in some varieties of English.

desyllabification (also **desyllabication**) Any process in which a syllabic segment loses its syllabic character, most commonly the conversion of a vowel to a glide, as in **glide-formation**. The opposite is **syllabification**.

determinative See under **Indo-European root theory**, item (7).

Deutlichkeitstrieb Striving for clarity, one of the supposed driving forces behind language change introduced by Georg von der Gabelentz in the nineteenth century. Compare *Bequemlichkeitstrieb*.

developmental linguistics The label applied by Bailey (1996 and elsewhere) and Markey (1990 and elsewhere) to their view that all linguistic description and theorizing requires explicit recognition of the diachronic dimension, that language change is in some sense deterministic, and that the study of language change should have some measure of predictive power. Proponents of this approach dismiss the quantitative studies of Labov and his colleagues as superficial, and argue instead for the importance of (certain versions of) iconicity, markedness and naturalness. Compare **panchrony** (sense 2), **emergent grammar**.

deverbal Of a lexical item, derived from a verb. For example, *arrival* is a deverbal noun derived from the verb *arrive*.

devocalization Any phonological process in which a vowel or a glide is converted into a consonant: one form of **fortition**. For example, in western Basque, the nouns *gau* 'night' and *ao* 'mouth', when combined with the article *-a*, yield *gaba* and *aba*.

devoicing Any phonological change in which a voiced sound is converted to the corresponding voiceless sound. For example, word-final /b d g/ have become /p t k/ in German, Russian and many other languages, and all voiced fricatives became voiceless in all positions in Old Spanish. The opposite is **voicing**.

diachronic correspondence The relation between two segments, one of which is directly descended from the other within a single line of linguistic descent. For example, Old Japanese /p/ and modern Japanese /h/ are in a diachronic correspondence, since modern /h/ derives from earlier /p/.

diachronic cycle Another term for the cycle posited in the **linguistic cycle hypothesis**.

diachronic trajectory See **trajectory** (senses 1 and 2).

diachronic universal Any generalization about the nature or direction of language change which is presented as holding true without exception, or at least as nearly so. Possible examples: intervocalic plosives may undergo voicing but not devoicing; independent words may become bound morphemes but not vice versa; a lexical verb may become an auxiliary but not vice versa; a passive construction may develop into an ergative construction but not vice versa. Few if any such statements are known to be totally without exceptions, but many are nevertheless excellent generalizations. A weaker version is a **universal tendency**.

diachrony The time dimension in language. A diachronic approach to a language is one which examines the ways in which the language has changed over some period of time. Compare **synchrony**.

dialect Any distinctive variety of a language spoken by some group of people. A particular style of pronunciation is an *accent*; in the USA, an accent is considered to be one part of a dialect, while in Britain accents are considered to be independent of dialects, which are characterized by lexicon and grammar. See **regional dialect** and **social dialect**.

dialect atlas A book containing a large number of **dialect maps**, each illustrating a particular linguistic variable within a certain geographical region.

dialect borrowing Another term for **dialect mixing**.

dialect chain Another term for **dialect continuum**, or sometimes more specifically for a continuum with an essentially linear structure, in which all the distinguishable varieties are arranged in a single line.

dialect continuum (also **family-like language**) A group of closely related speech varieties occupying a cohesive geographical area, in such a way that there are no sharp linguistic boundaries. Typically, every speaker can speak easily with near neighbours, with more difficulty with people farther away, and with great difficulty or not at all with people farther away still. Just such a continuum is the usual result of the **breakup** of a single language occupying a sizeable geographical area, as different but overlapping changes affect different parts of the region. An example is the Romance-speaking dialect continuum produced by the breakup of Latin. See the **wave model**.

dialect geography The study of regional variation, typically involving the mapping of the distribution and frequency of particular linguistic features in a geographical area. The findings are conveniently presented in the form of **dialect maps** which may be marked with **isoglosses** or **isopleths**. Dialect geography was developed in Europe in the second half of the nineteenth century, by Georg Wenker, Jules Gilliéron, and others; both questionnaires and interviews were tried, with the second winning out, and several **dialect atlases** were the result. The dialectologists were often strong opponents of the **Neogrammarians**, whose 'exceptionless sound laws' they could not find in the messiness of their data. See Andersen (1988). Compare **dialectology** and see the references there.

dialect interference The **diffusion** of linguistic features from one to another dialect of a single language. See Trudgill (1986), Thomason and Kaufman (1988).

dialect levelling Another term for **koinéization**.

dialect map A map which shows, for some linguistic **variable**, the different forms which predominate in different geographical areas occupied by a single language.

dialect merger A label applied by the proponents of **developmental linguistics** to the process by which a more or less unified **koiné** arises from the blending of several rather distinct dialects, usually with morphological simplification in the process. The rise of English from the several dialects of Old English is seen as a case in point.

dialect mixing (also **dialect borrowing**, **intimate borrowing**) A largely hypothetical process frequently invoked in the past by the proponents of the **Neogrammarian Hypothesis** in order to account for language varieties which do not appear to have undergone regular phonological change – that is, some words show the effect of a change while others do not. For a rigorous Neogrammarian, such a state of affairs can only result from a mixing of forms from two distinct varieties, each of which has undergone regular but different changes. With the recognition in recent years of more sophisticated models of phonological change, such as **lexical diffusion**, dialect mixing is appealed to less frequently, though its reality is not in doubt: note standard English *vat* and *vixen*, borrowed from a southwestern dialect and displacing the expected **fat* and **fixen*, and note

Hetzron's (1990) argument that the Afro-Asiatic languages show extensive evidence of dialect mixing. The term **dialect interference** is now preferred. An extreme form of dialect mixing is **endohybridization**. See Trudgill (1986) and see **bidirectional diffusion**.

dialectology The study of **dialects**, especially **regional dialect** but also **social dialects**. The term encompasses not only **dialect geography** but also purely descriptive work on regional non-standard dialects. Today a good deal of dialectology is done with large databases stored on computers. See **structural dialectology**, and see Chambers and Trudgill (1998) or Francis (1983) for an introduction.

diaphoneme A single abstract segment which occurs with the same distribution in several different varieties of a language but which is represented by a phonetically different phoneme in each. For example, the Basque diaphone |ĵ| appears in the several dialects as a phoneme /j/, /ɟ/, /dʒ/, /ʒ/, /ʃ/ or /χ/.

diastole [*rare*] The **lengthening** of an originally short syllable. The opposite is **systole**.

diatopy The geographical dimension in language. Diatopic variation is regional variation, and is the subject of **dialect geography**.

differential loss The state of affairs in which a linguistic form existing in an ancestral language survives in its daughter languages in two different reduced forms: in some, part A is retained and part B is lost, while in others part A is lost and part B is retained. See the examples under **portmanteau reconstruction**.

differentiation 1. The development of differences in meaning, function or register between potential synonyms, of whatever origin. English examples include *brothers* and *brethren*, *older* and *elder*, *cow* and *beef*, and *kingly* and *royal*. 2. Another term for **paradigmatic split**.

diffuse Of a speech community, exhibiting substantial internal divergence. Examples of diffuse communities include Belfast and many Caribbean islands. The opposite is **focused**.

diffusion The spread of a linguistic form or of a language change across the speech varieties occupying a considerable geographical area, sometimes especially when this occurs across the boundaries of languages or of families. For example, a uvular realization of /r/, apparently originating in Parisian French, has diffused into regional varieties of at least nine western European languages; the change of /k/ to /tʃ/ has diffused into several unrelated languages of the Pacific coast of North America; and numerals and agricultural terms have diffused across language boundaries in certain parts of Mexico. Large-scale diffusion can greatly complicate our elucidation of the prehistories of languages and even our assignment of languages to families.

diffusional cumulation The term used by Swadesh (1951) for **convergence** resulting from **language contact**.

diffusional linguistics The term used by Heath (1978 and elsewhere) for the study of *contact* (see **language contact**) phenomena.

diglossia The state of affairs in which two quite distinct languages or language varieties are spoken in a single community, with a high degree of specialization between the two, so that each variety is perceived as appropriate for certain functions. In every instance of diglossia, one variety, which we may call High (or H), has much greater overt prestige and is acquired through formal education, while the other, Low (or L), is the mother tongue of virtually the entire population. Typically, H is used for all or most publication, for news broadcasts, for university lectures and most public speeches, and for religious purposes (among other functions), while L is used for ordinary conversation and for the more popular types of entertainment (such as soap operas) (among other functions); often L may lack a recognized written form. The correct choice of variety is of great importance, since using the 'wrong' variety for a particular function is seen as comical or offensive; even speakers with a severely limited command of H prefer to hear H when H is appropriate. Diglossia was first identified by Charles Ferguson (1959). Among the diglossic communities which have existed in recent times are Paraguay (H = Spanish, L = Guaraní), Greece (H = Katharevousa, L = Dhimotikí; diglossia has now disappeared from Greece), German Switzerland (H = standard High German, L = Swiss German), Haiti (H = French, L = Haitian Creole) and the Arab countries (H = classical Arabic, L = colloquial Arabic).

diminutive A morphologically modified form of a word (usually a noun) which in principle denotes a smaller version but which in practice often acquires extended senses indicating affection or familiarity. In the history of Romance, many Latin nouns were completely displaced by their diminutives; for example, Latin *auris* 'ear' was displaced by *auricula*, the source of Spanish *oreja* and French *oreille*.

diphthongal root In some analyses, a label applied to a PIE root containing a vowel-glide sequence, such as *ghew-* 'pour'. Today it is more usual to analyse these as containing a sequence of two segments, a vowel plus a resonant, since doing so allows these roots to be regarded as participating normally in the **ablaut** system.

diphthongization Any phonological change in which a pure vowel is converted to a diphthong. For example, Proto-Romance stressed */ɛ/ and */ɔ/ were diphthongized in Spanish and Italian, the first as [eɛ] > [iɛ] > [je], the second as [oɔ] > [uɔ] > [wo] (and > [we] in Spanish), so that, for example, Proto-Romance **pɛtra* 'stone' yields Spanish *piedra*, Italian *pietra*, and Proto-Romance **bɔno* 'good' yields Spanish *bueno*, Italian *buono*. The opposite is **monophthongization**. A distinctive kind of diphthongization is **breaking**.

diplomatic See under **edition**.

disambiguating compound A **compound** which is constructed in order to distinguish homophones. For example, in southern American varieties of English, *pen* has become homophonous with *pin*, and speakers may use the compounds *ink-pen* and *stick-pin* to get round the potential ambiguity.

discontinuity problem The name given by Lass (1987: 170) to the puzzle of how long-term changes like **drift** and **conspiracies** can apparently pause for a few generations and then resume. Compare the **extension problem**.

discontinuous descent (also **discontinuous transmission**) The rare case in which a language dies out entirely as a mother tongue but is then, at some later date, revived as a mother tongue by deliberate efforts. The only truly successful instance of this is **Hebrew**, though it is reported that a few people have now learned the dead language Cornish as their mother tongue.

discontinuous spread In **dialect geography**, the phenomenon in which an innovation 'jumps' from one area to another without affecting the intervening area (at least initially). Many such cases are known, and all involve jumps from one urban area to another across intervening rural areas.

discontinuous transmission Another term for **discontinuous descent**.

discourse-based approach Any approach to the study of **grammaticalization** which sees this as essentially resulting from the **syntacticization** of discourse strategies. See Heine *et al.* (1991a: 238–243) for a survey with references.

disjunct The term used by Blust (1970, 1980) for either of two reconstructed forms which are supported by overlapping cognate sets. For example, Fijian *kumi* 'beard' can be derived either from Proto-Austronesian **gumi* or from Proto-Austronesian **kumis*, both of which are independently required.

dispersal of human language The spread of languages across the earth along with the original peopling of the planet. From the anthropological and archaeological evidence, it appears at present that our species arose in eastern and southern Africa between 100,000 and 200,000 years ago, and that it spread out from there, successively reaching northern Africa, the Near East, southeast Asia, New Guinea, Australia, Europe, northern Asia, the Americas and finally (much later) the Pacific islands. Countless incidents of **language shift** and **demic diffusion** have, however, greatly disturbed the original distribution of languages, and no one knows how much of that original distribution might still be recoverable from living and attested languages. Two major attempts at confronting this issue are **population typology** and the **Renfrew hypothesis**.

disproportionation [*rare*] An unusual type of **paradigmatic change**, in which a single phoneme disappears from the system by undergoing **merger**, in some cases with a second existing phoneme but in other cases with a third. For example, Old Turkish had (and some Anatolian varieties still have) the nine-vowel system /i e ɛ y œ ɯ a u ɔ/, in which /e/ spoils the otherwise perfect symmetry; in standard Turkish, this /e/ has disappeared, merging in some instances with /i/ but in others with /ɛ/, in a seemingly arbitrary manner.

dissimilation Any **syntagmatic change** in which one segment changes so as to become less similar to another segment in the same form. For example, Latin *arbore(m)* 'tree' yields Spanish *árbol* (with dissimilation of the second /r/ to /l/); Latin *libellum* 'level' yields French *niveau* (with dissimilation of the first /l/ to /n/, plus other changes); Latin *anima* 'soul' is borrowed into Basque as *arima* (with dissimilation of the first nasal). Most cases of assimilation, like these, involve non-adjacent segments (*dissimilation at a distance*), but dissimilation can also occur with adjacent segments, as with the change of Dutch /sxo:n/ 'clean' to Afrikaans /sko:n/, with dissimilation of the second of two fricatives to a plosive. The extreme case is *dissimilatory loss*, as when Basque **Santso* 'Sancho' (name of several Navarrese kings) became *Antso*, with dissimilatory loss of the first sibilant. The opposite is **assimilation**.

distant assimilation See under **assimilation**.

distant relationship Another term for **remote relationship**.

disyllabic root A label formerly applied to a PIE root which seemingly had to be reconstructed with two syllables, such as **perə-* 'allot, grant'. Today such roots are usually reconstructed as monosyllabic roots containing a cluster of a consonant and a laryngeal, and hence **perH$_2$-* in this case. It was only in certain daughter languages that a laryngeal in this position became a vowel, as in Greek *pera-*.

divergence 1. (also **diversification**) The process by which languages or dialects sharing a common ancestor become ever more different over time, as a result of accumulated changes. In the past, the prehistories of languages were commonly viewed as consisting of constant divergence, but see the remarks under **convergence**. 2. (also **split**) In **grammaticalization**, the coexistence of grammaticalized and ungrammaticalized forms of the same item, such as English *one* and *a(n)* or French *pas* 'step, pace' and *pas* 'not'. See Hopper and Traugott (1993: 116–120). 3. The split of what was originally a single lexical root into two or more distinct lexical items perceived as only feebly related or as unrelated, as has occurred with English *tree* and *true* and with German *Ameise* 'ant' and *emsig* 'busy' (originally 'antlike').

divergent 1. Of a language or dialect, differing markedly in form or structure from its closest genetic relatives. Among the **Indo-European** languages, the **Anatolian** languages are highly divergent;

among the **Germanic** languages, **English** is the most divergent; among the dialects of **Japanese**, the Ryukyuan varieties are by far the most divergent and are sometimes counted as distinct languages. 2. Of a linguistic form, differing in an irregular or inexplicable manner from its cognates.

diversification Another term for **divergence** (sense 1).

diversity The degree of typological or genetic variety observable within a language family or within a geographical area.

division sign The symbol '÷', sometimes used to represent *akin to*. Thus, 'Middle English *lomeren* "to lumber", ÷ regional Swedish *loma* "to move heavily"' means that the English word is related in an unspecified manner to the Swedish one.

documentation (also **attestation**) For a given linguistic form, the secure presence of that form in one or more documents written in the relevant language. We write things like this: 'Basque *emazte* "wife" is first documented in 1189, though in its earlier sense of "woman".' The documentation of forms is of critical importance in philological work, and the date of first attestation is often of the greatest importance.

Dolgopolsky list A list, compiled by Dolgopolsky (1964) and based on a survey of 140 Eurasian languages, of the fifteen words which are supposedly most resistant to **lexical replacement**. In order of decreasing stability, these are (1) *I/me*, (2) *two/pair*, (3) *thou/thee*, (4) *who/what*, (5) *tongue*, (6) *name*, (7) *eye*, (8) *heart*, (9) *tooth*, (10) *no/not*, (11) *fingernail/toenail*, (12) *louse/nit*, (13) *tear(drop)*, (14) *water* and (15) *dead*. Of these, (1) had been replaced in none of the languages examined, (15) in about 25 per cent of them.

Dolobko's Law (also **Vasiljev and Dolobko, Law of**) The statement, put forward by Dolobko (1927), that, at a certain stage in the prehistory of **Slavic**, the word-accent moved rightwards in adjectives in which a former enclitic had become a true adjectival suffix. See Collinge (1985: 29–30) for an account.

domal [*obsolete*] An old philological term for *retroflex*.

donor language In **borrowing**, the language which contributes the linguistic forms introduced into another language.

Dorsey's Law In the Siouan language Winnebago, a regular process in which Proto-Siouan *CRV acquires an **echo vowel**, yielding CVRV (with two identical vowels) whenever C is an obstruent and R a sonorant. In addition, C becomes voiceless and aspirated – surprisingly, since all instances were originally lenis and unaspirated. The observation was made by Dorsey (1885) and named by Wolff (1950–51). See Miner (1979).

doublet 1. A pair of **variants**, or a pair of distinct words deriving from variant forms of a single ancestor. A likely example is English *shade* and *shed*, which appear to derive from variant forms of Old English *sceadu* ~ *scead* ~ *sced* 'shade, shelter'. 2. A pair of phonologically similar forms which must apparently both be reconstructed in a proto-language for the same **cognate set**, such as Proto-Austronesian *akar* ~ *wakar* 'root', *kambiŋ* ~ *kandiŋ* 'goat', *Rataq* ~ *Ratas* 'milk' and *gilap* ~ *kilap* 'lustre'. See the *tooth* problem. 3. One of two words in a language which have been borrowed at different times from what is historically the same item in a single source language or family, such as English *castle* (from Old French) and *château* (from the modern French continuation of the same word). Larger sets are possible: English *gentile*, *gentle*, *genteel* and *jaunty* all derive from Latin *gentilis* and its continuations in French at various periods. 4. The term used by Hoenigswald (1960: 39) for the two forms arising in **paradigmatic split**.

drag chain See under **chain shift**.

Dravidian A major language family of southern India and Sri Lanka, with one outlier in Pakistan and several in eastern India. There are about twenty-eight Dravidian languages, of which four have over 25 million speakers each: *Tamil*, *Telugu*, *Malayalam* and *Kannada*. It is widely suspected that the extinct and undeciphered **Indus Valley language** was a Dravidian language, but no confirmation is available. The existence of the isolated northern outlier *Brahui* is consistent with the hypothesis that Dravidian formerly occupied much of northern India but was displaced by the invading **Indo-Aryan** languages, and the presence in the Indo-Aryan languages of certain linguistic features, such as retroflex consonants, is often attributed to Dravidian substrate influence. Attempts at linking Dravidian to the extinct **Elamite** in a larger **Elamo-Dravidian** family have not won general acceptance. See Steever (1997) for a survey of the family.

drift A term coined by Sapir (1921a: ch. 7) to denote either of two related but distinct phenomena. 1. The tendency of a language to keep changing in the same direction over many generations. An example is the steady loss of inflectional endings in English over several centuries. See Lass (1987, 1997: 300–303), and see **extension problem, discontinuity problem, chreod**. 2. Another term for **independent parallel innovation**.

duplicate changes Another term for **independent parallel innovation**.

dvandva (also **copulative compound, coordinate compound**) A type of **compound** in which every component is a head and no element modifies another: *Austria-Hungary, tragicomic, Metro-Goldwyn-Mayer*. Dvandvas are extremely frequent in **Sanskrit**, in which they are formed with seemingly total freedom: *ācārya-śisya* 'teacher-pupil', i.e. 'teacher(s) and pupil(s)'; *aśva-gaja-bāla-narā* 'horses, elephants, children and men'.

Dybo's Law A shift in the word-accent of common **Slavic**, identified by Dybo (1962), by which a non-acute accent falling on a short vowel was shifted one syllable to the right. See Collinge (1985: 31–33) for an account.

dysphemism A dismissive or offensive word or phrase used in place of another which is respectful or neutral. English examples include *nag* for 'horse', *mug* for 'face', *screw* for 'copulate' and *tart, bird, chick* or *sheila* for 'woman'. A dysphemism may replace its corresponding neutral term, as when Latin *caballus* 'nag' replaced earlier *equus* 'horse' in many Romance languages. The opposite is **euphemism**.

early-creolized creole A **creole** resulting from **abrupt creolization**.

Early Modern English The name given to a certain period in the history of English, conventionally dated from about 1500 to 1700.

ease-of-articulation explanation of change Any proposal that certain linguistic changes, especially phonological changes, occur because they make the language easier to pronounce as a result – because of fewer segments, less marked segment-types, smaller movements of the vocal organs, simpler sequences, or whatever. It is clear that *certain* changes result in some kind of phonological simplification, but others do not and may even have the opposite effect, as when vowel losses produce new and complex consonant clusters, or when /u/ is fronted to the highly marked vowel /y/. In any case, phonological simplification in particular forms may result in complex alternations or in the loss of bound grammatical markers; a language system involves far more than phonemes and sequences of phonemes. Finally, ease of articulation for the speaker does not correspond to ease of perception for the hearer; if every utterance had the form [m], life would be maximally easy for the speaker but maximally difficult for the hearer.

East Sudanic A large and possibly primary branch of **Nilo-Saharan**. Greenberg (1963b) assigns it to his controversial **Chari-Nile** grouping, and regards **Nilotic** as a branch of it.

Ebeling principle A slightly facetious observation about the behaviour of historical linguists. It says: the more exotic a language, and the fewer linguists who have analysed it, the more tractable and self-evident is its grammar. Proposed by Lightfoot (1979: 316–317), this observation is not inherently historical, but Lightfoot clearly intends it as a comment on work in historical grammar. In his view, the study of the grammatical history of English is characterized by a much greater degree of dispute and controversy than, say, that of the history of Georgian, merely because there are far fewer linguists who work on Georgian or who even know anything about Georgian. His general point is that historical facts do not exist in isolation, free of interpretation and debate.

Ebeling's Law The statement that, at some point in the prehistory of **Slavic** (or of **Balto-Slavic**), the word-accent in two-syllable verb-forms moved from the final to the initial syllable. This was proposed by Ebeling (1963); see Collinge (1985: 35–36) for an account.

Eblaite An extinct **Semitic** language spoken in northwestern Syria in the second half of the third millennium BC and later displaced by **Amorite**. The abundant texts, which date from about the twenty-fourth century BC, were discovered and deciphered only in the mid-twentieth century. Among Semitic languages, Eblaite is rather archaic and possesses a good deal of unique vocabulary; its classification within the family is difficult. See Gordon (1997).

echo vowel (also **copy vowel**) A vowel inserted by **anaptyxis** which is identical to a vowel in a neighbouring syllable. Examples include the vowel inserted in the change from Old Latin *faclis* to *facilis* 'easy', that inserted in the borrowing of Latin *fronte* as Basque *boronde* 'forehead', and the vowels inserted in *polnoglásie* (see **pleophony**).

echo word A word constructed by repeating an existing word with a fixed alternation (usually to the beginning). Echo words serve varied functions. Yiddish–influenced American English uses formations with *schm-* for dismissal, as in *Jaguar-Schmaguar*; Turkish uses formations with *m-* to express 'and the others', as in *Ali-mali* 'Ali and the others'; Basque uses formations in *ma-* for a variety of expressive purposes, as in *haundi-maundi* 'pompous, self-important' (*haundi* 'big'); Malay uses a range of formations to express 'all sorts of', as in *sayur-mayur* 'all sorts of vegetables' (*sayur* 'vegetables'). Compare **rhyming formation**.

eclipsis In modern Irish, a **mutation** in which /p t k f/ become /b d g v/ and /b d g/ become /m n ŋ/.

economy Any of various criteria which may be appealed to in **reconstruction**. For example, we prefer to reconstruct an ancestral phoneme system with as few segments as possible, and we prefer that reconstruction which requires the smallest possible number of distinct and independent changes. Compare **symmetry**.

economy-of-effort principle (also **least-effort principle**) Any of several related but distinct putative principles of language structure and change, according to which languages tend to change in such a way as to minimize the effort involved in speaking. See **ease-of-articulation explanation of change**, **Grammont's law**, **Zipf's principles**.

edited evidence In seeking **remote relationships** among languages, the use of irresponsibly selected data which appear to support a proposed grouping, while silently ignoring counterevidence. A typical example is the citation of a single regional variant form of a word which provides a good-looking match, when examination of other regional variants shows clearly that the earliest form of the word must have been such as to provide no support for the proposed match. This deeply unprofessional practice is common in the works of certain long-rangers, and it often produces spurious 'results' which look impressive on the page to anyone not a specialist in the languages cited.

edition A published version of an ancient text preserved only in the form of one or more manuscripts or of an inscription, often accompanied by the editor's notes and commentaries, by suggested emendations where the text appears to be defective or corrupt, and sometimes also by variant readings, where these exist. Very often the editor makes additions for the convenience of the reader; for example, in editions of Old English texts, length marks are added to long vowels, the letter wynn is replaced by <w>, abbreviations may be written out, and, in the case of poetry, the poems may be broken up into lines with line numbers added. All this work is the **critical apparatus**. An edition based upon two or more variant manuscript versions of a single text is a *critical edition*; an edition based upon a single manuscript rendered as faithfully as possible is a *diplomatic*.

e-grade See under **ablaut**.

Egyptian The principal language of ancient Egypt, forming one branch of the **Afro-Asiatic** family by itself. Egyptian is substantially recorded in the form of the monumental *hieroglyphic* inscriptions and also in an everyday **demotic** writing system. The discovery in 1803 of the *Rosetta Stone*, containing the same text in both written forms and in Greek, allowed Champollion to begin the decipherment of the hieroglyphs, and today we can read Egyptian texts easily – though neither writing system represented the vowels. Egyptian is divided into periods called *Old Egyptian* (3000–2000 BC), *Middle* (or *Classical*) *Egyptian* (2000–1300 BC) (the language of the great inscriptions), *Late Egyptian* (1300–700 BC), *Demotic* (seventh century BC–fifth century AD) and **Coptic** (fourth–fourteenth centuries AD), after which the language died out as a mother tongue. See Loprieno (1995).

elaboration 1. In **language planning**, the business of creating new vocabulary and possibly also new constructions, with the intention of making the language a suitable vehicle for all types of discourse. 2. A label sometimes applied to the construction of a **creole** from a **pidgin**, with accompanying expansion of grammar and vocabulary. Compare **simplification** (sense 4). 3. In the work of Johanna Nichols, the splitting of a language into distinct **daughter languages**.

elaboration rate The number of distinct *immediate* **daughter languages** typically arising from a single **ancestor language**. Nichols (1990), on the basis of an empirical study, estimates this number as two to three before extinction is allowed for, and as about 1.6 after. Nichols takes this result as casting doubt on the viability of searches for vast macro-lineages like **Nostratic**, which typically require six to ten major daughters of a single ancestor. **Indo-European**, with its ten or so major branches, is a problem, but perhaps results from exceptional circumstances; see, however, the **Pennsylvania model of IE**.

Elamite An extinct language formerly spoken in southwestern Iran and recorded in writing from about the twenty-third to the fourth century BC. It was routinely used in the trilingual inscriptions of the Achaemenid kings of Persia, and we can read the texts. Elamite is very probably also the language concealed in an earlier body of undeciphered texts dating from around 3200 BC. Elamite is usually regarded as an **isolated language**, but see **Elamo-Dravidian**.

Elamo-Dravidian A proposed genetic grouping of the **Dravidian** languages with the extinct **Elamite** language. Put forward by McAlpin (1974, 1975, 1981), this proposal has received some sympathy but does not at present command anything like general assent.

elevation Another term for **amelioration**.

elision Any of various processes in which phonological segments are lost from a word or a phrase. Specific varieties of elision are often given special names like **aphaeresis, syncope, apocope, synaeresis, synizesis** and **synaloepha**. Not infrequently this name is given to specific processes in particular languages, such as the French process that converts *la* + *amie* to *l'amie* 'the (female) friend', or to the Spanish process in which *Santa Ana* 'Saint Anne' is pronounced *Santana*. Compare **ellipsis**.

ellipsis Any construction in which some material which is required for semantic interpretation and which could have been overtly present is absent but immediately recoverable from the linguistic context, particularly when that material is overtly present elsewhere in the sentence. For example, the sentence *Susie can't speak Spanish but Lisa can* illustrates ellipsis of the repeated VP *speak Spanish*. Compare **elision**.

Elymian The extinct and very sparsely recorded language of western Sicily, attested between the sixth and fourth centuries BC. It was probably **Indo-European**, and is occasionally classed as **Italic**, though there is little evidence for this.

embedding problem The problem of determining how a given linguistic innovation comes to be embedded in the surrounding system of linguistic and social relations. See the **WLH model of language change**.

emblematic feature A linguistic feature which is present in one speech variety but absent from closely related varieties and which is perceived as identifying a speaker of the first variety. An emblematic feature may be acquired by a speech variety by means of an **act of identity**.

emblematic language In a multilingual society, a language which is perceived as the property of a particular group and which serves to identify a member of that group. A group's emblematic language is usually less prestigious and less widely used than one or more other languages used for inter-group communication, and linguistic features tend to flow from the inter-group language(s) into an emblematic language, but not the reverse. A group may change its emblematic language abruptly. See Grace (1996), M. Ross (1996).

emendation In philological work, and especially in an **edition** of a text, an alteration ('correction') made by the editor to the form of a word which appears to be clearly erroneous. For example, in the *Reja de San Millán*, a copy of a document of 1025 listing the towns and villages of part of the Basque province of Alava, the incomprehensible *Betollagaha* is emended by scholars to *Betollazaha*, an ancestral form of the modern town-name *Betolaza*.

emergent grammar A view of **syntactic change** which holds that the grammar of a language is never fixed and complete; instead, it is constantly in the process of being newly constructed out of discourse strategies. This view has been defended and developed by Hopper (1979a, 1979b, 1982, 1987). Hopper argues that 'grammar is always emergent but never specific,' rejects the view that speakers come to a discourse with a fixed grammar already in place, and defines **grammaticalization** as 'movement toward structure' (1987: 148).

emergent languages The term used by T. Kaufman (1994) to denote very closely related languages which are just 'emerging' from a chain of dialects and have progressed just beyond being mutually intelligible, as they formerly were.

emerging metaphor See under **metaphor**.

emphatic foreignization Another term for **hyperforeignism**.

enclave language The term applied by Maher (1985) to a **minority language** which is surrounded and/or dominated by one or more languages of greater prestige.

encliticization See under **cliticization**.

endangered language A language which is in grave danger of becoming extinct within the next two or three generations at most, even though it may still be being learned by children. Compare **moribund language**.

endocentric compound A **compound** with a *head*: a compound denoting a specific variety of something denoted more generally by its overt head. Examples include *blackbird* (a type of bird), *green olive* (a type of olive) and *olive-green* (a type of green). Compare *bahuvrīhi*.

endogenous innovation Another term for **internal change**.

endogenous pidgin A **pidgin** whose speakers continue to live in the area in which the languages which contributed to the pidgin are spoken. Compare **exogenous pidgin**.

endohybridization The term used by Leer (1990) to denote a hypothetical process by which several closely related but distinct language varieties are blended into a single language which is the descendant of all of them and which incorporates, in a rather unsystematic way, features inherited from all of the original languages: an extreme variety of **dialect mixing**. The result he calls a **portmanteau language**. Compare **exohybridization**.

Endzelin's Law A statement about the development of the PIE diphthongs in **Baltic**, put forward by Endzelin (1922, 1948). Endzelin himself argued only for a change of PIE */ei/ to Baltic /ie/ when accented, but others have attempted to generalize his analysis to treat the three PIE diphthongs */ei ai oi/. See Collinge (1985: 37–39) for a discussion with references.

English The world's premier language. English belongs to the **Germanic** branch of the **Indo-European** family, and it derives from the **Ingvaeonic** speech of the North Sea peoples who settled Britain in sizeable numbers after the Roman withdrawal in the early fifth century AD. The speech of these invaders (Angles, Saxons and Jutes) eventually came to be called *English*, and English gradually displaced the earlier **Celtic** language of Britain from most of the island. (This Celtic language, which we call *British*, is the ancestor of *Welsh*, *Breton* and the extinct *Cornish*.)

During the tenth century the Vikings conquered and settled much of England, and their **Old Norse** language had a significant effect upon the closely related English. In 1066, the French-speaking Normans conquered England, and Norman French replaced English as the prestige language for about two centuries. English eventually reasserted itself, but it acquired thousands of loan words from French in the process.

Until the seventeenth century, English was spoken nowhere but in Britain, and it was a language of no great prestige or importance elsewhere. Conquest and colonization, however, introduced English first into Ireland, North America and the Caribbean, and later into Australia, New Zealand and several parts of Africa and Asia. Continuous expansion by English-speakers spread the language across the greater part of the North American continent, obliterating or reducing to insignificance the indigenous languages, and the same thing happened in Australia and New Zealand.

In the twentieth century, and especially since 1945, the wealth and power of the English-speaking countries, and above all of the United States, have led to a state of affairs unprecedented in the history of our planet; English has become the first truly *global language* ever to exist. With perhaps 425 million native speakers, it is a distant second to Mandarin Chinese, but there are further hundreds of millions who speak English either as an everyday second language or as a fluent foreign language, and the total number of English-speakers is probably above one billion and growing rapidly. English now has some kind of special status in almost every country on earth, and it is by far the language most widely learned by speakers of other languages. In science, scholarship, technology, business, diplomacy, communications, transport and popular culture, English is everywhere the first language.

During the last thousand years the language has changed from a typical Germanic language, with a rich and complex morphology, to a predominantly analytic language with little morphology; its vocabulary has been transformed by massive importation from French, Latin, Greek and a hundred other languages; and its pronunciation has undergone some dramatic changes. The history of English is conventionally divided into periods called **Old English, Middle English, Early Modern English** and **Modern English**. See Price (1998: 137–150) for a brief survey. Among the numerous histories of English are Algeo and Pyles (1993), Barber (1993), Smith (1996) (mainly structural), Freeborn (1992) (mainly textual), Graddol *et al.* (1996), Leith (1997), McCrum *et al.* (1992) (mainly social) and Blake (1996) (structural and social). Denison (1993) and Traugott (1972) are studies of the history of English syntax, while Jespersen (1909–49) and Visser (1963–73) are major sources for the history of English grammar.

English Length Conspiracy A series of formally unrelated changes occurring in English between the West Germanic period and about the fourteenth century, by which vowel length, formerly contrastive, became predictable in almost all environments. See Lass (1987: 159–161).

enlarged reduplication See under **reduplication**.

enlargement See under **Indo-European root theory**.

entering element In a **chain shift**, a segment which moves into the phonological space formerly occupied by another segment moving out of it, the **leaving element**.

Entfaltungstheorie The view that many language changes can be attributed to 'inherited tendencies', by which the speakers of a language, over many generations, 'tend' to alter it in particular directions. This is one interpretation of **drift**; it was invoked on many occasions by Herbert Penzl.

entrenchment The 'freezing' of phrase-level and clause-level collocations into *speech formulas*, conventional expressions which must be learned and used as units, just like individual lexical items. English examples include *black and white* (not *white and black), *ham-and-cheese* (*sandwich*), *come to think of it* and *have a* Adjective *time*. The term was coined by Langacker (1991) but the phenomenon has been much discussed. M. Ross (1996: 203–206) draws attention to language-specific variation in this area (for example, English *I am cold* is rendered literally in other languages by such formations as *I have cold*, *To me is cold* and *Cold bites me*), and observes that extensive bilingualism tends to bring about convergence of entrenched patterns between the languages involved.

environment In a **conditioned change**, the totality of the phonological characteristics, other than the changing segments themselves, which are relevant in determining whether a given change will or will not apply in a given case. The environment most commonly involves the immediately preceding and/or following segments, but may also involve segments further away, suprasegmentals like stress, pitch and tone, word boundaries, morpheme boundaries, and rarely even grammatical information. In a simple example, earlier Basque */p t k/ were voiced to /b d g/ whenever immediately preceded by a nasal consonant or /l/; here the environment consists solely of the preceding segment. In a more complex case, earlier Basque */e/ was raised to /i/ in the first syllable of a word whenever the second syllable contained a high vowel and a third syllable existed. Here the environment includes the position of the initial word-boundary, the vowel in the following syllable and the number of syllables, but not either of the immediately adjacent segments.

epenthesis (also **insertion, intrusion**) Any phonological change which inserts a segment into a word or form in a position in which no segment was formerly present. Examples include the development of Latin *spina* 'thorn' to Spanish *espina*, of Old English *ǣmtig* to English *empty*, of Old Latin *faclis* 'easy' to classical *facilis*, of Middle English *thuner* to modern *thunder*, and of Middle English *betwix* to modern *betwixt*. Note that certain types of epenthesis are sometimes given more specific names, such as **prothesis, anaptyxis** (or *svarabhakti*) and **excrescence** (or **paragoge**), but these other labels are not always used in a consistent manner. Note also that some linguists restrict *epenthesis* to insertion in word-medial position, or to insertion of a consonant. Epenthesis is a **whole-segment process**. The opposite is **loss** (sense 1) or *deletion*.

Epigraphic South Arabian (also **Sayhadic**) A group of about four extinct **Semitic** languages recorded in southern Arabia between the beginning of the first millennium BC and the sixth century AD. See Kogan and Korotayev (1997).

epigraphy The study, decipherment and interpretation of ancient texts written on hard materials like stone and metal. Compare **palaeography**.

epithesis A rare synonym for **paragoge**.

eponym 1. A name, especially a place name, derived from the name of a real or mythical person, such as *Constantinople* from *Constantine*. 2. The name of the person from which such a name is derived. We say that Tristram Shandy is the eponymous hero of the novel of the same name.

equal sign The symbol '=', used to provide an identification or a clarification of a linguistic form. For example, the notation '*Aceari* (= *Aznar*)' indicates that the medieval Basque personal name *Aceari* is identical in origin to the modern Spanish surname *Aznar*, and the notation '*Cayçedo* (= *Quecedo* (?))' indicates that the obscure medieval place name *Cayçedo* is possibly to be identified with the modern town called *Quecedo*.

erosion Another term for **attrition**, in either sense but most commonly in sense 1.

err. An abbreviation for *erroneous*, an annotation added to a linguistic form or interpretation published by somebody else and here identified as wrong.

Eskimo-Aleut (also **Eskaleut**) A small language family of northern North America and eastern Siberia. The Eskimo languages are *Inuit*, a vast **dialect continuum** in which language boundaries are impossible to identify (though three or four main subgroups are sometimes recognized), and *Yupik*, which consists of three to five distinct languages, while the more distantly related *Aleut* is a single language. Eskimo-Aleut is usually considered to have no known relatives, but see **Eurasiatic**. Attempts at linking it to **Chukchi-Kamchatkan** remain unsubstantiated.

esoteric language The term used by Thurston (1989) for a language which has been deliberately engineered by its speakers in such a way as to make it maximally opaque to outsiders. Complex phonological processes and grammatical irregularities are embraced, as are opaque idioms and numerous near-synonyms. This is an extreme type of

emblematic language. The process of creating an esoteric language is *esoterogeny*. The opposite is **exoteric language**.

étalon language A language which is perceived or taken as a standard against which other languages are compared or evaluated, such as Latin in medieval and early modern Europe. The notion has been developed and elaborated by the Russian linguist Uspenskij (1965 and elsewhere).

Eteo- The combining form of Greek *eteós* 'true', occasionally used in constructing a name for a seemingly indigenous language in the eastern Mediterranean.

Eteo-Cretan The unknown language concealed in a modest number of inscriptions, in the Greek alphabet, dating from the fourth and third centuries BC, in Crete. It may possibly be a later form of **Minoan**, but this conclusion is not established, and the two terms should not be used interchangeably.

Eteo-Cypriot The unknown language concealed in some inscriptions in a syllabic script, dating from the Hellenistic period, in Cyprus.

ethnonym The name of a people. Such names may vary widely across languages; for example, the peoples we call the *Greeks* and the *Basques* call themselves the *Hellenes* and the *Euskaldunak*, respectively.

Etruscan An extinct language of north-central Italy, roughly modern Tuscany. Though important before the spread of **Latin**, Etruscan is poorly recorded, and we can read the texts only to a limited extent. At present there is no evidence that Etruscan is related to any other known language, save only for **Raetic**, **Lemnian** and perhaps **Camunic**. See Price (1998: 153–156), Bonfante and Bonfante (1983).

et seq. The abbreviation for 'and those that follow' (Latin *et sequentes* or *et sequentia*). For example, 'Agud and Tovar (1988 *et seq.*)' denotes a publication appearing in fascicles over a period of years beginning in 1988.

etymological Of a segment, descended from an ancestral segment. For example, the /f/ of English *father* is etymological, since it descends from PIE **p* in **pəter* 'father'. In contrast, the /b/ of *thimble* and the

/d/ of *thunder* are *unetymological*, since they were inserted by **epenthesis** into continuations of Old English *thymel* and *thunor*, respectively. Basque /h/ is almost never etymological, since it derives from a suprasegmental feature in an ancestral form of the language.

etymological dictionary A book which presents, in an organized manner, whatever is known or proposed about the origins and histories of the words of a particular language or family. Among the major etymological dictionaries are (for English) Partridge (1958), Onions (1966) and Klein (1971), (for Latin) Ernout and Meillet (1959), (for Spanish) Corominas and Pascual (1980), and (for IE) Pokorny (1959/1969). See Polomé (1990b) for a survey of etymological dictionaries of IE languages.

etymology 1. The origin and history of a particular word. 2. The branch of linguistics which investigates the origin and history of words. 3. An assembly of words or forms from several languages which are presented as putative **cognates** and hence as evidence either for a **systematic correspondence** or for a genetic link among the languages involved.

etymon (plural **etyma**) An earlier linguistic form from which a later one is directly derived. For example, English *father* derives from Old English *fæder*, which derives from Proto-Germanic **fader-*, which derives from PIE **pǝtér*. Each of these last three is an etymon of the English word. The opposite is **reflex**.

euphemism A word or phrase used as a polite replacement for another which is considered too vulgar, too painful or offensive to religious susceptibilities. English examples include *make love* for 'copulate', *pass away* for 'die', and *wee* or *powder one's nose* for 'urinate'. A euphemism may replace its corresponding neutral term, as has happened in American English with *restroom* for '(public) toilet', and in Spanish, in which earlier *preñada* 'pregnant' has been displaced by *embarazada*, originally 'encumbered'. The opposite is **dysphemism**. See also **taboo**.

Eurasiatic A putative macro-family including **Indo-European, Uralic, Yukaghir, Altaic, Korean, Japanese, Ainu, Gilyak, Chukchi-Kamchatkan** and **Eskimo-Aleut**. This idea has been put forward by Joseph Greenberg, but Greenberg's case is still in preparation at the time of writing. That case, when it appears, will be based on

multilateral comparison, and it will undoubtedly elicit opposition and hostility from specialists. Note that Eurasiatic somewhat overlaps the **Nostratic** proposal but is very different from it; a few linguists use the two names interchangeably, which is poor practice.

evaluation The social response to language change – that is, speakers' perceptions of innovations as desirable or not, and their decisions as to whether to adopt the new forms. See Milroy (1992: *passim*).

evaluation problem The problem of determining how speakers of a language evaluate a given change and what the effect of their evaluation is on the change. See the **WLH model of language change**.

'Every word has its own history' A slogan adopted by many opponents of the **Neogrammarian Hypothesis** and particularly by many dialectologists. The dialectologists of the late nineteenth and early twentieth centuries were troubled because they could not find the Neogrammarians' 'exceptionless sound laws' in the messiness of real dialect data. It is not clear who coined the slogan and several dialectologists have been credited with it.

evidence Hard linguistic data which can be adduced to support some particular conclusion, as opposed to other conceivable conclusions. All serious work in historical linguistics relies upon such evidence, and a proffered conclusion is only widely accepted when specialists are persuaded that the evidence supporting it is at least great enough to make it clearly preferable to any alternative – though not necessarily so overwhelming as to render all competing conclusions indefensible. In general, it is not enough that the available evidence should be *consistent* with some conclusion; rather, it must *actively support* that conclusion by tending strongly to exclude other conceivable conclusions. This is so because a body of evidence, especially a small body, may in fact be consistent with an almost limitless number of mutually incompatible conclusions. Speculations have their place in historical linguistics, as a way of encouraging discussion of problems, but only so long as they are clearly presented as speculations and as nothing more.

evolution of language A term used in several quite different ways.
  1. Another term for **language change**. This usage is perhaps unfortunate, since it conflicts not only with the other senses given here but

with the expression *origin and evolution of language*, denoting the rise of full-blown human language among our remote ancestors. 2. Any view of language change as predetermined, as in **stadialism** and some versions of **Darwinism**. Such views are rejected today. 3. A series of related changes in a language, all tending in the same direction, as in **drift** (sense 1) and **conspiracies**. See McMahon (1994: ch. 12).

evolutive innovation In the terminology of Andersen (1980), an innovation which arises wholly from the interaction of the grammar with underlying or surface forms and which lacks the kind of communicative motivation lying behind an **adaptive innovation**. An example is the Russian locative endings -*u* and -*ĕ*. These were originally equivalent and lexically selected, but today they are used with the same nouns in differing circumstances.

exaptation The use by a language for new purposes of **junk**, more or less functionless material left over from the decay of earlier systems. The term was borrowed by Lass (1990a) from evolutionary biology; one of his examples is the re-use in Germanic of fossilized aspectual stem-variations in verbs as markers of number. Schuh (1990) argues that gender-marked Proto-Afro-Asiatic determiners have lost their determining function in the daughter languages but have frequently become fused to nouns as overt markers of gender, without being incorporated into the stems. Compare *bricolage*, **demorphologization**, **incorporation**.

exbraciation Any word order change in which an element which was formerly obliged to be positioned in a 'brace' between two other items is moved to a different position. For example, Marchese (1984) reports that certain Kru languages have been shifting from a word order S AUX O V, in which the object O is located within the AUX–V brace, to a word order S AUX V O, in which the object has undergone exbraciation.

exception A linguistic form which has apparently failed to undergo an otherwise perfectly regular change. According to the **Neogrammarian Hypothesis**, real exceptions to sound changes are impossible, and we can only have *apparent* exceptions resulting from our failure to formulate the laws perfectly. The more recent discovery of such phenomena as **lexical diffusion**, however, reveals that exceptions to sound changes are possible and normal in certain types of change.

exclamation mark The symbol '!', used in an **etymological diction-ary** to mark a proposed etymology as improbable or absurd.

exclusion principle A principle sometimes invoked in addressing the **homeland problem**. It says this: the homeland should lie in a territory which was not demonstrably occupied by speakers of a different language family at a time close to the initial expansion of the family.

excrescence 1. The (usually sporadic) insertion of a consonant (usually a plosive, and some would define it this way) into word-final position, as in *vermin* > *varmint*, *no* > *nope* and Old English *betwihs* > *betwixt*. This is one type of **paragoge**. 2. [*rare*] Another term for **epenth-esis**. 3. [*informal*] A label applied to a segment (especially a con-sonant) whose presence in a particular linguistic form is surprising. 4. A largely functionless remnant of an otherwise vanished gramma-tical system, such as the English *-s* appearing on third-singular present-tense verb-forms.

exemplary language The term used by Grace (1981, 1990, 1996) for a language which is a 'well-behaved' member of its family. It retains a large number of cognates, it exhibits a large number of very con-sistent systematic correspondences, its phonological history is easy to reconstruct, and it is of great value in reconstructing the proto-language ancestral to the family. Compare **aberrant language**.

exit principle The principle that a language which exhibits a certain state of affairs can always undergo linguistic change which will eliminate that state of affairs, subject only to whatever constraints are uni-versally present in human languages: in effect, the principle that 'everything can change.'

exocentric compound Another term for *bahuvrīhi*.

exogenous innovation Another term for **external change**.

exogenous pidgin A **pidgin** which is chiefly spoken in a region in which the languages that contributed to it are not spoken. Compare **en-dogenous pidgin**.

exohybridization Another name for *creolization* (see under **creole**), coined by Leer (1990) and reflecting the observation that a creole typically arises from bits and pieces of two or more entirely distinct languages; the term is intended to contrast with **endohybridization**.

exoteric language In the terminology of Thurston (1989), a language which is widely used for communication between different groups, for only some of whom it is a mother tongue, and which has accordingly acquired a simple and regular structure making it easy to learn and use. The process of creating an exoteric language is *exoterogeny*. Compare **esoteric language**.

exotic language Any language which is substantially different in structure from your own.

expansion 1. A label sometimes applied to the period of rapid development leading from a stabilized **pidgin** to a **creole**, or to the **elaboration** (sense 2) of a creole to enable it to serve as a fully functional language. 2. Another term for **rule simplification**. 3. The spread of a language into a larger area than it formerly occupied.

explanation of change Any proposed answer to either of the following questions: (1) Why do languages change (in general)?; (2) Why do particular changes occur, instead of other conceivable changes? While historical linguists have made great progress in understanding *how* languages change, the *why* questions are generally regarded as more refractory and perhaps as impossible to answer. Most linguists would probably agree that no 'deductive-nomological' explanations of **language change** are possible – that is, that we can never declare that change C occurred because no other outcome was possible in the circumstances, a position expressly defended by Lass (1980). Many, however, are hopeful that we can provide weaker explanations, along the lines of 'change C occurred because there were identifiable factors favouring C.' The principal attempts at answering the two questions above include the **ease-of-articulation, expressive, external, functional, generative, perceptual, psychological, simplification, social, structural, substrate** and **teleological** explanations of change. Earlier attempts at explaining language change in terms of anatomy and ethnic background ('black people have thick lips'), climate and geography ('French has nasal vowels because of the damp climate') and social upheaval ('the Black Death induced surviving English-speakers to drop their inflectional endings') are now universally discredited, with only minor and specific

qualifications for the last. See also **functionality of change,
Darwinism**.

expressive explanation of change Any proposal for accounting for
language change in terms of speakers' constant desire to make their
speech ever more vivid and dramatic. Such proposals are of some
relevance for certain types of lexical change, such as the brisk
turnover in intensifying and evaluating terms with meanings like
'very' (good, bad, big, stupid, frightened or whatever), and the
frequent semantic bleaching of extreme terms like *awful*, *tragic* and
agony. They may also perhaps have something to say about certain
syntactic shifts, such as when topicalized or dislocated structures,
formerly marked, become unmarked and fixed. On the whole,
though, such approaches have little to say about most types of
change.

expressive form A label applied to a historical linguistic item which
appears to be irregular in form, on the assumption that the irregularity arises from some kind of emotional reinforcement. For example, PIE **gal-* 'call, shout' should appear in Proto-Germanic as **kal-*
but the form is in fact **kall-*, with an unexpected geminate /ll/.
Watkins (1969: 1503) calls this an *expressive form*.

expressive formation Either of two rather different cases. 1. A modified
form of a word possessing additional emotional colouring, such as
small size or affection. For example, Basque *zoko* 'corner' has an
expressive variant *(t)xoko* 'cosy little place', and Basque *hegal* 'wing'
once had an expressive variant *magal*, which has now lost its expressive colouring. 2. (also **descriptive form**) A lexical item which
is coined *de novo*, often in defiance of the ordinary phonological
structure of words, and often to denote something with intrinsic
emotional colouring. Basque examples include *zirimiri* 'drizzle',
tontor 'summit', *pinpirin* 'butterfly', *moxkor* 'drunk' and *zirti-zarta*
'decisively', all exhibiting phonological structures not found in
ordinary lexical items.

expressive gemination Unexpected and irregular **gemination** of a
segment, apparently for expressive purposes. For example, Old
English *liccian* 'lick' exhibits a geminate /kk/ which is etymologically unjustified; the suggestion is that our ancestors deliberately
lengthened the plosive for expressive purposes.

expressive renewal A label proposed by Hagège (1993: 150–156) for those cases of **renewal** which appear to be motivated by the desire to emphasize a semantic feature which is particularly important in discourse, such as negation in **Jespersen's cycle**.

expressive symbolism Another term for **affective symbolism**.

extended form Especially in IE studies, a linguistic form derived by adding an **extension** (sense 7 - see under **Indo-European root theory**) to a root, such as PIE **peld-*, an extended form of **pel-* 'thrust'.

extended sense A sense of a word which is different from, and later than, its original and central sense. For example, English *head* 'top part of the body' has acquired extended senses such as 'top part' (the head of a list), 'director' (the head of a corporation) and 'round thing' (a head of cabbage). An extended sense may entirely displace the original sense, as has happened with the German cognate *Haupt*. This poses problems in historical work. For example, Basque *agor* 'dry' has often featured in comparisons, but it seems clear that word has developed semantically from 'hard, unyielding' to 'barren, sterile' to 'exhausted, dried up' to 'dry', with the original sense now entirely lost, but it is the earliest known sense which should be invoked in comparisons, not the modern one. When the extended sense has no semantic features at all in common with the original sense, we speak of a **transferred sense**.

extension 1. Another term for **broadening**. 2. Any of various directional semantic developments, as in the **Traugott progression**. 3. See **analogical extension**. 4. The term used by Harris and Campbell (1995) for any change in the surface manifestation of a syntactic structure which does not intrinsically involve modification of the underlying structure. Unlike **reanalysis**, extension involves immediate changes in the surface forms of certain utterances. For example, Proto-Kartvelian had two different systems for case-marking verbal arguments, depending on the tense-aspect-mood of the verb, but in Laz one of these systems has been generalized to all tense-aspect-mood forms. 5. Another term for **actualization**. 6. See **rule simplification**. 7. See under **Indo-European root theory**.

extension problem The name given by Lass (1987: 170) to the puzzle of how a language can keep changing in the same direction over many generations, as in **drift** (sense 1) and **conspiracies**. Compare the **discontinuity problem**.

external change (also **exogenous innovation**, **contact-induced change**) Any linguistic change in a language which results from the influence of a distinct neighbouring language. See Thomason and Kaufman (1988) for a survey. Compare **internal change**.

external evidence Evidence about the history or prehistory of a language which is non-linguistic in nature, which is not derived from scrutiny of the language itself. Examples include evidence from archaeology and from comments about the language written by speakers of other languages. Compare **internal evidence**.

external explanation of change 1. Any proposal to account for **language change** in terms of **language contact**. 2. Any proposal to account for language change in terms of non-linguistic factors, usually changes in the world. Such accounts are obviously correct for certain types of lexical innovation, such as the introduction of new words for new objects, concepts and practices. They may also be relevant to certain types of semantic change, such as the extension of formerly purely religious terms like *cell, office, passion, sanctuary, clerk* and *novice* into various secular domains. It is clear, however, that most types of language change cannot be accounted for in terms of non-linguistic change; for one thing, change occurs even in the speech of isolated and conservative societies, such as those of pre-European Australia, New Guinea and Polynesia.

external history The history of a language from the point of view of its documents and its speakers. An external history starts with documentation: what texts exist in the language?; where and when were they written?; by whom, in what circumstances and for what reason? Very commonly (and increasingly today) an external history includes a **social history** of the language: who spoke the language, and to what social, cultural and political forces were they exposed? What attitudes were expressed by speakers towards particular forms or usages? Compare **internal history**.

extinction Another term for **language death**.

extinct language Another term for a **dead language**, especially in sense 1.

extrafamilial contact principle A proposed principle invoked in addressing the **homeland problem**. It says this: the homeland is to be found in the vicinity of the neighbouring family which exhibits the largest degree of contact with the family whose homeland is being sought. This principle has frequently been appealed to in connection with Indo-European, but unfortunately linguists are often unable to agree which language words are borrowed from, in which direction borrowing took place, or even which words are borrowed at all – and, of course, we can rarely be sure where the neighbouring families were located at the relevant time. See Mallory (1997: 97–98) for discussion.

extraparadigmatic force The term used by van Marle and Smits (1989) for the spread of an inflected form into a paradigm in which it was not previously present. An example, in American Dutch, is the spread of the infinitive into positions formerly requiring either a finite form or a participle. Compare **intraparadigmatic force**.

extraterritorial language variety A variety of a language spoken in a geographical region into which that language has only recently been introduced by immigration, such as English in Australia or South Africa.

extreme structural borrowing Another term for **metatypy**.

eye philology The practice of philology entirely upon the basis of written forms, without regard for the sounds those written forms imperfectly represent. An example is the fallacious derivation of French *bizarre* 'bizarre' from Basque *bizar* 'beard', overlooking the fact that Basque <z> spells [s] and would never be heard by a Romance-speaker as anything but [s]. Common in the eighteenth and nineteenth centuries, this practice is long since obsolete.

Fachliteratur Specialist literature: the writings on a language or family by knowledgeable specialists in it.

fadeout effect The remorseless tendency, over time, for the ordinary processes of linguistic change to obliterate all or virtually all traces of a common ancestry between languages sharing a common origin, with the result that evidence of genetic relatedness can no longer be detected, or at least can no longer be distinguished from **chance resemblances**. See the **time-depth problem**.

fading 1. See **bleaching**. 2. The disappearance of the earlier central sense of a word in favour of a **transferred sense**. 3. The name given by Schuh (1990) to the process in which a grammatical marker loses its original value or function without disappearing, as occurs, for example, within the **Greenberg progression**. Such a faded marker may undergo **absorption** into a stem or it may be assigned a new function by **exaptation**.

Faliscan An extinct **Italic** language attested in a number of inscriptions dating 400–240 BC just north of Rome. It was very closely related to **Latin** within the **Latino-Faliscan** subgroup.

falling together A general term for any linguistic change resulting in the loss of a former distinction. For example, phonemes which undergo **merger** are said to 'fall together', and formerly distinct words which become homophonous are said to 'fall together'.

Fall of the Jers Another term for the **Third Slavic Vowel Shift**.

false analogy A label sometimes applied by the linguists of the past to instances of **analogy** which they disliked. The term is emotive, not descriptive, and is no longer in use.

false cognates Two or more linguistic forms which look for all the world as though they must be **cognates** but are in fact unrelated. An example is Old English *habban* 'have' and Latin *habēre* 'have', which are not connected even though the languages are genetically related.

false reconstruction An erroneous **reconstruction** within a language or a family, often particularly one which is proposed specifically to make certain items look more similar than they really are to items in some other language or family with which the investigator is hoping to establish a **genetic relationship**. For example, it is entirely out of order to 'reconstruct' Basque *bi* 'two' as *$g^w i$ purely in order to make it look more like a word for 'two' in some other language, since no such reconstruction can be motivated by the facts of Basque.

false segmentation In **comparison**, the insertion into a cited linguistic form by the comparativist of erroneous or unjustified morpheme boundaries, in order to extract a non-existent morph which resembles something in another language. An example is the citation of western Basque *intzigar* 'hoarfrost' as *in-tzig-ar* in order to extract a putative morph **-tzig-* which resembles words for 'frost', 'snow' or 'cold' in various other languages, but the segmentation is preposterous and the word is surely an ordinary compound of *intz* 'dew' and *igar* 'dry'.

family A linguistic **taxon**. Like all such terms, this one is applied to taxa of varying sizes and depths, but it is most commonly applied to the maximal taxon of whose validity linguists feel confident, such as **Indo-European** or **Afro-Asiatic**. However, it is sometimes applied more narrowly to a smaller and more cohesive grouping like **Germanic** or **Bantu**. Nichols (1990: 477) proposes to apply the term to a grouping within which genetic relatedness is self-evident and systematic correspondences and cognates are numerous, such as Germanic. Compare **stock**.

family consistency A proposed guideline in **reconstruction**: no segment-type should be reconstructed for a proto-language that does not occur in at least one daughter language. This guideline cannot be applied rigidly – for example, laryngeals were successfully reconstructed for PIE before they were found in any daughter language – but it may be helpful in constraining over-exuberant reconstructions.

family-like language Another term for **dialect continuum**, or sometimes specifically for such a continuum in which widely separated varieties are very different indeed.

family resemblance [*informal*] A set of recurrent similarities among a group of languages which are so pervasive and so striking that there seems no alternative to regarding them as derived from common inheritance and hence to regarding the languages as constituting a **language family**. Family resemblances are prominent among closely related languages like **Germanic** and **Polynesian**, but usually less so among languages more distantly related.

family tree (Ger *Stammbaum*) A graphical representation of the structure of a **language family**, showing clearly the posited **subgrouping** of the family. Family trees have the great advantage of representing both ancestral and descendant languages simultaneously, but the drawback of positing unrealistically sudden and decisive splits between language varieties. Southworth (1964) offers some proposals for improving family trees, but these have rarely been taken up.

family-tree model Another term for the **genetic model**.

family universal A linguistic feature which is not particularly common in the languages of the world but which is very common in the languages belonging to a particular family. For example, the Pama-Nyungan languages of Australia consistently exhibit a very large number of contrasting places of articulation, with both plosives and nasals occurring at every available place, and laterals at every available place except labial and velar. Family universals may be invoked to justify **reconstructions** which would otherwise look very unusual. Family universals of **language change** may perhaps also exist; a possible example is the change /t/ > /k/, which has occurred independently in a geographically dispersed number of Austronesian languages, but is virtually unknown elsewhere.

feeding The state of affairs in which an earlier phonological change creates new cases for a later one to apply to. For example, the West Germanic change of */ð/ to */d/ created new instances of /d/ which were then regularly changed to /t/ by the **Second Germanic Consonant Shift**, as in *faðer* > *fader* > German *Vater* 'father'. In a rule-based account of phonological change, *feeding order* is an ordering between two changes such that the first creates new cases for the second to apply to. The opposite is **bleeding**.

Fennic (also **Finnic**) A group of about sixteen languages spoken in Scandinavia, along the Baltic coast, and in northern Russia, and forming one branch of the **Finno-Ugric** branch of the **Uralic** family. Among its members are *Finnish*, *Estonian*, *Mari*, *Komi* and the several varieties of *Saami* ('Lappish'), though the precise position of Saami is disputed. **Krevinian** and **Votic** are extinct.

filiation The process of establishing **genetic relationships** and of constructing **family trees**.

final devoicing (Ger *Auslautsverhärtung*) The **devoicing** of a consonant in word-final position, a particularly common development in languages.

Finnic Another form of **Fennic**.

Finno-Ugric The largest branch of the **Uralic** family, consisting of two branches: **Fennic** and **Ugric**.

first fronting Another name for **Anglo-Frisian brightening**.

First Germanic Consonant Shift (also **Grimm's Law**) A series of rather dramatic changes in the values of plosive consonants which occurred in Proto-Germanic and which made the consonantism of the Germanic languages rather different from that found in other branches of IE. Ignoring the controversial palatal plosives, the PIE plosives were voiceless */p t k kʷ/, voiced */b d g gʷ/, and 'voiced aspirated' */bh dh gh ghʷ/. These developed as shown in Table 2.

These changes must have happened in the chronological order given. The resulting */x/ and */xʷ/ were reduced to /h/ and /hw/ in word-initial position. Table 3 provides some examples; Latin, Greek, Lithuanian and Sanskrit represent the IE languages not undergoing the shift, and Old English represents Germanic. No examples are provided for PIE */ghʷ/, whose fate in Germanic is unknown.

These shifts were categorical, except in two circumstances: (1) after certain other consonants (Latin *noct-* 'night', OE *niht*, not **nihθ*); (2) when the consonant was neither word-initial nor immediately preceded by the accent; see **Verner's Law**. The date of the shifts is unknown, but most guesses involve the period between 500 BC and the beginning of the Christian era.

The correspondences were largely identified first by Rask (1818) but the classic presentation is that of Grimm (1822), whence the familiar name. Compare the **Second Germanic Consonant Shift**. Note that general acceptance of the **glottalic theory of PIE**, if that ever comes, will have the most profound consequences for the very reality of the First Germanic Consonant Shift; see Collinge (1985: 63–76) for an account. See also **bifurcational theory**.

(1)	/p/ > /f/	/t/ > /θ/	/k/ > /x/	/kʷ/ > /xʷ/
(2)	/b/ > /p/	/d/ > /t/	/g/ > /k/	/gʷ/ > /kʷ/
(3)	/bh/ > /b/	/dh/ > /d/	/gh/ > /g/	/ghʷ/ > /gʷ/

Table 2

First Palatalization A phonological change, occurring in common Slavic, by which inherited */k g x/ were palatalized to /tʃ ʒ ʃ/ before a following front vowel.

first palatal series A series of palatal plosives, */kʲ gʲ ghʲ/, sometimes reconstructed for PIE to account for the differing developments in the **centum** and **satem** languages. Not all specialists accept the reality of this series.

First Slavic Vowel Shift A phonological change, occurring in common Slavic, by which inherited */u:/ was changed to /ɨ:/ and all diphthongs were levelled to long vowels.

fixation Especially in **grammaticalization**, any change in which an item that was formerly free to occur in any of several positions in a sentence comes to be fixed rigidly in one position.

fl. The abbreviation for Latin *floruit* 'flourished', used with the name of a historical figure whose birth and death dates are unknown to indicate the time period when that figure was most active.

flapping Another term for **tapping**.

PIE	Germanic	Gloss
Lat *piscis*	OE *fisc*	'fish'
Lat *tenuis*	OE *þynne*	'thin'
Lat *cornu*	OE *horn*	'horn'
Lat *quod*	OE *hwæt*	'what'
Lith *trobà*	OE *þorp*	(Lith) 'house', (OE) 'village'
Lat *duo*	OE *twa*	'two'
Lat *genu*	OE *cneo*	'knee'
Lat *vivus* (< *gwiwos*)	OE *cwicu*	'alive'
Skt *bharami*	OE *beran*	'bear, carry'
Gk *thyra* (< PIE *dhwer-*)	OE *duru*	'door'
Gk *khloros* (< PIE *ghel-*)	OE *gealu*	(Gk) 'green-yellow', (OE) 'yellow'

Table 3

flip-flop rule A type of phonological change in which two segments exchange their phonetic values, so that, in effect, we have X > Y and Y > X. Permitted by the formalism of generative phonology, such changes are of uncertain reality, but a favourite example is the English of Utah, in which the phonetic values of the vocalic nuclei of *card* and *cord* have reportedly been exchanged.

florilegium (also **florilegy**) Literally, an anthology, but the term is occasionally used in philological work to denote a collection of quotations from a variety of authors expressing opinions on a matter under discussion.

focal area (also **core area**) In **dialect geography**, a geographical area in which the effects of a particular change are maximally prominent and in which the change appears to have originated. Typically a focal area serves as a source from which the change radiates out towards other areas. Compare **transition area**, **relic area**.

focused Of a speech community, exhibiting a high degree of internal homogeneity. The opposite is **diffuse**.

folk etymology (also **analogical reformation**) An arbitrary change in the form of a word of opaque formation which serves to make that word more transparent in form, if not necessarily in its semantics. English examples include *crayfish* from French *écrevisse*, *sparrow grass* from *asparagus*, *cowcumber* from *cucumber*, *woodchuck* from Cree *oček*, *shamefaced* from ME *schamfas*t 'firm in modesty', and *bride-groom* from ME *bridegome* after the loss of *guma* 'man'. Particularly successful are Old English *mere-grota* 'pearl' (literally 'sea-grain') from Latin *margarita* and regional Basque *zainhoria* 'carrot' (literally 'yellow-root') from Spanish *zanahoria*, of Arabic origin. See also **homonymic assimilation**.

font-name A name conferred upon a person at the time of baptism.

foreigner talk The distinctive style of speaking we adopt in talking to a person who does not speak or understand our language very well.

form-meaning asymmetry Especially in **grammaticalization**, the observation that semantic change precedes any changes in surface form, with the result that the overt form of a grammaticalized expression may be out of line with its meaning or function. The observation goes back at least to Sapir (1921a: 98).

form reduction Another term for *clipping* (see under **clipped form**), but one sometimes applied more specifically to the reduction of a phrase to a single word, as in *private soldier* to *private*, *commercial advertisement* to *commercial*, and *Havana cigar* to *Havana*.

formulaism Another term for **algebraism**.

fortition (also **strengthening**, rarely also **hardening**) Any phonological change in which a segment becomes less vowel-like and more consonant-like. Examples include the strengthening of */s/ to /t/ in a number of Austronesian languages, of */w/ to /b/, /g^w/ or /k^w/ in many Austronesian languages (this a case of **glide-strengthening**) and the various cases of **gemination**. The opposite is **lenition**.

Fortunatov's Law 1. A putative development in early **Indo-Aryan**, proposed by Fortunatov (1881), by which a sequence of /l/ plus coronal plosive was converted into a retroflex plosive. Example: PIE *$kult$-* 'cultivate' > Skt $kut^ha:ra$- 'axe' *(cf.* Latin *culter* 'plough-share'). The validity of this statement has been much debated; see Collinge (1985: 41–46) for a critical discussion with references. 2. A putative change in common **Slavic**, proposed by Fortunatov (1880), by which a word-accent falling on a non-final short syllable was shifted rightwards in certain circumstances. The proposal is controversial; see Collinge (1985: 232–233) for an account.

fossilization 1. (also **degrammaticalization**) The loss of its original grammatical function by a grammatical marker which none the less remains present. For example, in a number of American languages an old third-person possessive affix has become fossilized within body-part names or kinship terms. The old prefix **e-*, which appears in all non-finite forms of ancient Basque verbs, clearly once had a grammatical function (it was probably a nominalizer of verbal roots) but today it no longer has any discernible function: it is just there. 2. The loss of productivity of a grammatical paradigm which nevertheless remains in use with certain words. An example is the class of **heteroclitic nouns**, which was apparently productive in PIE and remained so in Hittite but was fossilized in other daughter languages like Greek and Latin, which retained the pattern only for a handful of nouns. 3. A label occasionally applied to the conversion of discourse strategies into syntax and morphology by **grammaticalization**.

fossilized form 1. Another term for **frozen form**. 2. A functionless grammatical marker resulting from **fossilization** (sense 1).

founder effect The phenomenon in which a region is colonized by one or more languages which happen by chance to possess certain features, and, over time, these features persist in the several daughter languages, even though they are not cognitively necessary and could, in principle, be eliminated by linguistic change. The possibility of founder effects has been particularly stressed by Johanna Nichols in her recent work. For example, Nichols (1994/95) sees several widespread grammatical features of the Pacific coast of the Americas as founder effects resulting from the peopling of the Pacific Rim from southeast Asia, where these very features are endemic. See the **exit principle**.

four-part analogy (also **proportional analogy**) Any instance of **analogy** which can be schematically represented as the solution to a proportion of the form A : B :: C : ? An example is eastern American *dove* as the past of *dive*, which can be represented as *drive* : *drove* :: *dive* : ?, with *dove* as the solution. Any other kind of analogy is **non-proportional analogy**.

fracture [*rare*] Another term for **breaking**.

French The principal language of France, also widely spoken in Belgium, Luxembourg, Switzerland, Canada, many present and former French possessions overseas, and also in Louisiana. The distinctive local varieties of Belgium, Canada and Louisiana are called *Walloon*, *Canadian French* and *Cajun French*, respectively. French is a **Romance** language deriving from the **Latin** spoken in northern Gaul but significantly influenced by the **Germanic** language of the Franks, who conquered the territory after the collapse of Roman power. When the Latin of Gaul began to break up into a **dialect continuum**, two major linguistic groups developed: French in the north and *Occitan* (commonly, but inaccurately, called 'Provençal') in the south, with a transitional region of *Franco-Provençal* speech in the east–central region. In the early Middle Ages, a literary version of Occitan was the most prestigious language in France, but the growing political preeminence of Paris eventually made Parisian French the dominant language of the country, and standard French, based originally upon Parisian speech, has for centuries steadily been displacing the other regional varieties of French, Occitan and the several other **minority languages** of France – though not yet completely.

The conquest of England by the French-speaking Normans in 1066 led to a huge influx of Norman French words into English. Centuries later, the French empire carried French into many corners of the world, and the brilliance of French civilization also made French for several centuries the premier European language of diplomacy and of high culture; it was routinely learned and used by educated speakers of English, German, Russian and other languages, and hundreds more French words flowed into English and other languages as a result. In the twentieth century, however, French has steadily given way to English in virtually every domain, and today educated French people routinely learn and use English. The French authorities spend vast sums of money to promote the use of French all over the world, and they struggle to coin French terms to replace what is now a tidal wave of English words pouring into French every year. Nevertheless, French still retains its position as the most widely learned foreign language in Britain, though no longer in many other countries. See Price (1998: 167–177) for a survey, Ewert (1933) or Price (1971) for a structural history, Harris (1978) for a grammatical history, and Lodge (1993) for a social history.

fricativization [*rare*] Another term for **spirantization**.

fronting Any phonological change in which a segment comes to be pronounced closer to the front of the mouth than formerly. An example is the fronting of /u/ to /y/, which occurred categorically in early Greek and in **umlaut** circumstances in early English. The opposite is **backing**.

frozen form (also **fossilized form**) A linguistic form representing a pattern or a construction which was formerly productive in the language but which has dropped out of use in general, remaining only in one or two cases, yet without being regarded as an **archaism** (sense 2). For example, the former English perfect in *be*, as in *He is come*, has disappeared except in the frozen form illustrated by *She is gone*, and the former use of finite *be*, as in *if she be fair*, is now generally dead except for one or two frozen forms like *be that as it may* and *so be it*. The German dative ending *-e* is now generally gone except in a few frozen forms like *zu Hause* 'at home' and *am Tage* 'in the daytime'.

frozen idiom Another term for **lexicalization** (sense 1).

fudged dialect (or **fudged lect**) The term used by Chambers and Trudgill (1998: 110–119) for a regional speech variety with the following characteristic: it is located between two regions in which a particular variable consistently has two quite distinct realizations, and it itself has an intermediate value which appears to represent a kind of compromise. For example, English words like *cut* and *money* have [ʊ] in the north of England but [ə] in the south, and an intermediate region has the 'fudged' realization [ɤ]. See also Trudgill (1986: 60–62) for a more complex case in East Anglia. Trudgill here concludes that *fudging* is both phonetically and lexically gradual, in contrast to **lexical diffusion**. Compare **mixed dialect**.

full grade See under **ablaut**.

functional explanation of change Any proposal to account for **language change** in terms of the communicative functions of linguistic units. Proponents typically argue that languages tend to keep contrastive units as different from one another as possible, and they maintain that phonemes tend to be kept as phonetically distinct as possible, that contrasts of high functional load (those distinguishing many pairs of items) tend to be retained, and that homophony tends to be resisted. While such ideas are undoubtedly useful in some cases, there are perhaps as many counterexamples as confirming instances: note, for example, the massive mergers of Tocharian or the massive homophony of Mandarin Chinese. Functionalist explanations were pioneered by the Prague School and developed by André Martinet, notably in Martinet (1955).

functionality of change The question of whether changes in language are typically functional, dysfunctional or neutral. Among non-linguists, of course, a common perception is that most changes are dysfunctional ('corruptions'), but perhaps no linguist would endorse such a view. Linguists do, however, differ strongly on the remaining options. See Milroy (1992) and the references there for the case that language change is typically functional, and see Lass (1997: 352–365) and the references there for the case that change is typically neutral.

functional load For a particular phonemic contrast, the number of linguistic forms which it alone serves to distinguish. For example, the English /p/–/b/ contrast has a high functional load, distinguishing numerous pairs like *pit/bit*, *nipple/nibble* and *lap/lab*, while the /ʃ/–/ʒ/ contrast has a very low functional load, confined to a couple of marginal pairs like *Aleutian/allusion*. It has often been suggested that contrasting phonemes of low functional load undergo **merger** readily, while those of high functional load resist merger, because of the massive homophony that would result, but in practice it is easy to find examples of mergers applying to contrasts of high functional load; see King (1967), Hock (1986: 150–151).

functional shift 1. Another term for **conversion**. 2. Any linguistic change in which the function of a grammatical marker is substantially altered, possibly making it difficult to identify with cognate elements in related languages. For example, the English suffix *-ing* has shifted from being a word-forming suffix deriving nouns from nouns to an inflectional element constructing non-finite forms of verbs.

function contiguity hypothesis A proposed constraint upon the course of **grammaticalization**, put forward by Blansitt (1988). It says this: an allative marker cannot serve as a direct-object marker unless it also serves as a dative marker, and a locative marker cannot serve as a dative marker unless it also serves as an allative marker. In other words, the grammaticalization of a motivated locational marker must proceed stepwise through increasing degrees of grammatical abstractness.

fusion 1. Any instance of **reanalysis** (either sense) in which a morpheme boundary or a word boundary is blurred or lost. Some simple examples are cited under **boundary loss**. Matisoff (1973: 32–34) cites a more complex case from Lahu. Here an ancient causative prefix **s-* has been lost, leaving behind alternations in voicing and tone: **dò* 'drink', **s-dò* 'give to drink', modern *dò*, *to*. 2. Another term for **coalescence**.

fusion creole A label occasionally applied to a language which has been heavily influenced by another, such as English (by Norman French) or Yiddish (by Hebrew and Slavic), but most linguists would not see these languages as creoles in any meaningful sense.

Gaelic See under **Celtic**.

Garde's principle 1. (also **irreversibility of merger**) The following principle: **mergers** are irreversible by linguistic means. This principle, long taken for granted in historical work, was explicitly formulated by Garde (1961) and named by Labov (1994: 311). See **reversal of merger** for discussion of apparent counterexamples. 2. A putative principle of language change, put forward by Garde (1961): a speech area which possesses a phonological or grammatical contrast will lose it under the influence of a neighbouring area which has already lost it, while the reverse will not happen. See Collinge (1985: 242–243) for discussion.

Garde's Rule A proposed accent-shift in the Slavic language Slovincian, put forward by Garde (1976): a word-final accent on a short vowel shifts to the penult in a polysyllabic word. See Collinge (1985: 233).

Gaulish An extinct and scarcely recorded **Celtic** language spoken in the larger part of Gaul (France) at the time of the Roman conquest.

Ge'ez An extinct south **Semitic** language, the language of the Aksum empire of Ethiopia in the first centuries AD and long used as a classical literary and liturgical language in Ethiopia. See Gragg (1997).

gemination Any phonological change in which a simplex segment is converted to a geminate. An example is the gemination of /b/ in the development of Latin *res publica* into Italian *repubblica*. The opposite is **degemination**.

generalization Another term for **broadening**.

generational change A type of **language change** in which each individual enters the speech community with a characteristic frequency for a particular **variable** and maintains this value unchanged throughout life, but in which each younger generation enters the community with an increasingly incremented value for the variable, leading to steady change over time. This appears to be a common pattern for phonological and morphological change. Compare **age-grading, communal change**.

generative explanations of change Any of various attempts at explaining **language change** in terms of the formalisms associated with the several versions of Noam Chomsky's generative grammar. In phonology, these attempts have focused on notions of economy and simplicity as formulated by means of phonological rules; see the entries in this dictionary between **rule addition** and **rule simplification**.

The major statement is King (1969); see McMahon (1994: 36–44) for a survey. In syntax, the leading figure is David Lightfoot; see the **Lightfoot framework**.

generic consonant A concept sometimes invoked in **comparison**, particularly in the **search problem**. A generic consonant is a combination of a small number of phonetic features covering a range of phonetically distinct consonants. For example, one might treat *labial obstruent* as a generic consonant, covering all of /p b p′ pʰ bh f v/ (at least). As a rule, the idea is that any member of a generic consonant counts as a match for any other in determining whether items in different languages count as a match or not, and so, for example, /vot/ in one language might be counted as a match with /patʃi/ in another. See Nichols (1995b).

generic resemblance The term used by Johanna Nichols (1997d and elsewhere) for a set of closely related meanings which are deemed to be acceptable semantic matches in identifying possible **cognates** within a **limited search**.

genetic affiliation Another term for **genetic relationship**.

genetic classification (also **taxonomy**) The classification of languages according to their ancestry. Genetically related languages belong to a single **language family**, the structure of which is typically exhibited in a **family tree**.

genetic density The number of genetic lineages per unit area in a geographical region. Nichols (1997b: 368) reports that the number of **stocks** (in her sense) per million square kilometres is 1–3 for Africa and Eurasia, 10–20 for Australia and Central and South America, and over 100 for New Guinea. These figures represent **stock density**, but genetic density can also be expressed in terms of smaller **taxa**. Compare **linguistic density**.

genetic diversity For a given geographical area, the number of distinct **taxa** and the degree of branching within those taxa.

genetic diversity principle Another term for the **age-area hypothesis**.

genetic linguistics Another term for **comparative linguistics**.

genetic marker In the work of Johanna Nichols, a linguistic form or set of forms whose probability of occurring in a language by chance is so low that its recurrence in two or more languages must be taken as powerful evidence of a common origin. She estimates this threshold probability as one in 100,000–500,000 (this is the *individual-identifying threshold* - see **individual-identifying criteria**), and she concludes that the presence of two genetic markers suffices to prove genetic relatedness. See Nichols (1992: ch. 6, 1994/95, 1995b, 1997c), Nichols and Peterson (1996). Compare **historical marker**.

genetic model (also **cladistic model**, **(family-)tree model**, *Stammbaum* **model**) The most venerable and familiar **model of linguistic descent**. Though generations of earlier linguists had obviously had some conception of this model, it was only explicitly introduced by Schleicher (1871); see W. P. Lehmann (1967: 87–96) for an extract including Schleicher's tree for IE. Since that time, it has remained the standard model for exhibiting **genetic relationships** among languages, because of its great convenience and perspicuity.

   In this model, a single ancestral language is viewed as splitting into two or more sharply distinct daughters, each of which in turn splits into sharply distinct daughters, and so on, as many times as required to include all the languages known to belong to the family. Typically the single language which is ancestral to all the others is unrecorded but reconstructed to some extent, and the same is typically true of many of its descendants. The resulting structure is readily displayed in a **family tree**, with the great advantages that both ancestral and descendant languages can be displayed simultaneously and that **subgrouping** can likewise be readily displayed – that is, the tree shows explicitly which languages are considered to be most closely related within the family. These advantages, however, come at the price of unreality; in practice, languages do not split up suddenly and sharply into daughter languages which immediately go their own way. Instead, a myriad of different but overlapping changes turns a language into a **dialect continuum**, in which varieties continue to influence neighbouring but partially distinct varieties, as posited in the **wave model**, and no sharp language boundaries exist until geographical separation intervenes or until some local varieties acquire sufficient prestige to displace other varieties. Still, the genetic model possesses enough truth as a model of **divergence** that we continue to make everyday use of it.

genetic relationship (also **genetic affiliation**) The relationship which holds between two or more languages which share a single common ancestor – that is, they all started off at some time in the past as no more than regional varieties of that ancestral language, but each has undergone so many changes not affecting the others that they have diverged into distinct languages. All the languages sharing such a common ancestor constitute a single **language family**, and all those languages which share a single common ancestor at some intermediate time constitute a single **branch** of that family. The identification of genetic relationships is the principal business of **comparative linguistics**.

genetic stability Especially in **population typology**, the tendency of a typological feature to remain unchanged within a linguistic lineage over a long period of time.

genetic unit Any **language family** or **isolated language** for which no wider relationship is known to exist: a maximal **taxon**.

geographical grouping The grouping together of languages occupying a particular geographical area, regardless of whether any **genetic relationships** can be shown to exist. Geographical groupings are often convenient in linguistically complex areas of the world (a prominent example is the **Papuan** languages), but it must be remembered that a geographical grouping is a purely *ad hoc* affair, and that the languages contained in one need not be genetically related at all.

geographical linguistics Another term for **linguistic geography**.

geolinguistics The term used by Harold Schiffman in his English translation of Breton (1991) for a variety of **linguistic geography** oriented towards the social, political and economic circumstances in which languages find themselves.

Georgiev's Law A proposed change in the common **Slavic** vowel length, put forward by Georgiev (1965 and elsewhere). It says: a stressed word-initial short vowel becomes long in certain tonal configurations. See Collinge (1985: 234).

Ge-Pano-Carib A proposed grouping of over 100 South American and Caribbean languages, put forward by Greenberg (1960) and supported by some shared morphological patterns. The grouping unites

Cariban with a number of smaller families; it has been received sympathetically, but is not fully accepted.

German A major language of central Europe, a member of the **Germanic** branch of **Indo-European**. German is not in fact a single language, but rather a very diverse **dialect continuum** whose numerous regional varieties are often not mutually comprehensible. The dialects are primarily classified into *Low German* in the north and *High German* in the south, distinguished by (among other things) the effects in the southern varieties of the **Second Germanic Consonant Shift**. What unites the speakers of German, apart from a measure of political unity, is the recognition by all of them of a single **standard language**, also called *High German*; the only reason that *Dutch* is considered a separate language from German, with which it forms part of the same dialect continuum, is its acceptance of a very different standard language. The history of High German is divided into three periods: **Old High German, Middle High German** and *modern High German*. A distinctive variety of German spoken in Pennsylvania is *Pennsylvania German* (informally, 'Pennsylvania Dutch'). See Price (1998: 193–206) for a survey and Lockwood (1965), R. E. Keller (1978) or C. J. Wells (1985) for a linguistic history.

Germanic A major branch of **Indo-European**, commonly divided into three branches: *Eastern* (**Gothic**, extinct), *Northern* (*Icelandic, Faroese, Norwegian, Danish, Swedish*) and *Western* (**English**, *Frisian, Dutch, Afrikaans*, **German**, *Yiddish*); a number of earlier forms of these are recorded in the late first millennium AD. The Germanic languages are distinguished by, among other things, the **First Germanic Consonant Shift**, the uniform assignment of word-stress to initial syllables (other than prefixes), the dental preterite (as in *love*, past tense *loved*), the presence of extensive **umlaut** (except in Gothic), and some distinctive items of vocabulary (*rain, blood, hand, finger*). See Ramat (1998) for a summary, Konig and van der Auwera (1994) for a survey of the modern languages, Robinson (1992) for a survey of the ancient Germanic languages, and Voyles (1992) for a structural history of Germanic.

ghost language 1. A non-existent language which, through error or fraud, has been wrongly reported as real, and possibly even provided with some vocabulary and/or a genetic classification. Campbell (1997a: 13–15) lists the ghost languages reported in the Americas.

2. A hypothetical language, usually a **substrate**, posited as the source of certain puzzling words or features in an attested language.

ghost word A non-existent word which has been entered in a dictionary or another reference work as a result of a misunderstanding. A famous example is *Dord*, defined in a 1934 American dictionary as 'density in physics or chemistry'; in fact, the typesetter had merely misread the intended entry *D or d, density in physics or chemistry*. Dr Johnson's dictionary contains the ghost word *foupe*, defined as 'to drive with a sudden impetuosity', but Johnson had in fact misread the word *soupe*, a dialect variant of *swoop*, printed with the long *s* favoured in the eighteenth century.

It is possible for a ghost word to become established. The Roman writer Cicero in one text used the Latin word *sittubas*, the accusative plural of *sittuba*, a word of Greek origin denoting a label on a manuscript recording its title and author. In a 1470 edition of Cicero's works, *sittubas* was misprinted as *syllabus*, and this form has not only come into use in English but acquired its own distinct sense of 'summary of a course of studies' – not to mention a pseudo-Latin plural *syllabi*. Something similar has happened to a Scots dialect variant of *twill*, *tweel*, which was misprinted in 1831 as *tweed* and, by a chance association with the River Tweed, became established as the name of the cloth. [I am indebted to Julian Burnside for these examples.] Compare **mumpsimus**.

Gilyak (also **Nivkh**) An **isolated language** spoken on Sakhalin Island off the coast of east Asia.

given name A personal name conferred upon an individual. Compare **surname**.

glide-cluster reduction The name given by J. Wells (1982) to the loss of /h/ in the word-initial cluster /hw-/ in English, so that, for example, *whine* becomes homophonous with *wine*.

glide-formation Any **syntagmatic change** in which a (syllabic) vowel is converted to a (non-syllabic) glide. For example, in Pre-Basque, word-initial */e/ changed to */j/ when followed by a non-high vowel: **eakin > jakin* 'know'; **eosi > josi* 'sew'.

glide-strengthening Any phonological change in which a glide is converted to a true consonant, usually an obstruent. For example, in most varieties of Basque, the ancestral glide [j] has been strengthened to one of [ɟ], [dʒ], [ʒ], [ʃ] or [χ].

global cline See under **cline** (sense 2).

global etymology A putative case of a single linguistic form which is attested in languages all over the world and which is interpreted as directly descended from the single ancestral language of all human-kind. For example, Ruhlen (1991: 261, 1994: 322–323, and else-where) has defended a supposed 'Proto-World' root *tik 'one, finger, point'. Such ideas are dismissed by most linguists as absurd fantasies; see Salmons (1992) for a critique of this particular case.

gloss 1. A brief translation into one language of a word or phrase in another language. Historical and other linguists routinely use glosses in citing words and forms, as in Basque *etxe* 'house' (note the convention), but medieval copyists also often inserted glosses of difficult forms into their manuscripts, as in the celebrated *Emilian glosses* into Basque and Spanish of certain phrases in a tenth-century Latin document. 2. In a continuous text translated from another language, a word selected to translate a particular item in the original, sometimes especially one which is difficult to translate adequately. See Lass (1997: 83–93) for an essay on this. 3. See **interlinear gloss**.

glossary A list of words in a language with approximate translations into another. Many extinct languages, or earlier stages of languages, are attested only in the form of one or more short glossaries drawn up by amateur investigators.

glossator The (possibly unknown) person who has provided a **gloss**, especially in sense 2.

glossogenetics (also **glottogony**) A label sometimes applied to the time period during which human language emerged for the first time, or to that emergence itself.

glottalic theory of PIE A proposed modification of the standard reconstruction of the PIE plosives. That standard reconstruction posits three series of plosives: voiceless unaspirated /p t (kʲ) k kʷ/, voiced /b d (gʲ) g gʷ/, and 'voiced aspirated' /bh dh (ghʲ) gh ghʷ/. This set appears to be typologically unusual, since a language normally only has a 'voiced aspirate' (murmured) series if it also has a voiceless aspirated series. Consequently, several linguists have proposed a major modification, as follows: the voiceless unaspirated series is reinterpreted as voiceless aspirated /p^h t^h (k^{hj}) k^h k^{hw}/, while the voiced series is reinterpreted as an ejective ('glottalized') series /p' t' ($k^{j'}$) k' $k^{w'}$/.

The glottalic theory makes the PIE plosive system look much more natural typologically. It also seems to account for the observation that PIE roots never contain two members of the voiced series – that is, there are no roots like *bed- or *deg- – and further for the observation that PIE *b was, at best, very rare; these now become the observation that a root cannot contain two ejectives (a common constraint in languages with ejectives, and having a good phonetic basis) and the observation that */p'/ was rare to non-existent (/p'/ is often rare or absent in languages with ejectives).

In spite of its apparent successes, the glottalic theory remains highly controversial. For one thing, whereas the standard reconstruction requires dramatic shifts in the consonants only in Germanic and Armenian, the glottalic theory requires dramatic shifts in all branches *except* Germanic and Armenian. For another, a few languages with exactly the three series of the standard reconstruction have now turned up, thus weakening the typological case.

The glottalic hypothesis was first suggested by Martinet (1953), but it was particularly developed by Hopper (1973) and, independently, by Gamkrelidze and Ivanov (1973, 1995). For critical discussion, see W. P. Lehmann (1993: 97–100), Szemerényi (1996: 151–153) and especially Collinge (1985: 259–269).

glottalization 1. The addition of a glottal closure to a segment which formerly lacked it, as in the common pronunciation of English *meet* as [miːʔt]. 2. The conversion of another segment to a glottal stop. An example is the conversion of English /t/ to [ʔ] in London and Glasgow, as in *bu*[ʔ]*er* for *butter*. 3. Especially in Romance linguistics, another term for **aspiration** (sense 2). Note: outside of historical linguistics, this term is also used in other senses.

glottochronology A proposed technique for estimating the date of separation of two languages known to be related. First, a standard word list such as the **Swadesh word list** is prepared for each language and the proportion of shared cognates is calculated (this much is **lexicostatistics**). Next, an estimate of the rate of vocabulary replacement is introduced, and the numbers are plugged into the **Lees equation** to calculate the date of separation. The chief difficulty with this approach is the requirement that the rate of vocabulary replacement should be constant, or at least capable of being reasonably estimated; since we know that rates of replacement vary dramatically among languages, many critics dismiss glottochronology as unworkable. However, see Embleton (1986, 1991) for a modified and more sophisticated version that appears to give better results. Glottochronology was developed by Morris Swadesh in a series of publications beginning in 1952; a classic presentation is Gudschinsky (1956). See Fox (1995: 279–291) for a critical survey, and see Hymes (1983) and Blench (1997a: 7) for historical antecedents.

glottogenesis The creation of a **non-genetic language**.

glottogony Another term for **glossogenetics**.

Goidelic (also **Gaelic, Q-Celtic**) See under **Celtic**.

gorgia toscana In Tuscan dialects of Italian, the conversion of intervocalic voiceless plosives /p t k/ to fricatives, typically [Φ θ h], though details vary: hence *catena* [kaθe:na] 'chain' but *la catena* [la haθe:na] 'the chain', and *pecora* [pɛ:hora] 'sheep' but *la pecora* [la Φɛ:hora] 'the sheep'.

Gothic An extinct **Germanic** language, the only known member of the *eastern* branch of Germanic. Gothic was spoken by many of the Germanic invaders who disrupted the Roman Empire; after about AD 270, the Goths were divided into two main groups, the *Ostrogoths* ('eastern Goths') and the *Visigoths* ('western Goths'). Apart from a few fragments, our only record of Gothic is a partial translation of the Bible by the Visigoth Wulfilas in the fourth century AD. Gothic died out in most of Europe around the eighth century, but a form of the language called *Crimean Gothic* was found to be still spoken in the Crimea in the sixteenth century, though this too died out not long after. Among the Germanic languages, Gothic is remarkably conservative, particularly in its verbal morphology, where it retains a number of contrasts lost elsewhere. The standard grammar of Gothic is J. Wright (1910). See Robinson (1992: 43–68), Price (1998: 208–211), Voyles (1992: ch. 4).

gradation, grade See under **ablaut**.

gradualness of change The issue of whether language change proceeds gradually, in small increments, or abruptly, at one fell swoop. At least four different kinds of gradualness must be distinguished, some of which apply only to sound change. In a *phonetically gradual* change, sound A changes to sound B via tiny increments; in a *phonetically abrupt* change, A changes directly to B, with no intervening forms. In a *lexically gradual* change, the change affects only a few words at first, spreading later to more and more words; in a *lexically abrupt* change, all relevant words are affected simultaneously. In an *individually gradual* change, an individual begins by using the newer form only occasionally but gradually increases its frequency at the expense of the older form; in an *individually abrupt* change, the individual at once totally replaces the older form by the newer. In a *socially gradual* change, only a few people in the speech community are using the newer form at first but, over time, more and more people come to use it; in a *socially abrupt* change, everyone in the community changes at the same time.

It is now clear that no one of these captures the whole truth about language change, and that all varieties and combinations are possible. For example, a case of **lexical diffusion** is always phonetically abrupt and lexically gradual, and it may be individually abrupt but socially gradual. See Trask (1996: 294–296) for discussion and see Lass (1997: 221–226) for phonetic gradualism.

Regardless of pathway, a linguistic change goes to **completion** when there is no scope for further change of that kind.

grammatical change 1. (Ger *grammatischer Wechsel*) A meaningless label applied in the nineteenth century to certain consonantal **alternations** for which no conditioning phonological environment could then be identified, particularly in the Germanic languages. These were cases in which verb-stems in some forms exhibited the regular outcome of the **First Germanic Consonant Shift** but in other forms exhibited quite different, and seemingly irregular, reflexes. Examples from modern standard German include *ziehen* 'pull' (infinitive) but preterite *zog, zogen* and participle *gezogen; leiden* 'suffer' but *litt, litten, gelitten;* and also *heben* 'raise' but noun *Hefe* 'yeast'. The discovery of **Verner's Law** successfully explained these apparently anomalous alternations, and the term *grammatical change* has now largely dropped out of use, except occasionally as a slightly facetious label for an unexplained alternation in some language. 2. A superordinate term for **morphological change** and **syntactic change** taken together.

grammatical conditioning See **morphologically conditioned sound change**.

grammatical correspondence A systematic match in morphological systems between languages. Grammatical correspondences, as a rule, constitute the most powerful evidence that the languages exhibiting them are genetically related, a conclusion particularly stressed by Antoine Meillet, for example in Meillet (1958: 91). A good example is the pronominal paradigm shared by **Algonquian** with the distant Yurok and Wiyot languages of California, recognized by Sapir (1913). In all these languages there are only three pronominal stems – first-person *n-*, second-person *k-*, and third-person zero – and moreover in all of them a *-t-* is inserted before a vowel-initial stem. This degree of grammatical correspondence is so great that it can hardly result from anything but common ancestry, and it led to the setting up of the **Algic** family.

Observe that a grammatical correspondence exists only when both the system of contrasts and the morphological material both match; one or the other by itself does not constitute a correspondence. The mere presence of shared typological features like vowel harmony or ergativity or a three-term tense system counts for nothing. (Note particularly the case of **metatypy**.) Likewise, the mere observation that two case-languages both have *some case-form or other* marked by, say, *-e, -i, -n* and *-k* is devoid of value, since grammatical affixes tend universally to be short and to contain unmarked segments. Nor does a single perfect match, like that between Basque *-k* (plural) and Hungarian *-k* (plural) carry any weight.

Note further that the correspondences must be exhaustive, or nearly so. In the Algic example, if it had merely been the case that each of the three members had possessed *several different person-markers*, of which only one matched anything in the other members, then the evidence for relating the languages would have been anything but persuasive, since **chance resemblances** would have been highly likely. The need for stringent requirements is illustrated by the following remarkable match, due entirely to chance, in the verb-agreement markers of Proto-Eastern Miwok and late PIE (Callaghan 1980); see Table 4.

Proto-Eastern-Miwok		Late PIE	
Singular	Plural	Sing	Plural
1 *-m	*-maṣ	*-m	*-me(s) / *-mo(s)
2 *-ṣ	*-tok	*-s	*-te
3 *-Ø	*-p	*-t < -Ø	*-nt ≈ *-r

Table 4

This is the kind of thing that is commonly taken as powerful evidence of a genetic relationship, but here we have excellent evidence that the Proto-Eastern Miwok forms are secondary within this branch of the Miwokan grouping, and hence that the apparent evidence for a relationship is entirely illusory; there is no reason to suspect a relationship between Eastern Miwok and IE.

See **multidimensional paradigmaticity**.

grammaticalization (also **grammaticization**, **grammatization**, **condensation**, rarely **subduction**) A generic label for any process by which a construction, a word or a form becomes more grammatical in nature than it formerly was. In such a development, the linguistic item being affected undergoes loss in one or more of pragmatic significance, semantic complexity, syntactic freedom, morphological structure and phonetic substance. For example, a discourse strategy may become a syntactic construction, a syntactic construction may become a single word-form, a lexical item may become a grammatical word, or a grammatical word may become a bound affix. A simple example is the English *be going to* pattern. Originally, *go* was strictly a lexical verb, and an utterance like *I am going to visit Mrs Pumphrey* could only mean 'I am now on my way to visit Mrs P.' Today, however, *be going to* has become grammaticalized as an expression of (a certain kind of) futurity, and it can be used even when no relevant motion is even conceivable, as in *I am going to be in trouble*; moreover, grammatical *I'm going to* can be reduced to *I'm gonna*, whereas lexical *I'm going to* cannot: *I'm gonna do it* but **I'm gonna the beach*. The term *grammaticalization* was introduced by Meillet (1912); though nineteenth-century linguists had noted the existence of grammaticalization and discussed it, the phenomenon has chiefly been investigated since about 1980, since when it has become a major area of investigation. Among the principal recent studies are Heine and Reh (1984), C. Lehmann (1985), Traugott and Heine (1991), Heine *et al.* (1991a), Hopper and Traugott (1993) and

Bybee *et al.* (1994). Models of grammaticalization are numerous and varied; Heine *et al.* (1991a: ch. 4) presents a survey with references. See the **linguistic cycle hypothesis** and **unidirectionality**. Note: some (but not most) linguists use the variant *grammaticization* to denote 'having become grammatically obligatory', as opposed to merely 'grammatically available'.

grammaticalization chain In Heine *et al.* (1991a, 1991b), the sequence of events or structures occurring in a particular instance of **grammaticalization**, along a particular **grammaticalization channel**, often particularly when this sequence is interpreted cognitively.

grammaticalization channel Any of several conceivable pathways along which an instance of **grammaticalization** may proceed.

grammatical reconstruction See **morphological reconstruction**, **syntactic reconstruction**.

grammaticization Another term for **grammaticalization**.

grammatischer Wechsel The German for **grammatical change** (sense 1).

grammatization Another term for **grammaticalization**.

Grammont's Law (also **law of the stronger**) The statement that, when a 'stronger' and a 'weaker' segment occur close together in a sequence of speech sounds, the weaker will tend to have its articulation modified - for example, by assimilation or lenition. Proposed by Grammont (1933: 169–171), this idea has been much discussed, and it has featured prominently in many theoretical attempts at formalizing phonological change, but proponents have been unable to agree on any absolute scale for measuring the 'strength' of segments. See Collinge (1985: 243–247) for a critical account with references.

Grassmann's Law (informally, also **ha-ha rule**) A development occurring in early Greek and Indic, first pointed out by Hermann Grassmann (1863: 110–111). With considerable oversimplification, it may be stated as follows: if two aspirated consonants occur in the same syllable, or in consecutive syllables, then the first loses its aspiration. Greek examples: $t^h riks$ 'hair' (nominative), genitive $trik^h \acute{o}s$ (for underlying $*t^h rik^h \acute{o}s$); $p^h e\acute{u}go$ 'flee', perfect $p\acute{e}p^h euga$ (for underlying

*$p^h \acute{e} p^h euga$). This 'law' has attracted perhaps more critical attention than any other process in IE languages; see Collinge (1985: 47–61) for a critical discussion with references. Note also that Grassmann's original formulation included a second statement, now known as **Aspiration Throwback**, and not regarded as part of Grassmann's Law.

graveyard An informal term for any development which freezes into place the last remnant of an ancient grammatical formative or pattern and thus prevents it from being totally lost by grammatical means. For example, in some Salishan languages the ancient body-part prefix *m- has been incorporated into some body-part names as part of the stem, so that no purely grammatical development can eliminate it. See Greenberg (1991).

Great Tone Split An informal label for a process, frequent in the tone languages of eastern and southeastern Asia, by which the number of tones present was doubled by splitting each inherited tone into a higher and a lower version, depending on the original voicing of the syllable–initial consonant; at the same time, the contrasts in the initial consonants were generally lost. The split affected all Tai languages and many others; it is dated to around the eleventh century AD.

Great Vowel Shift A major change in the phonetic values of the Middle English long (tense) vowels, a **chain shift**, which occurred mainly between about 1500 and about 1700. In sum, the two high vowels /iː/ and /uː/ diphthongized to /əɪ/ and /əʊ/, respectively; /eː/ and /oː/ raised to /iː/ and /uː/, respectively; /ɛː/ and /ɔː/ raised to /eː/ and /oː/, respectively; and /aː/ raised to /ɛː/, leaving a gap at the bottom of the vowel space. Later changes, including the raising of the new /eː/ (original /ɛː/) to /iː/ in most varieties and the diphthongization of most of the new long vowels, are often not counted as strictly part of the GVS. There has been considerable debate over just how the GVS proceeded; see Lass (1976: ch. 2) for a critical evaluation with references. Since English spelling was largely settled before the GVS, the GVS is the principal reason why the English vowel letters are out of line with those in the rest of Europe: spellings like *name, heat, feet, wine, goat, moon* and *loud* were designed to represent the Middle English vowels /aː/, /ɛː/, /eː/, /iː/, /ɔː/, /oː/ and /uː/, respectively. The name was coined by Jespersen (1909–49, vol. 1, § 8.1).

Greek A single language constituting a distinct branch of **Indo-European** all by itself; the branch is sometimes called **Hellenic**. An archaic form of Greek called *Mycenaean Greek* is attested from about 1400 BC in the Linear B texts; this syllabic writing system later died out. *Homeric Greek*, the language of the great Greek epics, is thought to date from around 800 BC, but the texts were only written down much later. *Classical Greek* is the language of the great literary works written around the fifth century BC. This was followed by *Hellenistic Greek*, the language of the empire of Alexander the Great, and by *New Testament Greek*, the post-classical variety in which the New Testament is written. The medieval language of the Byzantine Empire is *Byzantine Greek*, while the modern form of the language developed since Greek independence is *Modern Greek*. It is possible that the ancient **Macedonian** language was closely related to Greek, but we have too little information to reach any conclusions. For a historical summary, see Price (1998: 211–224), Hoenigswald (1998) or Horrocks (1997).

Greenberg progression A sequence of grammatical changes in determiners, identified by Greenberg (1978, 1991) as having occurred in very many languages. The determiner starts as a demonstrative, is then reduced to an article marking its noun as definite or identifiable, is then further reduced to a largely superfluous marker of gender or another category, and finally either disappears entirely or is absorbed by nouns as additional phonological material.

Gresham's law of semantic change A slightly facetious observation about **semantic change**. It says: bad meanings drive out good ones. In other words, when a word acquires a sense which is offensive or at least potentially embarrassing, that sense prevails over other, neutral, senses of the word, which disappear. For example, the sense of *boor* as 'uncultivated lout' has completely displaced the earlier sense of 'farmer', and the sense of *gay* as 'homosexual' has made the earlier sense of 'cheerful' almost totally unavailable.

Grimm's Law Another term for the **First Germanic Consonant Shift**.

Grimston hybrid A place name composed of Anglo-Saxon and Old Norse elements, such as *Grimston*, from *Grim*, a Viking personal name, and Old English *tūn* 'village'.

Grundriss The German for 'compendium', commonly applied to a **hand-book** describing the prehistory and structure of a family of languages. When used without qualification, the word usually denotes Brugmann and Delbrück's (1886–1900) comparative grammar of the IE languages.

Guanche The extinct and sparsely recorded indigenous language of the Canary Islands. It seems to have been a variety of **Berber**.

Gulf A speculative grouping of **Muskogean,** *Natchez, Tunica, Atakapa* and *Chitimacha* in the southeastern USA, proposed by Mary Haas in several publications. Gulf is not generally accepted as a valid grouping; see Campbell (1997a: 306–308) for a critical review.

guṇa See under **ablaut**.

Gur (also **Voltaic**) One of the primary branches of **Niger-Congo,** containing about eighty-five languages in west Africa.

guttural In IE studies, another term for **tectal**.

ha-ha rule A jocular term for **Grassmann's Law**.

half-contrast Another term for **near-merger**.

Hamitic [*obsolete*] A label formerly applied to all members of the **Afro-Asiatic** family except **Semitic**. It is now known that Semitic is only one of a number of coordinate branches of the family.

Hamito-Semitic A former name for the **Afro-Asiatic** family. The name is no longer in use, since it was based upon the false assumption that the family consisted of just two branches, **Semitic** and everything else.

Hamp's principles of comparison A set of principles for **comparison** put forward by Hamp (1998). There are thirteen, the most important being these: (1) all linguistic forms cited must be acceptable to specialists in the relevant languages; (2) all linguistic forms cited must be segmented in a way acceptable to specialists; (3) a linguistic form may not be adduced in a comparison at a higher level unless it is securely reconstructible at the next lower level; no **'reaching down'** is permitted; (4) all linguistic forms cited must be presented with full phonological and grammatical information; (5) the **total accountability principle** must be upheld.

handbook A reference book containing an organized presentation of certain facts about a language or family. Examples are Pokorny (1959/69), a dictionary of PIE roots with their reflexes in the various daughter languages, and Horrocks (1997), an internal and external history of Greek.

hapax (also **hapax legomenon**, plural **hapax legomena**) A word or form which is attested in writing in only one single case, and whose reality may therefore be in doubt.

haplology A type of phonological change (or of phonological constraint) in which one of two adjacent syllables of identical or similar form is lost (or fails to appear in the first place). For example, Latin *nutri-* 'nourish' plus *-trix* 'female agent' should have yielded **nutritrix*, but the form is *nutrix* 'nurse'; Basque *sagar* 'apple' plus *ardo* 'wine' should yield **sagar-ardo*, but the form is *sagardo* 'cider'; English *library* is pronounced in England as though it were *libry*; Greek *amphi-* 'on both sides' plus *phoreus* 'bearer' yields Homeric Greek *amphiphoreus* 'amphora', reduced in classical Greek to *amphoreus*; Old English *Anglaland* 'land of the Angles' yields modern English *England*.

hardening A rare synonym for **fortition**. The term is particularly applied to the fortition of earlier voiced fricatives */β ð γ/ to voiced plosives /b d g/ in certain circumstances in some Germanic languages.

hare-and-tortoise principle A putative principle of language changes involving the gain and subsequent loss of a feature, advanced by Bailey (1996): roughly, first in, last out. For example, in rounding umlaut, high vowels round before low vowels, but low vowels unround before high vowels.

harmonic change An extreme type of **assimilation** in which a phonetic feature is extended to all instances of certain segments in a word. Crowley (1997: 53–54) cites the Indonesian language Enggano, in which the presence of a nasal consonant in a word has induced nasalization of every following voiced stop or vowel in the word.

Hartmann's Law A statement about the word-accent in common **Slavic**, put forward by Hartmann (1936), according to which the accent of a class of denominal adjectives is predictable from the accent of the nominal stems from which they are derived. See Collinge (1985: 77–79) for a critical survey with references.

Hattic An ancient and poorly recorded language of Anatolia, spoken by a people we call the *Hatti*; it was apparently the dominant language in the area before the rise of **Hittite**, which borrowed a number of words from it. Some bilingual Hattic-Hittite texts are preserved in the Hittite archives, and we can tell that Hattic was not an Indo-European language, but its genetic affinities (if any) are unknown; some scholars favour a link with one or another of the **Caucasian** families, but nothing has been established.

h-dropping An informal name for the disappearance of the historical /h/ in English, especially for its total loss from some accents. Old English /h/ was lost early before most consonants, as in *hnutu* 'nut', *hræfn* 'raven', *hlud* 'loud' and *hring* 'ring', and later in a few other cases, as in *hit* 'it'. More recently, /h/ has been lost before /w/ in England, as in *when* /hwɛn/, now /wɛn/, and this loss is increasingly frequent in American English as well. Such losses are accepted in standard English, but the majority of vernacular speakers in England have gone further and lost *all* instances of /h/, so that, for example, *hair* is homophonous with *air* and *harm* with *arm*. Such '*h*-dropping' is strongly stigmatized in England, but there is good evidence that it has been a prominent feature of English speech for centuries. See Milroy (1983, 1992: 137–145) for an account of the evidence.

heavy base Another term for **laryngeal base**.

heavy close law A proposed universal tendency, advanced by Hagège (1990: 142–143, 1993: 58), according to which, in a fixed expression of the form 'X or Y' or 'X and Y', the phonologically 'heavier' member tends to come last, even when this would violate the usual tendency for an item closer to ego to come first. Examples: English *by gosh and by golly*, *up and down*, Russian *tam i sjam* 'there and here', Spanish *tarde o temprano* 'late or soon'. The tendency is not exceptionless: English *hither and yon*, Basque *hemen eta han* 'here and there'.

Hebrew The traditional language of the Jews. Hebrew belongs to the northwestern branch of the **Semitic** languages, and it is recorded in writing from about the end of the eleventh century BC, though the familiar Hebrew alphabet was not developed until some centuries later. The language was spoken in Palestine until about the third century BC, when it died out as a mother tongue in favour of **Aramaic**. The classical written form of the language, known as *Biblical Hebrew*, was used in writing most of the Old Testament. After its disappearance as a spoken language, Hebrew continued to be used as a **liturgical language** by Jews, and it continued to be written in modified forms called *Mishnaic Hebrew* and later *Medieval Hebrew*. Remarkably, the Zionist settlers of Palestine in the nineteenth century managed to revive Hebrew as a mother tongue, and today *modern Hebrew* (or *Israeli Hebrew*) is the mother tongue of most Jewish inhabitants of Israel. This is the only case on record of the **discontinuous descent** of a language. For religious reasons, Hebrew has long been important to both Jews and Christians, and it has also been a favourite candidate for crankish ideas like 'the original language of humanity' and 'the source of all languages'. See Price (1998: 225–228), Steiner (1997).

heir-apparent principle See under **clause fusion**.

Hellenic A name sometimes given to the branch of **Indo-European** whose sole known member is **Greek**, though it is conceivable that ancient **Macedonian** may also have belonged to this branch.

Herkunfthypothese The hypothesis that all of the categories absent from **Anatolian** but present in all other branches of IE were formed only after Anatolian split off from the rest of the family, and that Anatolian is accordingly archaic. The opposing view is the *Schwundhypothese*. See the **Indo-Hittite hypothesis**, and see Luraghi (1988: 190–191).

heteroclitic noun One of a class of nouns in PIE and the older IE languages which exhibit an **alternation** in the consonant of the stem. Almost all of these nouns exhibit an r/n alternation. Examples: PIE $*i\acute{e}k^w\text{-}r$, genitive $*i(e)k^w\text{-}\acute{e}n\text{-}s$ 'liver', Sanskrit $y\acute{a}k\text{-}r\text{-}t$, $yak\text{-}n\text{-}\acute{a}s$ 'liver' (with an extra /t/), Latin *iec-ur*, *iec-in-oris* 'liver' (with contamination of the genitive by the nominative), Greek *hēp-ar*, *hēp-at-os* ($< *h\bar{e}p\text{-}nt\text{-}os$, also with an extra /t/) 'liver', Latin *it-er*, *it-in-eris* 'road' (also with contamination), PIE $*p\acute{e}H_2\text{-}ur$, $*p(e)H_2\text{-}u\acute{e}n\text{-}s$ 'fire', Hittite *pahh-ur*, *pahh-uen-as* 'fire', Avestan *rāz-arǝ, rāz-ǝng* 'instruction', Sanskrit *údh-ar, údh-n-as* 'udder', Greek *oûth-ar, oúth-at-os* (< **oúth-nt-os*) 'udder', Hittite *wat-ar, wet-en-as* 'water', Greek *hýd-or, hýd-at-os* (< **hýd-nt-os*) 'water', Sanskrit *śák-r-t, śak-n-ás* 'excrement'. One noun exhibits an *l/n* alternation: PIE **séH₂-ul, *sH₂-uén-s* 'sun', Avestan *hvarǝ, xvǝng* 'sun'. The heteroclitic class is very large in Hittite and seemingly productive there, but elsewhere, even in other Anatolian languages, it is rare and fossilized.

heteronomy The status of a language variety which is regarded merely as a version of another language variety, instead of as a distinct language. For example, the divergent Flemish dialects of western Belgium are heteronomous with respect to standard Dutch. A heteronomous variety may be shifted from one reference language to another; for example, the speech of southern Sweden was regarded as dialects of Danish when the territory was part of Denmark, but came to be regarded as dialects of Swedish shortly after the region passed under Swedish control in 1658, even though there were no significant linguistic changes in the local speech. Heteronomy can also develop into **autonomy**, as when Afrikaans changed from being regarded as a dialect of Dutch to an independent language in the 1920s.

Hetzron's principle Another name for (the principle of) **archaic heterogeneity** (version 2).

heuristic comparison The term used by Nichols (1995b, 1997d) to denote any procedure, whether **closed comparison** or **limited search**, which is intended to suggest or to demonstrate a **genetic relationship** between languages. Compare **Neogrammarian comparison**.

High German See under **German**.

High German Consonant Shift Another term for the **Second Germanic Consonant Shift**.

Hindi-Urdu The most important modern **Indo-Aryan** language, spoken by well over 250 million people, mainly in India and Pakistan. At the spoken level, *Hindi* and *Urdu* are the same language (called *Hindustani* before the political partition), but the two varieties are written in different alphabets and differ substantially in their abstract and technical vocabulary, as a result of the religious differences between Hindi-speaking Hindus and Urdu-speaking Muslims.

Hirt's law Either of two statements about the development of the PIE word-accent in certain daughter languages put forward by Herman Hirt. 1. The statement that, in a PIE word of the shape ... V:CV:# or ... V:CVC#, a word-accent on the final vowel shifted to the preceding vowel in Balto-Slavic: hence Sanskrit *dhūmá-*, Greek *thymós*, but Russian *dýma* (gen. sg.) (Hirt 1895: 165–166). With modifications, this is widely accepted. 2. The statement that, in early Greek, a three-mora pattern of the type śśs shifted to śss, as in PIE *welútrom*, Sanskrit *varútram*, but Greek *élytron* 'container' (Hirt 1904). This now finds little support. See Collinge (1985: 81–87) for discussion of both.

historical connection (also **historical relatedness**) The term used by Nichols and Peterson (1996: 358–359) to denote any kind of resemblance among languages resulting from any kind of common history, including at least **genetic relationship, diffusion, substrate** effects and any combination of these. Their prime example is the curious distribution of *n/m* pronouns around both sides of the Pacific Rim. See Campbell (1997b) and Nichols and Peterson (1998) for discussion.

historical linguistics The branch of linguistics which investigates the processes of **language change**, which attempts to identify all types of historical and prehistoric connections between languages, and which tries to establish **genetic relationships** between languages. Though there were a few earlier efforts of note, historical linguistics largely got going with the rise of **comparative linguistics** in the late eighteenth century, and it was the first branch of linguistics to be placed on a firm scholarly footing; indeed, it was almost the only kind of linguistics pursued before the rise of general linguistics towards the end of the nineteenth century. Classical historical linguistics was chiefly concerned with the study of **internal history**, but the subject was revolutionized in the 1960s by the introduction of sociolinguistic techniques, and today **external history** is seen as equally important. Among the major textbooks on the subject are Anttila (1989), Campbell (1998), Crowley (1997), Hock (1986), Hock and Joseph (1996) and Trask (1996); McMahon (1994) focuses more specifically on language change.

historical marker In the work of Johanna Nichols, a linguistic feature or set of features which recurs in two or more languages or families and which is unlikely to derive from anything other than a common origin, but which fails to meet **individual-identifying criteria** and is thus not sufficiently distinctive to constitute a **genetic marker**. See, for example, Nichols (1992: ch. 6, 1994/95, 1997c), Nichols and Peterson (1996), and see also **population typology**.

historical pragmatics A general label for any kind of historical linguistic work in which pragmatics plays a major role. See, for example, Sweetser (1990), and see also **grammaticalization** and **metaphor**.

historical relatedness Another term for **historical connection**.

historical spelling A conventional spelling of a word which represents its earlier pronunciation more or less accurately but which fails to represent the current pronunciation with any fidelity. For example, English *knight* is spelled with the graphs <k> and <gh>, representing two consonants which were pronounced a few centuries ago but which have disappeared in the modern pronunciation. Languages with long written traditions and little spelling reform, like English, French and Irish, often make heavy use of historical spellings.

historicization The more or less conscious process of constructing a past for a language variety, especially for a **standard language**. Milroy and Milroy (1985a) argue that there is a tendency for historical studies to focus on those forms which are directly ancestral to those of the modern standard language and to ignore or reject all other forms as 'not part of the story'. In other words, there is a tendency to project the modern standard language backwards in time, and to see the whole complex history of the language as a vast conspiracy to arrive at the modern standard form; sometimes the very existence of the modern standard is projected centuries back into the past to a time when no standard variety existed. Just to cite one example, a particular change may be assigned a firm date, reflecting its appearance in the ancestor of the standard variety, even though this change may have occurred centuries earlier or later, or not at all, in other varieties. Historicization is one aspect of **legitimization**. See also Milroy (1992: 124–129).

Hittite An extinct language, the principal language of the Hittite Empire, copiously attested in the middle of the second millennium BC, mainly about 1600–1200 BC. Hittite is the best-recorded member of the **Anatolian** branch of **Indo-European**. It preserves some archaic features of PIE, including the **heteroclitic noun** class and some of the **laryngeal** consonants. Its precise relation to the rest of the family has been disputed; see the **Indo-Hittite hypothesis**. See Friedrich (1952, 1960).

Hjelmslev's Law A putative change in the word-accent of common **Baltic**, put forward by Hjelmslev (1932: 5, 234), by which an accented syllable acquired the pitch contour (rising or falling) of the following syllable. The details are controversial; see Collinge (1985: 89–91) for a critical account.

hlonipha A word used as a polite replacement for a **taboo** word, particularly one which has no other existence in the language, such as English *heck* for *hell*. The term comes from Zulu, which, like many Bantu languages, has a distinctive set of such words, often exhibiting phonological forms not found in ordinary lexical items.

Hmong-Mien Another term for **Miao-Yao**.

Hochstufe See under **ablaut**.

Hokan A deeply controversial proposed grouping of a variable number of languages in western North America and Mesoamerica. It was put forward by Dixon and Kroeber in a series of articles in the 1910s, then picked up by Sapir, and both Sapir and others have frequently proposed expanding the grouping to include ever more languages. A conservative view recognizes about two dozen Hokan languages, while more generous views recognize many more, but it remains to be established that Hokan is a valid family at any level. See Campbell (1997a: 290–296).

Hokan-Siouan A vast putative language family of North America, proposed by Sapir (1929). It includes **Siouan**, **Iroquoian**, **Hokan** (itself far from established), **Caddoan**, *Tunica-Chitimacha* and *Natchez-Muskogean*, plus the four isolates *Yuki*, *Keres*, **Yuchi** and *Timucua*. Sapir himself called it his 'wastepaper basket stock'; this is where he placed everything he couldn't fit into any other large construct. It is now generally abandoned. A less ambitious grouping of Siouan, Iroquoian and Caddoan has obtained a somewhat higher degree of assent under the label **Macro-Siouan**, but is still controversial.

hole in the pattern (also *case vide*) A gap in an otherwise symmetrical set of phonemes, such as the absent /o/ in the vowel system /i e a u/. There is evidence that such holes in the pattern may encourage **chain shifts**, an idea developed most vigorously by Martinet (1955), but criticized by King (1969).

holokinetic See under **accent in PIE**.

Holtzmann's Law (also **sharpening**, *Verschärfung*) A development in the early Germanic languages, first pointed out by Holtzmann (1835), by which a geminate obstruent was inserted between a vowel and a following glide. This obstruent was usually spelled <gg> but occasionally <dd>; its phonetic value has been much disputed, but one possibility is [ɟɟ]. Examples: PIE **drew-* 'true' > Gothic *triggws*, *triggwa*, ON *tryggr*, *tryggva*; PIE **dwey-* 'two' > Gothic *twaddjē*, ON *tveggja*. The process is not totally regular; it is most pervasive in Gothic and Old Norse but only sporadic in West Germanic. See Collinge (1985: 93–101) for a critical account with references.

homeland (also **core area**; Ger *Urheimat*) The geographical area once occupied by an unrecorded language which is the ancestor of a language family.

homeland problem The problem of determining the geographical area in which the single language ancestral to a **language family** was anciently spoken. This problem is generally difficult and a number of criteria have been proposed for helping to identify it. Among these are the **age-area hypothesis** (or **centre-of-gravity principle**), the **conservatism principle**, the **extrafamilial contact principle**, the **linguistic relationship principle**, the **total distribution principle**, the **temporal plausibility principle**, the **exclusion principle**, the **relationship principle**, the **minimal-migration principle** and the **archaeological plausibility principle**. See Mallory (1997) for a critical discussion of these, and Nichols (1997a) for a critique of the first. The single most celebrated example is the **Indo-European homeland problem**.

homomery A term coined by Dyen (1965) to denote a collection of **cognate sets** distributed over exactly the same set of languages.

homonymic assimilation One type of **folk etymology**, as follows: a loan word of opaque formation is reshaped so that it consists of elements which are familiar in the borrowing language, though typically senseless in the context. For example, Old French *moisseron* was borrowed as English *mushroom*, French *lustrin* as English *lutestring*, Irish *seamrog* as English *shamrock*, Italian *marzapane* as English *marchpane*, and Cree *oček* as English *woodchuck*. The name was coined by Hagège (1993: 11). Compare **allonymic dissimilation**.

homonymic clash See under **isomorphy**.

homoplasy Any of several types of change which can obscure the historical development of languages or the nature of the genetic links between them: **convergence, transfer** (sense 2) or **reversal**. The term is taken by Lass (1997: 118–123) from biological cladistics.

hotbed In **linguistic geography**, a geographical region in which some typological feature is far more prominent than on the planet generally.

Humboldt cycle A posited and seemingly well-supported pattern of change in the morphological typology of languages. An isolating language becomes agglutinating; an agglutinating language becomes fusional; and a fusional language becomes isolating. Egyptian/Coptic is reported to have passed from fusional to isolating to agglutinating back to fusional again during the 3000 years in which it is recorded.

Humboldt's Universal See under **isomorphy**.

Hunnic The extinct and unrecorded language of the Huns who invaded Europe in the fourth century AD; it was possibly an early **Turkic** language.

Hurrian An extinct language recorded in a cuneiform script in northeastern Mesopotamia between about 1500 and 1000 BC; the most important Hurrian text is the *Mitanni letter*. Hurrian was closely related to **Urartian**, but otherwise seems to have no known relatives. Attempts at linking it to the **Nakh-Dagestan** languages have so far been inconclusive at best.

hybrid form 1. A lexical item which is constructed from elements originating from different languages, such as English *because* (English *bi* 'by' plus French *cause*) and *television* (Greek *tele* 'far' plus Latin *visio* 'seeing'). 2. (also **linguistic hybrid**) A linguistic element which is in the middle of **grammaticalization** and which exhibits both its earlier behaviour and its new grammatical behaviour at the same time, sometimes even in the same sentence. For example, Kenyan Pidgin Swahili is converting the distal demonstrative *ile* 'that (one)' into an invariable marker of a relative clause, and the sentence *mimi na-ona ile gari kwisha fika* [I Tense-see Dem/Rel car Perf arrive] can mean either 'I saw that car; it has arrived' or 'I saw the car that has arrived.' Heine *et al.* (1991a: 172–174) cite the example of Ewe *megbé* 'back', which variously functions as noun, postposition or adverb.

hydronym In **onomastics**, the name of a body of water, such as a river or a lake.

hyperbole Overstatement, such as the use of *fantastic* to mean 'very good'. The opposite is **litotes**.

hypercorrection 1. (also **hyperurbanism**) An error resulting from a faulty attempt at avoiding another error, with consequent 'over-shooting of the mark'. For example, an American trying to acquire a British accent might attempt to replace his native /uː/ with /juː/ in words like *dew*, but might overdo it and wrongly produce /djuː/ also for *do*; this is hypercorrection. English-speakers who have /n/ in place of /ŋ/ in unstressed syllables in words like *loving* may, in attempting to acquire /ŋ/, also wrongly produce *oving* for *oven*. Compare **hypocorrection** (sense 1). 2. In the work of William Labov, another term for **lower-middle-class crossover**.

hyperdialectalism A type of **hypercorrection** (sense 1) in which a speaker attempts to imitate the pronunciation of a non-standard regional accent and overgeneralizes. Peter Trudgill, reported in Hock and Joseph (1996: 188), notes a case from Norwich, England. Older Norwich speakers distinguish *daze* and *days* as [deːz] and [dæiz], respectively. Younger speakers who have lost the contrast, and pronounce both words as [dæiz], sometimes attempt to use the older style of pronunciation, but wind up pronouncing both words, wrongly, as [deːz].

hyperforeignism (also **emphatic foreignization**) A historically irregular or unexpected pronunciation of a word or name of foreign origin deriving from a mistaken attempt to make it 'sound more foreign'. Examples include the pronunciation of *mah-jong* and *Taj Mahal* with

/ʒ/ rather than with /dʒ/ (/ʒ/ is more 'foreign' than /dʒ/), of *Punjab* with /ʊ/ rather than / ʌ / (in foreign words, <u> often spells a rounded vowel), of *deity* and *academia* with /eɪ/ instead of /iː/ (<e> often spells a mid vowel in foreign words), and of *coup de grâce* as /kuː də grɑː/ ('French drops final consonants').

hypernativism A word which is deliberately constructed in a language from elements which are native or perceived as native and intended to replace an existing word which is a **loan word**: the most familiar type of **purism**. English-speakers have at times proposed hypernativisms in English, seriously or not; examples include *gainrising* 'resurrection', *yeasay* 'affirmation', *unthingsome* 'abstract', *yearday* 'anniversary', *deepthinker* 'philosopher'. Almost none of these has found a place in the language, but hypernativisms are numerous and prominent in some other languages, such as Icelandic, Turkish and Basque. Compare **inkhornism**.

hypertaxon The term used by Lass (1997: 160) for a large and speculative proposed genetic grouping, such as **Amerind**, **Austric** or **Elamo-Dravidian**.

hyperthesis See under **metathesis**.

hyperurbanism Another term for **hypercorrection** (sense 1).

hyphen The symbol '-', used in a set of **systematic correspondences** to indicate the position in a word in which a particular segment participates in a correspondence. For example, /s-/ represents word-initial /s/, /-s-/ word-medial /s/, and /-s/ word-final /s/. An unhyphenated /s/ represents /s/ in all positions.

hypocorism (also **hypocoristic**) A diminutive, especially one used as an endearment or pet name, such as *Mikie* or *Lucykins*, or as a **euphemism**, such as *undies* or *hanky*.

hypocorrection 1. An attempt at 'correcting' a vernacular form to a prestige form which fails to go far enough and produces something intermediate between the two. For example, writers of Arabic attempting to produce the verb-initial order of classical Arabic sometimes fail to remove the subject-agreement in the verb, as required in the classical construction. Compare **hypercorrection** (sense 1). 2. A label applied to a phonological change which results from hearers' failure to perceive accurately what they hear. For example, Proto-Austronesian */k/ and */g/ have undergone **voicing crossover** in some words in some daughter languages (/g/ for */k/ and /k/ for */g/), and they merge completely in some other languages. These developments presumably result from the difficulty of perceiving voicing contrasts in velar plosives.

hysterodynamic inflection In PIE, an inflectional class in which the word-accent regularly fell at or near the end of the word-form, as in *$pH_2té:r$* 'father', accusative *$pH_2tér$-m*, genitive *pH_2tr-ós*. Compare **proterodynamic inflection**. See Beekes (1995: 174–183).

hysterokinetic See under **accent in PIE**.

Iberian An extinct language attested in writing in eastern Spain and southern Gaul from about the sixth to the first centuries BC. Most of the texts are written in an indigenous script; this was deciphered by Manuel Gómez-Moreno in the first half of the twentieth century, and proved to be of mixed alphabetic-syllabic type. We can now read the texts at the phonological level but we cannot make the slightest sense of them, and Iberian does not appear to be related to any other known language, not even to **Basque**.

Ibero-Caucasian The name used in the former USSR for the **Caucasian** languages.

ibid. The abbreviation for 'in the same place' (Latin *ibidem*), used to make a further reference to that work which has most recently been cited. Compare *loc. cit.*

iconic coding principle (also **complexity principle**, **quantity principle**) Any of various principles of the following form: the phonological bulk or morphological complexity of a linguistic form correlates with its degree of semantic or cognitive complexity. Thus, for example, a lexical item is likely to be bulkier or more complex than a grammatical marker, and a linguistic form meaning 'for what purpose?' is likely to be more complex than one meaning 'what?' See **isomorphy**, and see Givón (1991).

iconicity A direct link between the form of a linguistic item and its meaning. An iconic form may resist regular phonological change or become re-established. For example, Middle English *pipe* /piːp/ and *tine* /tiːnə/ have become *pipe* and *tiny* in modern English, but *peep* and *teeny* have been recreated; ancient Greek /bɛː/ for the sound of a sheep would become */viː/ in modern Greek by regular change, but a sheep-sound is still /bɛː/ today.

id. The abbreviation for 'the same (meaning)' (Latin *idem*). In a list of words from various languages, with **glosses**, this indicates that the meaning of a word is the same as that of the preceding one. For example, the sequence 'Latin *mare* 'sea', Old Irish *muir* id.' means that the Irish word also means 'sea'.

identical correspondence A **systematic correspondence** involving identical segments, such as Latin /p/ : Greek /p/ : Sanskrit /p/. Common among very closely related languages, identical correspondences are less usual among more distantly related languages; for example, the three just cited are further matched by Germanic /f/, Armenian /h-/ ~ /-w-/ and Celtic zero. One reason for scepticism about many proposed **remote relationships** is the astonishing number of identical correspondences involved, even at astounding time depths; for example, in the version of Proto-**Nostratic** presented in Dolgopolsky (1998), a putative PN */-r-/ simply remains /-r-/ in all ten of the daughter branches recognized, and such patterns are quite typical of Dolgopolsky's book, even though the author assigns PN to the late Palaeolithic or early Mesolithic era – 15,000 or more years ago. Many critics find such correspondences just too good to be true.

ideophone Any one of an exceptional class of lexical items occurring in certain languages which typically express some particular and distinctive type of sound, appearance, behaviour or movement. In some such languages, ideophones are phonologically exceptional in permitting segments or sequences not permitted elsewhere. Among the ideophones of the Carib language Apalai are *kui kui* 'screaming', *seky seky* 'creep up', *ty ty ty* 'person walking' and *tututututu* 'fast approach'. Ideophones are not normally available as **comparanda** in **comparison**.

idiomatization (also **routinization**) A label sometimes applied to the first stage in **grammaticalization**, in which a particular form or construction comes to be used routinely to express a particular meaning or function.

IE See **Indo-European**.

Ijoid A branch, possibly a primary branch, of **Niger-Congo**, containing about ten languages spoken in the Niger delta.

Illič-Svityč's Law The proposal, put forward by Illič-Svityč (1979: 103–104), that the mobile stress-pattern of the word-accent in Slavic masculine *o*-stems can be explained by analogical extension of the mobile pattern from other noun-classes to this one. See Collinge (1985: 103–104) for an account.

Illyrian An extinct and virtually unrecorded **Indo-European** language anciently spoken along the east coast of the Adriatic Sea. Some specialists subdivide Illyrian into three varieties: *Illyrian proper* in the east, *Dalmatian-Pannonian* in the west, and *Liburnian* in the north-west (but see **Liburnian** for a major qualification). It is widely suspected that **Albanian** may be a continuation of Illyrian, but we lack the data to investigate this. See also **Messapian**.

imitative word Another term for **onomatopoeia** (sense 1).

immigrant language A language which is spoken in some country by a sizeable group of people who have recently immigrated into that country, such as Arabic in France or Bengali in Britain. Compare **minority language**.

imperfect learning A notion which has sometimes been appealed to as a possible way of accounting for certain linguistic changes: for some reason, children or adults learning a language fail to master it. See **acquisition explanation of change, abrupt creolization, linguistic obsolescence**, and see also the work in natural phonology, such as Stampe (1969), Donegan and Stampe (1979).

implementation of change (also **propagation of change, spread of change**) The transmission of a linguistic innovation from speaker to speaker within a community or across a geographical area. At present we still know little about how this occurs, but our most successful approaches are sociolinguistic in nature; see for example Milroy (1992) or McMahon (1994). In the **WLH model of language change**, implementation is decomposed into more specific issues.

implicational scaling The proposal that, in a **post–creole continuum**, linguistic change from the *basilect* towards the *acrolect* will proceed in a predictable order. See Romaine (1988).

imposition The introduction of a prestigious speech variety into an area in which it was formerly absent, as occurred with Latin in the western Roman Empire. Van der Wurff (1995) distinguishes between **borrowing** and *imposition* as two different ways in which one language can influence another.

incoming change In a particular geographical area, an **innovation** which has established itself elsewhere and which is now beginning to appear in the area in question.

incoming form In any kind of language change, a segment or a form which is replacing an earlier one.

incorporation Any change in which an independent word-form is reduced to a bound morph within a larger word-form. For example, the subject- and object-agreement markers in the finite verb-forms of many languages result from the incorporation of originally independent personal pronouns. Compare **demorphologization, exaptation.**

increasing weakness, law of A putative principle of **reconstruction**, advanced by Lass (1997: 228). It says this: in the absence of clear evidence to the contrary, always reconstruct the strongest character-state for a segment and assume that the observed segments, where they differ, result from **lenitions**.

increment A general term for any linguistic change in which a phonologically less bulky form is replaced by a phonologically bulkier one, as when Latin *auris* 'ear' was replaced by *auricula*, originally 'little ear', or when Latin *homo* '(a) man' was replaced in French by *un homme*. Hoenigswald (1960: 40) regards this as a conditioned split of zero.

independent parallel innovation (also **drift, parallel development, duplicate changes**) Identical changes occurring in two or more languages, especially in related languages after they have already separated. For example, English and German have independently diphthongized /i:/ and /u:/ to /ai/ and /au/, and have independently converted inherited */sk/ into /ʃ/; a number of Oceanic languages have independently lost word-final consonants. Such developments constitute one kind of **convergence** and may constitute a potential obstacle to **subgrouping**. Our normal reliance upon **shared innovations** in subgrouping assumes that, apart from some natural and frequent changes, such parallel innovations are sufficiently rare to be largely dismissed from consideration. See the **seeds-of-destruction paradox**, *Entfaltungstheorie*.

indeterminacy 1. In **reconstruction**, a case in which we cannot tell which of two proto-phonemes should be reconstructed. For example, Pre-Basque */l/ merged categorically with Pre-Basque */r/ in intervocalic position, with the result that, except in those cases in which other evidence is available, we are unable to tell whether a modern word with intervocalic /r/ should be reconstructed with */l/ or */r/. This indeterminacy applies to a sizeable number of words, such as *bero* 'hot' and *ira* 'fern'. 2. The property of a surface form of uncertain or potentially ambiguous interpretation, especially when this leads to **abductive change** (see under **abduction**).

Indic Another term for **Indo-Aryan**.

indicator A linguistic **variable** which correlates with personal characteristics like age, sex or social class but is independent of degree of formality. An indicator is typically involved in a **change from below**. Compare **marker**.

indigenous language (formerly also **aboriginal language**) For any given geographical region, the earliest language spoken there of which we have any knowledge, such as **Basque** along the Bay of Biscay, **Iberian** in eastern Spain, or the whole constellation of local languages encountered by European settlers in North America and Australia. Note that there is generally no suggestion that a language labelled 'indigenous' was the first language *ever* spoken by human beings in that area.

indirect diffusion The borrowing of grammatical patterns without the borrowing of any morphological material. If this is taken to an extreme, the result is **metatypy**. The term was coined by Heath (1978).

individual-identifying criteria Any kind of evidence adduced in support of a **genetic relationship** which meets the following requirement: the probability that the feature could occur purely by chance in unrelated languages is so low as to be negligible. The topic has been investigated by Johanna Nichols in a series of publications; Nichols (1996: 49) estimates that an *a priori* probability that a given feature will occur in an arbitrary language of one in 100,000 or less is sufficient to make the recurrence of the feature excellent evidence for genetic relatedness. See **multidimensional paradigmaticity** and the **search problem**, and compare **type-identifying criteria**.

Indo-Aryan (also **Indic**) The sub-branch of the **Indo-Iranian** branch of the **Indo-European** family including most of the IE languages of the Indian subcontinent; among these are **Hindi/Urdu**, *Gujarati*, **Bengali**, *Sindhi*, *Marathi*, *Oriya* and *Nepali*, as well as *Romany*, the language of the Gypsies, or Travellers.

Indo-European (formerly also **Aryan**, **Indo-Germanic**) A vast language family occupying most of Europe and much of western and southern Asia and formerly also occupying much of Anatolia and central Asia; since the European expansion, IE languages now also predominate in the Americas, Australia and New Zealand, and are prominent elsewhere. Today the family has more speakers than any other family on earth. Its principal branches include **Celtic, Germanic, Italic, Albanian, Greek, Balto-Slavic, Armenian, Indo-Iranian**, and the extinct **Anatolian** and **Tocharian**. The extinct **Illyrian** and **Phrygian** are also usually counted as separate branches of the family. A number of extinct IE languages are sparsely recorded and often difficult to classify.

The IE family began to be recognized in the eighteenth century; the English physician James Parsons was aware of it in his 1767 book *Remains of Japhet*, but Sir William Jones is usually credited with making the first public declaration of the family, in 1786. Latin, Greek and Sanskrit were the first members to be recognized, followed in the next few years by most of the other branches, though Albanian was not recognized as IE until 1854, and the two main extinct branches only turned up in texts discovered around the turn of the twentieth century.

For surveys of the family and its prehistory, see Lockwood (1969, 1972), Baldi (1983), Giacalone Ramat and Ramat (1998), Beekes (1995) and Szemerényi (1996), in order of increasing detail and density. See **Proto-Indo-European** and the **Indo-European homeland problem**.

Indo-European fallacy The fallacious belief that huge and far-flung
language families like **Indo-European** are the norm, while tiny
families are unusual and isolates are positively anomalous. The truth
is otherwise. True, only a handful of families represent the great
majority of *speakers*. With around 2.5 billion speakers, Indo-European represents about 50 per cent of the world's population; the
addition of Sino-Tibetan, with its 1.1 billion, already represents over
70 per cent of the total speakers. Only six more families have as many
as 100 million speakers: Austronesian, Afro-Asiatic, Niger-Congo,
Dravidian, Japanese and Altaic (whose genetic unity is denied by
some). Only a further three families have over 30 million: Austro-
Asiatic, Tai and Korean. These eleven families therefore represent
close to 98 per cent of the world's population. (Figures from Crystal
1997: 289.)

However, counting languages gives a very different result. There
are perhaps 6500 living spoken languages (Grimes 1992). Only
Niger-Congo and Austronesian contain as many as 1000 languages;
otherwise, only Indo-European, Afro-Asiatic and Nilo-Saharan contain as many as 100 languages (and the genetic unity of Nilo-Saharan
is again debatable). Most families are very small, with six languages
or fewer, and isolates are very numerous. (Crystal cites 296, but this
includes some dead languages.) The linguist Johanna Nichols has
repeatedly stressed the observation that between 35 and 50 per cent
of the world's languages are isolates or members of tiny families, and
condemns ambitious macro-groupings that sweep up isolates as
'pathological' (1990: 492).

There are therefore grounds for suspecting that the growth and
spread of huge families is a relatively recent development in human
affairs, and that, until only a few thousand years ago, most of the
planet was occupied by an enormous diversity of small families and
isolates. Such a conclusion would have the most profoundly negative
consequences for the search for **remote relationships**. Compare
the **Nostratic fallacy**.

Indo-European homeland problem The problem of identifying the
geographical area in which PIE was spoken. The issue has been
debated for a century or more, with no consensus in sight. The single
most popular proposal is the Pontic steppes (see the **Kurgan
hypothesis**), but the Near East, Anatolia, central Asia and the
Balkans have all been vigorously defended, while some have argued
for east central Europe, the Baltic coast, northern Europe and Egypt,
and the more implausible suggestions include Africa, the Pacific

coast of Asia and the North Pole. For critical surveys of the proposals, see Mallory (1973, 1989: ch. 6, 1998); for the most recent defence of central Asia, see Nichols (1997a). See the **homeland problem**.

Indo-European root theory The body of theoretical work upon the nature of verbal roots in PIE. Our current understanding has been assembled by generations of work, but by far the most influential contribution has been that of Émile Benveniste (1935: 147–173). The main points are as follows. (1) A root is monosyllabic and always has the basic form *CeC-*. (2) The two consonants are subject to certain constraints: they may not be identical (hence no **pep-*) (exception: **ses-* 'lie', with two sibilants, is permitted); they may not both be voiced plosives (hence no **beg-*); they may not consist of a voiceless plosive and a voiced aspirated plosive, in either order (hence no **bhet-* or **tebh-*) (exception: after *s*, forms like **steygh-* 'go up' are possible). (3) A resonant may be present before or after the vowel, as in **lewbh-* 'love' and **gwey-* 'live', but there may not be two consecutive resonants (hence no **tewrk-* or **teyw-*). (4) The root may be optionally preceded by *s*-**mobile**, as in **teg-* ~ **steg-* 'cover' (possibly from metanalysis of a preceding inflectional *-s*). (5) The root is subject to **ablaut**. (6) The root may be followed by an ablauting suffix, in either of two patterns, or *themes*, or *stems;* in *theme one*, the root is in full grade and accented, and the suffix is in zero-grade, while in *theme two* the root is in zero grade and the suffix is in full grade and accented (hence **pet-* 'fly' plus suffix **-er-* can yield either **pét-r-* or **pt-ér*). (Suffixes generally have identifiable grammatical functions.) (7) A root with no suffix, or a suffixed root in theme one, may take one *determinative* (*extension, enlargement*) of unknown function; this consists only of a single consonant, so that **wel-* 'wish, hope' can form **wel-p-* or **wel-d-*, and **yew-* 'join' can take a suffix to form **yew-g-* and then a determinative to form **yew-g-s-*. (8) A suffixed root in theme two may take a **nasal infix**, so that **yew-*, with suffix **-eg-* in theme two appearing as **yw-eg-*, may form **yu-n-eg*. (9) The addition of any further suffixes or determinatives renders the result nominal, rather than verbal. (10) In some contexts a root can exhibit a reduced form, as for example with **steH₂-* 'stand', which has a reduced form **st-* in some formations. Though highly attractive, and rather successful, this account runs into a number of difficulties, and Szemerényi (1996: 130–133) concludes that some PIE roots simply did not adhere to the usual patterns. See **laryngeal base, diphthongal root, original long vowel**.

Indo-Germanic An obsolete name for **Indo-European**, based on German *Indogermanisch*, which is still current.

Indo-Hittite hypothesis The hypothesis that Proto-Anatolian is not a daughter of Proto-Indo-European but a sister of it. Proposed by Edgar Sturtevant in 1926, but only published posthumously in 1962, this hypothesis is by no means obviously distinct from the view that Anatolian was simply the first branch of IE to split off from the rest. Indo-Hittite has found little support among specialists, but there is much more sympathy for the view that **Anatolian** was indeed the first branch to split off, and Warnow *et al.* (1995) have made an explicit case for this. See Sturtevant (1962), and see the *Herkunfthypothese* and the *Schwundhypothese*.

Indo-Iranian A huge branch of the **Indo-European** family, itself consisting of three branches: **Indo-Aryan**, **Iranian** and the small **Nuristani**.

Indo-Pacific A proposed language family put forward by Greenberg (1971) and including all the **Papuan** languages plus **Andamanese** and the extinct and poorly recorded **Tasmanian languages**. The proposal has won little support, and has indeed been fiercely criticized.

Indo-Uralic A proposed language family including **Indo-European** and **Uralic**. Put forward by Vilhelm Thomsen in 1869 on the basis of similar personal pronouns and occasionally embraced since, this hypothesis enjoys almost no support today, at least as a single taxon, but note that both the **Nostratic** and **Eurasiatic** hypotheses include both these families within larger groupings. See Oswalt (1991: 397–401) for a brief survey with references.

Indus Valley language An extinct and unidentified language spoken in the Indus Valley and Baluchistan, possibly from the fourth millennium BC, and recorded in a number of texts written between 2500 and 1900 BC in a unique and undeciphered script related to no other. The Indus civilization, whose main sites were Mohenjo-Daro and Harappa, was apparently destroyed around 1900 BC. The language's affinities are naturally unknown, though the favourite guess is a link with **Dravidian**, and many have seen the destruction as the work of invading speakers of **Indo-Aryan**.

infixation A morphological process in which a grammatical morpheme is inserted into the middle of a lexical morpheme, as when the Tagalog verb-stems *basag* 'break' and *sulat* 'write' take the past-tense infix *-um-* to yield *bumasag* 'wrote' and *sumulat* 'wrote'. The historical origin of infixes is well understood only in some cases.

Ingvaeonic A name sometimes given to the Germanic dialects spoken along the North Sea coast of continental Europe in the early centuries AD; it was the Ingvaeonic speech of the Germanic tribes who invaded Britain that became English, while the Ingvaeonic varieties remaining behind became Frisian and Low German. The terms *Istvaeonic* and *Erminonic*, formerly applied to central and southern Germanic dialects, respectively, are now little used. All three names derive from a classification of the Germanic peoples provided by Tacitus.

inheritance The retention in a language (possibly with some alteration in form) of a feature which was present in an ancestor of that language. For example, English *father* is inherited from Old English *fæder*, which in turn is inherited from PIE **pətér-*.

initial branching The splitting of a single language into some number of immediate daughter languages. Linguists often prefer to draw **family trees** in which any given language has only two or three daughters, on the ground that the simultaneous fission of a language into eight or ten daughters is historically implausible. For discussion of this point, see Nichols (1998). The case of IE, with its customary ten or twelve major branches, is puzzling, but see the **Pennsylvania model of IE**.

initial dropping An unusual type of phonological change in which word-initial consonants or even word-initial syllables are systematically lost. A number of Australian languages have undergone initial-dropping, with dramatic consequences for the forms of words. For example, Proto-Pama-Nyungan **gudaga* 'dog', preserved unchanged today in some languages, occurs in Uraði as /utaɣa/, in Mpalityan as /twa/, in Ntraʔɲit as /uʔa/, in Mbiywom as /two/ and in Mbabaram, amusingly, as /dɔg/. See Dixon (1980: 195–207).

initialism A word constructed by combining the initial letters of the significant words in a phrase of the same meaning, in such a way that the result cannot be pronounced as a word and must be spelled out letter by letter, such as *BBC* for *British Broadcasting Corporation*. Compare **acronym**.

injunctive A set of verb-forms, marked for person and number but not for tense or aspect, found in Sanskrit and, more marginally, in some other early IE languages. Their PIE status is debatable; see Hoffmann (1967).

inkhornism (also **aureate word**) A word which is deliberately constructed on the basis of a classical language. Very many of these were proposed in English during the sixteenth and seventeenth centuries. Some have found a secure place in the language: *affirmation*, *maturity*, *persist*. Most, however, failed to gain acceptance: *commixture* 'blending together', *adiuvate* 'help', *obtestate* 'beseech', *disgregation* 'separation'. Compare **hypernativism**.

inlaut The interior of a word, or a segment in this position. Compare **anlaut**, **auslaut**.

innovating 1. Of a linguistic form, exhibiting the effects of a change; newer, as opposed to an earlier version of the same form or to an earlier form of the same meaning or function. 2. Of a language, exhibiting the effects of one or more changes which have not occurred in related languages, either in general or in a particular respect. The opposite in both cases is **conservative**.

innovating-centre principle Another term for the **peripheral-region criterion**.

innovation (also **apomorphy**) Any change in a language; but see the qualification under **speaker-innovation**.

innovation-defined subgroup A subgroup (branch) of a language family which is defined by one or more shared innovations found within that branch but not elsewhere in the family. This is normally considered the most secure way of defining a subgroup, providing the innovations invoked are not so natural and frequent that they could easily occur independently; but see **independent parallel innovation**.

inorganic See under **organic**.

input A linguistic form, or a set of linguistic forms, which is present in a language at a given moment and which is affected by a change. In a rule-based account of change, the input is the form to which the rule applies directly. In the case of sequential changes (rules), the output of an earlier one may serve as the input to the next one; see **rule ordering**.

inscription A written text carved on to a hard and durable material such as stone, bone or metal. Compare **manuscript**. The study of inscriptions is **epigraphy**.

insertion 1. Another term for **epenthesis**. 2. See **rule insertion**.

inspection The first step in **comparison**: merely casting one's eye over lists of words or forms in the languages of interest, in order to see whether any apparent similarities or patterns present themselves. Unless we have chosen our languages shrewdly, we are unlikely to find anything of interest, but this step is still necessary to allow an investigator to get a handle on material that may be genuinely promising. Most linguists see inspection as only the prelude to the real work of identifying grammatical and phonological correspondences and performing **reconstruction**, but the proponents of **multilateral comparison** claim that inspection alone is sufficient to establish subgroups and even totally new families.

intensification The use of linguistic means to add stress, intensity or importance to what is being said. This is an area of rapid linguistic change, since speakers are constantly searching for ways of underlining their remarks above and beyond those which are already established.

intensity of contact In a case of **language contact**, the degree of bilingualism on the part of speakers. The greater the proportion of bilingual speakers, the greater their fluency in both languages and the longer the time over which bilingualism is maintained, then the greater the linguistic effects of contact are likely to be.

interference (also **transfer**) The non-deliberate carrying of linguistic features from your mother tongue into a second language which you also speak. Many (not all) linguists are careful to distinguish this from **borrowing** (sense 2).

interlanguage A language system created by someone learning a foreign language, typically a reduced version of that foreign language with many features carried over from the learner's mother tongue. It is possible in principle for an interlanguage to become a mother tongue, leading to a **semi-creole**.

interlect Any speech variety used as a vehicle of communication between speakers of different languages, such as a **koiné** or a **pidgin**.

interlinear gloss A **gloss** written between the lines of the main text, as opposed to within the body of the text or in the margin.

internal change (also **endogenous innovation**) Any linguistic change in a language which does not result from the influence of another language. Some have doubted whether internal change ever occurs at all, but there is little doubt that it does. For example, voicing of intervocalic plosives recurs constantly in languages, while devoicing of intervocalic plosives is virtually unknown; this is scarcely comprehensible unless intervocalic voicing is the result of obvious internal factors. Compare **external change**.

internal evidence Evidence about the history or prehistory of a language obtained by scrutinizing the language itself. For example, the vowel alternations typical of **Trisyllabic Laxing** provide evidence about the earlier nature of the English vowel system. Compare **external evidence**.

internal explanation of change Any proposal to account for language by appealing to nothing but the linguistic system and possibly also universal tendencies, with no appeal to **language contact** or to changes in the world. See **explanation of change** for the various internal explanations which have been proposed.

internal history The history and prehistory of a language as a linguistic system – that is, the development over time of its vocabulary, phonology, morphology, syntax and semantics, without reference to its geographical location, to its speakers or to their political or social circumstances. Compare **external history**.

internal reconstruction Any type of **reconstruction** which works exclusively with the forms existing in a single language, with no comparison involving forms from other languages or dialects. In the most straightforward case, the method works like this: we note that a pattern exists in a language but that some forms are exceptions to the pattern; we hypothesize that the exceptional forms once conformed regularly to the pattern but were disturbed by regular phonological change; we therefore reconstruct regular forms for the exceptional cases and identify the changes which have disrupted the pattern in their case.

When conditions are favourable, internal reconstruction can be an extremely powerful method; it was, for example, the method used by Saussure to reconstruct the **laryngeal** consonants of PIE. Nevertheless, some historical linguists have often been sceptical of the method, regarding it as less reliable than the **comparative method** and sometimes dismissing it altogether. For example, linguists as eminent as Saussure (!) and Meillet declared in print that no historical work could be done on the isolated language **Basque** for want of any relatives to compare it with. In fact, specialists in Basque have applied the internal method with some considerable success in reconstructing the prehistory of the language. Here is an example from Trask (1990).

Most ancient Basque verbs exhibit the form *e-Root-i, where e- and -i are identifiable affixes and the root recurs in finite forms. (This conclusion itself was arrived at by internal reconstruction.) Yet a sizeable number exhibit the different pattern *e-Morph[n], in which the suffix -i is absent and the morph following the prefix always ends in -n. The verbs in this second class further exhibit a number of anomalies absent from the more regular first group: for example, the -n is schizophrenic, behaving sometimes like part of the root but at other times like a suffix; finite forms of these verbs do not exhibit the -n and regularly end in a vowel but yet take the variants of suffixes which normally occur after consonants rather than after vowels, as though the verbal root ended in an invisible consonant; the word-forming suffixes -te and -le unexpectedly appear as -ite and -ile with these verbs. For a long time, specialists simply assumed that Pre-Basque had two different classes of verbs, but there is a better explanation. Early medieval Basque underwent the categorical loss of intervocalic /-n-/, a conclusion also reached by internal reconstruction, since the loss resulted in a number of alternations; and the verbs in the first (regular) group do not have roots ending in /n/.

We may therefore conclude that the second (anomalous) class of verbs were originally perfectly regular members of the first group, those which happened to have roots ending in /n/. The loss of /n/ produced several anomalies in the paradigms of these verbs, anomalies which were then acted on by various instances of **analogy** to produce the patterns we see today.

For textbook accounts of internal reconstruction, see Fox (1995: ch. 7), Trask (1996: ch. 9), Lass (1997: 232–241) or Hock (1986: ch. 17). See **alternation** and compare **comparative reconstruction**.

internationalization The tendency, over time, for languages (especially politically important languages) to become more similar in their vocabularies, because of the worldwide spread of scientific terms like *geology* and *plutonium* and of terms pertaining to popular culture, like *pizza*, *striptease*, *ski*, *whisky*, *video* and *sex-appeal*.

intimate borrowing Another term for **dialect mixing**.

intraparadigmatic analogy An instance of **analogy** involving different inflected forms within a single paradigm, as when, in certain West Saxon nouns, the nominative plural ending -*a* was extended to the accusative plural, displacing earlier -*e*, thereby making the two forms identical, by analogy with other noun-classes in which the two forms were already identical.

intraparadigmatic force The term used by van Marle and Smits (1989) to denote the spread of a particular linguistic form within a single paradigm. An example, in American Dutch, is the spread of third-singular verb-forms to first singular and third plural. Compare **extraparadigmatic force**.

intrusion Another term for **epenthesis**.

intrusive language A language which has spread into an area in which it was formerly not present, particularly when by doing so it has separated earlier languages which were formerly spoken in a contiguous area, or when it has left itself isolated from the remainder of its own family. For example, the discontinuous distribution of the Dravidian and Munda languages in the Indian subcontinent is consistent with the common view that the Indo-Aryan languages are intrusive into the region formerly occupied by these two groups, and the Uralic language Hungarian has moved deep into IE-speaking territory, leaving its nearest relatives far to the east. Compare **relic language**.

intrusive *r* In some non-rhotic accents of English, an /r/ which appears at the end of a word ending in one of certain vowels when the next word begins with a vowel, even though no /r/ was ever historically present there, as a result of the generalization of the **linking** *r*. President John Kennedy famously said things like *Cuba*[r] *and China*; in the south of England, the name of the squash player *Lisa Opie* is pronounced (apparently) *Lisa Ropie*, and the American football team is (apparently) called the *Philadelphia Regals*. This can even happen in the middle of a word, as in *draw*[r]*ing*.

intrusive segment A segment introduced by **epenthesis**.

invasion zone (also **sump**) A term used by T. Kaufman (1990) to denote a geographical region most of whose languages have originated elsewhere. Kaufman finds several such zones in South America.

invented language A language which is consciously and deliberately constructed by the adults in a single speech community and which is usually intended to be used exclusively in ritual or ceremonial contexts. The frequency of such inventions is unknown, but a particularly clear case appears to be the Australian language *Damin*, used in ritual contexts by initiated males of the Lardil tribe; Damin's tiny vocabulary and remarkable inventory of unusual segment-types leads most investigators to conclude that the language was deliberately invented (Dixon 1980: 66–67). No case is known of an invented language becoming a mother tongue. See **non-genetic language** and compare **artificial language**. Compare **secret language**.

invention Another term for **word-manufacture**.

inverse spelling (or **inverse graphy**) An unetymological spelling which arises as follows: two distinct phonemes A and B, which traditionally have distinct spellings, undergo merger as B, and as a result the traditional spelling of A comes to be used in cases in which B is etymological. For example, early Latin /ei/ (spelled <ei>) merged with /iː/ (spelled <i>), and as a result the spelling <ei> came to be used for some words which had always had /iː/. See **back spelling**.

inverted reconstruction Another term for **top–down reconstruction**.

invisible hand A view of **language change** developed by Keller (1990). Keller argues that the accumulation of individual tiny decisions by large numbers of people produces a result neither intended nor envisaged by any of them: a change in the language.

iotacism Any phonological change, or more commonly a set of changes, in which other vocalic nuclei develop into the high front vowel /i/. The term is particularly applied to Greek, in which no fewer than eight distinct vocalic nuclei of the pre-classical period (/i iː e ɛː u uː ei oi/) have merged as /i/ in modern Greek.

Iranian A group of nearly fifty languages, some of them extinct, forming one branch of the **Indo-Iranian** branch of **Indo-European**. The two ancient Iranian languages called **Avestan** and **Old Persian** are of great linguistic importance. Among the modern languages are *Persian* (*Farsi*), *Kurdish* and *Pashto*. The extinct **Scythian** was probably Iranian. See N. Sims-Williams (1998) for an account.

Iroquoian A family of about fifteen languages in eastern North America, about half of them now extinct. Among them are *Huron*, *Mohawk*, *Seneca* and *Tuscarora*. Apart from **Algonquian**, these were the first indigenous languages encountered by European settlers. Attempts at grouping Iroquoian further with such families as **Caddoan, Siouan, Hokan** and **Muskogean** in macro-families variously called **Macro-Siouan** or **Hokan-Siouan** have attracted interest, but no such proposal is established.

irreversibility of merger Another term for **Garde's Principle** (sense 1).

isogloss A line drawn on a **dialect map** to represent a fairly sharp boundary between two competing linguistic forms used in neighbouring areas. Isoglosses cannot always be drawn, because the boundaries between competing forms are not always sharp. Compare **isopleth, typological isogloss**.

isogloss bundle A group of **isoglosses** which all fall in roughly the same place. Such a bundle, when it exists, may be evidence for a fairly sharp boundary between two adjoining but distinct speech varieties, or **dialects**.

isolate Another term for **isolated language**.

isolated form A linguistic form which was formerly a regular part of a paradigm but which, as a result of some combination of changes, has become detached from that paradigm and is no longer regarded as part of it. For example, the Basque noun *goi* 'high place, height, summit' took the allative case-suffix *-ra* 'to' to produce **goira* 'upwards', but this frequently used form has undergone irregular reduction to *gora*, which is now a distinct lexical item meaning 'up' and no longer regarded as related to *goi*, which remains in the language. The process leading to this is **relexicalization**. Compare **demorphologization**.

isolated language (also **isolate**) A language which does not appear to be genetically related to any other known languages at all. As has been stressed by Johanna Nichols in several recent publications, isolates are much more numerous than is commonly supposed; Crystal (1997: 289) counts nearly 300 of them. Among the best-known isolates are **Basque** in western Europe, **Burushaski** in the Himalayas, **Nahali** in India, **Yukaghir** and *Ket* in Siberia (though Ket has some recorded but extinct relatives; see **Yeniseian**), **Yuchi** and **Zuni** in North America, **Bai** in China, and possibly **Songhai** in north Africa (this is debated). **Japanese**, **Korean** and **Ainu** are commonly regarded as isolates, in spite of attempts at linking them to one another and to **Altaic**. Many dead languages of ancient Europe and the Near East were apparently isolates, including **Iberian**, **Etruscan**, **Sumerian** and **Hattic**. See the **Indo-European fallacy**.

isomorphy (also **one-meaning-one-form**, **semantic transparency**, **transparency**) The state of affairs in a language in which a single form always has the same meaning or function, and a single meaning or function is always expressed by the same form. Many linguists have maintained that languages (or their speakers) tend strongly to prefer this state of affairs, to resist changes that would produce violations, and to remove violations, when these do arise, by further changes; the putative principle that this is so is called the *Transparency Principle* or the *uniqueness principle*. However, phonological change tends to disrupt isomorphy in two ways. First, it introduces **alternations** into the forms of stems and affixes; *Humboldt's Universal* claims that such alternations tend to be eliminated by the action of **analogy**. (For a critique of this, see Lass 1997: 340–352.) Second, phonological change may convert words of distinct meaning into homophones, a state of affairs called *homonymic clash* or *polysemic clash*. The transparency principle maintains that such clash should be eliminated, usually by replacing one of the affected words, and there are confirming instances of this.

For example, Latin *cattus* 'cat' and *gallus* 'rooster' fell together in Gascon as *gat*, after which the word for 'rooster' was replaced variously by /azã/ (originally 'pheasant'), /begej/ (originally 'vicar') or /put/ (originally 'chick'). Old English *lætan* 'prevent' and *lettan* 'permit' fell together in Middle English as *let*, after which the first was replaced by *forbid* and *prevent*. Old English *cwēn* 'queen' and *cwene*, originally 'woman' but later 'hussy, harlot', fell together in Early Modern English as the homophonous *queen* and *quean*, after which the second was lost.

The notion of linguistic isomorphy was introduced by the philosopher C. S. Peirce but has been pursued by many others; see Givón (1991) for a summary with references.

isopleth On a **dialect map**, a line separating the frequencies of occurrence of some linguistic form above and below a specified reference value. For example, on a map of southern England, where rhotic and non-rhotic pronunciations coexist, a 75 per cent isopleth would mark the boundary between regions in which non-rhotic pronunciations are above and below 75 per cent in frequency. Compare **isogloss**.

Italian The major language of Italy, also spoken in some neighbouring regions, a **Romance** language. Italian is not really a single language, but rather an extensive **dialect continuum** whose regional varieties are often mutually incomprehensible. What unites the speakers is the recognition of an agreed standard form of the language, which itself is largely based upon a literary version of the Tuscan variety. The highly divergent *Sardinian* is normally counted as a separate language, not as a dialect of Italian, while both *Corsican* and *Sicilian* usually are counted as forms of Italian. See Price (1998: 251–276) for a summary and Maiden (1995) or Migliorini (1984) for a history. Devoto (1978) is a linguistic history of the Italian peninsula from pre-Roman times to the present.

Italic A major branch of the **Indo-European** family. Its best-known languages are divided into two main subgroups: **Latino-Faliscan**, consisting of **Latin** and its close relative **Faliscan**, and **Sabellian** (or *Osco-Umbrian*), consisting of **Oscan** and **Umbrian** and some others. The possible Italic status of a number of other very sparsely recorded languages of ancient Italy is uncertain, and specialists differ as to which languages they recognize as Italic. Among the languages sometimes regarded as Italic are **Aequian, Elymian, Marrucinian, Marsian, Paelignian, Pre-Samnite, Sabine, Sicel, South Picene, Venetic, Vestinian** and **Volscian**. Note that many specialists today prefer to use the term *Italic* to denote all the family except Latin and its **Romance** descendants. See Silvestri (1998) for a summary.

Italo-Celtic A proposed grouping of the **Italic** and **Celtic** languages into a single branch of **Indo-European**. Few specialists take this proposal seriously today.

Japanese The principal language of Japan, recorded since about AD 700. Japanese has long been regarded as an **isolated language,** but today an increasing number of scholars are beginning to believe that it belongs to the **Altaic** family, or at least that it belongs with **Tungusic** (and possibly **Korean**) in a **Macro-Tungusic** family, though these conclusions are still far from generally accepted. Some Japanese linguists have preferred to try to link Japanese to various families of southern and southeastern Asia, or even to see Japanese as a **mixed language** in origin. Many specialists prefer to regard the highly divergent *Ryukyuan* dialects as one or more distinct languages, and hence to see Japanese as a tiny family.

Japhetic [*obsolete*] 1. A name applied centuries ago to the languages of Europe, in contrast to the **Hamitic** languages of Africa and the **Semitic** languages of the Middle East. The idea was that these three groupings represented the languages descended from the speech of the three sons of Noah: Shem, Ham and Japheth. 2. An early name for the **Indo-European** family. 3. A hypothetical language family proposed by the eccentric Georgian linguist Nikolai Marr, including most of the non-IE languages of Europe and western Asia, plus Celtic and some American languages. No one takes this seriously today.

Jaqi Another term for **Aymaran**.

jargon 1. The distinctive and special vocabulary of a particular social group, such as lawyers or truck-drivers, consisting of technical terms and markers of solidarity like in-jokes. 2. A speech variety, usually a **pidgin**, which is not a mother tongue but which is used as an **interlect**.

jer (also **yer**) In the ancestor of **Slavic** languages, either of two reduced vowels /ĭ ŭ/, deriving from Proto-Slavic short */i u/. See the **Third Slavic Vowel Shift**.

Jespersen's cycle The tendency of a negative item to be reinforced by a second item, with the result that the negative sense is transferred to the reinforcing item, with the original negative losing its negative force and perhaps even disappearing. A familiar example is the reinforcement of French *ne* 'not' with *pas* '(a) step', with *pas* now having acquired the negative sense and *ne* having largely disappeared from spoken French except in contexts in which it is not perceived as a negative. The cycle was proposed in Jespersen (1917: 4) and named by Dahl (1979); it represents one form of **renewal**.

jocular formation (also **playful formation**) A word which is deliberately coined for humorous effect. Three examples are English *wasm* 'an outdated doctrine', derived from *ism* 'a doctrine', itself extracted from nouns like *Marxism;* English *hypocynophile* 'person who habitually supports the underdog', from Greek elements; and Spanish *feministo* 'man who supports the feminist agenda', with alteration of the normally invariant suffix *-ista* '-ist' to include the overtly masculine ending *-o*. Such formations may become established: the English city of *Liverpool* is affectionately known as *Liverpuddle*, and from this the word *Liverpudlian* has been coined and is now the normal word for denoting an inhabitant of the city; and the word *bikini* 'tiny two-piece bathing costume' was the source of *monokini* 'bikini with no top', which is fully established in French, where it has already been clipped to *mono*.

jodization The conversion of another segment to jod, [j]. An example is the Basque conversion of initial */e/ to /j/ before a non-high vowel, as in **eosi* to *josi* 'sew'.

juncture displacement Another term for **metanalysis**.

Junggrammatiker The German term for the **Neogrammarians**.

junk A slightly facetious term for the fossilized and unsystematic remnants in a language of what was formerly a fully productive grammatical system. Such junk may provide a source for **exaptation**. But see Vincent (1995) for a criticism of the concept of junk.

$$\boxed{\text{K}}$$

Kadai (sometimes also **Daic**) A group of about seven languages spoken along the border of China and Vietnam. It is included in the **Tai-Kadai** hypothesis.

Kafiri An obsolete term for **Nuristani**.

Kam-Sui A group of six languages spoken in southern China. It is included in the **Tai-Kadai** hypothesis.

Kam-Tai Another term for **Tai-Kadai**.

Karen A group of about twenty closely related languages spoken in Burma and western Thailand. The Karen languages clearly belong to **Sino-Tibetan**, but their position is disputed; some see them as part of **Tibeto-Burman**, others as coordinate with Tibeto-Burman in a larger *Tibeto-Karen* grouping coordinate with **Sinitic**.

Kartvelian (also **South Caucasian**) A family of five languages spoken on the southern slopes of the Caucasus; its best-known member is *Georgian*. Kartvelian has no known relatives, but it is included in the **Nostratic** hypothesis.

Keltic An old-fashioned spelling of **Celtic**.

Keresan A language spoken in about seven distinct dialects in New Mexico. Attempts at linking Keresan to other families, notably the **Keresiouan** hypothesis, do not command general assent.

Keresiouan A proposed grouping of **Keresan, Caddoan, Siouan, Iroquoian** and the isolate **Yuchi**, put forward by Greenberg (1987). This proposal has found little support.

Kernwortschatz The German for **basic vocabulary**.

Khoisan A proposed language family of southern Africa, consisting of the *Khoi* ('Hottentot') group, the *San* ('Bushman') group, and the outliers *Hadza* and *Sandawe*; all of these languages are rich in click consonants. Put forward in the 1920s and endorsed by Greenberg (1963b), Khoisan has not been shown to be a valid family, and its genetic validity is doubted by some. See Ruhlen (1991: 114–120) for a historical survey.

Kiowa-Tanoan A family of about nine languages spoken in Oklahoma and New Mexico; its best-known member is *Kiowa*. See **Aztec-Tanoan**.

Kiparsky's Principle In rule-based descriptions of phonological change, the principle that rules tend to change their order so as to maximize **feeding** order – that is, so as to maximize the number of forms to which each rule can apply. The principle was formulated by Kiparsky (1968: 197).

Klingenheben's Law The statement that, in the Chadic language Hausa, an original syllable-final stop becomes /r/ if dental, /w/ otherwise.

koiné A more-or-less uniform variety of a language which develops by the levelling out of originally significant dialectal variation. The term was originally applied to the levelled variety of **Greek** which spread through the empire of Alexander the Great.

koinéization (also **dialect levelling, deregionalization**) The creation of a koiné. Compare **swamping, endohybridization**.

Komuz A primary branch of **Nilo-Saharan**, consisting of seven languages in eastern Sudan and western Ethiopia.

Kordofanian A group of about thirty-two languages spoken in and near southern Sudan. They are now usually regarded as belonging to the **Niger-Congo** family, but perhaps the branch most distant from the entire rest of the family (hence the label *Niger-Kordofanian*). However, the divergent subgroup of Kordofanian called the *Kadugli* languages is still controversial; some specialists see these as not Kordofanian and not even Niger-Congo, and some would place them into the **Nilo-Saharan** family. The Kordofanian languages are not closely related, and the validity of the taxon is queried, even without Kadugli.

Korean The principal language of Korea, also spoken in adjoining parts of China. Korean has long been regarded as an isolated language, but today an increasing number of scholars are beginning to believe that it belongs to the **Altaic** family, or at least that it can be joined to **Tungusic** and **Japanese** in a **Macro-Tungusic** family, though these conclusions are still far from generally accepted.

Kortland's Law A statement about word-accent in the **Baltic** language Old Prussian, put forward by Kortland (1974: 303). It says that a short stressed vowel lost the ictus to the following syllable. See Collinge (1985: 234–235).

Kreislauf Jacob Grimm's famous circular representation of the **First Germanic Consonant Shift,** by which *tenues* changed to *aspiratae*, *mediae* changed to *tenues*, and *aspiratae* changed to *mediae*. For example, with the labials, **p* changed to *f*, **b* to *p*, and **bh* to *b*. This circular arrangement depends upon the mistaken assumption that both voiceless fricatives and voiced aspirates can be reasonably lumped together as 'aspirates'.

Krevinian An extinct and little-known **Fennic** language spoken in parts of Latvia between the fifteenth and nineteenth centuries.

Kronasser's Law The statement that word-meanings tend universally to move from the concrete to the abstract. This is common enough, as when Basque *akats*, originally just 'nick, scratch', acquired the more abstract sense of 'defect' (of any kind), but movements in the opposite direction are by no means unknown. This universal was proposed by Kronasser (1952: 116–117) and named by Kovács (1961).

Kru A primary branch of **Niger-Congo,** containing about forty languages spoken in Liberia and the Ivory Coast.

Kuchean See under **Tocharian**.

Kurgan hypothesis The hypothesis that the Kurgan culture, which flourished in the steppes north of the Black Sea from about the fifth millennium BC, represented the speakers of **Proto-Indo-European**. These people built no permanent settlements but left behind their highly distinctive burial mounds, or *kurgans*. The hypothesis was championed for much of her career by the Lithuanian-American archaeologist Marija Gimbutas; it remains the single most popular solution to the **Indo-European homeland problem**, but it has never commanded anything like general acceptance.

Kwa A primary branch of the **Niger-Congo** family, including about seventy-five languages spoken in west Africa, from the Ivory Coast to Nigeria. Among its best-known members are *Igbo*, *Yoruba* and *Ewe*.

Kwanyama Law See under **Meinhof's Law**.

labialization The addition of lip-rounding to a segment which formerly lacked it. The opposite is **delabialization**.

labio-velar Any one of the PIE consonants commonly reconstructed as a labialized velar: */k^w/, */g^w/, */gh^w/.

Labov-Yaeger-Steiner paradox Another term for the **Bill Peters effect**.

Lachmann's Law A development in early Latin by which a short vowel in a verb-stem was lengthened in certain forms (notably the perfective participle) in certain circumstances. Examples: *ăgō* 'drive', participle *āctus*; *ĕmō* 'buy', *ēmptus*. The conditions are obscure, and the phenomenon has been much debated; commentators cannot even agree whether it is phonological or morphological in nature. It was inexplicitly noted by Lucretius, whose puzzling account was interpreted by Lachmann (1850). See Collinge (1985: 105–114) for a critical discussion with references.

lacuna In a manuscrupt or an inscription, a piece of text which is illegible or missing, because of damage. In an **edition**, a lacuna is marked off by **square brackets** (sense 2).

Lady Mondegreen Another term for **pullet surprise**.

lag [*rare*] Another term for **perseveration**.

Lallwort The German for **nursery word**.

lambdacism Any phonological change in which another segment develops into a lateral. Lambdacism occurs sporadically in Basque: Latin *theca* 'pod' is borrowed as *leka*, French *danger* 'danger' as *langer*, and Spanish *naranja* 'orange' as *laranja*.

landmark model In Heine *et al.* (1991a), the name for a type of **grammaticalization** in which nouns denoting features of the landscape are converted to grammatical items, such as 'sky' to 'on' and 'earth' to 'under'.

Langobardic An extinct and generally unrecorded west **Germanic** language spoken by a people who occupied first Hungary and then, in the sixth century AD, northern Italy.

language as organism The view that a language can be profitably viewed as an independent organism with a kind of 'life of its own'. Strongly associated with certain earlier writers, such as Hermann Paul (1920 [1880]), this conception is arguably also present in the **Neogrammarian Hypothesis** and in Saussure's structuralism. In its most extreme form, this metaphor holds that all language change can be fully understood in terms of internal factors, without reference to any external forces.

language birth (also **language genesis**) The creation of a new natural language. The term is most commonly applied to the appearance of a **non-genetic language**, such as a **creole**.

language builder A speaker perceived as a more or less conscious and deliberate agent engaged in the business of constructing and renewing a language system for the purpose of serving communicative goals. The idea has been developed at length by Claude Hagège (1993).

language chain The term used by Crowley (1997: 252) for a group of geographically adjacent and genetically related languages in which each language appears to be particularly closely related to its own neighbours and no coherent **subgrouping** is possible. This is the logical consequence of a **dialect continuum**.

language change The central object of study in historical linguistics. Every living language is always changing; indeed, it is always in the middle of a number of changes – hence the **Saussurean paradox**.

Historical linguists seek both to elucidate the long sequences of changes which have occurred in the past in particular languages and families and to extract general principles of language change; we have been rather successful in both enterprises. Since the introduction of sociolinguistic techniques in the 1960s, we have also begun to understand something about how language change occurs. McMahon (1994) is a textbook of the study of language change, but see also the textbooks listed under **historical linguistics**.

language cluster The term used by T. Kaufman (1994: 68) for a group of languages or families which have frequently been the object of as-yet unsubstantiated proposals of a remote **genetic relationship**.

language contact (or **contact**) Any change in a language resulting from the influence of a neighbouring language of which the speakers of the first have some knowledge; the passage of linguistic objects or features from one language into another. The effects of contact may range from the trivial to the overwhelming, and may involve vocabulary, phonology, morphology, syntax or just about anything else. The simplest type of contact is **borrowing**, but far more radical types are possible, including (for example) **metatypy**, the creation of **non-genetic languages** and (the ultimate) **language shift**. Weinreich (1953) proposes that this term should be restricted to cases involving substantial bilingualism; compare **culture contact**. See **rule borrowing**.

language death (also **extinction**) The disappearance of a language as a mother tongue. This usually results from peaceful **language shift**, but may involve more dramatic circumstances, as in **language suicide** and **language murder**. See **linguistic obsolescence**.

language family (Ger *Sprachfamilie*) A group of languages which all derive from a single common ancestor – that is, they all started off at some time in the past as no more than regional dialects of that ancestral language. The languages in a family are therefore linked in a **genetic relationship**. The number of secure language families currently spoken on the planet is around 300; further research will doubtless succeed in reducing this number by combining some families into larger families, but it is most unlikely that we will ever get the total below about 200, if that. Ambitious and often speculative attempts at combining recognized families into huge macro-families are not lacking, but few such proposals enjoy any significant support, for lack of persuasive evidence. Even the **Nostratic** hypothesis, the most sober of all these proposals, enjoys only very limited support at present. Note that an **isolated language** forms a family all by itself.

language fissure See under **social-network model**.

language fusion See under **social-network model**.

language genesis Another term for **language birth**.

language maintenance 1. The retention of a language as a mother tongue, in the face of pressure from a more prestigious language threatening to displace it. 2. The tendency of a language to remain as it is and to resist change.

language missionary An individual who, as a result of moving from one place to another, is influential in spreading speech-forms from one community to another. The term was introduced by the dialectologist Anders Steinsholt; see Milroy (1992: 198–199).

language murder A type of **language death** brought about by savage persecution of the language's speakers by those in power. This persecution may range from severe discrimination against the language's speakers up to and including murdering them. Two cases in point are the Yahi language of California and the indigenous languages of Tasmania, both of whose speakers were slaughtered by white settlers who coveted their land.

language-oriented framework (also **system-oriented framework**) An approach to historical linguistics which views languages as objects existing independently of their speakers and as the proper domain of investigation. This approach has long been the norm in historical work (and see Lass 1997 for a defence), but it is now being challenged by the **speaker-oriented framework**.

language planning (also **linguistic engineering**) Making deliberate decisions about the form of a language, especially when this is done more or less officially and on a large scale. As a result of political changes in the twentieth century leading to greater importance for their languages, speakers of Finnish, Basque and Belarusian (for example) have undertaken large-scale programmes of language planning, both to establish standard forms (previously lacking) and to permit the use of these languages for all purposes (for example, by constructing technical vocabularies). In the Belarusian case, there was a further factor: the desire to distance the language from the closely related Russian (see *Abstand*). Language planning may be divided into *selection* (choosing the language or variety to be planned), *codification* (determining the linguistic forms to be accepted as standard), *elaboration* (introducing new vocabulary and other features to allow the language to be used for any purpose), *implementation* (teaching the new form and persuading people to accept it) and *acceptance* (use by the community).

language shift The process in which a speech community makes steadily decreasing use of its ancestral language and increasing use of another language seen as more valuable or more prestigious. This process typically occurs over several generations, with the ancestral language being confined to fewer and fewer contexts; often there are linguistic consequences for the ancestral language, as it loses ever more features which it formerly had (see **linguistic obsolescence**), and the final outcome is usually **language death**. This is one form of **acculturation**. Nichols (1997b: 372) argues that language shift should be the default explanation for the displacement of one language by another, rather than major population movements. See Thomason and Kaufman (1988: ch. 5).

language spread The movement of a language into an area in which it was formerly not spoken. There are three known mechanisms: **language shift, demic diffusion** and **migration**, though perhaps none of these ever occurs in a 'pure' form.

language succession In **linguistic geography**, the chronological sequence of languages which are dominant over time in a particular geographical region.

language suicide A type of **language death** in which the speakers of a language consciously and deliberately abandon it in favour of another language seen as more prestigious or more valuable; typically such speakers refuse to let their children learn or use the language being abandoned.

lapsus calami A slip of the pen; an error made by a scribe in writing or copying a document. On occasion, it can be difficult to decide whether we are looking at a rare or unusual form or only at a *lapsus*.

laryngeal Any one of several hypothetical consonants posited as having existed in PIE and as having been lost in most of the IE languages. Laryngeals were proposed by Ferdinand de Saussure (1879); he counted them among his *coefficients sonantiques*, and he recognized two of them. Today three laryngeals are commonly recognized, notated H_1, H_2 and H_3, though a few specialists prefer four or some other number, and one or two specialists still reject laryngeals altogether. Saussure originally proposed these hypothetical consonants in order to account for the forms of certain roots which departed from the usual PIE form, but they later came to be invoked in accounting for a number of puzzling phonological and morphological problems. Saussure arrived at his hypothetical consonants purely by **internal reconstruction**, but in 1927 Jerzy Kuryłowicz pointed out that the recently discovered **Hittite**, still unknown in Saussure's day, appeared to preserve H_2 as a consonant written *h*. (It is possible that **Armenian** and **Greek** also preserve overt reflexes of laryngeals in a few cases, notably in their 'prothetic vowels'; see Clackson (1994: 32–49).) The name *laryngeal* is arbitrary and meaningless; the precise phonetic nature of the sounds is unknown, though there is no shortage of speculations, with the favourite guesses being $H_1 = [ʔ]$, $H_2 = [x]$ and $H_3 = [ɣ^w]$. See Lindemann (1987) for a presentation of the laryngeal theory, Szemerényi (1973) for a history, Szemerényi (1996: 121–130) for a critical review, Anttila (1989: 266–273) for an account of the internal reconstruction, and Beekes (1995: 142–148) for a survey of the historical development of the laryngeals in the daughter languages. The term *laryngeal* is occasionally applied also to reconstructed consonants of uncertain phonetic nature in other language families, such as Austronesian and Dravidian.

laryngeal base (also **heavy base**) In PIE, a root containing a **laryngeal**. Such roots typically retain a distinctive word–accent in Lithuanian, Latvian and Serbo-Croatian. The Sanskrit *seṭ*-roots are generally laryngeal bases.

Latin The language of the city of Rome in the first millennium BC, which later became the principal language in much of the Roman Empire. Latin belongs to the **Italic** branch of **Indo-European**, and we have records of several of its close relatives, all spoken in Italy and all long extinct. The language is sparsely recorded from the fifth or sixth century BC, and copiously attested for centuries after. The early inscriptions, and some early literary works, are written in a variety of the language called *Old Latin*. By the time the Roman Republic was extending its political control around the Mediterranean, a codified literary variety called *classical Latin* was in regular use; this variety was undoubtedly already noticeably conservative and somewhat distant from everyday speech. During the centuries of the Roman Empire, and long after its breakup, educated people continued to write in classical Latin as best they could, even though the spoken language was steadily becoming ever more different from the written standard; we apply the name *Vulgar Latin* to the spoken language, which is occasionally recorded in writing, though only in fragments, and we give the name *Late Latin* to the written language in use from about the third to the seventh centuries AD. Eventually, of course, spoken Latin broke up into a dialect continuum of regional varieties which became ever more different from one another and increasingly lacking in mutual intelligibility, and the more prominent of these regional varieties evolved into conspicuously different languages, the **Romance** languages. Meanwhile, educated people all over Europe continued to write in an approximation to classical Latin, though this *Medieval Latin* was often influenced by the local spoken languages, and it acquired a sizeable number of new words from various sources. See Price (1998: 286–293) and Vineis (1998), and see Roger Wright (1982) for a case that Latin as we know it was invented during the Carolingian Renaissance.

Latino-Faliscan A branch of **Italic** consisting of **Latin** and **Faliscan**.

Lautgesetz The German for **sound law**.

Lautschieber The German for 'sound-shifter': a term of abuse hurled at the **Neogrammarians** by those opponents who prefer to see language change as more complex, more 'organic' and more human-centred than is seemingly permitted in an approach based on 'exceptionless sound laws'.

Lautverschiebung See under **sound law**.

law 1. A statement which purports to describe a particular change, or set of changes, which took place in the past in some particular language or languages. This is the most usual sense of *law* in historical linguistics; it is the sense present in **sound law**, but not all such statements pertain to phonological changes, and it is also the sense present in the majority of named laws, such as **Grimm's Law**, **Bartholomae's Law** and **Grassmann's Law**. Note carefully that the presence in the handbooks of a named law does not imply that the process was exceptionless, or that specialists agree on the precise formulation of the law, on the languages in which the change occurred, or even on whether any such process ever occurred at all. See Collinge (1985: 1–2) for critical discussion. 2. A statement which purports to express some general principle of language change – that is, a statement that, if anything happens at all, certain changes are far more likely to occur than others. This is the sense of the term in the phrase *laws of analogy* (see **analogy, laws of**). See Fox (1995: 194–206) for discussion.

law of the stronger Another term for **Grammont's Law**.

laxing Any change in which a tense vowel becomes lax. Often this term is used as a synonym for **shortening**, but laxing can occur without shortening: for example, in Canadian French, which generally lacks contrasts of vowel length, the high vowels /i y u/ are laxed to [ɪ ʏ ʊ] in closed syllables. The opposite is **tensing**.

layering Especially in **grammaticalization**, the simultaneous existence within a language of several grammatical patterns within a single subsystem, all reflecting the outcomes of several temporally distinct changes. For example, the English verbal system exhibits ablauting inflections, the dental preterite, modal and non-modal auxiliaries, and recently grammaticalized forms like *keep V-ing* and *be going to V*. See Hopper and Traugott (1993: 124–126).

learnèd word (also **learnèd borrowing**) A word which is borrowed into a language from a prestigious ancestral form of that language and which fails to exhibit the phonological developments which would have occurred had it been transmitted normally. For example, Spanish *fábula* 'fable' is a learnèd borrowing from Latin *fabula(m)*, since normal transmission would have produced **habla*. (Compare the Spanish verb *hablar* 'speak', from a late Latin **fabulare*.) Compare **semi-learnèd word**.

least-effort principle Another term for the **economy-of-effort principle**.

leaving element In a **chain shift**, any segment which moves out of a phonological space it formerly occupied, that space often being occupied in turn by another segment, the **entering element**.

lect Any distinguishable variety of a language.

lectal differentiation See under **social-network model.**

lectal linkage See under **social-network model.**

lectio difficilior   The Latin for 'the more difficult reading'. Among
   different manuscript copies of a single text, it sometimes happens
   that the copies differ substantially at some point, with one copy
   having an opaque or largely unintelligible word or phrase where
   another has a different and transparent one. The more opaque
   version is the *lectio difficilior*, while the more transparent one is the
   lectio facilior, or 'easier reading'. It is often assumed that the *lectio
   difficilior* represents the earlier and more authentic version, and that
   the transparent one results from the effort of puzzled copyists to
   'make sense' of it by replacing it with something they can understand. In **etymology** and **onomastics**, the label *lectio difficilior* is
   also applied to a variant form of a word or name which is harder to
   understand or explain than another variant.

Lees equation The equation used in **glottochronology** for calculating
   dates of separation of related languages. It is this: t = (log C)/(2 log
   r), where t is the time elapsed since separation (in thousands of
   years), C is the percentage of cognates shared by the two languages
   (expressed as a decimal), and r is the *glottochronological constant*, a
   measure of the rate of retention of vocabulary, most often taken as
   about 0.80. For the derivation, see Lees (1953).

legitimization The term used by Milroy (1992) for the process by which
   certain linguistic forms come to be accepted as constituting a
   standard language, particularly when this is done by legislation
   rather than through a consensus of speakers. See **historicization.**

Lehnwort The German for **loan word.**

lemma 1. A headword entered in a dictionary. 2. A reconstructed or
   attested form which serves to head a list of linguistic forms which are
   historically descended from it. 3. A historically attested form representing a reconstructed root, when this is presented in an etymological dictionary. For example, the PIE root *kel- 'cover, conceal' is
   attested in such lemmas as English *hell, hall, hole, hull* and *helm*, Old
   Norse *höll* 'hall', Latin *color* 'colour' and *cēlāre* 'conceal', and Greek

kalyptein 'cover, conceal', among others. 4. A cited linguistic form accompanied by a **gloss**. In the example of Old Spanish *asmar* 'invent, think up', *asmar* is the lemma.

Lemnian The language of a single inscription found on the Greek island of Lemnos and dating from the seventh or sixth century BC. Largely unintelligible, Lemnian is suspected of being related to **Etruscan**.

lengthened grade See under **ablaut**.

lengthening Any phonological change in which a formerly short segment (usually a vowel) becomes long. For example, in Middle English, certain short vowels were lengthened before certain consonant clusters; the ancestors of *gold, child, mild, fiend, bind, climb* and *comb*, all with long vowels, had short vowels in Old English. The opposite is **shortening**. The lengthening of a consonant is more usually called **gemination**. See also **compensatory lengthening**.

length of compared forms The number of segments present in linguistic forms offered in a **comparison**. When the compared forms are very short – only one or two segments – the comparison is less convincing than with longer forms, since a **chance resemblance** is highly possible. For example, it is trivial to find 'matches' for the short Basque word *ar* 'male': Nama *aró* 'masculine', Yakut *är* 'male', Mongolian *ere* 'male', Old Hungarian *erj* 'male', Mande *yar* 'man', Songhai *aru* 'man', and many more.

lenition (also **weakening**) Any phonological change in which a segment becomes less consonant-like than previously. A shift in character from left to right along any of the scales in Table 5 may be regarded as a lenition; a lenition all the way to zero is **loss** (sense 1) or **deletion**.
   See Trask (1996: 55–60) for a survey with examples. The opposite is **fortition**. See **stepwise shift**.

Lepontic An extinct **Celtic** language sparsely recorded in northern Italy between the sixth and first centuries BC, the first Celtic language recorded.

Leskien's Law In Lithuanian, the apparent shortening of an originally long vowel in a final syllable bearing a falling (acute) accent, as in accusative plural *rankàs*, instrumental singular *rankà* (both with

(1) geminate > simplex
(2) stop > fricative > approximant > zero
(3) stop > liquid > zero
(4) oral stop > glottal stop > zero
(5) non-nasal > nasal
(6) voiceless > voice

Table 5

short vowels in the final syllable) versus nominative plural and genitive singular *rañkōs* (with a long vowel), all being derived from original long *$\bar{a}$*. The phenomenon was pointed out by Leskien (1881). See Collinge (1985: 115–116) for a critical account with references.

levelling 1. Any phonological change in which a diphthong (or an even more complex vocalic nucleus) is converted to a pure vowel whose quality is roughly halfway between the initial and final elements of the original diphthong: one type of **monophthongization**. An example is Latin /au/, which was levelled to /o:/ or /o/ in western Romance: Latin *causa*, but Spanish and Italian *cosa*, French *chose* 'thing'. Compare **reduction** (sense 1). 2. See **analogical levelling**. 3. See **paradigm levelling**. 4. The reduction of differences among the dialects of a language.

lexical change Another term for **lexical replacement**, or sometimes for **borrowing** (sense 1).

lexical copying Another term for **borrowing** (sense 1).

lexical diffusion A type of phonological change in which the new pronunciation is introduced suddenly into just a few words of the relevant form and then spreads over time to more and more of the relevant words, possibly (but not necessarily) being finally extended to all relevant words, at which point the change has gone to **completion**. In effect, what was formerly a single phonological class of words is split into two different classes, one of which is initially empty, and words are steadily transferred from one class to the other. Lexical diffusion is phonetically abrupt but lexically gradual; compare *fudging* (under **fudged dialect**). The existence of lexical diffusion had long been suspected, but its reality was only finally demonstrated by Wang (1969) and Chen and Wang (1975). For summaries, see McMahon

(1994: 47–56) and Labov (1994: ch. 15). For an example, see **lexical split**. Note that Campbell (1998: 198–200) doubts the frequency of lexical diffusion. See **probabilistic phonetic conditioning** and **bidirectional diffusion**.

lexical fading The disappearance of an **alternation** from the paradigm of a lexical item. For example, the voicing alternation seen in *leaf / leaves* has disappeared in some varieties of English from certain nouns, such as *house, truth* and *moth*.

lexical innovation [*rare*] Another term for **lexical replacement**.

lexicalist method The name given by Campanile (1998) to the simplest kind of **linguistic palaeontology**: if we can reconstruct PIE **reg-s* 'king' and **owis* 'sheep', then the PIE-speakers must have recognized kings and reared sheep, and, if we can't reconstruct a PIE word for 'sea', then the PIE-speakers were not near a seacoast. Though much practised in the past, this approach runs into a number of difficulties, such as the **beech-tree problem**. Compare the **textual method**.

lexicalization 1. (also **frozen idiom**) Any change in which an inflected or derived form, a compound word or a syntactic construction is reduced to a single simplex lexical item, with consequent loss of earlier morpheme boundaries or word boundaries. Examples include the reduction of Old English *hlæf-dige* 'loaf-kneader' to *lady* and the reduction of the Middle English prepositional phrase *bi cause* 'by cause' to *because*. 2. Any change in which a formerly fully productive alternation becomes confined to certain lexical items only, as has happened in English with **Trisyllabic Laxing**. This is one type of **morphologization**. 3. Another term for **lexification**.

lexical reconstruction See under **reconstruction**.

lexical replacement (rarely also **lexical innovation, lexical change, morpheme decay**) The disappearance from a language of a word (at least in its central sense) in favour of a new word (of whatever origin). For example, native English *andwlita* and *here* were replaced by the French loans *face* and *army*, respectively; native English *hie* was replaced by the Scandinavian loan *they*; British English *wireless* has recently been replaced (for most speakers) by the competing term *radio*; Basque *estudiante* 'student' (a loan from Spanish) has recently been replaced by the neologism *ikasle*, formed from native elements.

The replaced term need not disappear entirely; native English *deer* 'animal' has been replaced in its original sense by the Latin loan *animal*, but remains in use to denote a specific kind of animal. Lexical replacement is pervasive in languages over time, and it constitutes one of the most severe obstacles to the identification of **remote relationships** between languages; it may be true (as often claimed) that words in the **basic vocabulary** are particularly resistant to replacement, but appeals to **lexical sets** (sense 2) like the **Swadesh word list** and the **Dolgopolsky list** must nevertheless be formulated very carefully, with statistical testing, if they are to be of any value.

lexical set 1. A set of words from related languages which exhibit **systematic correspondences** and are presented as **cognates**. 2. A fixed list of specific meanings whose lexical realizations are sought in various languages - for example, to test whether those languages might be genetically related. A familiar example is the **Swadesh word list**, though various other such sets are used by specialists in particular languages or geographical areas. See Nichols (1996: 61–62) for a brief account of the proper use of such sets in seeking genetic links. 3. A set of vocabulary items forming a structured system, such as kinship terms, numerals, colour terms, or words denoting levels of social organization. With such sets, especially in a **proto-language**, it is often more illuminating to study the structure of the system than to ponder the words individually; see W. P. Lehmann (1993: 248–255) for an account.

lexical split 1. A type of phonological change in which a single phoneme undergoes a split into two phonemes under typically complex conditions which are partly predictable and partly arbitrary. An example is the split of earlier /æ/ into /æ/ and /ɑ:/ in the south of England; the low back vowel is now found in *dance* and *chance* but not in *fancy* or *romance*, in *plant* but not in *ant*, in *class* but not in *bass* (fish), in *sample* but not in *ample*, in *demand* and *slander* but not in *land* or *pander*; the back vowel is variably present in *mass* 'religious service' but never present in *mass* 'material', and it is categorical in *plaster* but variable in *plastic*. Lexical split probably results in most cases from **lexical diffusion**. 2. The separation of a single word into two words of distinct meaning which are no longer felt to be related. This has happened, for example, with *pipe* 'tube' and *pipe* (for tobacco), and with *flower* and *flour*.

lexical stratification The division of the vocabulary of a language into words of differing ages, sometimes also including attempts at correlating the various layers of words with different levels of culture. For example, in the early IE languages, -*a*-stem and -*o*-stem nouns are the most numerous, productive and regular type, and were therefore presumably the last type to be formed, while the consonant-stems are less productive and less regular, and therefore presumably represent an older layer of vocabulary. Specht (1947) concludes that most items of the **basic vocabulary** of PIE belong to the second (older) group, while (for example) words pertaining to transport and vehicles belong to the first (newer) group and must therefore represent later additions to the PIE vocabulary, allowing us to infer that the PIE-speakers acquired wheeled vehicles only at a late stage.

lexicostatistics 1. A simple statistical technique for estimating the degree of linguistic divergence between related languages, once **cognates** have been securely identified. It uses a standard word list, typically the **Swadesh word list**. The proportion of cognates shared by two related languages is taken as an indication of their degree of relatedness; the higher the proportion of shared cognates, the closer the languages are linguistically. A celebrated instance is Dyen's (1965) use of lexicostatistics to provide a tree structure for Austronesian; the results are very much in conflict with the subgrouping suggested by all other evidence. Far more dubiously, lexicostatistics has also been applied on occasion to try to discover previously unknown genetic links by a simple process of counting resemblances between the languages, in the hope that these might prove to be 'cognates'. Lexicostatistics was proposed by Morris Swadesh in a series of papers beginning with Swadesh (1950). Note: some people use *lexicostatistics* interchangeably with **glottochronology**, but this is poor practice. 2. Very broadly, any statistical approach to the vocabularies of two or more languages.

lexification (also **lexicalization**) Any development which leads to the creation in a language of a phonological form which must be counted as a lexical item and must therefore be assigned to the lexicon of the language.

lexifier language A language which provides a large proportion of the lexical items found in a **pidgin** or a **creole**.

Liburnian An extinct and sparsely recorded language spoken on the coast of Croatia in Roman times, probably related to **Illyrian** or to **Venetic** (opinions differ).

Lightfoot framework A theory of language change, especially **syntactic change**, developed by David Lightfoot in a series of publications, notably in Lightfoot (1979). The framework lies within the Chomskyan tradition of generative linguistics, which typically posits abstract underlying representations for surface linguistic forms. In Lightfoot's conception, at some stage in the history of a language, surface forms are rather close to their underlying representations. Over time, accumulated linguistic changes in surface forms tend to make those forms increasingly remote from their underlying forms, which become therefore ever more abstract. Lightfoot posits a *Transparency Principle*, by which there exists some kind of (unspecified) principled limit upon the allowable distance between underlying and surface forms. When this limit is reached, *restructuring* (or *radical reanalysis*) occurs, as the next generation of speakers constructs a radically new set of underlying representations, very different from those of their parents and much closer to the surface forms.

This view predicts that syntactic change should be very abrupt, with marked discontinuities between the syntactic structures used by one generation and the next. Lightfoot claims to have found evidence for this, but critics have strongly queried his account and at present his framework enjoys no more than modest support. For criticism, see the special issue of *Lingua* (vol. 55, 1981), and also Bennett (1979), Aitchison (1980), Warner (1983) and Plank (1984). Lightfoot revises his ideas in Lightfoot (1981) and presents a summary of his views in Lightfoot (1988). McMahon (1994: ch. 5) provides an overview of the whole issue. Lightfoot modifies his views further in Lightfoot (1998).

Ligurian An extinct and poorly recorded language spoken along the Mediterranean coast from the Rhône to the Arno in early Roman times. We know almost nothing about it, and we cannot tell if it was **Indo-European** or not.

limitation law In ancient Greek or Latin, the statement that the word-accent could only fall on one of the last three syllables of a word.

limited-scope comparison Another term for **'reaching down'**.

limited search The term used by Nichols (1995b, 1997d) to denote a restricted variety of **open-ended comparison** in which principled and identifiable limits are placed, in advance, upon the semantic matches which can be accepted.

Lindemann's rule The statement that **Sievers's Law** (sense 1) applies in word-initial position after an initial consonant only in monosyllables. For example, in the *Rigveda*, the divine name *Dyáus* must often be read *Diyáus*.

lineage A linguistic **taxon** of any size.

linearization Another term for **unpacking**.

lingua franca (plural **lingue franche**) A language which is routinely used in some region for dealings between people who have different mother tongues. In the past this term was often applied to any **interlect**, even a **pidgin**, but today it is more usually restricted to a mother tongue, though possibly to a version different from that used by native speakers. The original *Lingua Franca* was a variety of Italian, laced with words from a number of other languages, used as a trade language in the eastern Mediterranean in the late Middle Ages.

lingua franca **model** Another term for the **crystallization model**.

linguistic age In Nichols (1998), an estimate of the time depth required to account for the observed **genetic density** in a geographical region. When the linguistic age is substantially less than the time of known human habitation, as established by archaeology, she takes this as indicating that the area has seen considerable extinction of linguistic lineages.

linguistic archaeology A term occasionally applied to the use of philological data to shed light on a social or sociolinguistic state of affairs in the past. For example, the study of naming practices in medieval England can tell us things about the use of English, Norman French and Old Norse.

linguistic area (also **convergence area**, Ger *Sprachbund*) A geographical region in which a number of languages which are unrelated or only distantly related have converged significantly as a result of **language contact**, with the result that these languages, in many respects, resemble one another more strongly than they resemble their own closest relatives elsewhere. (This is **areal convergence**.) Among the best-known linguistic areas are the Balkans, the northwest Pacific coast of North America, and southeast Asia. The study of linguistic areas is **areal linguistics**.

linguistic cycle hypothesis The hypothesis that linguistic elements tend to develop over time in a cyclical manner, being created, integrated, reduced and finally obliterated, while **renewal** feeds new elements into the cycle. Many versions of this hypothesis have been advanced, but a global summary looks something like this: discourse strategies become syntactic structures; syntactic structures become morphological markers; morphological markers become phonological alternations; phonological alternations become obliterated, requiring renewal. See Heine *et al.* (1991a: 243–247) for a survey with references. Compare **stadialism**.

linguistic density The number of distinct languages per unit area. Compare **genetic density**.

linguistic ecology The attempt to identify, in a **proto-language**, words for specific wild animals (*salmon, camel*), wild plants (*oak, palm*) and geographically restricted natural phenomena (*monsoon, northern lights*), particularly in the hope of addressing the **homeland problem**. This is one type of **linguistic palaeontology**, and it runs into familiar difficulties like the **beech-tree problem**.

linguistic engineering Another term for **language planning**.

linguistic geography (also **geographical linguistics**) The study of the distribution of languages and language families over the planet, including changes in that distribution over time, sometimes also including attempts at explaining that distribution in terms of nonlinguistic factors. For various attempts at getting to grips with linguistic geography, see the **Bulging Hub Principle**, the **Renfrew hypothesis, population typology** and the **New Synthesis**. **Geolinguistics** is a specific variety of linguistic geography.

linguistic hybrid Another term for **hybrid form** (sense 2).

linguistic marker In **population typology**, a structural feature of grammar that has sufficient genetic and geographical stability to identify populations of languages that have some historical, geographical or cultural unity even though they lack detectable genetic unity. A useful linguistic marker must be persistent within a genetic family, must have a demonstrated but modest ability to diffuse areally, and must have uneven worldwide frequency.

linguistic market The term used by Milroy (1992) to denote the variety of competing linguistic forms which coexist within a speech community and which are available for selection by speakers to meet their purposes.

linguistic obsolescence The term used by Dorian (1989) for the purely linguistic consequences accompanying **language shift**: speakers engaged in shifting become ever less fluent in their ancestral language, which gradually loses vocabulary, grammatical constructions, alternations, irregular forms, marked segment-types and elevated registers.

linguistic palaeontology The use of linguistic data (lexical items) to draw conclusions about the environment and the culture of the people who spoke an unrecorded but reconstructed language. The idea is simple in principle: if we can reconstruct a word for 'sheep' for the proto-language, then its speakers must have known sheep. In practice, however, there are major pitfalls, notably the **beech-tree problem**, and the reliability of the approach is questioned by many linguists. The approach may be more trustworthy when we can reconstruct a whole set of semantically related items, such as 'sheep', 'goat', 'wool', 'pasture' and 'small cattle'. Compare *Wörter und Sachen* and see **lexical stratification**.

linguistic phylogeny In the **genetic model** of linguistic descent, the ancestry of particular languages; the identification of **genetic relationships** and the construction of **family trees**; a family tree resulting from decisions about ancestry. For example, the phylogeny of English might be summarized as English < Northwest Germanic < Proto-Germanic < PIE.

linguistic prehistory The historical development of languages before they come to be adequately written down: the chief subject matter of **historical linguistics**.

linguistic relationship principle A putative principle sometimes invoked in addressing the **homeland problem**. It says this: the proposed solution must be consistent with the major isoglosses – that is, it must be consistent with the major branching structure visible in the family. For example, a proposed IE homeland must account for the early separation of Anatolian from the rest of the family.

linguistic seriation The provisional determination of the direction of a particular change by appeal to known universals of change. For example, a systematic correspondence between /s/ and /h/ in two languages points to original */s/ and a lenition */s/ > /h/ in one of them, since this is a frequent and natural change, while the reverse is virtually unattested. Similarly, cognation between an independent word in one language and a bound morpheme in another points to reduction of the independent word to an affix in the second language, since such a process is common, while the reverse is extremely rare. See Anttila (1989: 296–297).

linguistic stratigraphy Especially in **dialect geography**, the enterprise of determining the relative ages of competing linguistic forms. For example, the Romance of France shows three different words for 'mare', reflexes of Latin *equa*, *caballa* and *jūmentum*; both the distribution of these forms on the map and independent historical evidence point to the conclusion that *equa* was once widespread, that it was later displaced from much of its territory by *caballa*, and that this last in turn has been largely displaced by *jūmentum*.

linguistic variable See **variable**.

linguoarchaeology A particular approach to correlating the findings of historical linguistics and of archaeology, developed in the then USSR in the 1980s. See Shnirelman (1997).

linkage breaking See under **social-network model**.

linkage rejoining See under **social-network model**.

linking *r* In some non-rhotic accents of English, an instance of non-prevocalic /r/ which has been lost in isolation but which reappears when the position of the lost /r/ is directly followed by a vowel, as in *far* /fɑ:/ but *far away* /fɑ:rəweɪ/. Compare **intrusive** *r*.

link language The term used by Hock and Joseph (1996: ch. 13) for a supraregional language learned and used by speakers of a variety of languages. Examples include Latin in Roman and medieval Europe, Greek in the Hellenistic and Roman east, French in the French empire and in early modern Europe, Sanskrit in pre-colonial India, and English in much of the modern world. A **koiné** is considered to be a special type of link language.

Lislakh The name given by Hodge (1998) to a putative genetic grouping of **Indo-European** and **Afro-Asiatic**.

Lisramic An obsolete term for **Afro-Asiatic**.

litotes Understatement, such as the use of *not bad* to mean *very good*. The opposite is **hyperbole**.

liturgical language A language, most often a **dead language**, which is used in some community for religious purposes.

loan adaptation Another term for **loan nativization**.

loanblend A **loan word** in which at least one element is replaced by a corresponding element in the borrowing language. For example, Pennsylvania German borrows English adjectives in -*y* but replaces this suffix with native -*ig*: *bassig* 'bossy', *fonnig* 'funny', *tricksig* 'tricky'.

loan nativization (also **loan adaptation, correspondence mimicry**) A distinctive type of **borrowing**, as follows. When there is well-established bilingualism between speakers of two closely related languages, speakers will often be keenly aware of the phonological and morphological correspondences holding between the two languages. In such circumstances, a loan word may be nativized by replacing each of its segments with the regularly corresponding segment in the borrowing language, and a morphologically complex form may be borrowed by constructing a **calque**. As a result, the borrowed items may be indistinguishable from native formations in the borrowing language. Leer (1990: 88) reports that Michael Krauss, in unpublished work, has discussed the possibility of just such loan nativization among the Athabaskan languages, and Nash (1997: 191–192) reports some examples from Australia.

loan shift The use of an existing native word to render a new meaning which is itself being borrowed from another language. For example, Old English *heofon* 'sky', *hel* 'underworld' and *god* 'pagan deity' were loan-shifted, under the influence of Latin words used by Christians, to yield (in modern form) *heaven* 'Christian paradise', *hell* 'Christian inferno' and *God* 'Christian deity'.

loan translation Another term for **calque**.

loan word (Ger *Lehnwort*) A word which has been taken into one language from a second language in which it was already present; see **borrowing** (sense 1) for examples.

loan-word trajectory The path followed by a word which is borrowed from language to language to language. For example, *coffee* appears to have travelled from an Ethiopian language to Arabic to Turkish to Italian and from there to English and other European languages.

localism The doctrine that spatial expressions are linguistically more basic than other kinds of expression, and that spatial expressions accordingly constitute the primary raw material for such processes as **metaphor** and **grammaticalization**. See Heine *et al.* (1991a: 113–118) for discussion with references.

loc. cit. (also *op. cit.*) The abbreviation for 'in the work cited' (Latin *in loco citato*). Attached to an author's name, this indicates that another reference is being made to the last work cited from that same author, possibly many pages ago. It should not be used. Compare *ibid.*

locus (also **centre of innovation**) A small part of the total geographical extent of a language or a family which functions as an epicentre from which innovations tend to spread out. Compare **range**.

locus of diachronic process The object that changes during **language change**. There has been much discussion of whether this object is speakers' mental grammars, speakers' social behaviour, the language independent of its speakers, or something else. See, for example, Lightfoot (1998) for a defence of the first, Milroy (1992) for a defence of the second, and Lass (1997) for a defence of the third.

Lolo-Burmese Another term for **Burmese-Lolo**.

long-range comparison The **comparison** of established language families in the hope of finding very distant genetic links among them.

long-ranger A whimsical self-designation adopted by some practitioners of **long-range comparison**, often especially by those who try to work solely by **inspection**.

long resonant In early reconstructions of PIE, a contrastively long version of any of */y w r l m n/; the first two are often called *long semivowels*. Many of these are now known to have been instances of a short resonant followed by a **laryngeal**; for example, the source of Latin *gratus* 'pleasing', formerly reconstructed as $*g^w\bar{r}\text{-}t\acute{o}\text{-}$, is now reconstructed as $*g^wrH\text{-}t\acute{o}\text{-}$. Some linguists maintain that all long resonants can be so interpreted, but others disagree.

lookalikes Linguistic forms in different languages which are noticeably similar in form and meaning but which are not known to be related and which cannot be fitted into **systematic correspondences**. The great majority of lookalikes are **chance resemblances**, and hence few linguists attach any importance to them in **comparison**.

'Look for Latin etymologies on the Tiber' A dictum in **etymology**. It means 'when seeking the origin of a doubtful word, prefer obvious and mundane sources to fanciful speculations, particularly those involving faraway languages.'

loss A label applied to two quite different types of phonological change. 1. (also **deletion**) In the case of a **syntagmatic change**, loss is the total disappearance of a segment from some particular words and forms, as when /t/ was lost in certain clusters in English (*soften, fasten, castle, rustle*). Note that certain types of syntagmatic loss are sometimes given more specific names, such as **aphaeresis, syncope** and **apocope**. The opposite here is **epenthesis**. 2. (also **merger with zero**) In the case of a **paradigmatic change**, loss is the total disappearance of a phoneme from the language, as when /h/ disappeared at various times in Greek, Latin, French, Spanish and Hawaiian, leaving nothing behind. This second case has no opposite, since phonemes are not created from nothing.

loss of the conditioning environment Any linguistic change which partly or wholly removes the phonological environment governing a conditioned alternation and thus renders that alternation unconditioned and unpredictable. Very often the result is that an allophonic variation is converted into a phonemic contrast. For example, in Pre-Old-English, /k/ was palatalized to [tʃ] always and only before a front vowel, and [tʃ] was therefore only an allophone of /k/. Thus, /kinn/ 'chin' became phonetically [tʃinn] and /keaff/ 'chaff' became phonetically [tʃeaff], while /katt/ 'cat' remained phonetically [katt]. Then, however, the first element of the diphthongs /ea/ and /eo/ was lost after [tʃ], so that the word for 'chaff' was now phonetically [tʃaff]. As a result, [k] and [tʃ] now contrasted before back vowels, as in [katt] and [tʃaff], and hence [tʃ] was no longer an allophone of /k/, but rather a distinct phoneme /tʃ/, and the three words were now phonemically /tʃinn/, /tʃaff/ and /katt/. This is an example of **split** (sense 1).

Lower Exit Principle A putative principle governing the movement of low vowels during **chain shifts**, put forward by Labov (1994: 280). It says this: in a chain shift, low non-peripheral vowels become peripheral. Compare **Mid Exit Principle**, **Upper Exit Principle**.

lowering (also **opening**) Any phonological change in which a non-low vowel changes to a lower vowel, as when short /i/ and /u/ changed to /e/ and /o/, respectively, in early western Romance. The opposite is **raising**.

lower-middle-class crossover (also **overadjustment, hypercorrection**) The following phenomenon, widely attested. In a stratified society possessing a linguistic variable with more and less overtly prestigious realizations, every social group will use a higher frequency of the more prestigious version as the context becomes more formal, and every group will consistently use a higher frequency of the more prestigious version than the next lower group in any given context, with one exception: in the most formal context, the second-highest group will use a higher frequency of the prestige version than the highest group.

Low German See under **German**.

lucus a non lucendo **etymology** A crazy way of guessing the etymology of a word, in which the word is (wrongly) derived from another word of similar form but virtually opposite meaning. The classic case is the derivation of Latin *lūcus* 'grove of trees' from *lūcēre* 'shine, be bright', since a grove is *not* bright. Much favoured by some Romans, this approach has long been dismissed as ridiculous.

Ludolf's rule The statement that comparative work on languages is most secure when carried out with grammar, rather than with phonology or lexicon.

lumper An informal label applied to a comparative linguist who is perceived as eager to unite recognized language families into larger families on the basis of a modest amount of evidence. The opposite is **splitter**.

Luorawetlan Another term for **Chukchi-Kamchatkan**.

Lusitanian An extinct and poorly-known language recorded in northern Portugal during the first two centuries AD. It appears to be **Indo-European** but not **Celtic**.

Luwian (also **Luvian**) A group of two extinct **Anatolian** languages. *Cuneiform Luwian* is recorded in fragments associated with the **Hittite** texts, while *Hieroglyphic Luwian* is more extensively recorded in south and west Anatolia and north Syria in the second millennium BC. **Lycian** and **Milyan** are sometimes also considered members of the Luwian group.

Lycian An extinct **Anatolian** language, recorded in the fifth to fourth centuries BC in southwest Anatolia. It was apparently descended from a variety of **Luwian**, and is sometimes classified as Luwian. **Milyan** was formerly regarded as a variety of it.

Lydian An extinct **Anatolian** language, recorded in the sixth to fourth centuries BC in western Anatolia.

Lyman's Law See under *rendaku*.

Macedonian The ancient language of the Kingdom of Macedonia, the mother tongue of Alexander the Great. Virtually nothing is known about it, but it seems to have been an **Indo-European** language and possibly one closely related to **Greek**. Note: the modern *Macedonian* language of the Republic of Macedonia is a **Slavic** language, not a descendant or close relative of ancient Macedonian.

Mac Neill's Law The observation, put forward by Mac Neill (1908/09), that certain word-final sonorants in Irish undergo fortition when preceded by another sonorant itself preceded by an unstressed or lost vowel. Hamp (1974) proposes to reformulate the observation, and renames it the *Mac Neill–O'Brien Law*. See Collinge (1985: 235–236).

Macro- A prefix attached to the name of a **language family** to denote a proposed larger grouping including that family, most often one which is speculative and not established.

Macro-Algonquian A putative genetic grouping linking **Algonquian** with **Muskogean** and other small families of the southeastern USA. It enjoys little support.

macro-family An exceptionally large **language family**. The term is commonly applied to a speculative and unestablished grouping of several established families, such as **Austric, Amerind** and **Nostratic**.

Macro-Gê (also **Macro-Je**) A proposed grouping of thirty-odd languages spoken in eastern South America, proposed by T. Kaufman (1990, 1994). While not established, this proposal is supported by evidence and enjoys a good deal of support.

Macro-Mayan A proposed genetic grouping of **Mayan** with **Mixe-Zoquean**, *Totonacan* and sometimes also *Huave*. It is not established, but it is regarded as promising by some specialists.

Macro-Penutian See under **Penutian**.

Macro-Siouan A proposed genetic grouping of **Siouan, Iroquoian, Caddoan** and sometimes also **Yuchi**, put forward on numerous occasions since the nineteenth century. Campbell (1997a: 262–269) concludes that the existing evidence for any part of this hypothesis is sparse to non-existent.

Macro-Tungusic A proposed genetic grouping of **Tungusic, Japanese** and **Korean**, currently favoured by some specialists who seek Asiatic links for the two eastern languages but are hesitant about accepting the validity of **Altaic**.

Maipurean (also **Arawakan**) A large language family linking a number of highly dispersed languages ranging from Belize to Paraguay. Though the core membership of the family seems secure, there are disputes about the possible membership of dozens of languages, and the number of languages assigned to the family ranges from a conservative 50 to a generous 120. Today the name *Maipurean* is applied to the secure core, and *Arawakan* to the speculative larger grouping. See Campbell (1997a: 178–182).

malapropism (also **catachresis**) The erroneous use of a word in place of an intended word which is somewhat similar in form but typically unrelated in meaning, such as the use of *facilities* for *faculties*, of *prostrate* for *prostate*, or of *epitaph* for *epithet*. Very rarely does a malapropism become established in a language, though one or two cases, such as *fortuitous* for *fortunate*, are at present very widespread.

Malayo-Polynesian An obsolete term for the **Austronesian** family of languages. The term is still in use to denote the major branch of Austronesian, the one including all but the Taiwanese languages.

mama-papa **vocabulary** See under **nursery word**.

Manchu–Tungus Another term for **Tungusic**.

Mande A group of about fifty languages spoken in west Africa. The Mande languages are generally (but not universally) thought to belong to the **Niger-Congo** family, but are classified as one of the branches most distant from all the others; moreover, they are at best only distantly related to one another, and the validity of the taxon is not certain. Among the best-known Mande languages are *Bambara*, *Mandinka* and *Kpelle*.

manuscript A handwritten text on paper or a similar soft material. Compare **inscription**. The study of manuscripts is **palaeography**.

mapping In the terminology of Lass (1978), the procedure, in diagramming phonological change, of moving forwards in time from a proto-segment to its various descendants – for example, from PIE initial */s-/ to English /s-/ on the one hand and to ancient Greek /h-/ and then modern Greek /Ø-/ on another. The reverse is **projection**.

marginalia Notes written in the margin of a **manuscript**.

margin of safety The putative tendency of languages to maintain the greatest possible phonetic distance between phonemes, often especially vowels. This is sometimes taken as a principle of **reconstruction**: unless we have strong evidence to the contrary, we prefer to reconstruct */i u a/ rather than, say, */e o a/.

markedness shift (also **shift of markedness, markedness reversal**) 1. A certain type of syntactic change, as follows. A language has an unmarked construction used in most circumstances and a competing marked construction used in certain special circumstances. Over time, more and more functions are transferred from the unmarked construction to the marked one, until finally the originally marked construction is used in most circumstances and is therefore unmarked, while the originally unmarked construction is confined to a few special functions and is marked. Givón (1977) cites the example of biblical Hebrew. Early biblical Hebrew had an unmarked VSO word order with a marked SVO order confined to a few functions. Over time, more and more discourse functions were transferred to the SVO pattern, until by late biblical Hebrew the now unmarked SVO order was used for most purposes, with the now marked VSO order confined to a few functions. 2. A switch in productivity from one pattern to another. For example, English nouns ending in voiceless fricatives formerly voiced those fricatives in the plural, as in *leaf/leaves*; early French loans like *chief*, which did not undergo this voicing, were originally marked as exceptions, but today the great majority of such nouns show no voicing (*bus, graph, myth*), and now it is the nouns like *leaf* which must be marked as exceptions.

marker A linguistic variable which correlates both with degree of formality and with social factors like sex or social class. It is suggested that markers are typically involved in **change from above**. Compare **indicator**.

Marrucinian An extinct and sparsely recorded language attested on the central Adriatic coast of Italy in the third century BC; it was apparently **Italic**, though this is not certain.

Marsian An extinct language, sparsely recorded east of Rome in about 300–150 BC, and sometimes classed as **Italic**.

mass comparison An older term for **multilateral comparison**.

mathematical methods Any of various approaches to **comparative linguistics** which depend upon the use of mathematical methods, most often statistical ones. In most cases these methods are applied in an attempt to determine whether there exists good evidence for a **remote relationship** between certain languages (the **search problem**), though sometimes linguists are interested in determining the degree of closeness between related languages, in **subgrouping**, or in the **time depth** at which related languages separated. Named methods include **lexicostatistics**, **glottochronology**, the **probabilistic approach** (including the **Monte Carlo test** and the **Oswalt shift test**) and **best-tree approaches**. See these entries for details and references; see Bender (1969) and Nichols (1995b); and see Embleton (1986, 1991, 1992) and Wang (1994) for surveys.

maximal coding [*rare*] Another term for **portmanteau reconstruction**.

Mayan A family of about thirty languages spoken in southern Mexico and Guatemala. A Mayan language called *classical Mayan* occurs in the inscriptions left behind by the vanished Mayan civilization. No secure links exist with any other languages, though Mayan is included in the **Macro-Mayan** hypothesis and often in the **Penutian** hypothesis.

Mechanical Principle A putative principle governing the course of phonological change, formulated by Labov (1994: 603) as follows: the relative progress of a sound change is determined by phonetic factors alone, without regard to the preservation of meaning. In other words, the principle holds that **avoidance of merger** is not, in general, a primary force in dictating the course of a sound change. This is one aspect of the **Neogrammarian Hypothesis**; see the **Regularity Principle**.

media (plural **mediae**) A voiced plosive, such as /b d g g^w/. The term is traditional in IE studies. Compare **tenuis**, **aspirata**.

media aspirata (plural **mediae aspiratae**) Any one of the PIE consonants traditionally reconstructed as 'voiced aspirated' plosives and notated */bh dh (gh') gh gh^w/.

mediation The passage of a word or form in a language through another language, possibly with consequences for its form. For example, the

Basque word *hanka* 'haunch' derives from Frankish, but it was not borrowed directly from Frankish; instead, the Frankish word was borrowed into Gallo-Romance and from there into Basque, and so it entered Basque via Romance mediation. The Basque personal name *Xabier* 'Xavier' is thought to be of native origin, but we would have expected **Xaber*; the non-native /ie/ points to Romance mediation of the name – that is, the name appears to have been taken into Romance, where it acquired the Romance diphthongization of stressed /ɛ/ to /ie/, and then to have been taken back into Basque in this modified form.

Mediterranean A hypothetical extinct language invoked by some Romanists as the source of certain words in Romance languages for which no etymology is available. Like all such hypothetical substrate languages, this one is dubious.

Meeussen's rule A process occurring in many Bantu languages by which the second of two adjacent high tones becomes low.

megalocomparison A dismissive term sometimes applied to the work of linguists who ambitiously attempt to unite huge numbers of languages into vast and speculative **macro-families** on the basis of little evidence. The term was coined by Matisoff (1990) with reference to the work of Joseph Greenberg, particularly his **Amerind** hypothesis.

Meillet's Law A statement about word-accent in common **Slavic**, put forward by Meillet (1902). Essentially, it proposes that a Balto-Slavic acute accent becomes a Slavic circumflex. See Collinge (1985: 117–118) for a critical survey with references.

Meillet's principle (also **three-witness principle**) In **comparative linguistics**, the principle that apparently cognate words must be present in at least three different languages before the words can serve as the basis of a proposed **reconstruction**.

Meinhof's Law In Bantu, the statement, put forward by Meinhof (1932), that a voiced plosive is lost when immediately preceded by a nasal and immediately followed by a vowel plus a nasal. A version of this applying only to /mb/ and /nd/, but not to /ŋg/, is the *Kwanyama Law*.

melioration Another term for **amelioration**.

merger (also **dephonologization**) The loss of a contrast which formerly existed between two (or more) phonemes. In an *unconditioned merger*, the contrast disappears in every case, and the number of phonemes is reduced. For example, the historical Basque contrast between laminal /s/ and apical /ś/ has been lost in western varieties in favour of /ś/ – that is, the laminal has become apical in every case. In a *conditioned merger*, the contrast only disappears in specified environments. For example, in southern varieties of American English, the contrast between /e/ (as in *bed*) and /ɪ/ (as in *bid*) has been lost in favour of /ɪ/ before a nasal, but not otherwise, making *pen* and *pin* homophones, but not *bed* and *bid*. Trudgill and Foxcroft (1978) distinguish two mechanisms for merger. In *merger-by-transfer*, lexical items shift individually and abruptly from the class defined by one phoneme to the class defined by the other phoneme, until the first class is empty; this is a kind of **lexical diffusion**. In *merger-by-approximation*, the phonetic realizations of the two phonemes move steadily closer together until they coincide. Labov (1994: 321–323) adds a third type: *merger by expansion*, in which the contrast is abruptly abandoned, and the phonological space formerly occupied by two phonemes is reassigned to the single new phoneme. The opposite is **split** (sense 1). Compare **coalescence**, **near-merger** and see **reversal of merger**.

merger with zero Another term for **loss** (sense 2).

mesolect See under **post-creole continuum**.

Messapic An extinct and poorly recorded **Indo-European** language attested in southeastern Italy between the sixth and first centuries BC. Some specialists suspect it may be the same language as **Illyrian**.

metanalysis (also **juncture displacement, recutting**) A type of morphological **reanalysis** (sense 1) in which segments are transferred from the end of a word or morpheme to the beginning of a following one or vice versa. Familiar English examples include the development of earlier *a naddre, a napron, a noumpere, an ewt, an ekename* into modern *an adder, an apron, an umpire, a newt, a nickname*. In Basque, a verb-form can take the suffix *-(e)z* (phonetically [-(e)s]) plus the postposition *gero* 'after' to express 'since' (in the causal sense); in western varieties, *-ez* has been moved from the verb to the postposition, producing a new causal postposition *ezkero*.

metaphony Another name for **umlaut**. Note, however, that the term is often applied more widely to any kind of assimilation involving non-adjacent vowels, both to the historical changes and to the resulting alternations.

metaphor Any extension in the semantic value of a linguistic form resulting from a perceived resemblance, as when *head* 'body part' is extended to denote things which are on top, in charge or just rather round: *the head of a valley, the head of a company, a head of cabbage*. Heine *et al.* (1991a: 60–61) distinguish between a *creative metaphor*, which involves a totally new utterance (as in *Susie is a rock*), and an *emerging metaphor*, in which a familiar utterance is given a new sense (as in *Susie let the cat out of the bag*).

metaphoric iconicity The term used by Mannheim (1986) for the introduction, for expressive purposes, of phonetic features into words which formerly lacked them. As example is the introduction of glottalization and aspiration into Quechua words in which these are not etymological.

metathesis Any **syntagmatic change** in which the order of segments (or sometimes of other phonological elements) in a word is altered. In the simplest case, a single segment changes its position, as in the development of Latin *crocodilus* 'crocodile' to Spanish *cocodrilo*, with metathesis of the /r/. In more elaborate cases, two segments exchange their positions; for example, Latin *miraculum* 'miracle' should have yielded Spanish *miraglo, but the form is *milagro*, with metathesis of the two liquids. The label *hyperthesis* is sometimes applied to an instance of metathesis between two segments very far apart. An instance of *quantitative metathesis* is provided by the development of earlier Greek /neːós/ 'new' into Attic /neóːs/, with metathesis of the length. A still more complex example is provided by the Basque word for 'swallow' (the bird): common *ainara ~ enara* must derive from earlier *ainːala, but western *elae* points equally clearly to earlier *ailːana, with metathesis of /n/ and /l/ plus transfer of the length from one to the other. Metathesis is a **whole-segment process**. Note that certain sequences of changes can produce *apparent* cases of metathesis; see **unpacking** for an example.

metatony Any of several shifts in the position or nature of the word-accent in early **Balto-Slavic**. The term was used by Saussure in his various writings on the subject. See Collinge (1985: 271–277) for a survey of the phenomena.

metatypy (also **extreme structural borrowing**) An extreme case of the grammatical restructuring of a language under the influence of a neighbouring language. In the classic case, the restructuring is so thorough that every sentence in the affected language becomes a morpheme-by-morpheme calque of the corresponding sentence in the influencing language. As a rule, no morphological material is borrowed from the influencing language, but exceptions may occur when speakers of the affected language can find no suitable morphemes in their own language to calque morphemes in the other. An outstanding example is the Austronesian language Takia, whose grammar has been entirely remodelled to match that of the neighbouring Papuan language Waskia (M. Ross 1996). The phenomenon of metatypy has been recognized for years, and various names have been applied to it, such as *extreme structural borrowing* (Thomason and Kaufman 1988); the term was coined by Malcolm Ross (1996), and Ross has been a major investigator of it (1996, 1997). Compare **accommodation** (sense 3).

metonymy A type of **semantic change** in which a word acquires the sense of something else with which its referent is commonly associated. Examples include *the stage* for the theatrical profession, *the White House* for the US President and his or her staff, and *red-light district* for a sleazy area of town (from the former practice of putting red lights in the windows of brothels).

metronymic An additional name conferred upon a person to indicate the name of the bearer's mother. Compare **patronymic**.

Miao-Yao (also **Hmong-Mien**) A family of about fifteen languages spoken in southeastern China and probably representing a remnant of the languages spoken in the area before the Chinese settlement. Miao-Yao is usually thought to have no relatives, but see **Austric**.

Michelena's Law The statement that, in early medieval Basque, intervocalic /n/ was categorically lost, leaving behind nasalized vowels, with the nasalization then meeting different fates according to variety: retention, loss or reinterpretation as a *following* /n/. For example, Pre-Basque *zani* 'watchful, expectant' developed to *zã̃i, leading variously to modern zã̃i, zai and zain. The definitive statement is Michelena (1977: 299–305).

Middle Preceding a language name, a label used in some conventional chronological classification to denote an intermediate period in the recorded history of that language, as in **Middle English**. Compare **Old, Modern**.

Middle English The name conventionally given to the English used between about 1100 and 1500.

Middle High German The name given to that period in the history of (High) German between about AD 1100 or 1200 and 1500. This is the language of the *Niebelungenlied* and of the Minnesingers.

Mid Exit Principle A putative principle governing the raising of mid vowels in **chain shifts**, put forward by Labov (1994: 284). It says this: in chain shifts, peripheral vowels rising from mid to high position develop inglides (centring glides). Compare **Lower Exit Principle, Upper Exit Principle**.

migration 1. The movement of a group of people from one geographical region to another. An example is the migration of (some) Athabaskan-speakers from Canada to the western USA. This is one possible mechanism of **language spread**. 2. In **migration theory**, such a movement of people which causes the area occupied by a language to become discontinuous.

migration theory An approach to the study of **language spread**, put forward by Dyen (1956). Dyen defines a **homeland** as a continuous area; any movement that causes that area to become discontinuous is a **migration** (sense 2), while a movement that only changes its shape or area is an **expansion** (sense 3). For Dyen, a homeland should be reconstructed in accordance with the **minimal-migration principle**.

Milyan An extinct **Anatolian** language known chiefly from a single text. It was formerly regarded as a variety of **Lycian** ('Lycian B') but is now often regarded as a distinct language.

minimal-migration principle A putative principle invoked in addressing the **homeland problem**, put forward by Dyen (1956). It says this: the homeland should be reconstructed so as to require the fewest **migrations** (sense 2) and the smallest number of migrating branches.

Minoan The language used in Crete in the second millennium BC and recorded in the Linear A texts. We cannot read these texts and we know next to nothing about Minoan, though most scholars are satisfied that it was not Indo-European. Innumerable 'decipherments' have been published but none has won any acceptance. Compare **Eteo-Cretan**.

minority language A language which has long been spoken as the mother tongue in a geographical region of a nation in which the national language is something else. For example, Corsican, Catalan, Basque, Breton, Dutch and Alsatian German are all minority languages in France. Compare **immigrant language**.

Mischsprache The German for **mixed language**.

mitian **phenomenon** The name given by Nichols (1992) to the striking correspondence of first- and second-person markers in Indo-European and in Uralic. In both families, first-person pronouns and verbal agreement markers (both singular and plural) commonly involve the consonant /m/, while the second-person ones likewise show /t/. This has often been taken as evidence for some kind of link between the two families, but only a minority of linguists are prepared to see this as evidence for a remote genetic relationship in the absence of further confirmation, especially since the families are known to have been in contact for a long time.

mixed dialect (or **mixed lect**) The term used by Chambers and Trudgill (1998: 110–119) for a regional speech variety with the following characteristic: it is located between two regions in which a given variable has consistently different values, and it itself sometimes uses one value and sometimes the other, in a complex manner. For example, English words like *cut* and *money* consistently have [ʊ] in the north of England but [ə] in the south, and some intervening varieties use both. This appears to be a classic case of what has been called **dialect mixing**. Compare **fudged dialect**.

mixed language (Ger *Mischsprache*) A language which does not descend from a single ancestor in the normal way but which has instead been assembled by combining large chunks of material from two (or more) existing languages: one type of **non-genetic language**. The term is commonly applied only to mother tongues and not to **pidgins**, which otherwise may have a similar origin, and it is not usually applied to **creoles** either. At least since the days of Hugo Schuchardt in the late nineteenth century, linguists have wondered whether mixed languages truly exist, and many linguists have doubted their reality. In the last few years, however, increasingly persuasive cases have come to light: among them are *Media Lengua* in Ecuador (constructed from Quechua grammar and Spanish lexical stems; see Muysken 1997a); *Ma'a* (or *Mbugu*) in Tanzania (Bantu and Cushitic, plus some Maasai; see Thomason 1997c and references therein); *Mednyj Aleut* on Copper Island (Aleut and Russian; Thomason 1997b); and, perhaps the most spectacular case of all, *Michif* in the USA and Canada (Cree and Canadian French; Bakker and Papen 1997, Bakker 1997). The status of some of these has been questioned, but Michif, at least, appears to be beyond dispute a mixed language. In general, the creation of a mixed language seems to require a high degree of bilingualism plus some unusual social factors. See Bakker and Mous (1994) and Thomason (1997a). The clearest examples, like Michif and Mednyj Aleut, are characterized by the presence within them of large and monolithic blocks of material imported wholesale from each of the ancestral languages (for example, Michif has an entirely Cree verbal system and an entirely French nominal system), but a **portmanteau language** (if any such exists) shows a much more highly integrated structure. Note: the term *mixed language* has sometimes been applied far more broadly to any language which has been significantly influenced by another (such as English), but this broad usage seems objectionable, since in this sense there are hardly any unmixed languages.

mixed lect Another term for **mixed dialect**.

Mixe-Zoquean A family of eighteen languages spoken in southern Mexico. A Mixe–Zoquean language was apparently spoken by the Olmecs, founders of Meso-American civilization. See **Macro-Mayan**.

mixoglotty [*obsolete*] An older term for *creolization* (see **creole**).

Moabite An extinct and sparsely recorded northwestern **Semitic** language apparently spoken in what is now Jordan from about the fourteenth to the sixth centuries BC. The single most important inscription, the *Moabite stone*, dated to the ninth century BC, contains one of the earliest examples of alphabetic writing.

mobile *s* Another term for *s* **mobile**.

model of linguistic descent Any of various idealized schemas which attempt to capture major aspects of the way in which languages descend from earlier languages. More or less standard in the field is the **genetic model**, based upon the **family tree**, and introduced in the mid-nineteenth century. The **wave model** was advanced around the same time, while the **rake model** is very recent. The **rhizotic model** has been defended occasionally since the early twentieth century (though the label is recent). The **crystallization model** has been defended by various people since the 1960s. Very recently, the **social-network model** and the **punctuated-equilibrium model** have been proposed. None of these models can claim to do more than to capture important aspects of particular cases of descent, and they are best seen as complementary, rather than as competing. The first three are essentially models of **divergence**, while the last four emphasize **convergence**; only the last four have anything to say about **non-genetic languages**.

Modern Preceding a language name, a label used in some conventional chronological classification to denote the most recent period of the recorded history of that language, as in **Modern English**. Compare **Old, Middle**.

Modern English The label conventionally given to the English used from 1700 to the present. A few people are beginning to apply the label *Global English* to the English of the present day.

modular depotentiation A hypothetical type of phonological change, by which a maximally strong segment which is obliged to undergo **fortition** is converted to a maximally weak segment. The notion was introduced by J. Foley (1977).

Mongolian (also **Mongolic**) A group of about a dozen closely related languages spoken in central Asia, the most important being the standard *Khalka Mongolian* of the Mongolian People's Republic. All the Mongolian languages appear to be descended from the *classical Mongolian* of Genghis Khan. Mongolian forms one branch of the controversial **Altaic** family.

Mon-Khmer One of the two main branches of the **Austro-Asiatic** family, containing about 140 languages, the best known being *Khmer* (*Cambodian*) and *Vietnamese*.

monogenesis The idea that language arose only once in human history, and hence that all the languages ever spoken are descended from a single common ancestor. Most linguists consider monogenesis a plausible idea, but there is no way we can test it, since tens of millennia of geographical dispersion and language change are enough to obliterate all traces of a common ancestry many times over. A few linguists, notably Vitaly Shevoroshkin and Merritt Ruhlen, have recently been claiming that we can still recover traces of the ancestral 'Mother Tongue' in modern languages, in the form of **global etymologies**, but the vast majority dismiss such suggestions as absurd beyond comment. Note that the **Proto-World hypothesis** is technically distinct from monogenesis, though the distinction is utterly academic. The opposing view is **polygenesis**.

monophthongization The conversion of a diphthong to a pure vowel. There are two main types: **reduction** (sense 1) and **levelling** (sense 1). The opposite is **diphthongization**. See also **smoothing**.

Monte Carlo test A particular statistical approach to evaluating the evidence for remote relationships among languages, put forward by Ringe (1992), with further development and examples of application in Ringe (1995a, 1995b, 1996, 1998). (Ringe now regards his original 1992 version as obsolete.) The test involves seeking statistically significant correlations between phonemes in specific phonotactic positions, without reference to phonetic similarity. For critiques, see Baxter and Manaster Ramer (1996), Baxter (1998).

Moravcsik universals of borrowing A set of proposed universal constraints on the borrowing of grammatical forms, put forward by Edith Moravcsik (1978). Among them are the following: grammatical morphemes cannot be borrowed until after some lexical morphemes have been borrowed; bound morphemes can be borrowed only as parts of complete words; verbs cannot be borrowed directly; inflectional morphemes cannot be borrowed until after some derivational (word-forming) morphemes have been borrowed; a preposed grammatical item may not be borrowed as a postposed one, and vice versa. These principles do appear to represent the most typical cases, but counterexamples are known to most of them, and possibly to all of them.

more-frequent-more-grammaticalizable principle (MFMG) A label proposed by Hagège (1993: 213) for the observation that lexical items (especially verbs) of very high frequency (typically those with very general meanings like 'be', 'do', 'come', 'go', 'give', 'take', 'finish') are the ones most likely to undergo **grammaticalization**.

moribund language A language which is in danger of imminent extinction, usually one which is no longer being learned by children. Compare **endangered language**.

morphanization A term used by James Matisoff (1973 and elsewhere) to denote any process in which a formerly transparent morpheme is converted to an opaque and seemingly unique morph, an 'orphan morph' or '**cranberry morpheme**'. Examples include the loss of OE *thryl* 'hole', leaving the *-tril* of *nostril* an orphan; the loss of OE *twi-* 'half', leaving the *twi-* of *twilight* an orphan; and the loss of earlier English *whelm*, leaving the *-whelm* of *overwhelm* an orphan.

morpheme decay Another term for **lexical replacement**. This label has the advantage that the replacement of bound morphemes is obviously included.

morpheme doubling (also **morphological refilling**) The addition of a productive grammatical marker to a word-form which already contains an affix of identical function, particularly when the earlier marker has become obscure. Examples include the change of Middle English *childer* to modern *children* and the change of Latin *esse* 'be' to Vulgar Latin *essere*. It is possible for the identical morpheme to be added a second time: Basque *non* ~ *nun* 'where?' consists of the interrogative stem *no-* plus locative *-n*; the addition of *-bait* created *nunbait* 'somewhere', in which the locative ending is no longer word-final, as normally, with the result that some western varieties have re-added the locative to produce *nunbaiten*. See Haspelmath (1993), Koch (1996: 246).

morphocline Another term for **transformation series**.

morphological change Any change in the morphological form or structure of a word, a word-form or a set of such forms. See Anderson (1988) for a summary, and Andersen (1980) for a proposed typology of morphological changes.

morphological integration A type of **borrowing** in which the borrowed word is inserted into an existing paradigm in the borrowing language and hence equipped with a set of inflected forms it did not have in the source language. Anttila (1989: 157–158) cites the example of the Spanish adjectives *loco* 'crazy' and *rico* 'rich', borrowed into Chiricahua Apache (which has no adjectives) as third-person verb-forms and outfitted with complete verbal paradigms.

morphologically conditioned sound change Any phonological change which occurs regularly except in some morphologically distinguished environment, or, less commonly, which occurs only in a morphologically distinguished environment. Campbell (1996: 78–80) cites the cases of northern Estonian, in which final /n/ was lost everywhere except when it was the marker of first-singular in finite verbs, and of the Mayan language Kekchi, in which a short vowel in the final syllable of a polysyllabic word-form was lost everywhere except when it was the vowel of a verbal root. (Kekchi verbs are inflected by prefixation.) A particularly striking example is **Aitken's Law**. Regarded as impossible by the Neogrammarians but as unremarkable in much generative work on sound change, this type of change is of debated frequency. See Campbell (1996) for a critical summary with references, and see Anttila (1989: 78 *ff.*) and Crowley (1997: 242–244) for further examples.

morphological reconstruction The **reconstruction** of morphological forms and paradigms. See Fox (1995: 92–103) for a survey, and see Beekes (1995: *passim*) or W. P. Lehmann (1993: chs 7, 8) for examples from PIE.

morphological refilling Another term for **morpheme doubling**.

morphological shift Another term for **regrammaticalization**.

morphologization 1. Any change in which a formerly productive phonological process or alternation ceases to be productive and becomes confined to certain morphological environments or to certain lexical items only, thus becoming part of their morphology. Examples include Germanic **umlaut**, as in English *foot/feet*, in which the formerly automatic vowel alternation has become merely a marker of number, and the Celtic **mutations**. Some linguists apply the term more narrowly to the introduction of a semantic distinction between two allomorphs of a morpheme. A possible example is PIE dative *-ei* and locative *-i*, if these derive from umlaut variants of a single original ending. 2. (also **compacting**) Any instance of grammaticalization in which an independent word or a clitic is reduced to a bound affix. See Hopper and Traugott (1993: ch. 6) for a survey.

morphosyntactic status, change in Any change in the status of a linguistic form along the free/bound axis, such as **cliticization, affixization, demorphologization** or the creation of a **phrasal compound.**

Mosan A putative language family linking three families of the Pacific coast of North America: **Chimakuan, Salishan** and **Wakashan.** Put forward by Edward Sapir in the 1920s, the proposal has now been generally abandoned.

movable *s* Another term for *s* **mobile.**

ms. (or **MS**) The abbreviation for *manuscript*. Next to a linguistic form, it indicates that the form occurs in an unpublished manuscript, which is itself frequently identified by a following label known to specialists; thus, 'MS Cotton Vitellius A.XV' identifies a particular Old English document in the British Museum. The notation '*healde* for MS *healdne*' means that *healdne* appears in the manuscript, but that the editor of a published version has chosen to emend this to *healde*.

multidimensional paradigmaticity The presence of consistent and recurrent patterns, in two or more languages, in morphological paradigms involving two or more grammatical dimensions. Consider, for example, the main set of adjective endings in Latin and in Attic Greek, as shown in Table 6.

The very high degree of consistent patterning is obvious here; the same distinctions are made within the three dimensions of case, gender and number, **syncretism** occurs in the same positions, and there are conspicuous recurrent correspondences in sound. Such shared multidimensional paradigmaticity is generally taken as the most powerful kind of evidence available in identifying a **genetic relationship.**

multilateral comparison (also **mass comparison**) A particular approach to the issue of identifying subgroups of languages within language families and, in some hands, even of identifying genetic links in the first place. Not all practitioners employ the technique in the same way, but the general idea is to collect hundreds of

	Masculine	Feminine	Neuter
Latin			
Sg. Nom.	-us	-a	-um
Sg. Acc.	-um	-am	-um
Pl. Nom.	-ī	-ae	-a
Pl. Acc.	-ōs	-ās	-a
Greek			
Sg. Nom.	-os	-ē̄	-on
Sg. Acc.	-on	-ēn	-on
Pl. Nom.	-oi	-ai	-a
Pl. Acc.	-ūs	-ās	-a

Table 6

vocabulary items, and sometimes also grammatical morphemes, from a very large number of languages, and then to look for resemblances of form and meaning among the items in the resulting lists. Languages which appear to exhibit sizeable numbers of such resemblances are assumed to be genetically related, and those languages showing the largest number of resemblances are assumed to be most closely related. Many (not all) linguists are prepared to admit that MC might be of some use in identifying (at least provisionally) subgroupings within an established family. Recently, however, the American linguist Joseph Greenberg has been arguing that MC is, all by itself, capable of identifying previously unrecognized genetic groupings, and he has employed the technique in proposed classifications of the languages of Africa, Australia, New Guinea and the Americas. While Greenberg's classification of African languages is widely accepted, his other proposals, such as his suggested **Indo-Pacific** family, are widely rejected, and his proposed **Amerind** family has been greeted by most specialists with undisguised hostility. Very few linguists follow Greenberg in believing that MC can actually identify previously unknown genetic groupings.

multiple-birth model A particular model of language change. In this model, several competing forms or sounds emerge within different areas, styles or social groups and coexist for a time, but eventually some options become more favoured and therefore more frequent, while others atrophy or become specialized. This model is introduced by Aitchison (1995), who cites some examples of it. Compare the **tadpole-into-frog model** and the **young-cuckoo model**.

multiple incompatible comparisons In comparison, the citation of a single linguistic form, or of derivatives of a single linguistic form, in one language or family with two or more entirely different and unrelated forms in another; citing the same form in different proposed **cognate sets**. Examples include the citation of Basque *egun* 'day' and its two regular derivatives *eguzki* 'sun' and *ekhi* 'sun' in three totally different comparison sets, and the citation of Central Pomo *ča[:]č[']* 'man' and its Eastern Pomo cognate *ka:k^h* 'man' in two entirely different comparison sets, purely on the basis of their surface forms.

mumpsimus A word which has come into existence as a result of a misreading or a misprinting. In the King James Bible, in Genesis ii.18, God decides 'to make an help meet for him' [Adam]; here *meet* simply means 'suitable', but a seventeenth-century printing wrongly gave 'to make an help-meet for him', and the new word *helpmeet* entered the language and was invested with a suitable meaning. In 1871, as the Prussians were poised to bombard Paris, a German newspaper commented on *das psychologische Moment* of the proposed bombardment. This means 'the psychological momentum', but it was mistranslated into French as *le moment psychologique*, whence English *the psychological moment*, with the new sense of 'the moment at which the mind is aware of something about to happen'. [I am indebted to Julian Burnside for these examples.] Compare **ghost word**.

Munda A group of about two dozen languages spoken in discontinuous regions in eastern India. Munda forms one branch of the **Austro-Asiatic** family, and is thought to represent a remnant of the pre-Indo-Aryan languages of India.

Muskogean A family of about nine languages in the southeastern USA; its best-known members are *Choctaw*, *Creek* and *Seminole*. Muskogean is included in the **Gulf** hypothesis, in some versions of the **Penutian** hypothesis, and in the **Macro-Algonquian** hypothesis, none of which has won acceptance.

muta [*rare*] Especially in IE studies, another term for *plosive*. The term is most prominent in phrases like *muta cum liquida* (a plosive-liquid cluster).

mutation 1. In the Celtic languages, any one of a number of **alterna-tions** in the nature of certain word-initial consonants. These alter-nations were originally phonologically conditioned, but, with the loss of certain word-endings, they came to be grammatically conditioned instead. The details vary from language to language. Those in Welsh are called the **soft mutation**, the **spirant mutation** and the **nasal mutation**; those in Irish are called **aspiration** (sense 3) and **eclipsis. 2.** A term used by Benveniste (1968) to label certain cases of morphological and syntactic change. He distinguishes between *innovating mutation*, in which a new grammatical form or pattern is created by analogy with existing ones, and *conservative mutation*, in which a purely morphological form is replaced by a syntactic (peri-phrastic) one.

mutual assimilation See under **assimilation**.

Na-Dene A proposed language family of North America, consisting of the large **Athabaskan** group plus the three languages *Eyak*, *Tlingit* and *Haida*, put forward by Sapir (1915). The Athabaskan-Eyak grouping is considered secure; the addition of Tlingit is considered plausible but doubtful; and the further addition of Haida is widely rejected.

Nahali (also **Nehali, Nihali**) An **isolated language** spoken in central India.

Nakh-Dagestan (also **Northeast Caucasian**) A family of about thirty languages mainly spoken in and near the Caucasus, just west of the Caspian Sea. There are three main subgroups: *Nakh*, *Dagestanian* and *Lezgian*. Among the best-known members are *Chechen*, *Ingush*, *Avar* and *Tabasaran*.

narrowing (also **specialization, restriction**) A type of **semantic change** in which a word comes to be restricted to fewer cases than formerly. An example is English *deer*, which formerly meant 'animal' (in general) but now means only 'cervine animal'. The opposite is **broadening**.

narrow-scope comparison The term used by Manaster Ramer and Hitchcock (1996) for a type of comparison in which the investigator searches the languages under examination *only* for apparent matches to forms and meanings determined in advance. Compare **wide-scope comparison**.

n-ary comparison In **comparative linguistics**, comparing more than two languages at a time, particularly in the hope of finding genetic links. There has been some statistical work on the circumstances in which n-ary comparison gives better results than strictly **bilateral comparison**; see the references under the **probabilistic approach**. Note that the term **multilateral comparison** commonly denotes only a type of n-ary comparison based purely on **inspection**.

nasal infix In PIE and in some of the older IE languages, a segment /n/ which is infixed into the middle of a verbal root for certain grammatical purposes, especially to construct a present active form of a transitive verb. The system is best preserved in Indo-Iranian but is still visible in Latin, which has verbs like *pingere* 'paint', supine *pictum* (< PIE **peig-*) and *tangere* 'touch', supine *tactum* (< PIE **teg-*).

nasalization Any phonological change in which a segment acquires a nasal character which it formerly lacked. For example, /b/ was nasalized to /m/ in early Basque in the configuration */bVn/, and the later categorical loss of intervocalic /n/ left behind contrastively nasalized vowels, both developments being illustrated by the word */bini/ 'tongue' > */mini/ > /mĩhĩ/ (modern Souletin; other varieties have undergone further developments). The opposite is **denasalization**.

nasal mutation In Welsh, a **mutation** which changes /b d g/ to /m n ŋ/ and /p t k/ to voiceless versions of /m n ŋ/.

Nasite An accurate but little-used name for **Hittite**, reflecting the discovery that the speakers of Hittite called themselves *Nas*.

nativization 1. Another term for **adaptation**. 2. See **loan nativization**.

natural change A linguistic change which is frequent in languages and easy to understand in terms of motivation and pathway. Examples of natural phonological changes include the palatalization of velars before front vowels, the devoicing of word-final obstruents, and the voicing, lenition or loss of intervocalic consonants. The opposite is **unnatural change**.

naturalization Another term for **adaptation**.

naturalness 1. The property of a linguistic change which is frequent and easy to understand. An example is the palatalization of velar consonants before front vowels, which is easy to understand in terms of the movements of the speech organs. The degree to which natural changes can be securely identified has been much debated, and not all linguists are satisfied that a concept of naturalness has any part to play in historical linguistics. See **process naturalness**. 2. A principle of **reconstruction**, by which a reconstructed phoneme system should be natural (similar to those found in attested languages). See **system naturalness**.

natural serialization principle A putative principle of **syntactic change**, by which languages tend strongly to conform to the word-order universals of Greenberg (1963a), notably in conforming across the board to one of the orders modifier–head or head–modifier. A language which fails to conform is deemed to be unstable and in the middle of a **word-order change** from one pattern to the other. The principle was named and defended by Vennemann (1974), though he was not the first to propose it. See McMahon (1994: 138–160) for critical discussion.

Naturwissenschaft-Geisteswissenschaft **debate** The nineteenth-century debate about whether linguistics (in practice, historical linguistics) was one of the natural ('hard') sciences or one of the humanities. The first, 'etymological', view, defended by Schleicher and by the **Neogrammarians** and their successors, has generally been triumphant and is the modern orthodoxy. The second, 'ideological' or 'psychological', view, espoused by Humboldt, is associated with an emphasis on typology and above all with **stadialism**, and it regards language as part and parcel of race and culture; today it is effectively dead. See the **language-oriented framework** and the **speaker-oriented framework**.

near-merger (also **half-contrast**) The phenomenon in which the speakers of a particular language variety consistently produce an objectively observable distinction between the phones (usually vowels) occurring in two sets of words while at the same time they deny the existence of any difference between the phones in question and are unable to hear the difference in the speech of their neighbours or in recordings of their own speech. Among the reported examples are *source* and *sauce* in New York City, *pool* and *pull* in Albuquerque, *too* and *toe*, and also *beer* and *bear*, in Norwich, *line* and *loin* in Essex, *meat* and *mate* in Belfast, and *ferry* and *furry* in Philadelphia. The phenomenon was discovered, and has been chiefly investigated, by William Labov and his colleagues (Labov *et al.* 1972, 1991; Labov 1975, 1994: chs 12–14). Labov (1975) suggests that many problematic historically reported **mergers** may in fact have been near-mergers of this kind.

neglect of known history (also **ancestral disparity**) In **comparison**, the practice of extracting a form blindly from a language or family and using it as a **comparandum** in seeking wider genetic links, when specialists can show clearly that the cited form cannot possibly be ancient or cannot possibly have had its cited form or meaning at an earlier stage. For example, regional Basque *mihi* 'tongue' has been compared with somewhat similar-looking forms in other languages, even though specialists can show that it derives from Pre-Basque **bini*; Arapaho *hiii'* 'snow' has been compared with similar-looking words in other languages, even though it derives from Proto-Algonquian **okoona*. This intolerable practice is all too prevalent among those **long-rangers** who work entirely by **inspection**. See **transferred sense**.

Nehali Another form of **Nahali**.

Neogrammarian comparison The term used by Nichols (1995b, 1997d) to denote any procedure that establishes **systematic correspondences** and then uses these to identify and trace **cognates** and to set up a **family tree** with substantial **subgrouping**. In her characterization, this involves **closed comparison** on the phonological side but open-ended and often extremely wide-ranging semantic comparisons, and it can be done only after the basic fact of relatedness is established. Compare **heuristic comparison**.

Neogrammarian Hypothesis (also **regularity hypothesis**) The hypothesis that all **phonological change** is regular, often formulated as follows: every sound change takes place according to laws that admit no exception. In this view, a phonological change must apply absolutely and simultaneously to every single linguistic form in the language which exhibits the relevant phonological form. That is, neither the meaning nor the grammatical nature of a form is of the slightest relevance, and no tendency to the **avoidance of merger** can interfere Apparent exceptions to a sound change are only that: *apparent* exceptions indicating only that we have not yet succeeded in formulating the sound law with complete accuracy.

Propounded by the **Neogrammarians** in the 1870s, the doctrine was at first opposed by older linguists who preferred to see sound changes as mere 'tendencies' that might or might not apply in particular cases, rather than as absolute 'laws'. However, the hypothesis has one great advantage as a heuristic. If you believe that exceptions are normal, then you will take no interest in explaining them; but if you believe that real exceptions cannot exist and that apparent exceptions must have an explanation, then you will devote your energies to finding those explanations, and, if they exist, you will very likely find them. The success of the Neogrammarians in doing just this, together with a wide perception that their doctrine was more 'scientific' than the older approach, led to the adoption of the Neogrammarian Hypothesis as linguistic orthodoxy, a position it retained until the 1960s and in large measure still retains today. Nevertheless, the work of the sociolinguists, who have uncovered such anti-Neogrammarian phenomena as **lexical diffusion**, has shown that the hypothesis cannot be strictly true. Even so, the majority of historical linguists still prefer to adopt it as their normal working procedure. Labov (1994) decomposes the hypothesis into two parts: the **Mechanical Principle** and the **Regularity Principle**. See Kiparsky (1988) for a critical review of the hypothesis.

Neogrammarians (Ger *Junggrammatiker*) A label originally applied to a group of young historical linguists at Leipzig University who first proclaimed the **Neogrammarian Hypothesis,** seen by most established linguists at the time as foolish. The most prominent Neogrammarians were Karl Brugmann, Berthold Delbrück, August Leskien and Hermann Osthoff. The label is sometimes applied more broadly to all linguists who espouse the hypothesis.

Neolinguistics An approach to linguistics developed by the Italian Matteo Bàrtoli in the first half of the twentieth century. Its proponents were interested in maps, and often maintained that the study of **dialect maps** and other maps could be used to establish a valid diachronic perspective independent of Neogrammarian methods.

Their **peripheral-region criterion** has been widely accepted, but otherwise the movement has had little influence outside Italy.

neologism (also **coinage**) A recently coined word, especially one constructed consciously and deliberately by one person or by an official body.

neutralization Another term for **syncretism**.

New Synthesis, The A label which has been applied to recent efforts at combining the findings of historical linguistics, genetics and physical anthropology, and sometimes also archaeology, in the hope of obtaining information about the ancient movements of peoples and languages. Most prominent here are the linguist Joseph Greenberg and the geneticist Luigi Luca Cavalli-Sforza, who, sometimes with the anthropologists Christy Turner and Stephen Zegura and others, have argued that linguistic, genetic and physical anthropological groupings of the peoples of the world correspond so closely that we may reasonably interpret these groupings as representing prehistoric populations which settled the various parts of the earth. Though it has found some support, this work is deeply controversial, and it has been subjected at times to fierce criticism from a number of angles. In particular, Greenberg's proposed linguistic groupings, based upon **multilateral comparison**, have been attacked as unsubstantiated; Cavalli-Sforza's methodology and conclusions have been called into question; and, most importantly, the claimed fit has been dismissed as illusory. See Greenberg *et al.* (1986), Cavalli-Sforza *et al.* (1988), O'Grady *et al.* (1989), Bateman *et al.* (1990), Cavalli-Sforza (1991), and Cavalli-Sforza *et al.* (1992); see also the **Renfrew hypothesis** and the references under **multilateral comparison**.

Nichols progression The tendency of languages to renew their possessive markers from free pronouns, with the new pattern extended to most nouns and marking alienable possession, while the older one remains fossilized on a small number of nouns and marks inalienable possession. This is noted by Nichols (1988, 1992: 270).

nickname An additional name, often a humorous or affectionate one, conferred upon an individual, often in recognition of some quality of the recipient. For example, the baseball player George Herman Ruth was known as *Babe Ruth*; the politician Margaret Thatcher was known as *The Iron Lady* and as *Attila the Hen*; and the golfer José María Olazábal is known as *Ollie*.

Nicobarese A group of two languages spoken in the Nicobar Islands. Nicobarese is assigned to the **Austro-Asiatic** family, though its position within the family is debated.

Nieminen's Law The proposal, put forward by Nieminen (1922: 125–170), that certain accentual alternations in Baltic, such as in Lithuanian *diẽvas* 'God' (nom. sg.), *dievaĩ* (nom. pl.), result from a leftward shift in certain (not all) singular forms. (Compare PIE *deiwós* (nom. sg.).) See Collinge (1985: 119–120) for an account.

Niger-Congo A vast language family occupying most of sub-Saharan Africa, also called *Niger-Kordofanian* when the problematic **Kordofanian** languages are regarded as coordinate with the rest of the family, as proposed by Joseph Greenberg (1963b). The family contains between 1000 and 1500 languages. Though the validity of the family is accepted by most specialists, the large number of languages and the seemingly great time depth at which they are related has posed difficulties: subgrouping is controversial, and only limited progress has been made in reconstructing the ancestral language; a few sceptics have wondered whether Niger-Congo is a secure family at all. The widely extended **Bantu** group forms just one low-ranking branch of Niger-Congo. Generally recognized as primary or major branches of Niger-Congo are **Mande, Kordofanian, West Atlantic, Ijoid, Kru, Gur, Adamawa-Ubangi, Kwa** and the vast **Benue-Congo**, while the single language *Dogon* has so far resisted all attempts at placing it within any subgrouping. See Bendor-Samuels and Hartell (1989).

Niger-Kordofanian See under **Niger-Congo**.

Niger-Saharan Another term for **Congo-Saharan**.

Nihali Another form of **Nahali**.

Nilo-Saharan A large language family (perhaps 160 languages) proposed by Joseph Greenberg (1963b) and including all those languages spoken in or near the African Sudan which cannot be assigned either to **Afro-Asiatic** to the north and east or to **Niger-Congo** to the south. The family extends in a discontinuous belt from northeastern

Nigeria and southern Libya to eastern Tanzania, with a single remote
outlier (**Songhai**) in west Africa. Greenberg originally proposed six
coordinate subgroups, including a huge **Chari-Nile** group, but later
work has reorganized his classification and usually rejected Chari-
Nile. While many subgroups are secure, the validity of the whole
family is controversial; it is accepted by some specialists but queried
or rejected by others. Particularly controversial is the inclusion of
Songhai, which some specialists prefer to regard as an isolate. In fact,
Greenberg himself originally recognized no fewer than ten distinct
phyla before deciding to lump all of them into Nilo-Saharan. Among
the major languages assigned to the family are *Maasai*, *Dinka*,
Kanuri, *Luo*, **Nubian** and *Acholi*. See Dimmendaal (1992) or Sim
(1994) for a survey.

Nilotic A major branch of the **Nilo-Saharan** family, containing about
fifty languages. It was originally classed by Greenberg (1963b) as a
subgroup of the **East Sudanic** branch of his huge **Chari-Nile**
grouping. Among the best-known Nilotic languages are *Maasai*,
Acholi and *Luo*.

Nivkh Another term for **Gilyak**.

nomination The process of creating new names for either old or new
things.

nonce borrowing A word which is borrowed from language A into
language B on an *ad hoc* basis by a speaker of B who knows A. For
example, educated speakers of Tok Pisin who know English often
borrow technical terms from English in just this way; such borrowings are intelligible only to speakers of Tok Pisin who know English,
and do not constitute an ordinary part of the Tok Pisin lexicon.

nonce formation A word which is coined on a particular occasion for
special effect and which does not find a place in the language.

non-cognates Linguistic forms which are not **cognates**. The term is
particularly applied to similar-looking forms in a single language
which look as if they might be historically related and which are
treated by some investigator as related in seeking broader genetic
links for the language, but which in fact are not related at all. This is
a common problem in comparison by **inspection** alone. See **neglect
of known history**.

non-genetic language A language which cannot reasonably be regarded as descending directly from a single ancestor in the normal way. Two types of non-genetic mother tongue are commonly distinguished – **creoles** and **mixed languages** – but naturally there are languages which do not fit neatly into any pigeonhole. M. Ross (1996) suggests that languages which have undergone **metatypy** should also be regarded as non-genetic. Also non-genetic, but not mother tongues, are **pidgins, invented languages** and **artificial languages**. See also **portmanteau language**. Other languages are **normally transmitted languages**.

non-peripheral track See under **peripheral track**.

non-proportional analogy Any instance of **analogy** other than **four-part analogy**.

non-rhotic accent Any accent of English in which the historical /r/ is lost everywhere except before a vowel, so that *farther* becomes homophonous with *father* and *star* rhymes with *Shah*. Non-rhotic accents are typical of most of England, Wales, the eastern and southern USA, parts of the Caribbean and all the Southern Hemisphere countries. Compare **rhotic accent**.

NORM A non-mobile, older, rural male – the sort of person considered the ideal informant in a traditional kind of **dialectology**. Earlier dialectologists were inclined to think that such people spoke the 'purest' form of a dialect, one from which other speakers had strayed. This idea is no longer taken seriously.

normalization The development of norms in a language, sometimes particularly in a **contact language**.

normally transmitted language A language which is not a **non-genetic language**; a language which is descended from a single ancestor in the ordinary way.

Normalstufe See under **ablaut**.

normative change A language change which is consciously introduced by a small but influential group of people and then spreads more widely through the language. Ebert (1992) cites the case of verb-position in German subordinate clauses, which was highly variable before a group of chancery administrators standardized verb-final order, which then became general in the language.

Norn The extinct north **Germanic** language of the Shetlands, the Orkneys and parts of mainland Scotland, introduced by Viking settlers from Norway in the ninth century AD or earlier. It died out around the eighteenth century.

Northeast Caucasian Another term for **Nakh-Dagestan**.

Northern Cities Shift A major and vigorous vowel shift currently affecting up to six vowels in urban areas in a part of the USA ranging from New England to Chicago. In this shift, peripheral vowels are rotating clockwise, while non-peripheral vowels are rotating anticlockwise: /æ/ is being raised toward [i], /aː/ is being fronted toward [æ], /ɔː/ is being fronted toward [aː], /ɪ/ is being lowered toward [ɛ], /ɛ/ is being lowered and backed toward [ʌ], and / ʌ / is being backed toward [ɔ]. As a result, a speaker who has not undergone the shift, when listening to one who has, may mishear *Ann* as *Ian*, *socks* as *sax*, *chalk* as *chock*, *steady* as *study*, *sing* as *sang*, *bus* as *boss*, and so on. See Labov (1994: 177–201) for an account. Compare **Southern Shift**.

North Picene An extinct language recorded in four inscriptions near the Adriatic coast of Italy in the sixth and fifth centuries BC. The texts are unintelligible, and nothing whatever can be concluded about the language. Compare **South Picene**.

Northwest Caucasian Another term for **Abkhaz-Adyge**.

Northwest Indo-European A hypothetical subgroup of **Indo-European**, including **Germanic**, **Celtic** and **Italic**, and sometimes also **Balto-Slavic**, posited as having constituted a single language at a date when the other branches of IE had already split off.

Nostratic A proposed macro-family consisting of **Indo-European**, **Uralic**, **Altaic**, **Afro-Asiatic**, **Kartvelian** and **Dravidian**, and in some versions additional languages and families, such as **Eskimo-Aleut**, **Gilyak**, **Chukchi-Kamchatkan**, **Elamite** and **Sumerian**. The Nostratic hypothesis was put forward by the Danish linguist Holger Pedersen in 1903, but Pedersen did little work on it. (Pedersen's version excluded Kartvelian and Dravidian, but included

Eskimo-Aleut.) The idea languished half-forgotten until the 1960s, when the Russian linguists Vladimir Illič-Svityč and Aharon Dolgopolsky independently began to work seriously on it; it was Illič-Svityč who added Dravidian and Kartvelian. Before his early death, Illič-Svityč was reportedly able to compile some 700 Nostratic etymologies and to propose phonological changes relating Proto-Nostratic to all six putative daughters. Much of this work has now been published, and it is currently being extended by several Russian and American linguists, including Dolgopolsky, Vitaly Shevoroshkin, Alexis Manaster Ramer and Mark Kaiser. In contrast to this mainstream, or 'Moscow–Ann Arbor', development of Nostratic ideas, the American Allan Bomhard has been developing a substantially different version involving mostly the same languages but different correspondences. The reaction to the Nostratic hypothesis has been mixed, ranging from enthusiasm to open hostility; most linguists appear to be adopting a wait-and-see attitude. See Manaster Ramer (1993a) for a critical review of Illič-Svityč's work, Kaiser and Shevoroshkin (1988) for a representative presentation of Nostratic work, Dolgopolsky (1998) for a presentation stressing linguistic palaeontology, and Bomhard (1990), Bomhard and Kerns (1994), or Bomhard (1996) for Bomhard's version. See Salmons and Joseph (1998) for a collection of articles pro and con. At the time of writing, Dolgopolsky's comprehensive *Nostratic Dictionary* is in preparation. See also **Eurasiatic, Sibero-European**.

Nostratic fallacy A label applied by sceptics to the two related views that the **genetic model** is the most appropriate **model of linguistic descent** for all work in historical linguistics, and that **language families** can be identified and **proto-languages** reconstructed back into the past without any principled limit on time depth. Compare the **Indo-European fallacy**.

Notker's Law (also **Notker's Canon, Notker's** *Anlautgesetz*) A highly distinctive spelling convention in the voluminous writings of the medieval German monk Notker III Teutonicus, who wrote in Old High German. Briefly, the ordinary spellings <p t k/c f> were replaced by <b d g v> (respectively) in syllable-initial position if the segment in question was preceded by a vowel, a liquid or a nasal. For nearly two centuries historical linguists have debated the possible significance of this orthography, without reaching any conclusions. See Collinge (1985: 121–125) for critical discussion with references.

Nubian A cluster of closely related languages or dialects spoken in southern Egypt and northern Sudan. Nubian is the only **Nilo-Saharan** language with a long written tradition; there are texts from the eighth to the fourteenth centuries AD.

nuclear zone The geographical heart of the region occupied by a language or language family, where it is protected by distance from significant contact with adjoining languages or families. It has been suggested that the speech of a nuclear zone is characterized by internal change alone and by almost totally regular phonological change of the Neogrammarian kind. Compare **transitional zone**.

null hypothesis (of language relatedness) Any logical starting position in **comparative linguistics**. For most linguists, the null hypothesis is 'no languages are related (until proven otherwise).' A few **long-rangers**, however, adopt the opposite null hypothesis: 'all languages are related (and the only issue is **subgrouping**).' The second position is anathema to the great majority.

Nullstufe See under **ablaut**.

Nuristani (formerly **Kafiri**) A group of five or six languages spoken in the upper reaches of the Afghan Hindu Kush. They are clearly **Indo-Iranian**, but their place is disputed; most see them as forming a third coordinate group with Indo-Aryan and Iranian, but some suspect them of being an archaic branch of Iranian.

nursery word (Ger *Lallwort*, rarely also **teknolalic word**) A word which is coined by adults for the purpose of addressing small children, often one which deliberately imitates the child's first utterances. Nursery words of such forms as *mama, ama, tata, ata, dada, papa, baba*, often called *babbling words* or *mama-papa vocabulary*, are exceedingly common in the world's languages in such senses as 'mother', 'father' and 'breast'; such words are useless as comparanda in **comparative linguistics**, because they are so often independently created.

obelos Another term for the **dagger**.

oblique cognates Two or more words in related languages which continue alternant forms of a single root in the ancestral language.

An example is English *feather*, from PIE **pet-rā-*, and Greek *pteron* 'feather, wing', from PIE **pt-ero-*, both PIE forms representing PIE **pet-* 'fly'. Compare **partial cognates, root cognates**.

obsolescence The gradual disappearance of a linguistic form. Most obviously, words pass out of use when their referents disappear, as has happened with the English words pertaining to falconry, like *jess* and *haggard*. Obsolescence need not reflect real-world developments, however. Denison (1992) argues that the English modal *may* is obsolescent in many varieties, being steadily displaced by *might* – though in vernacular British English it is *might* which is being displaced by *may* in certain functions, as in *I thought we may still have a chance* and *We may have won* (= *We might have won* [but didn't]).

Ob-Ugric The eastern branch of **Ugric**, containing the two languages *Khanty* and *Mansi*.

Oceanic A huge branch of the **Austronesian** family, containing nearly all the languages of the Pacific and many of those of New Guinea – well over 400 languages in all. **Polynesian** constitutes one small branch of Oceanic.

oddity condition The label given by Lass (1997: 230) to the following principle of **reconstruction**: the rarer a segment is cross-linguistically, the more evidence we need to reconstruct it in a given case (unless it is frequent in the relevant family or the relevant area).

o-grade See under **ablaut**.

Old 1. Preceding a language name, a label used in some conventional chronological classification of a language to denote the earliest period for which substantial material is recorded in the language, as in **Old English**. Compare **Middle, Modern**. 2. An element conventionally included in the names of certain languages which are attested in writing in the more or less distant past and which have given rise either to no descendants or to several descendants with different names, as in **Old Church Slavonic**.

Old Church Slavonic The language of the first texts written in a **Slavic** language, between AD 863 and about 950. This was a south Slavic language, and it is sometimes called *Old Bulgarian*.

Old English (also **Anglo-Saxon**) The name given to the earliest recorded period of English, from the first texts around 800 to about 1100. See Lass (1994), Robinson (1992: ch. 6), Voyles (1992: ch. 6).

Old European An unrecorded and hypothetical language which, in the view of Krahe (1962), underlies almost all river names in a vast area of Europe, and must have been spoken in the second millennium BC. Krahe sees this language as clearly **Indo-European**, a conclusion endorsed by Schmid (1987), but critics like Beekes (1995: 31–32) argue that no single language could ever have covered such an enormous extent of territory, while Vennemann (1994 and elsewhere) has argued instead that Old European existed but was non-Indo-European; he favours a connection with **Basque**. Vennemann's case is countered by Kitson (1996).

Old Frisian A **Germanic** language attested in writing about AD 1275–1600 along the North Sea coast of Europe and more or less directly ancestral to modern *Frisian*. See Voyles (1992: ch. 7), Robinson (1992: ch. 7).

Old High German The name given to the earliest recorded form of the Germanic varieties which underwent the **Second Germanic Consonant Shift**, the varieties which are the more-or-less direct ancestors of modern standard **German**. The name is applied to the language from the appearance of the first substantial texts in the eighth century AD until AD 1100 or 1200, after which the later forms are called **Middle High German**. See Robinson (1992: ch. 9), Voyles (1992: ch. 9).

old language A meaningless term. Except for **non-genetic languages**, which are a special case, all spoken languages are equally 'old' in that all are descended, without interruption, from the remote ancestor(s) of human speech. Of course, some languages are more **conservative** than others, some have been established in their present positions longer than others, and some are recorded in writing earlier than others, but none of these conditions makes a language 'older' than another.

Old Low Franconian A **Germanic** language attested in the form of a few religious texts of uncertain date but apparently associated roughly with what is now eastern Belgium. The language is more or less the direct ancestor of some eastern varieties of *Dutch*, and is sometimes called *Old Dutch*, but standard Dutch in fact derives from a little-known relative called *West Franconian*. See Robinson (1992: ch. 8).

Old Norse The language of the Vikings, a **Germanic** language ancestral to *Icelandic*, *Faroese*, *Norwegian*, *Danish* and *Swedish*. The language is abundantly attested in writing from about the ninth to the thirteenth centuries AD, chiefly in Iceland, though some of the poems were probably composed earlier. Among the writings are the *Elder Edda* (or *Poetic Edda*), the *Younger Edda* (or *Prose Edda*), the sagas, skaldic poetry, and a number of historical and religious works. Repeated Viking invasions of England, and its conquest by the Danes in 1016, led to the substantial introduction of Old Norse vocabulary into Old English. See Price (1998: 332–335), Robinson (1992: 69–99), Voyles (1992: ch. 5).

Old Persian An early **Iranian** language, the principal language of the Persian Achaemenid Empire, abundantly recorded between the sixth and fourth centuries BC. Old Persian is one of the most important early IE languages for comparative purposes. Compare **Avestan**.

Old Prussian An extinct **Baltic** language, spoken until the seventeenth century in the former German region of East Prussia. See Price (1998: 371–372).

Old Saxon A **Germanic** language formerly spoken in much of north-western Germany and substantially recorded from about the eighth to tenth centuries AD. The chief text is a life of Jesus called the *Heliand*, dated to AD 830–850; also important is the *Hildebrandslied*, whose language departs somewhat from that of other Old Saxon texts. Old Saxon is the more or less direct ancestor of some northern (Low) varieties of **German**. See Robinson (1992: 100–135), Voyles (1992: ch. 8).

om. The abbreviation for 'omits' (Latin *omittit*). In an **edition** of a text, an annotation like '*a triur*: *om.* Y' means that the words *a triur*, found at this point in other copies of a text, are missing from a particular copy abbreviated here as 'Y'.

Omotic A group of about thirty-four languages spoken in and near western Ethiopia. Formerly classified as **Cushitic**, the Omotic languages are now widely regarded as a distinct coordinate branch of **Afro-Asiatic**.

'once a language boundary, always a language boundary' Grace's (1996) term for a familiar assumption of historical linguistics: two distinct languages cannot merge into a single language. This assumption is challenged by some recent work; see, for example, **portmanteau language**, **mixed language** and several of the entries under **model of linguistic descent**.

one-meaning-one-form Another term for **isomorphy**.

one-vowel theory of PIE The hypothesis that PIE possessed only a single phonemic vowel, commonly represented as *e, and that the remaining four vowels usually assigned to it (*a, *o, *i, *u), plus the long counterparts of all five, can all be derived from other sources by internal developments, chiefly from **ablaut**, from the **vocalization** of the glides *y and *w, and from the effects of **laryngeals**. In spite of its considerable success, this hypothesis is generally rejected today, partly on the typological ground that no genuine one-vowel language has ever been discovered. Nevertheless, versions of it are still defended for **Pre-Proto-Indo-European**; see for example W. P. Lehmann (1993: ch. 6).

'only six' argument Any claim of the following general form: 'Only six (or fifteen, or thirty-five) good-looking matches between linguistic forms in two or more languages are enough to prove genetic relatedness beyond all reasonable doubt.' Such claims have been advanced many times, with numbers ranging from two to 100, sometimes with further qualifications, such as 'in the **Swadesh word list**' or 'according to certain phonological criteria'. At present, no version of this argument appears to have sufficient statistical underpinning to persuade sceptics.

onomastics The study of names, particularly of the origins and histories of names; one branch of **philology**.

onomastic sound change A phonological change which occurs in names but is not otherwise usual in the language, at least not at the time. Clark (1991) argues that such changes may include accelerated early manifestations of later and more general changes, especially **attrition** (sense 1).

onomatization The conversion of a linguistic form into a name.

onomatopoeia 1. (also **imitative word**) A word which is coined in an attempt to represent a non-linguistic sound by a combination of segments selected from the ordinary phoneme inventory of the language. Examples include English *buzz*, *clink*, *cock-a-doodle-do*, *meow* and *tinkle* and Basque *tu* 'spit' and *usin* 'sneeze'. Since they are so often independently created, such words are not available as **comparanda** in comparison. In a dead language, onomatopoeias may provide clues to pronunciation. For example, Aristophanes' use of *βῆ* to represent the sound of a sheep confirms that <β> represented /b/ and <η> something like /ε:/. (The same sequence spells /vi/ in modern Greek.) 2. More broadly, any type of **sound symbolism**. This second sense is probably objectionable.

op. cit. The abbreviation for 'in the work cited' (Latin *in opere citato*); see *loc. cit.*

open-ended comparison A particular procedure sometimes used in searching for **remote relationships** among languages. The investigator chooses a word or form from language A and then 'trawls' through the lexicon of language B, checking items which are increasingly remote in meaning (and form) from the first word, in the hope of eventually finding a possible cognate. For example, if 'woman' is chosen in A, then B is checked for 'woman'; if the result is not deemed to be a match, then 'wife' is checked; if there is still no match, the investigator proceeds to check 'female', 'aunt', 'daughter', 'sister', 'grandmother', 'old woman', 'crone' and so on. Typically, finding a 'match' at any point is deemed to be a 'hit', and the search is terminated. This methodology, much favoured by some (not all) self-styled **long-rangers**, is deeply suspect, since it is subject to no controls and recognizes only positive evidence; there is no such thing as negative evidence. See Nichols (1995b) for a critique, and compare **closed comparison**. A restrictive variety of open-ended comparison is a **limited search**.

opening Another term for **lowering**.

Open Syllables, Law of (also **Rising Sonority, Law of**) A series of formally unrelated phonological changes in common **Slavic** which had the combined effect of making all syllables open. This is a famous example of a diachronic **conspiracy**.

order A group of consonant phonemes in a language which have more or less the same place of articulation but differ in voicing and/or in manner; hence, for example, the labial order in PIE consists of */p b bh/. Compare **series**.

organic Of a segment, constituting part of a lexical root, and not part of an affix or inserted for phonological reasons. When dealing with complex word-forms in **comparison**, it is essential to distinguish the organic segments from such *inorganic* ones to avoid being misled. See the **total accountability principle**.

original long diphthong In earlier reconstructions of PIE, a diphthong such as */ōi/ or */ēi/, which apparently had to be reconstructed with a long first element. Most of these have more recently been reanalysed as sequences of the form */eHi/, where /H/ is a laryngeal, but one or two instances, such as *$p\bar{o}i$- 'drink', seemingly cannot be so reconstructed, and the question remains open.

original long vowel In PIE, any contrastively long vowel which must be reconstructed as primitive. The frequency of occurrence of these things was greatly reduced by the **laryngeal** theory, in which many of them were reanalysed as sequences of a short vowel followed by a laryngeal; for example, *$dh\bar{e}$- 'put' has been reinterpreted as *$dheH_1$-. Some long vowels, however, seemingly cannot be so reinterpreted, and most specialists today still posit a set of contrastive long vowels for PIE.

oronym In **onomastics**, the name of a mountain.

Oscan An extinct **Italic** language recorded in southern Italy from about 400 BC to AD 79, and closely related to **Umbrian** in the **Sabellian** grouping.

Osco-Umbrian Another term for **Sabellian**, but see the qualifications under that entry.

Osthoff's Law A vowel-shortening process occurring in early **Greek** (and possibly in other IE languages; this is debated), pointed out by Osthoff (1879, 1881, 1884). By this process, a long vowel underwent shortening when it occurred in the environment V:RC, where R is a liquid or a nasal (or possibly also a glide; this is disputed) and C is any plosive or /s/. This change preceded the loss of most word-final consonants in Greek. See Collinge (1985: 127–131) for a critical survey with references.

Oswalt shift test A simple statistical procedure for testing whether the resemblances in vocabulary between two languages are significantly greater than chance, and hence evidence for a possible genetic link. The test operates with a standard word-list, typically the 100-word version of the **Swadesh word list**, and it works as follows. First, compile word lists for the two languages under scrutiny. Second, choose any criteria of phonological resemblance you like. Third, make a series of passes. On the first pass, compare word 1 in language A with word 2 in language B, word 2 in A with word 3 in B, and so on, concluding with word 100 in A and word 1 in B. In each case, determine whether the words do or do not match according to your selected criteria. Calculate the percentage of matches in the 100 comparisons.

Make a second pass, this time comparing word 1 in A with word 3 in B, word 2 in A with word 4 in B, and so on, and again calculate the percentage of matches. Do this 99 times, in the obvious way, and then average the 99 results. This is the *background score*, representing the probability that two arbitrary words in A and B will match according to your criteria. Then make one more pass, this time comparing word 1 in A with word 1 in B, and so on, and thus calculate the percentage of matches between words of identical meaning. If the result is significantly greater than the background score, you may have evidence for a genetic link.

The test was proposed by Robert Oswalt (1991); see also Oswalt (1998).

Oto-Manguean An exceptionally large and deep (but secure) American language family extending from central Mexico to Costa Rica; it has eight principal branches, and it numbers anywhere from about thirty to eighty languages, depending chiefly on how the large and messy *Zapotecan* branch is counted. The family may be over 6000 years old, but its proto-language has been reconstructed in exceptional detail. The Oto-Manguean languages are among the most typologically divergent of all American families, and even Greenberg hesitated to include them in his **Amerind** construct. See Campbell (1997a: 157–159).

overadjustment Another term for **lower-middle-class crossover**.

overlapping correspondences The state of affairs in which two related languages exhibit multiple **systematic correspondences** in which a single segment in one language corresponds to two (or more) different segments in the other. For example, the Algonquian languages Fox and Plains Cree exhibit the correspondences F /hk/ : PC /sk/ and F /hk/ : PC /hk/, and also F /ʃk/ : PC /sk/ and F /ʃk/ : PC /hk/, with complex overlaps in the corresponding segments. Such overlaps may result either from **splits** or from **mergers** in some of the languages, and they constitute a potentially difficult problem in **reconstruction**.

overlapping sound changes The state of affairs in which one phonological **change in progress** tends to create new cases for a second change in progress to apply to. Anttila (1989: 191) cites the case of seventeenth-century English, in which the change /ʊ/ > / ʌ / was in progress at the same time as /uː/ > /ʊ/. Both *good* and *blood* had /uː/, but only the second underwent shortening frequently enough to participate in the unrounding; the vowel of *good* was eventually shortened, but too late to be unrounded. Compare **competing changes**.

oxytone In ancient Greek, a word with an acute accent on the last syllable; more generally, a word in any language accented on the last syllable. Compare **barytone**.

P

pace Preceding someone's name, a polite way of indicating that you are disagreeing with that person. For example, '*pace* Krahe' indicates that you are about to disagree with some view of Krahe's for which you nevertheless have some respect. Latin *pace* means 'with peace (towards)'. Compare *contra, apud*.

Paelignian An extinct **Italic** language of east-central Italy, closely related to **Oscan**.

Paeonian An extinct language anciently spoken in Thrace; virtually nothing is known about it.

Paezan A family of about six languages in Colombia and Ecuador. Paezan is widely thought to be distantly related to **Barbacoan**. See **Chibchan-Paezan**.

Pakawan See under **Coahuiltecan**.

palaeography The study of **manuscripts** (hand-written texts). Sometimes this term is applied to the study of ancient writing systems generally. Compare **epigraphy**.

palaeolinguistics 1. The term proposed by Décsy (1983) and Hegedűs (1997) for reconstruction performed upon **proto-languages** themselves reconstructed by comparing attested languages (**proto-linguistics**). See also **archaeolinguistics**. 2. The term used by Lass (1997: 235) for contemplation of the nature(s) of the first human language(s) ever spoken.

Palaeo-Sardinian A collective label for the little-known languages spoken in Sardinia before the Roman conquest. Some specialists have suggested connections with **Basque**, with **Iberian** and with **Berber**, but nothing can be established.

Palaeosiberian A geographical designation sometimes applied loosely to the several small language families of Siberia, including **Chukchi-Kamchatkan**, **Yeniseian**, **Yukaghir** and the isolate **Gilyak**. There is no suggestion that these four groups form a genetic family.

Palaic An extinct language of ancient Anatolia, closely related to **Hittite** within the **Anatolian** branch of **Indo-European**, but seemingly even more archaic than Hittite.

palatalization A cover term for any phonological change in which one of the following happens: a segment acquires a palatal component which it formerly lacked (as when [p] become [pʲ]); the articulation of a segment moves closer to the palate (as when [k] becomes [kʲ]); a segment articulated in some other position is converted into a palatal or palato-alveolar segment (as when [t] becomes [c] or [k] becomes [tʃ]). Palatalization phenomena are pervasive in languages, and are highly natural in certain circumstances, notably when the segment in question is followed (or less commonly preceded) by a front vowel or glide. Non-phonological palatalization is also frequent in the formation of diminutives and affective forms, as when Basque *zezen* [sesen] 'bull' gives rise to *xexen* [ʃeʃen] 'little bull' and *zoko* [soko] 'corner' gives rise to *xoko* [ʃoko] or *txoko* [tʃoko] 'nook, cosy little place'. The opposite is **depalatalization**.

palatals, law of (Ger *Palatalengesetz*) The realization, in the 1870s, that the Sanskrit vowel system /i a u/ derived from an earlier system */i e a o u/, and that problematic instances of Sanskrit palatal consonants before /a/ represented cases of the palatalization of velars before */e/, which had then later merged with /a/, destroying the conditioning environment. This discovery had many important consequences: it solved a major problem in comparative IE, it dethroned Sanskrit from its allegedly 'archaic' status among IE languages, it allowed a five-vowel system to be reconstructed for PIE, and it neatly accounted for previously puzzling Sanskrit formations like *cakára*, the reduplicated perfect of *kr-* 'make', for expected **kakára* – the PIE form was **ke-kor-e*. More or less the same insight struck a number of linguists at the same time and it has proved impossible to assign priority of discovery, which is why this observation, uniquely among the 'laws' of IE, has no one's name attached to it. See Collinge (1985: 133–142) for a lengthy account with references.

Pāli An early **Indo-Aryan** language, one of the **Prākrits** and the language of the Buddhist scriptures.

palimpsest A document from which an earlier text has been erased in order to make way for a new one.

Pama-Nyungan The name given to a group of **Australian languages** occupying the larger part of the Australian continent. The Pama-Nyungan languages are typologically rather similar to one another, and typologically different from the remaining languages of Australia, collectively called *non-Pama-Nyungan* and concentrated in the northern corner of Australia. It is not known whether Pama-Nyungan constitutes a valid taxon or whether it merely represents those members of a larger Australian family which have not happened to undergo any radical changes in their morphology. Dixon (1997) argues that the Pama-Nyungan languages do not constitute a valid genetic family at all, but merely represent the result of tens of millennia of **diffusion** of linguistic features across language boundaries; other specialists disagree.

pan-Americanism A linguistic item which seems to recur with similar form and meaning in a number of American languages not known to be related. See Campbell (1997a: 257–259) for a discussion with references.

panchrony 1. For Saussure (1916) and others since, the universal principles of language structure, which cannot be violated by the consequences of any linguistic change. 2. A label applied to several distinct but related views put forward in recent years, by which **diachrony** cannot be rigidly separated from **synchrony**, and language use is seen as fundamentally creative, with the synchronic state of a language always involving decisions currently being made by speakers and hence as always involving a diachronic element. For representative examples of such work, see Christie (1982) (the first to use the term in this sense), Hopper (1979a, 1979b, 1982, 1987), Heine *et al.* (1991a), Nichols and Timberlake (1991) and Hagège (1993). See also **retextualization**.

panda principle A very general constraint upon **reconstructions**. It says this: in the absence of powerful evidence, an implausible reconstruction should be rejected in favour of a plausible one. (Here *plausible* means 'frequent in attested languages'.) This principle has long been recognized, and it forms the basis of typological constraints on reconstruction; the slightly facetious label was borrowed by Lass (1997: 30) from the palaeontologist Stephen Jay Gould.

pandemic irregularity The term applied by Blust (1996) to instances of irregularity which occur in a whole language family or a major branch of it, typically affecting different words in different languages. For example, alongside reflexes pointing consistently to Proto-Austronesian *-VCV- or *-VNCV-, Austronesian languages have hundreds of words in which some languages require *-VCV- but others *-VNCV-, in a completely haphazard manner; that is, no single language consistently requires one or the other.

Pannonian A variety of **Illyrian** anciently spoken in the Danube valley.

Papuan The name given to all the languages of New Guinea and some neighbouring islands which are not known to belong to any recognized family. Since this includes all the languages of New Guinea which do not belong to **Austronesian**, the Papuan languages are sometimes called the *non-Austronesian* languages (of New Guinea). New Guinea has the highest **linguistic density** on earth (there are about 1000 languages spoken in an area not much bigger than Texas), and no one knows if the Papuan languages are all related or not. The **Indo-Pacific** hypothesis claims that they are, but most specialists dismiss this hypothesis as unsubstantiated. At present the Papuan languages are classified into about sixty recognized genetic groupings. Wurm (1982) proposes a number of ambitious large-scale groupings, but these are at present unsupported by comparative evidence. See W. Foley (1986) for a survey.

paradigmatically structured morphemes Paradigmatic sets of morphemes, in languages undergoing **comparison**, which match closely enough to be regarded as evidence of a **genetic relationship**. Examples are numeral names and kinship terms. Nichols (1996: 63–64) suggests that such sets might prove useful in comparing languages having no morphology, but only in cases in which entire sets of terms match.

paradigmatic change Any type of phonological change which has consequences for the phonological system of a language, particularly one which increases or decreases the number of phonemes or which markedly changes the phonetic character of one or more of the phonemes. Among the most prominent types of paradigmatic change are **merger**, (secondary) **split** and the disappearance of a phoneme from a system (**merger with zero** - see **loss** (sense2)); **chain shifts** represent particularly dramatic paradigmatic changes. Compare **syntagmatic change**.

paradigmatic split (also **differentiation**) A change in which a single lexical item exhibiting an alternation in its stem within its paradigm splits into two distinct lexical items, each preserving one of the alternants and each typically equipped with a full paradigm. For example, Old English *stæf*, plural *stafas* [stavas], developed regularly into *staff*, plural *staves*, and this then split into two words: *staff*, plural *staffs*, and *stave*, plural *staves*. Similarly, Pre-Latin **deiwos* 'god', plural **deiwī*, developed regularly into singular *deus* and plural *divī*, and these then split into two distinct lexical items: *deus*, plural *deī*, *diī* or *dī*, and *divus*, plural *divī*. Other English examples include *shade* and *shadow* and *mead* and *meadow*. Compare **doublet** (sense 1).

paradigmatization Any change or set of changes leading to the construction of a full morphological paradigm which previously did not exist. See Hopper and Traugott (1993: 150–156) for some examples.

paradigm levelling 1. Reduction or elimination of alternations in stems within a paradigm. For example, older Frisian *kies* 'tooth', *kjizzen* 'teeth' has been replaced by *kjizze, kjizzen*, removing the alternation, and in many Polish place names the stem alternant found in the local cases has been extended to other cases which formerly had different alternants. 2. Any development which tends to obliterate morphological distinctions within a paradigm. Paolillo (1994) describes a process in classical Singhalese in which person-marking was levelled in favour of invariant third-singular marking in certain sentences.

paragoge (rarely also **epithesis**) The addition of one or more segments to the end of a word, as in English *against* from earlier *againes*. The addition of a vowel is **proparalepsis**; that of a consonant is **excrescence**.

parallel development Another term for **independent parallel innovation**.

parametric theory of change An approach to **language change** in terms of the 'parameter-setting' idea developed by Noam Chomsky. See the **Lightfoot framework**.

parasite vowel (also **parasitic vowel**) A vowel inserted by **anaptyxis**.

parasitic consonant A consonant inserted by **epenthesis**, sometimes especially an unusual instance of this. Andersen (1988) cites a Hessian dialect of German which has *iks* 'ice' (< **i:s*), *likp* 'body' (< **li:p*), *fukst* 'fist' (< **fu:st*), and so on for other former long high vowels.

parentheses The notational device '( )'. 1. A device used to represent **variants** succinctly, as in Basque *mintz(a)* 'membrane', showing that the form is variously *mintz* or *mintza*. Compare **swung dash**. 2. An alternative to **square brackets** (sense 1). 3. In a form cited as a **comparandum**, an indication that the material enclosed is not cognate. For example, we write 'Latin *centum* "100", Greek *(he)katón* "100"' to indicate that the first syllable of the Greek word is not considered to be cognate with any material in the Latin word. 4. In an etymology, an indication that the enclosed material does not form part of the etymology, as when French *pêche* 'peach' is derived from Latin *(malum) persicum* 'Persian (apple)', or that it appears to have disappeared without trace, as when western Basque *bari(a)ku*

'Friday' is derived from *(a)bari-ba(ga)ko-egun 'day without dinner'. 5. In a published version of a text, an indication that the material enclosed is the spelling out of an abbreviation in the original.

parent language A language which is the direct and immediate ancestor of another language, its **daughter language**.

paronomasia The technical term for a pun, or play on words.

paroxytone In Greek, a word with an acute accent on the penult; more generally, a word in any language accented on the penult. Compare **oxytone**.

partial assimilation See under **assimilation**.

partial cognates Linguistic forms which contain morphological material that is narrowly **cognate** but at least some of which contain additional material not present in the others. For example, taking *cognate* in the broader sense 2, we might say that English *wit* and *video* are partial cognates, since both contain PIE **weid-* 'see' but the second also contains additional material. See **root cognates**, and compare **oblique cognates**.

partial reduplication See under **reduplication**.

particulization The conversion of a lexical item into a grammatical particle. See Matisoff (1991: 387–402) for a case study in Lahu.

passim In citing a reference, an indication that the required material is scattered about within the pages of the work cited, as in 'Beekes (1995: *passim*)'. Latin *passim* means 'scattered about'.

pastoralist model Another term for the **zoomorphic model**.

past-present verb Another term for **preterite-present verb**.

patch-up rule Another term for **adaptive rule**.

pathway Another term for **trajectory** (senses 1 and 2).

patronymic An additional name conferred upon a person to indicate the name of the bearer's father. Compare **metronymic**.

P-Celtic See under **Celtic**.

Pedersen's Law 1. An attempt by Pedersen (1895) to explicate the **ruki** phenomenon in Slavic. See Collinge (1985: 143–145) for an account. 2. The proposal, by Pedersen (1933: 25), to account for a certain accent retraction in Balto-Slavic. In a nominal lexeme with mobile accent, in a word of more than two syllables, the accent shifts from the penult to the antepenult; Pedersen sees this as the result of paradigmatic pressure. See Collinge (1985: 147–148).

pejoration (also **degeneration**) A type of **semantic change** in which a word comes to denote something more offensive than formerly. For example, all of English *churl*, *villain* and *boor* originally meant only 'farm-worker', but all have come to be insults, and much the same is now happening to *peasant*. The opposite is **amelioration**.

Pelasgian The name given by the ancient Greeks to a language which they believed had been spoken in Greece before the arrival of the Greek-speakers. Nothing whatever is known about it, but the presence in ancient Greek of apparent loan words suggests an **Indo-European** language not closely related to Greek.

Pennsylvania model of IE A proposed **family tree** for **Indo-European** which is derived by a *best-tree* computer program (see **best-tree approach**) from a selected set of **characters** and which exhibits only binary branching at every point. The tree is given in Warnow *et al.* (1995) and is reproduced in Trask (1996: 369). See also *http://www.cis.upenn.edu/~histling/*.

Penultimate Law The stress rule of classical Latin. A word of fewer than three syllables is stressed on the first syllable; a word of three or more syllables is stressed on the penult if that is heavy but on the antepenult otherwise. This rule was an innovation, since pre-Latin apparently had consistent word-initial stress.

Penutian A speculative grouping of North American families. Penutian was first mooted by Dixon and Kroeber (1913), who included within it several small families of California. Since then, others have embraced and expanded this proposal, adding to it further coastal languages, a number of languages of southern Mexico (including **Mayan**), and sometimes even the **Gulf** grouping (itself speculative) and various South American languages. The more ambitious versions are sometimes called *Macro-Penutian*. The maximal version includes over ninety languages (many of them extinct), but it must be stressed that even the original more modest version is not at present regarded as established, and some linguists argue that the name itself should be dropped as meaningless. See Campbell (1997a: 309–320) for a critical account.

perceptual explanation of change Any proposal to account for **language change** by appealing to the perceptions of speech by hearers. For example, Ohala (1981, 1987) proposes that **dissimilations** typically arise when hearers 'correct' what they perceive to be assimilations, and Bever and Langendoen (1971, 1972) argue that certain syntactic constructions disappeared from English because they were perceptually difficult. Some of these proposals look interesting, but no one is proposing that all language change can be explained perceptually. See McMahon (1994: 151–160) for a survey of work on **syntactic change** from this point of view.

perceptually motivated sound change (also **acoustically motivated sound change**) Any instance of a phonological change which appears to be motivated by perception. For some examples, see **voicing crossover** and **acoustic assimilation**.

perceptual strategy A strategy used by a hearer to interpret utterances. Some linguists have argued that perceptual strategies play a part in language change. For example, Bever and Langendoen (1971) consider English relative clauses of the type illustrated by Chaucer's *He sente after a cherl was in the toune* 'He sent for a man (who) was in the town'. In Old English, the noun *cherl* 'man' would have been overtly case-marked as an object, but, by Chaucer's day, the case-marking had disappeared and *a cherl* could be equally taken as the subject of *was*. Bever and Langendoen argue that the resulting perceptual difficulty caused this construction to disappear from English in favour of other constructions posing fewer perceptual problems.

peripheral-region criterion (also **innovating-centre principle**) In **dialect geography**, a putative principle according to which most **innovations** appear in the central part of a **dialect continuum** and spread out from there, so that peripheral dialects of a language tend to be most conservative while central dialects tend to show the greatest number of innovations. Championed by the proponents of **Neolinguistics**, this rule of thumb appears to be broadly valid, but of course it is not true that peripheral dialects never exhibit innovations of their own.

peripheral track In some conceptions of the vowel space, either of two elongated areas (front and back) occupying the outer region of that space, surrounding the more central *non-peripheral tracks*. Labov (1994: ch. 6) argues for the importance of these concepts in interpreting certain sound changes involving vowels, notably **chain shifts**.

peripheral vocabulary That part of the lexicon of a language which is not **basic vocabulary**.

perispomenon In Greek, a word bearing a circumflex accent on the last syllable. Compare **properispomenon**.

permeability The susceptibility to **borrowing** of a linguistic subsystem, such as lexicon or syntax.

perseveration (rarely also **lag**) The phenomenon in which a segment or a feature present earlier in an utterance is continued or repeated later in that utterance, where it is not necessary or appropriate. This includes both perseverative **assimilation** and slips of the tongue like *bread and brutter* for *bread and butter*.

perseverative assimilation See under **assimilation**.

persistence 1. In **grammaticalization**, the retention by a grammaticalized item of some of its original lexical properties. For example, in Malay, many nouns have become classifiers used to count classes of nouns, but a classifier is not used in counting a noun which is itself the source of the appropriate classifier. 2. The retention in a language of a linguistic form or pattern over a long period of time, sometimes especially an unusual one, such as the English construction illustrated by *The more Susie complains, the less attention her boss pays*. 3. The term used by Lass (1997: 117) for a 'vacuous change', such as the development of Old English /b/ into modern English /b/.

persistent rule A phonological rule which remains active in a language over a long period of time and continues to apply to new items meeting its structural description. A simple example is the final devoicing of obstruents in German.

pharyngealization Any phonological change in which a segment comes to acquire a pharyngeal character it formerly lacked. This has occurred in some dialects of Arabic.

Philippine languages The indigenous languages of the Philippines, totalling about 135, and constituting three or four major branches of the **Malayo-Polynesian** branch of the **Austronesian** family. Best known are *Tagalog*, *Ilokano* and *Cebuano*.

Philippi's Law The statement that, in the northwest Semitic languages, original */i/ changes to /a/ in an originally closed accented syllable.

philology A term which has been used differently at different times. Originally it was applied very broadly to the study of literature, of written texts, of grammar and of language matters generally; this sense is now obsolete. Later it came to be applied to historical and comparative linguistics generally, or even to linguistics generally; this usage still finds some currency in Britain, but is not usual there, and it is unknown in the USA. Today the term is understood as denoting all those aspects of historical linguistics which crucially depend upon the scrutiny and interpretation of written documents. Certain branches of the subject, such as **etymology** (sense 2) and **onomastics**, are overwhelmingly philological in nature; these are the areas which are typically chiefly concerned with the particular histories and prehistories of individual linguistic items. See Anttila (1989: ch. 17) for an essay on the importance of philology to historical linguistics, and see the papers in Fisiak (1990) for representative examples.

Phoenician An extinct northwest **Semitic** language formerly spoken in Lebanon and Syria and recorded in writing from about the eleventh century to the first century BC, in an alphabetic script. The Phoenicians appear to have introduced the alphabet to the Greeks. A variety of Phoenician called *Punic* was spoken in Carthage and in the Punic Empire; Punic is recorded from the ninth century BC to the first century AD, but was probably spoken for several centuries longer. See Segert (1997).

phonaestheme A sound or sound sequence which is used frequently in a language in coining words in a particular semantic area. A familiar English example is /sl-/ 'wet, slippery, mucky', as in *slime*, *slop*, *slush*, *sludge*, *slip*, *slide*, *slosh*, *slurry* and *slug* (the creature). The use of phonaesthemes is *phonaesthesia*; phonaesthesia constitutes one type of **sound symbolism**, and phonaesthetic words must be used with caution in **comparison**.

phonemic shift The outcome of a phonological change in which a segment changes its phonetic nature in such a way as to shift from one phoneme to another. For example, in the history of Spanish, intervocalic [p], representing /p/, shifted to [b], now representing the previously existing /b/. Compare **reassignment**.

phonemic split See **split** (sense 1).

phonemic substitution The term used by Hoenigswald (1960: 25) for the more or less systematic replacement of unfamiliar segments in loan words by some native segments apparently perceived as the 'nearest match', such as the frequent rendering of English /sw-/ in loans into German as /tsf-/, as in *Zwetter* 'sweater'.

phonetic change (also **subphonemic change**) Any phonological change which affects only the phonetic realization of one or more segments and has no consequences for the phonological system. For example, the English vowel /æ/ has undergone various types of raising, backing and diphthongization in many accents, but this is purely a phonetic change so long as /æ/ remains distinct from all other vowels and retains its distribution in words. See Ohala (1993) and the references there for a survey of the phonetic aspects of sound change. Note: in some European languages, the literal equivalent of *phonetic change* is used for **phonological change**.

phonetic drift A prolonged tendency, over several generations, for the phonetic character of a phoneme to shift steadily in one direction; one kind of **drift**. An example is the steady lowering and backing of English /æ/ in the accent called *Received Pronunciation*.

phonetic legality A proposed constraint upon **reconstruction**: no segment type or segment sequence which is not attested in a living language may be reconstructed.

phonetic plausibility criterion A proposed constraint upon phonological **reconstruction**: no reconstruction should be posited which requires unattested phonological changes to have occurred in one or more daughter languages. For example, a posited change like */k/ >

/m/ or */m/ > /s/ would usually be regarded as too implausible to accept. This criterion must be used with caution, however, since **unnatural sound changes** do occur, if usually only as the end-product of a series of more natural changes.

phonogenesis The term used by Hopper (1994 and elsewhere) to denote the process by which a word or form acquires additional syntagmatic phonological material by the **accretion** of morphemes to it. An outstanding example results from the prefixation of particles to verbs in early Old Irish: *to-thēg* 'to-go' (modern *tag-* 'come'), *imb-thēg* 'about-go' (*imigh* 'go, leave'), *frith-to-thēg* 'against-to-go' (*friotaigh* 'resist'), *fo-ad-gab* 'under-toward-take' (*fág-* 'leave'), and many others. Such phonogenesis counteracts the tendency of words to be phonologically reduced, eventually perhaps to almost nothing. See **reinforcement**.

phonological change Any kind of change in the phonological system of a language, in the phonological structures of particular linguistic forms, or in the phonetic nature of particular segments. (This last is **phonetic change**.) See Kiparsky (1988) for a survey, and see any textbook of historical linguistics for a textbook account.

phonological correspondence Another term for **systematic correspondence**.

phonological reduction The term used by Hopper and Traugott (1993: 145) for two kinds of phonological development within items undergoing **morphologization** (sense 2). Such items become syntagmatically reduced (they lose segments and hence phonological bulk) and they become paradigmatically reduced (the segments remaining in the item are drawn only from the small set of universally unmarked segments). Such reduction is a primary reason why bound grammatical morphemes are of limited value in **comparison** except when they exhibit substantial **grammatical correspondences**.

phonologization 1. The conversion of a phonetic phenomenon into a part of the phonological structure of a language. For example, the natural palatalization of [k] in the sequence /ki/ to [kʲ], [c] or [tʃ] may become obligatory, producing a change in phonological structure. Compare **rephonologization**. 2. Especially in Prague School terminology, another name for **split** (sense 1).

phonosymbolism The use, with significantly greater than chance probability, of particular segments in linguistic items with particular meanings or functions. There exist suggestions that words for 'nose' tend universally to contain nasal consonants, and that words for 'tooth' tend universally to contain dental consonants; if valid, such claims might constitute evidence for the reality of phonosymbolism.

phrasal compound A lexical item which is derived from a complete phrase, or sometimes from an even larger syntactic structure. English examples include *lady-in-waiting*, *toad-in-the-hole* (an item of cuisine), *love-lies-bleeding* and *forget-me-not* (both flower names). English *good-bye* derives from the complete sentence *God be with ye*, and Basque *eztabaida* 'argument, dispute' derives from the two complete sentences *Ez da! Bai da!* 'No, it isn't! Yes, it is!'

phraseologism A term introduced by C. Lehmann (1991), and taken from earlier use in German, to denote a syntactic construction which has been to some degree frozen into a fixed collocation, usually with some kind of metaphorical extension of its original meaning, and usually with restrictions on its wider collocability. Since about 1975, a number of German prepositional phrases have begun to exhibit varying degrees of reduction to single compound prepositions. For example, *im Vorfeld* (the noun *Vorfeld* is a military term denoting the area ahead of the front line) has come to mean 'in the run-up (to)' (a meeting or social event); *im Gefolge* 'in the suite (of)' has come to mean 'in the wake (of)' (a trend-setting activity); *im Wege* 'in the way (of)' (analogically replacing the otherwise categorical *auf dem Wege*) has come to mean 'on the way (to)' (a technological breakthrough). These new formations may eventually become fully lexicalized, just as older *auf Grund* 'on the basis (of)' has been lexicalized as *aufgrund*. Similar processes have introduced many new prepositions into English, such as *beside*, *because of* and *in front of*.

Phrygian An extinct **Indo-European** language of ancient Anatolia. It is not **Anatolian** but appears to form a separate branch of Indo-European all by itself; attempts at linking it to **Thracian** and to **Armenian** have been inconclusive at best.

phylogeny See **linguistic phylogeny**.

phylum A linguistic **taxon**. Like all such terms, this one has no precise definition, but it is most commonly applied to a maximal taxon: that

256 PHYLUM PHILOLOGY

is, to a taxon which is not known to be part of a larger taxon, such as
Indo-European, Afro-Asiatic, Eskimo-Aleut or **Basque**. Especially in the Americas, the term is often applied to a proposed large
grouping which is speculative and unestablished.

phylum philology A possibly somewhat dismissive term for attempts at
grouping languages into huge genetic families on the basis of inspection, comparable to **megalocomparison**. The term was used
by C. F. and F. M. Voegelin in various places.

Pictish An extinct language which is very sparsely attested in some
inscriptions in Scotland dating from the first millennium AD. It is
clear that most of these inscriptions conceal a **Celtic** language, but
opinion is divided over whether a few of them might represent an
entirely different language. See Price (1998: 357–358).

pidgin An auxiliary language constructed from bits and pieces of one or
more existing languages by people who have no language in common.
A pidgin is not a natural language; it has a tiny vocabulary and no
grammar to speak of. The construction of a pidgin is *pidginization*. A
pidgin may develop into a **creole**. See Romaine (1988), Holm (1988/
89) or Sebba (1997).

PIE See **Proto-Indo-European**.

pipe The symbol ' | ', used in a **reconstruction** to separate two segments,
either one of which may have been present in a particular position,
with the choice being unresolvable. For example, a reconstruction
$*g| \gamma awV$ indicates that either $*gawV$ or $*\gamma awV$ is possible; this is
equivalent to $*gawV \sim *\gamma awV$.

pitfalls of comparison Any of various phenomena which, especially
(but not only) in the absence of sufficient rigour, can be badly
misleading in an attempt at searching for possible **genetic relationships** or even in **comparative reconstruction**. Among the most
difficult to deal with are the **semantics control problem**, the *tooth*
problem, the **beech-tree problem, affective symbolism, indeterminacy, conflicting reconstructions**, and the possible presence of **loan words** and other **convergence** phenomena. Easier to
exclude by rigorous methodology are **nursery words, onomatopoeia**, 'reaching down', inadequate **density of attestation**, and
chance resemblances. Largely typical of the work of linguists who

pursue possible remote relationships among families they are not specialists in are (besides the last group) the use of inadequate **length of compared forms**, **false segmentations**, violation of the **total accountability principle**, citation of demonstrable **non-cognates**, **neglect of known history**, **edited evidence**, **false reconstructions**, citation of **spurious forms**, **multiple incompatible comparisons**, an unacceptable degree of **portmanteau reconstructions**, misuse of **alternations** and occasionally even the use of non-linguistic information such as cultural similarities. A final potential pitfall is the **circularity problem**. See Campbell (1997a: ch. 7) for a survey of many of these pitfalls, and see **Hamp's principles of comparison**.

place name Another term for **toponym**.

playful formation Another term for **jocular formation**.

pleonasm (also **pleonastic formation**) A formation containing two elements bearing the same meaning, such as *the hoi polloi* (Greek *hoi* = 'the'), the British word *fruiterer*, containing two instances of the suffix *-er*, or regional German *gingte* 'went', in which past-tense *-te* has been added to the already past-tense form *ging*.

pleophony (Ger *Pleophonie*, Russ *polnoglásie*) In eastern Slavic, the insertion of an **echo vowel** between /r/ and a following tautosyllabic consonant, as in *perd > *pered* 'before'.

plesiomorphy A technical term for **retention** (sense 1), borrowed by Lass (1997) from biological cladistics.

plus sign 1. The symbol '+', used in an etymological entry to indicate that a word is composed of smaller identifiable elements. For example, an etymology for Basque *lauburu* 'swastika' of the form 'LAU + BURU' indicates that the word is composed of two elements which can both be looked up in the same dictionary, while one for English *contralto* of the form '< It : *contra* 'pitched below' (< Lat *contrā* 'against') + ALTO' indicates that the word is borrowed from Italian, in which it is composed of two elements, the first of which is explained here and the second of which can be looked up in the same dictionary. 2. See under **asterisk** (sense 1).

pluti intonation In early Sanskrit, a special accentuation pattern in which a syllable that would normally receive falling pitch receives sustained pitch instead. This appears to represent some kind of marked intonation or sentence-stress.

Polabian An extinct west **Slavic** language spoken southeast of the city of Hamburg until the eighteenth century.

Polivanov's Law The statement that phonemic **splits** need **mergers** as their motivation, but not vice-versa – that is, that a phoneme can only split if it results from an earlier merger. Proposed by Polivanov in the 1920s, notably in Polivanov (1928), this statement formed part of its author's larger view that **convergence** is the norm in linguistic evolution while **divergence** can only be the result of an earlier convergence. This idea has been taken seriously by Jakobson and others, though not always in quite such a general form. See Collinge (1985: 253–255) for a critical discussion with references, and see the **crystallization model**.

polnoglásie The Russian for **pleophony**.

polygenesis The view that human language arose more than once in the remote past, and that the living or attested languages therefore do not necessarily share a common origin. The opposing view is **monogenesis**; see the remarks under that entry.

polygrammaticalization A label applied by Craig (1991) to cases in which a single linguistic form undergoes **grammaticalization** into different functions in different constructions. She cites the case in the Chibchan language Rama of **bang* 'go', which has become a tense-marker in verbs, a purposive adposition with noun phrases, and a conjunction linking clauses in complex sentences.

Polynesian A subgroup of the **Austronesian** family, containing about twenty-eight languages mostly spoken in the eastern and southern Pacific, such as *Hawaiian*, *Tahitian* and *Maori*.

polysemic clash See under **isomorphy**.

Pomoan A family of seven languages formerly spoken in northern California. Pomoan is suspected of being related to **Yuman**, and it is included in the **Hokan** hypothesis.

population In **population typology**, a group of language families occupying a coherent geographical area and exhibiting a shared set of **population markers**.

population marker In **population typology**, a highly stable linguistic feature which tends to persist in a language family and which is readily borrowed from one language to another. For a proposed list of such features, see Nichols (1992, 1994/95 and 1995a).

population typology An approach to **linguistic geography** developed by Johanna Nichols in a series of publications. This involves the quantitative examination of selected typological features (of presumed great stability) in languages across the globe, in the hope of uncovering evidence for the ancient movement of languages. See Nichols (1990, 1992, 1993, 1994/95, 1995a, 1995b, 1997b, 1997c, 1997e), and see Heath (1994) for a critique. See **population, population marker, historical marker** and **genetic marker**.

portmanteau Another term for a **blend**.

portmanteau language A single language which has emerged from a mixture of elements contributed by what were originally several quite distinct but closely related languages; one kind of **mixed language**. No certain case of this is known, but Leer (1990) argues that the several puzzling characteristics of Tlingit are best explained by supposing that it is the result of just such a blending of once-distinct varieties, via the process he calls **endohybridization**.

portmanteau reconstruction (also **maximal coding**) An individual reconstruction which combines seemingly conflicting information from the several presumably cognate forms in the languages under comparison, thus requiring **differential loss** in those daughter languages. The /k/ ~ /p/ variation seen in cases like Sanskrit *krī-*, Greek *priasthai*, Old Welsh *prinit*, all 'buy', is resolved by reconstructing a PIE labio-velar */kʷ/, with differential feature loss in the daughter languages. Old English *fīf* 'five' and Old Norse *fimm* 'five' are derived from a reconstructed Proto-Germanic **fimfi* by differential segment loss. The singular masculine definite articles *el* (Spanish) and *le* (French) are derived from a reconstructed **ille*, with differential syllable loss. Linguists differ in the extent to which they are prepared to tolerate such reconstructions in the absence of hard evidence. For example, Haas (1968: 41) derives both Creek *iłu* 'squirrel' and Choctaw *fani* 'squirrel' from a Proto-Muskogean **ix^w aNi/u*, with differential segment loss, but is able to support this with reflexes from other Muskogean languages. Benedict (1975), however, proposes to derive both Proto-Tai **hma* 'dog' and Proto-Hmong-Mien **klu* 'dog' from a putative Proto-Austro-Tai **[wa] kləm[a]*, again with differential syllable loss, but the sparsity of support for such a reconstruction induces deep scepticism in some critics. In the absence of strong supporting evidence, clearly *any* arbitrary linguistic forms can be combined in an arbitrary portmanteau reconstruction.

Portuguese One of the world's major languages, the first language of Portugal and of Brazil, also widely spoken in the former Portuguese colonies in Africa. Portuguese is a **Romance** language fairly closely related to Spanish. The language appears to have arisen in what is now Galicia in northwestern Spain and to have spread southwards into modern Portugal with the Reconquest. Due to the political boundary, the speech of Galicia (*Galician*) is commonly regarded as a distinct language from Portuguese, though some linguists prefer to regard the two as dialects of a single language.

Written records of Portuguese first appear in the twelfth century, and a literary tradition has existed since the thirteenth century. In the early fifteenth century, Portugal began building a colonial empire, first in Africa, then in Asia, finally in South America. Today close to 90 per cent of all Portuguese-speakers live in the huge country of Brazil. See Camara (1972) for a history.

post-creole continuum The result of substantial, but not total, **decreolization** of an original **creole**. The creole is strongly adjusted towards the local prestige language on which it is largely based, and as a result the community exhibits a wide variety of speech styles, ranging from the *basilect* (the unmodified creole) through a range of *mesolects* (intermediate styles) to the *acrolect* (the variety of the creole which is closest to, or possibly even identical to, the prestige language).

pragmatic change Change in the pragmatic values of linguistic forms, or a switch from structural to pragmatic value or vice versa. The **Traugott progression** is a well-known example.

pragmatic unmarking The process by which a stylistically or expressively marked construction loses its marked value as a result of frequent use.

Prākrits A group of **Indo-Aryan** languages recorded as literary languages in India between about 300 BC and AD 200; the single most important of them is **Pāli**. The Prākrits are not directly descended either from **Vedic** or from classical **Sanskrit**, though they are broadly more closely related to Vedic; the parallel tradition leading to the Prākrits is called the *Vedic Prākrits*. With a few qualifications, the Prākrits may be reasonably regarded as literary forms of the spoken languages which are ancestral to the modern Indo-Aryan languages.

Pre- An element prefixed to the name of a single language to denote a significantly earlier, and unrecorded, stage of that language. Thus *Pre-Basque* is a prehistoric form of Basque reconstructed by specialists, *Pre-Old English* is a stage of English some centuries earlier than the first Old English texts, and *Pre-Proto-Indo-European* is an ancestral form of PIE which is significantly earlier than, and different from, the version of PIE which is directly ancestral to the IE languages. Compare **Proto-**.

prediction of change The task of predicting what changes, if any, will occur in the future in a given language. Most linguists see this as an impossible task, and consider that we can hope to do no more than to conclude that certain types of change are more likely to occur than others. However, the proponents of **developmental linguistics** claim that some measure of predictive power is possible.

prehistory, linguistic See **linguistic prehistory**.

Pre-Indo-European Another term for **Pre-Proto-Indo-European**.

prenasalization A phonological change in which an oral consonant (most often a plosive) acquires a nasal onset, as when /b/ develops to /^{m}b/ or /mb/. This has possibly happened in a number of Austronesian languages, though the historical facts are obscure and debated.

Pre-Proto-Indo-European (also **Pre-Indo-European**) A stage of **Proto-Indo-European** which is significantly earlier in time than the PIE which is reconstructed on the basis of the daughter languages. Some specialists believe that it is possible to apply **internal reconstruction** to PIE to recover significant information about this earlier stage. See W. P. Lehmann (1993: ch. 6) for an attempt at reconstructing the phonology of Pre-PIE.

preruptive [*rare*] Any unaspirated voiceless obstruent.

Pre-Samnite An extinct and sparsely recorded **Italic** language attested in southern Italy in the sixth and fifth centuries BC; it was closely related to **Umbrian**.

prescriptivism The introduction into linguistic description of value judgements deriving, not from observation, but from personal taste and prejudice. Prescriptivist declarations have been at least partly responsible for driving such widespread vernacular forms as *I ain't got none* and *Me and him was there* out of standard English, though condemnations of *It's me* and of so-called 'split infinitives' have had more limited effect.

preservation by contact (also **retention by contact**) The state of affairs in which an ancestral contrast which has been lost in many related languages or dialects is preserved precisely in those varieties which are in contact with other languages possessing the contrast. For example, the historical /ʎ/ has merged with /j/ in all varieties of American Spanish except in the Andean varieties, where Spanish is in contact with Quechua and Aymara, both of which have /ʎ/.

prestige A fundamental but elusive notion in language change. It is a truism to say that speakers adopt such innovations as they consider prestigious, but the sources of prestige are numerous and conflicting. At the very least, we must distinguish between *overt prestige* (the property of a linguistic form which is regarded in the community as appropriate to educated standard usage) and *covert prestige* (the property of a form which is deemed appropriate to the speech of a particular group by the members of that group), and these two types frequently conflict.

prestige language A language which is perceived by speakers of a different language as in some way superior or preferable to their own – most commonly, perhaps, because its speakers enjoy greater power or wealth.

preterite-present verb (also **past-present verb**) Especially in the **Germanic** languages, a verb in which an original past-tense (preterite) or perfect form has become the present tense, and a new past tense has been created. Old English had a number of such verbs, such as *cunnan* 'be able' and *witan* 'know'. All of those which survive in modern English have become modal auxiliaries, like *can, may* and *must*, and this origin is the reason these verbs never take the ending *-s* in the third-person singular; historically, *he can* is parallel to *he sang*, not to *he sings*.

preventive analogy Another term for **analogical maintenance**.

primary endings One of the two sets of agreement suffixes found in verbs in all the early IE languages and reconstructible for PIE. The primary endings are found in the present indicative and in the subjunctive mood. In the three singular persons and in the third plural, the primary endings consisted of the **secondary endings** plus *-i*; the remaining two plural persons were more complex. See Beekes (1995: 232–234).

primary source In philological work, a document written in the language under investigation. For example, for Old English, the primary sources include the various poems, chronicles, religious texts and other material written by the Anglo-Saxon scribes and surviving long enough for us to study them. Primary sources are the principal source of information for philologists. Compare **secondary source**.

primary split See under **split**.

primitive 1. Of a linguistic feature, **conservative** (sense 1), **archaic** (sense 1). The term is particularly applied to a feature of language L which was inherited from the ancestor of L and which was still present in an early stage of L but which was later lost from L. Note that there is no suggestion that a 'primitive' feature is in any way 'cruder' or 'less advanced' than what followed it. 2. [*often capitalized*] Preceding a language name, a label used to denote an unrecorded early form of that language which has been to some degree reconstructed. Thus, for example, *primitive Latin* denotes a stage of Latin at which it already existed as a language distinct from its close relatives but at which it had not yet undergone several important changes which were complete by the time of our earliest Latin texts. In this sense, the term is equivalent to **Pre-**. 3. [*often capitalized*] Preceding the name of a language family, as in *Primitive Germanic*, equivalent to **Proto-** or **common** (sense 1).

primitive language A meaningless term. Every human language ever discovered has a large vocabulary and a rich and complex grammar.

The notion that, somewhere out there, there are people speaking primitive languages with tiny vocabularies and little grammar is a fantasy born of ignorance and prejudice.

probabilistic approach Any approach to the question of testing possible **remote relationships** which depends upon the use of probability theory. At present there are several such approaches, none of them generally regarded as entirely satisfactory. Most typically, such an approach sets out to test the **null hypothesis** ('the languages are not related') and looks for evidence at a high level of confidence that this hypothesis should be rejected. For representative examples of such work, and critiques, see Ringe (1992, 1995a, 1995b, 1996, 1998, forthcoming), Oswalt (1991, 1998), Baxter (1995, 1998), Manaster Ramer (1992, 1993b, 1996b, 1999), Manaster Ramer and Hitchcock (1996), Baxter and Manaster Ramer (1996), Michalove *et al.* (1998) and Manaster Ramer *et al.* (1998). See also the **Monte Carlo test** and the **Oswalt shift test**.

probabilistic phonetic conditioning A phenomenon often observed in cases of **lexical diffusion**: the change is strongly favoured in certain phonological environments and disfavoured in others, but in neither case is the environment fully decisive in determining whether the change occurs.

process naturalness The degree to which a particular linguistic change is frequent and easy to understand. For example, the change of /p/ to /f/ is natural, while /f/ to /p/ does not appear to be natural. Process naturalness is invoked in **reconstruction**; given a correspondence /p/ : zero, we prefer to reconstruct */p/ with loss in one branch, rather than zero with a highly unnatural shift of zero to /p/.

procliticization See under **cliticization**.

productivity The degree to which a linguistic process may be freely invoked in order to create new forms. The term is most frequently used with reference to **word-formation**; for example, in English, the derivation of abstract nouns in *-ness* is highly productive (it can be done almost at will), while the derivation of such nouns with *-th* is totally unproductive (no new cases can be constructed at all). The formation of adverbs with *-wise* was until recently almost totally unproductive, but today it is highly productive: *clotheswise, money-wise, fitnesswise*.

proethnic [*obsolete*] In IE studies, pertaining to the period at which PIE was still spoken as a single language, before the breakup into daughter languages. Today the term is usually replaced by **common** (IE).

profligacy The tendency of a language to 'sprout' a large number of competing forms for a single function, after which *selection* must take place. See the **multiple-birth model**.

progressive assimilation See under **assimilation**.

projection (also **triangulation**) In the terminology of Lass (1978), the procedure, in diagramming phonological change, of moving backwards in time from the attested segments in several daughter languages to a single ancestral segment. An example is the projection of Greek and Latin /p/, Germanic /f/ and Celtic zero into PIE */p/. The opposite is **mapping**.

Prokosch's Law The statement that phonological change applies more readily to certain places of articulation than to others. At least in the case of the **Second Germanic Consonant Shift**, the proposal is that coronals were affected first, most generally and in the widest area, while velars were affected last, least generally and in the smallest area. The proposal was put forward by Prokosch (1939) and named by Beade (1974: 68). See Collinge (1985: 254–255).

pronunciation pronunciation A term proposed by Anttila (1989: 190) for the behaviour of a speaker who, in place of his own native pronunciation of a word, attempts to reproduce faithfully a different pronunciation which he regards as more prestigious than his own. The term is coined by analogy with **spelling pronunciation**.

proof-by-anachrony principle The principle that an instance of **grammaticalization** may be seen to have gone to **completion** when the grammaticalized item can co-occur with its lexical source. For example, the Japanese verb *simau* 'put away' has been grammaticalized as a verbal marker meaning 'finally', and both functions can occur simultaneously, as in *kami o hikidasi ni simatte-simatta* 'he finally put the paper away in the drawer', in which the first occurrence of *simau* is the lexical verb and the second is the grammaticalized marker. English *I am going to go home* illustrates the same principle. The term was coined by Hagège (1993: 200), who provides a number of examples. Compare the **unheeded-contradiction principle.**

propagation of change Another term for **implementation of change.**

proparalepsis The addition of a vowel to the end of a word; one form of **paragoge.**

proparoxytone In Greek, a word bearing an acute accent on the antepenult; more generally, a word accented on the antepenult in any language.

properispomenon In Greek, a word bearing a circumflex accent on the penult. Compare **perispomenon.**

proportional analogy Another term for **four-part analogy.**

prosthesis Another term for **prothesis.**

proterodynamic inflection In PIE, an inflectional class in which the word-accent regularly fell at or near the beginning of the word, as in *H_2éu-i-s* 'bird', accusative *H_2éu-i-m*, genitive *H_2u-éi-s*. See Beekes (1995: 175, 183–187). Compare **hysterodynamic inflection.**

proterokinetic See under **accent in PIE.**

prothesis (also **prosthesis**) The addition of a segment to the beginning of a word, as in the development of Latin *stannum* 'tin' into Spanish *estaño*, the borrowing of Latin *regem* 'king' into Basque as *errege,* or the development of pre-Motu **au* 'me' to Motu *lau.* Some linguists restrict this term to the addition of an initial vowel. The opposite is **aphaeresis.**

proto- A combining form used to indicate reference to the properties of an unrecorded **proto-language.** We may speak, for example, of the *proto-phonemes* or the *proto-lexicon* of such a language.

Proto- An element prefixed to the name of a **language family** in order to denote the single language which is the common ancestor of that family. Thus **Proto-Romance** is the common ancestor of the Romance family, and **Proto-Indo-European** (PIE) that of the IE family. There is a certain ambiguity in the use of this term; hence *PIE* may denote either the real ancestral language itself (unrecorded, as in almost all cases), or it may instead denote the approximation to that language reconstructed by linguists. In practice, the ambiguity is rarely a problem, but its existence should not be forgotten. Compare **Pre-**.

proto-form Another term for **reconstruction** (sense 2).

Proto-Germanic The unrecorded ancestor of the **Germanic** languages, thought to have been spoken in southern Scandinavia around 500 BC.

Proto-Indo-European (PIE) The hypothetical language which is the ancestor of the **Indo-European** family of languages. Linguists have been very successful at reconstructing PIE, thanks to the large number of living and recorded IE languages, some of which are substantially recorded in the second and first millennia BC. PIE is unrecorded, since its speakers were aliterate, but it is usually thought to have been spoken about 6000 years ago (around 4000 BC). This estimate derives from the observation that PIE words can apparently be reconstructed for terms pertaining to horse-drawn chariots, which were seemingly not in use before about 4000 BC, and from the estimate that a significantly later date would leave too little time for the divergence observed in the earliest IE languages. However, *where* PIE was spoken is unknown and controversial; see the **Indo-European homeland problem**. See Watkins (1998) for a brief survey of PIE, Beekes (1995) for a more substantial one, Szemerényi (1996) for a scholarly study, and Gamkrelidze and Ivanov (1995) for an ambitious attempt at a synthesis which, however, argues for some very particular views by no means universally accepted. See also W. P. Lehmann (1952) for a traditional survey of PIE phonology, Vennemann (1985) for more recent ideas about PIE phonology, W. P. Lehmann (1974) for a proposed reconstruction of PIE syntax, Comrie (1998) for a typological study, and W. P. Lehmann (1993) for a survey of outstanding problems with some suggested solutions. The standard etymological dictionary is Pokorny (1959/69), which is, however, dated.

proto-language (Ger *Ursprache*) An unrecorded and hypothetical language which is ancestral to one or more attested languages and whose properties are deduced by some process of **reconstruction**, most often **comparative reconstruction** in characterizing the ancestor of a **language family**. Note the systematic ambiguity in the use of this term; we apply it both to the result of our reconstruction and to the unrecorded but historically real language which our reconstruction imperfectly represents.

proto-linguistics The term used by Décsy (1983) and Hegedűs (1997) for work in historical linguistics within a time depth that allows substantial and secure reconstruction of proto-languages like PIE and Proto-Uralic: comparative linguistics in the most familiar sense. Compare **palaeolinguistics**.

proto-pidgin hypothesis The hypothesis that all or most known **pidgins** are descended from a single ancestor, a Portuguese-based pidgin created during the Portuguese expansion, by **relexification**. This hypothesis is no longer taken seriously.

Proto-Romance The ancestor of the **Romance** family of languages. Reconstruction of Proto-Romance reveals a language which is obviously very close to classical **Latin** but nevertheless distinct from it in a number of respects, and we naturally conclude that Proto-Romance should be identified with a popular spoken form of Latin. See the discussion under **Latin**.

Proto-World hypothesis The hypothesis that all known languages are descended from a single common ancestor, or sometimes more particularly the hypothesis that this can actually be proved. The truth or falsehood of the first is unknown, while the second is dismissed by nearly all linguists as an absurd fantasy.

provection 1. The devoicing of a voiced obstruent. The term is mainly used in connection with **Celtic** languages. 2. The transfer of a segment (usually a consonant) from the end of one word to the beginning of a following word; one type of **metanalysis**. Examples: *for then once* to *for the nonce*; *an other* to *a nother*, as in *a whole nother story*.

pseudoreconstruction A reconstructed form of largely arbitrary shape, devised merely to provide a **lemma** for a set of items claimed to be cognate, but with no claim to accuracy; sometimes marked by a **dagger**.

psychological explanation of change Any attempt at accounting for **language change** in terms of the psychological behaviour of speakers. A prominent exponent is Hermann Paul, for example in Paul (1920). One of Paul's ideas, later picked up by Hockett (1958: ch. 52), is that minor departures from a phonetic 'target' may become cumulative and directional, resulting in sound change. There is little support for this idea today.

pull chain Another term for *drag chain*; see under **chain shift**.

pullet surprise (also **Lady Mondegreen**) A phrase, especially a comical one, derived by mishearing an ordinary phrase, such as *pullet surprise* for *Pulitzer Prize*, *sly drool* for *slide rule*, and *four-stair system* for *forced-air system*. Occasionally one of these becomes established, such as *spitting image* for the earlier *spit and image*.

punctuated-equilibrium model A model of linguistic descent advanced by Dixon (1997). In this model, the languages of a defined geographical area are characterized by long periods of equilibrium, during which linguistic features diffuse across language boundaries, and all the languages tend to converge upon a common prototype. On occasion, however, the equilibrium is punctuated by some more or less dramatic event (such as drought, the introduction of agriculture, or invasion), and as a result some languages spread out and then diverge into daughter languages. It is only during these comparatively brief periods of punctuation and divergence that the familiar **genetic model** (or *family-tree model*) is valid. Note that Lightfoot (1998) also uses the term *punctuated equilibrium* in connection with language change, but from a very different point of view.

Punic See under **Phoenician**.

purism The view that loan words and other linguistic features of foreign origin (or so perceived) constitute a kind of 'contamination' sullying the 'purity' of a language and should be eliminated in favour of 'native' features. Purism has at times been a significant force in the development of Icelandic, German, French, Greek, Basque, Bulgarian, Hungarian, Turkish, and many other languages, though it has been of little importance in English. Two examples must suffice. The Ottoman Turkish word for 'international' was *beyn-el-milel*, a complete Arabic phrase meaning 'between the nations'. The language planners replaced this with *milletlerarası*, a typical Turkish formation, but one based on Arabic *millet* 'nation'. So this was in turn replaced by *uluslarası*, derived from a Turkic word *ulus* 'tribe, people'. (The modern Turkish word is *enternasyonal*, borrowed from French *international!*) The English computing term *debug* was at first borrowed into French as the awkward *débugger*, but the authorities altered this to *déboguer*, which at least looks more French. This yielded the obvious derivative *débogage* 'debugging', but recently the authorities have proposed to replace this with the delightful creation *déverminage*. Purists frequently make use of **calques** in their efforts.

push chain See under **chain shift**.

Q-Celtic See under **Celtic**.

qq.v. The abbreviation for 'which (things) see' (Latin *quae vide*). This follows a list of two or more named works and instructs the reader to consult these for further information, as in 'The evidence for this conclusion is presented in Michelena (1977) and Trask (1997) (*qq.v.*).' Compare *q.v.*

qualitative ablaut See under **ablaut**.

quantitative ablaut See under **ablaut**.

quantitative approach to variation A method of investigating **variation** in speech, including the involvement of that variation in language change. It rests on the premises that variation is normal in language and that particular instances of variation often have social significance. The central technique is to select speakers belonging to the social groups of interest and to obtain a corpus of utterances from those speakers in varying contexts, after which a statistical examination is carried out to obtain correlations between the choice of variant and both the social factors and the context. This approach, devised by William Labov in the 1960s, has been applied to a number of speech communities, with illuminating results. Among other things, it has led to a great increase in our understanding of the mechanisms and pathways of language change, it has resolved the **Saussurean paradox**, and it has uncovered or elucidated a number of striking phenomena, such as **lexical diffusion** and the **Bill Peters effect**. See **indicator, marker**.

quantitative metathesis See under **metathesis**.

quantitative methods in reconstruction Any of various statistical approaches to linguistic prehistory. See Fox (1995: ch. 11) for a survey of proposals, and see **mathematical methods**.

quantity principle Another term for the **iconic coding principle**.

quantum The term used by Lass (1997: 221) for a hypothetical unit of phonological change: the minimal or maximal amount by which a segment may change its phonological nature in a single step. See **stepwise shift**.

quasi-stock A linguistic **taxon**. The term is not traditional, but it has been introduced by Johanna Nichols in several publications (e.g. 1997b) to denote a taxon whose genetic unity seems secure, but for which clear cognates are few, systematic sound correspondences cannot be demonstrated, and substantial reconstruction of the ancestral language is not possible. Nichols takes **Niger-Congo** as a paradigm case of a quasi-stock. Compare **stock**.

Quechuan A vast dialect continuum extending through most of the length of the Andes, with some varieties not at all mutually comprehensible with others. With around 8.5 million speakers, Quechuan has more speakers than any other American family. A Quechuan language was the chief language of the Inca empire. See **Quechumaran**.

Quechumaran A proposed genetic link between the **Quechuan** and **Aymaran** families of South America. Often proposed, this grouping has been fiercely attacked, mainly on the ground that the shared features probably result from contact, but Campbell (1997a: 273–283) concludes that this is one of the more promising larger groupings in the Americas, though not as yet substantiated.

question mark The symbol '?', enclosed in parentheses in philological work to mark something as doubtful, or occasionally unknown. Attached to a form extracted from a text or an inscription, it indicates that the reading of that form is uncertain. Attached to a date, it indicates that the date is not known with certainty. Attached to a gloss of a linguistic form, it indicates that the gloss is doubtful. Attached to a linguistic form in place of a gloss, it indicates that the meaning is unknown. Attached to an etymology, it indicates that the etymology is questionable or speculative. A double question mark indicates a greater degree of uncertainty.

q.v. The abbreviation for 'which (one thing) see' (Latin *quod vide*). This follows a single named work and instructs the reader to consult that work for further information, as in 'The phonological history of Albanian is summarized in Demiraj (1998) (*q.v.*).' Compare *v.* and *qq.v.*

R

radical change Any instance of language change which is unusually dramatic, which makes the later form of the language substantially different from the earlier one in some respect. The term is impressionistic and has no well-defined content.

radical language [*obsolete*] A very early term for **language family**. Genetically related languages were commonly described as *radically the same*, unrelated languages as *radically different*.

radical reanalysis See under the **Lightfoot framework**.

radoppiamento sintattico (also *rafforzamento sintattico*) In Italian, the phenomenon in which a word-initial consonant is geminated in certain phonological or syntactic environments, as in *come lui* [kome llui] 'like him' and *da capo* [da kkapo] 'from the start'. The historical origin of this is debated, and it may have multiple origins; see Maiden (1995: 72–76) for a survey.

Raetic An extinct language recorded in about 200 inscriptions in the Tyrol during the last half of the first millennium BC. It is distantly but clearly related to **Etruscan**. See Price (1998: 373–374).

rafforzamento sintattico Another term for *radoppiamento sintattico*.

raising Any **phonological change** in which a vowel is converted to a higher vowel. The English **Great Vowel Shift** involved a number of unconditioned paradigmatic raisings, such as /e:/ > /i:/ and /o:/ > /u:/, converting, for example, /be:/ to /bi:/ *bee* and /go:s/ to /gu:s/ *goose*. Conditioned raisings may occur syntagmatically, as in those dialects of Basque in which a mid vowel is raised before a following non-high vowel, as in *lore* 'flower' + *-a* 'the' to give *loria* 'the flower' and *asto* 'donkey' + *-a* to give *astua* 'the donkey'. The opposite is **lowering**.

rake model A **model of linguistic descent** put forward by Bellwood (1997: 127). In this model, a single language expands suddenly and rapidly in several directions; **shared innovations** are localized and geographically non-coterminous; regional splintering produces a large number of coordinate daughters differing from one another in complex ways; the **family tree** looks more like a rake; and reconstruction of the ancestral language is difficult or impossible. Bellwood cites **Pama-Nyungan** as a possible case in point.

range The total geographical extent of a language or a family at some particular point in time, often the time of its greatest extent. Compare **locus**.

'reaching down' (also **limited-scope comparison**) In **comparison**, the procedure of citing as a **comparandum** a form which is found in only one branch of a family, or even in only one language, and projecting it up to the ancestor of the whole family, in order then to use it in seeking cognates with other families. While a measure of this is acceptable in recovering overlooked cognates between languages which are indisputably linked, 'reaching down' is totally unacceptable in setting up genetic links in the first place, since it is capable of yielding any number of spurious 'cognates'.

realism (also **realistic reconstruction**) In **comparative reconstruction**, the belief that a reconstructed segment, such as PIE */p/ or */bh/, genuinely represents ancient phonetic reality with a high degree of reliability: for example, that PIE */p/ really was a voiceless bilabial plosive. This is by far the majority view among linguists; the competing view is **algebraism**. See Lass (1993).

real time Ordinary time; calendar time. **Language change** can be usefully studied in real time, by examining written texts of different periods, by consulting descriptions of the same community compiled at long intervals, or merely by watching speakers over many years to see what happens. The third is rarely convenient, while the second is possible only when suitable descriptions already exist, as in the case of Martha's Vineyard, studied by Labov (1963). Compare **apparent time**.

reanalysis 1. Of a lexical item, the moving of a historical morpheme boundary to a different location, or the insertion of a morpheme boundary not formerly present, in order to extract a word or morpheme not present in the original formation. For example, the adjective *darkling*, historically *dark* + *-ling*, was reanalysed as *darkle* + *-ing*, leading to the use of a new verb *darkle*; *hamburger*, originally *Hamburg* + *-er*, was reanalysed as *ham* + *-burger*, leading to the extraction of *-burger* and its use in new formations like *cheeseburger*; the noun *bikini*, from a place name containing no morpheme boundary, was waggishly reanalysed as *bi-* 'two' + *-kini*, leading to the formation of *monokini* 'bikini with no top'. 2. The historical process by which a syntactic structure comes to be assigned a different structure from the one it formerly had, with no change in its surface form and with little or no change in interpretation. It is generally impossible to tell that reanalysis has taken place until the new structural assignment leads to the production of utterances which were previously not possible, a step called **actualization**. For example, the older English structure *It will be* [*easy for us*] *to do that* was reanalysed as *It will be easy* [*for us to do that*], leading eventually to the innovating structure [*For us to do that*] *will be easy*. For a survey, see Harris and Campbell (1995: ch. 4).

reassignment The label applied by Hoenigswald (1960) to the outcome of a phonological change in which a particular segment is shifted from one phoneme to another without undergoing any change in its phonetic realization. For example, when PIE */p/ shifted in Proto-Germanic to */f/, and PIE */b/ shifted to */p/, those instances of original */p/ immediately preceded by */s/ remained unshifted as [p], and were thus reassigned from original */p/ (new */f/) to original */b/ (new */p/). Compare **phonemic shift**.

rebracketing Any instance of **reanalysis** (especially sense 2) which involves a change in the way in which the constituent elements of a construction are grouped (bracketed). For example, the original prepositional phrase [*in* [*back*] [*of the house*]], with two simple prepositions *in* and *of* and a noun *back*, has been rebracketed by many speakers as [[*in back of*] [*the house*]], with a single complex preposition *in back of*.

recategorialization In **grammaticalization**, the shift of an item from one class to another, as when a noun shifting to an adposition loses all of its former nominal properties but gains all the properties of a typical adposition. Compare **decategorialization**.

recessive Of a linguistic feature, tending to disappear from a speech variety in which it was formerly prominent. For example, the *oil/earl* merger, formerly very prominent in New York City, is said now to be sharply recessive, meaning that it is virtually gone except in the speech of some older speakers.

recessive accent A notable tendency for the position of word-stress to be shifted towards the first syllable. Recessive accent is pervasive in the Germanic languages, including modern English, in which words like *cigarette*, *magazine*, *research* and *ice cream*, formerly with final stress, now commonly have initial stress. British (but not American) English assigns initial stress to recent French loans like *ballet*, *café*, *croquet*, *pastel* and *débris*.

recomposition The re-formation of a compound word whose inherited form has become phonologically opaque or semantically shifted. For example, Old English *hūswīf* 'housewife' developed into modern *hussy*, with a different meaning, and we have now re-formed *house-wife* for the original sense. English *forehead* developed the opaque pronunciation /fɔrɪd/, which many speakers have now replaced by the recompounded form /fɔ(r)hed/.

reconstruction 1. Any of various procedures which are used to arrive at conclusions about the nature of an unrecorded language which is the ancestor of one or more attested languages. The term is most commonly encountered in respect of determining the forms of individual words and morphemes (this is *lexical reconstruction*) and of determining a phonological system; the two chief methods are **comparative reconstruction** and **internal reconstruction**. However, **morphological reconstruction, syntactic reconstruction** and **semantic reconstruction** can also be undertaken when conditions are favourable. See Fox (1995) for an account. A reconstructed language which is the common ancestor of two or more languages is a **proto-language**. Among the principles sometimes invoked in reconstruction are **archaic heterogeneity**, the **default procedure, economy, family consistency**, the law of **increasing weakness**, a **margin of safety**, **Meillet's principle, naturalness** (sense 2), the **oddity condition**, the **panda principle, phonetic legality**, the **phonetic plausibility criterion, process naturalness, simplicity, symmetry** (sense 1), **system naturalness**, and the existence of **universals**. Among the difficulties are the **beech-tree problem, conflicting reconstructions, indeterminacy, overlapping correspondences**, the *tooth* problem, and the possible overuse of **portmanteau reconstructions**. See **algebraism** and **realism, pitfalls of comparison**, the **textual method**, the **time-depth problem, typologically based reconstruction** and **witness** (sense 1). 2. (also **proto-form**) A single linguistic form posited as a result of the process of reconstruction; a reconstructed form. Such a form is marked with an **asterisk** (sense 1). See **pseudo-reconstruction** and **false reconstruction**.

recreolization The name given by Romaine (1988: 192) to the phenomenon in which speakers refocus their norms away from the local prestige speech and towards a **creole** to which they have access. For example, many young black people of West Indian origin in London choose deliberately to adjust their speech strongly towards the maximally basilectal forms of the Jamaican Creole spoken by their parents; the resulting London Jamaican is by no means identical to Jamaican Creole, but involves the conscious selection of those forms which are maximally distant from standard English.

recurrent correspondence Another term for **systematic correspondence**.

recutting Another term for **metanalysis**.

Redefinition Principle A putative principle of phonological change. It says this: peripherality is defined relative to the vowel system as a whole. In other words, the peripheral/non-peripheral contrast among vowels is not merely a matter of objective phonetics, but may be substantially determined by phonological changes. The principle is advanced by Labov (1994: 285).

reduced form A form of a linguistic item which contains less phonological material than the item normally does. See **Indo-European root theory**, item (10), for an example.

reduced grade See under **ablaut**.

reduction 1. A phonological change in which a diphthong (or a more complex vocalic nucleus) is reduced to a pure vowel by the loss of one element of the diphthong. An example is the reduction of the diphthong /ai/ to /a:/ in many southern American varieties of English. In the history of Germanic, this is called **smoothing**. See **deflection**, and compare **levelling** (sense 1). 2. Very broadly, any development which removes phonological material from a linguistic form. The term can be applied, for example, to the loss of an unstressed vowel or of a whole syllable, to the simplification of a consonant cluster, or even to the conversion of another vowel to schwa. 3. In *pidginization* (see under **pidgin**), the elimination of most of the lexicon and virtually all of the grammar of the source language(s) observed in the resulting pidgin.

Reduktionsstufe See under **ablaut**.

reduplication Any process in which some phonological material is repeated within a single linguistic form for lexical, grammatical or expressive purposes. Reduplication may be *total* (as in Basque *mara-mara* 'gently and continuously'), *partial* (Basque *zirimiri* 'drizzle') or *enlarged* (Basque *aiko-maiko* 'pretext'). Reduplication serves a variety of purposes. Malay uses it to form adverbs (*baik* 'good', *baik-baik* 'well'), for indefinite plurality (*bunga* 'flower', *bunga-bunga* 'flowers') and for word-formation (*mata* 'eye', *mata-mata* or *memata* 'police-man'). Certain Latin verbs form their perfect stem by reduplication: *curr-* 'run', perfect stem *cucurr-*. Chukchi derives certain absolutive case forms by reduplication: *nute-* 'tundra' (stem), absolutive *nutenut*. Tagalog uses reduplication in its verbal inflection: *sulat* 'write', future *susulat*. Turkish uses it to express 'and so forth': *Ali-Mali* 'Ali and the others'. Yiddish-influenced American English uses it to express dismissal: *Jaguar-Schmaguar!*

referent change A type of **semantic change** in which the identity of the referent of a word changes, typically because of a change in the world. Examples include the shift in referent of *car* from a cart pulled by animals to a self-propelled motor vehicle, of *tennis* from a game played on an indoor court with obstacles to a game played on grass with a net, and of *hockey* (in North America) from a game played on grass to a game played on ice.

referential salience The putative degree of prominence associated with the referent of a linguistic form, sometimes appealed to in discussions of semantic change. For example, it has been suggested that hands are referentially more salient than arms, and hence that a semantic shift from 'hand' to 'arm' is normal, while the opposite shift is very unusual. See Brown (1979), Brown and Witkowski (1983), Witkowski and Brown (1985) and Wilkins (1996).

reflex (also **descendant**) A word or other linguistic form which is directly descended within a particular language from an ancestral form taken as a reference point. For example, English *loaf* is a reflex of Old English *hlāf*, from which it is directly decended, and Italian *donna* 'lady' is a reflex of Latin *domina(m)*. The opposite is **etymon**.

regional dialect A **dialect** which is characteristic of a particular geographical area.

regrammaticalization (also **regrammatization**, **morphological shift**) The shift of a grammatical morpheme from one function to another. Examples include the shift of a demonstrative to an article, of a perfect-aspect marker to a past-tense marker, of a case-form of a verbal noun to an infinitive, of a comitative case to an instrumental case, and of a stem-forming suffix to a plural suffix. Compare **degrammaticalization**.

regressive assimilation See under **assimilation**.

regularity The property of a phonological change which applies without exception to every single linguistic form which meets its structural description. The issue of whether sound changes are normally regular or not has occupied linguists for generations. As early as 1535, Claudio Tolomei drew attention to the regular development of Latin /pl-/, /kl-/, /fl-/ to Italian /pj-/, /kj-/, /fj-/, as in Italian *fiore* 'flower' from Latin *florem*, and he correctly identified Italian *plebe* 'people' as a direct borrowing from Latin *plebem*, with dialectal *pieve* 'church for the common people' representing the regular development. Nevertheless, the founding fathers of historical linguistics, finding apparent exceptions to their sound laws, were inclined to believe that sound changes were only 'tendencies' which did not always apply. However, the successful explanation of some of the exceptions led to the promulgation in the 1870s of the **Neogrammarian Hypothesis**, according to which all sound change is

regular. Even though this new doctrine was rejected by the dialectologists, who could not find 'exceptionless sound laws' in the messiness
of their data, it became the orthodoxy in the field until the 1960s. At
that point the sociolinguists began their revolutionary study of
linguistic changes in progress, and discovered that many sound
changes are not regular at all, but proceed by more complex pathways, as in **lexical diffusion**. That sound changes are not always
regular is now established, but a debate continues among linguists
over whether regular or irregular changes are the norm; some see
regularity as the rule and phenomena like lexical diffusion as rare
exceptions, while others believe that observed regularity most often
results only when an irregular change finally goes to completion.

regularity hypothesis Another term for the **Neogrammarian Hypothesis**.

Regularity Principle A putative principle of phonological change,
formulated by Labov (1994: 603) as follows: sound change is a
change in the phonetic realization of a phoneme, without regard to
lexical identity. A central component of the **Neogrammarian
Hypothesis**, this principle is falsified by **lexical diffusion**. See
the **Mechanical Principle**.

regularization The removal of alternations or irregularities from a
grammatical paradigm.

reinforcement (also **compensatory accretion**) The addition, to a form
which has become semantically weakened (and possibly also phonologically reduced), of new morphological material which more or less
restores the lost semantics. C. Lehmann (1985) cites the striking
example of Latin *in* 'in', which was replaced by the adverb *intus*
'inside', which acquired a prefixed *de* to give *de-intus*, which was
phonologically reduced in French to *dans*, which then acquired a
second instance of *de* to yield modern French *dedans* 'inside'. This is
one type of **phonogenesis**.

reinterpretation 1. A type of semantic change in which the referent of a
linguistic form is shifted from one thing to another which occurs in
the same context. For example, English *bead* originally meant
'prayer', but, since Christians regularly 'counted their beads' by
using a rosary, the referent of *bead* was shifted to one of the small
balls on the rosary, and today *bead* means only 'small ball'. 2. A shift

in the categorial status of a linguistic form resulting from its occurrence in ambiguous positions, as when the English noun *fun*, occurring in utterances like *This is fun*, was reinterpreted as an adjective, leading to new utterances like *This is a fun game*.

relationship principle A principle invoked in addressing the **homeland problem**. It says this: the required expansions from the posited homeland should conform to the branching structure of the family tree.

relative chronology The placing of linguistic changes into the order in which they apparently occurred. Sometimes this is easy; for example, the Basque loss of intervocalic */n/ must have preceded the reduction of */nn/ to /n/, since intervocalic */nn/ appears as /n/ in modern Basque, not as zero. In other cases it is difficult, and perhaps even impossible without textual evidence. Compare **absolute chronology**.

relexicalization The conversion into a new lexical item of a morphological form which has become isolated from its paradigm. If the original paradigm is lost, the process is **demorphologization**; if the original paradigm remains, the result is an **isolated form**. See those entries for examples.

relexification The massive replacement of the words of a language by new words taken from a different language. The term is most commonly applied to **pidgins** and **creoles**, but it can also be applied to the importation of words from the local prestige language in a case of **language shift** or even to massive borrowing generally, leading to loss of most of the ancestral vocabulary, as has occurred in Albanian.

relic Another term for **archaism** (sense 1).

relic area In **dialect geography**, a geographical region in which the local speech has not been affected by a language change which has affected most other areas in which the same language is spoken. Compare **focal area, transition area**.

relic form A linguistic form which preserves a fossilized remnant of what was once a productive process or regular alternation in the language. An English example is the pair *was/were*, which preserves the ancient, and formerly regular, /r/ ~ /z/ alternation. See **Verner's Law**.

relic language A language which is surrounded by unrelated languages and which appears to represent the last remnant of a family formerly spoken more widely but otherwise obliterated by the spread of new families into the area. Examples include isolates like **Basque, Burushaski** and **Ainu**, the two non-Bantu languages of Tanzania (*Hadza* and *Sandawe*), and *Brahui*, a lone **Dravidian** outlier in Pakistan. Compare **intrusive language**.

remorphologization Any change in which a grammatical morpheme is switched from one grammatical function to another. For example, the English suffix *-ing*, which formerly derived nouns from nouns, as in *bedding*, now derives participles and gerunds from verbs, as in *eating*.

remote relationship (also **distant relationship**) A **genetic relationship** which is considerably deeper than those which are commonly regarded as securely established and which is perhaps at the very limit of detectability. Such relationships must surely exist, but opinions differ greatly as to whether they can be confidently identified and as to how this might be done. The mainstream view is that the only safe way of pursuing the matter is to carefully reconstruct the **proto-languages** ancestral to secure families and then to compare these to see if any of them can be linked by conventional methods, via **systematic correspondences** and shared grammatical paradigms; this has been called **palaeolinguistics**. A minority view is that it can be successfully done merely by **inspection**, and particularly by **multilateral comparison**. Among the most prominent remote proposals at present are **Nostratic, Eurasiatic, Amerind, Dene-Caucasian, Austric** and **Indo-Pacific**, but many others exist. All are deeply controversial at best. See Robert Wright (1991) and P. Ross (1991) for popular presentations of recent work, Shevoroshkin and Manaster Ramer (1991) for a survey of recent proposals, Michalove *et al.* (1998) for a survey of the issues, and Trask (1996: ch. 13) or Hock and Joseph (1996: ch. 17) for a textbook summary.

rendaku In Japanese, the phenomenon in compound formation by which an initial obstruent in the second element undergoes voicing: *ami* 'net' + *to* 'door' > *amido* 'screen door'; *ori-* 'fold' + *kami* 'paper' > *origami* 'paper-folding'. By *Lyman's Law*, this voicing is blocked if the second element already contains a voiced obstruent, so that *kami* 'god' + *kaze* 'wind' yields *kamikaze*, not **kamigaze*, because of the /z/.

renewal Any of various phenomena in which a linguistic form or system whose semantic value has become less overtly marked than formerly is replaced by a new one which expresses that value more overtly. The label is most commonly applied to the replacement of a morphological form or system by a syntactic construction. For example, Pre-Latin apparently had a periphrastic future constructed with 'be', of the approximate form *kanta bhumos* 'we are to sing'. By the historical period, this had fused into a morphological form, *cantabimus*. In Romance, this was replaced by a new periphrastic form constructed with 'have': *cantare habemus* 'we have to sing'. This in turn has fused into morphological forms like Spanish *cantaremos*. This form is likewise now giving way to a new periphrastic form constructed with 'go': *vamos a cantar* 'we are going to sing'. This kind of repeated renewal illustrates the **linguistic cycle**. Another instance of renewal involves the English second-person pronouns. The old number contrast between singular *thou* and plural *you* has been destroyed by the loss of *thou*, but many varieties have renewed the contrast by inventing a new plural form, such as *youse*, *y'all* or *you guys*.

Renfrew hypothesis The hypothesis, put forward by the archaeologist Colin Renfrew, that the spread of both peoples and languages over the earth can be understood in terms of certain climatic, economic and technological developments. Renfrew sees four major periods of spread: an *initial migration*, during which the first modern humans spread out over most of the planet; a *farming dispersal*, during which certain language families spread out over huge areas along with the spread of agriculture; a *late climate-related dispersal*, during which humans spread for the first time into previously uninhabitable sub-Arctic regions; and finally a period of *elite dominance*, during which certain societies acquired enough wealth and technology to conquer their neighbours and establish empires. Chief among these is the farming dispersal; Renfrew sees the great language families of the Old World, such as **Indo-European, Niger-Congo, Afro-Asiatic, Dravidian, Sino-Tibetan** and **Austronesian,** as the result of the systematic spread of originally small languages over vast areas together with the spread of agriculture into those regions. Renfrew's ideas have found some support, but they have also encountered some hostility, particularly from linguists, on the ground of time depth; for example, Renfrew is obliged to push PIE some 3000 or 4000 years further back into the past than the linguists are willing to countenance, in order to get the required fit with the spread of agriculture from the Near East. See Renfrew (1987), Renfrew *et al.* (1988), Renfrew (1989, 1991, 1992a, 1992b, 1994, 1995, 1997, 1998). Compare the **New Synthesis**.

reordering of morphemes Any morphological change in which the order of morphemes in a word-form is changed. This most often happens when the accretion of a clitic or an affix to an inflected form produces an anomalous result with the inflectional marker buried in the middle of the form. For example, earlier Basque *nor* 'who?', as in *nor zen?* 'who was it?', could also mean 'anyone', but in this use it required a verbal prefix *bait-*, as in *nor baitzen* 'somebody was'; by a **boundary shift**, the *bait-* was transferred to the pronoun, producing *norbait zen* 'somebody was'. This left case-inflections trapped internally, however, as, for example, *nork baitzuen* 'somebody had it', with ergative *-k*, became *norkbait zuen*; hence reordering of morphemes took place to shift the case-suffix to its ordinary place at the end, producing modern *norbaitek zuen* 'somebody had it'. For further examples, see Comrie (1980a), Haspelmath (1993) and Koch (1996: 244–246).

rephonemicization Any phonological change which results in a redistribution of the phones of a language among phonemes: **split** (sense 1), **merger, phonemic shift** or **reassignment**. Some might include **rephonologization**.

rephonologization The term used by Jakobson (1931) for a type of phonological change in which the phonetic relations among the phonemes of a language are changed but not their number or their distribution. For example, some Slavic languages formerly had three velar phonemes /k g x/, in which /k/ but not /x/ had a voiced counterpart; the development of /g/ into /ɣ/ reversed this situation. See **Grimm's Law** for another example.

repidginization The creation of a **pidgin** from an existing **creole** which itself derives from an earlier pidgin.

resegmentation A cover term, used by Langacker (1977), for all of **boundary shift, boundary loss** and **boundary creation**.

resemanticization Another term for **semantic shift**.

residual zone Another term for **accretion zone**.

residue 1. In historical phonology, a set of forms which have apparently
failed to undergo an otherwise regular phonological change. An English example is the set *great*, *break*, *steak*, which has failed to undergo
the regular vowel-raising seen in *meat*, *beak*, *sea* and *tea*. In the past,
linguists were inclined to see such residues as the result of **dialect
mixing**, but today we are more likely to interpret them as resulting
either from the action of **competing changes** or as representing
instances of **lexical diffusion** which have failed to go to completion.
2. In historical grammar, a set of forms, or a construction, which is
anomalous with respect to the system as a whole. Examples include
the presence of feminine *o*-stems in Latin and Greek (in which *o*-stems are almost invariably masculine or neuter), the absence of
third-singular -*s* in the English modals like *can* and *will*, the presence
of **heteroclitic nouns** in several early IE languages, the Old Irish
construction called **Bergin's Law**, and the Greek use of singular
verb-forms with neuter plural subjects. Such residues provide valuable evidence about the ancient grammatical system of a language or
family, and may shed light upon the origin of individual forms. (For
example, the Greek case suggests that IE plurals were originally
collective singulars, a conclusion reinforced by other evidence.)

resistance to borrowing The property of a linguistic form which is
difficult to transfer from one language to another. Nothing is absolutely resistant to borrowing, but pronouns, low numerals and other
basic vocabulary are often thought to be relatively difficult to
borrow, and verbs are sometimes thought to be more difficult to
borrow than nouns. The former belief that syntactic patterns were
particularly resistant to borrowing has been undermined by the
discovery of phenomena like **metatypy**.

resistant phoneme A phoneme which is more than averagely resistant to
phonological change. It is questionable whether any such phonemes
exist, though several linguists have suggested that /m/ might be one
such, at least in word-initial position.

resonant (also **sonant**) In PIE, any one of the consonants */w y m n l r/,
which had a somewhat distinctive role in the phonology and morphology of that language.

restoring reanalysis The term used by Claudi (1994) to denote the
following type of change. First, there is an instance of **grammaticalization** which involves shifting one or more items from one

syntactic category to another. After this, there occurs a **reanalysis** in which the shifted items are returned to their original categories, the ones matching their semantics; this is the restoring reanalysis. Claudi cites the case of the Mande languages of Africa, which are historically Subject-Verb-Object (SVO) and Genitive-Noun (GN), but which have largely shifted to SOV order. The proposal is that grammaticalized constructions of the type S V [G N] (PostP), with a main verb marked for tense/aspect (T/A) and a complement containing a nominalized verb taking a genitive complement, have been reanalysed as S (T/A) O V (T/A), with both the original main verb and the original postposition either reduced to a T/A marker or lost, the nominalized verbal complement reanalysed as the main verb (and thus restored to verbal status), and its genitive complement reanalysed as its direct object.

restriction Another term for **narrowing**.

restructuring 1. In phonology, any reorganization of the phonological system of a language, often particularly **rephonemicization** or **rephonologization**. 2. In grammar, the term used by Vennemann (1974) for an instance of **analogical levelling** which changes the basic form in a paradigm. An example is the change of early Latin nominative singular *honōs* 'honour', whose stem was *honōr-* in every other form in the paradigm, to *honor*. 3. See under the **Lightfoot framework**.

retailoring A cover term applied by Anttila (1989: 156–158) to any kind of phonological, morphological, syntactic or semantic modification applied to a **loan word** in order to fit it into the structure of the borrowing language. Examples include **loan nativization,** **loanblends, calques, loan shifts** and **morphological integration**.

retention 1. (also **plesiomorphy, archaic residue**) A linguistic form or feature which has persisted in a language over a long period of time, or a set of such features; that part of a language which has not undergone loss or replacement since the period of some ancestral language. 2. Another term for **archaism** (sense 1).

retention by contact Another term for **preservation by contact**.

retention rate In **glottochronology**, the (supposedly fixed) percentage of vocabulary items retained by a language per unit time, usually per thousand years.

retextualization The term used by Nichols and Timberlake (1991) to denote a *panchronic* (see **panchrony**) view of **grammaticalization** in which **innovation** and **idiomatization** are simultaneously active. In this view, speakers generate new tokens of text which are analogous to, but not identical to, existing exemplars (instances of use), after which these new tokens become conventionalized and may themselves serve as exemplars for producing further new tokens by extrapolation. As a result, the fixing of new grammatical patterns goes hand in hand with innovating patterns.

retraction 1. Another term for **backing**. 2. The movement of word-accent from right to left within a word. This is pervasive in English; see under **recessive accent**. It is also very common in the prehistory of **Balto-Slavic**, in which it poses formidable difficulties of analysis; see Collinge (1985: 271–277 and references therein) for an account.

retroflexion Any **phonological change** in which another segment is converted into a retroflex. In Swedish, for example, an earlier sequence of /r/ plus coronal has generally given rise to a retroflex, as in *fart* [fɑːʈ] 'speed', *korn* [kɔːɳ] 'grain' and *kvarts* [kvaʈʂ] 'quartz'.

retrograde formation [*rare*] Another term for **back-formation**.

reversal (Ger *Rückverwandlung*) Any linguistic change which simply reverses the effect of an earlier change. For example, the ancestor of Swedish underwent the usual Germanic change of PIE */t/ to /θ/, but Swedish has undergone the reverse change of /θ/ to /t/, as in *tre* 'three' and *ting* 'thing'. Such reversals can obscure the historical development of a language; in the Swedish case, if we lacked documentary evidence of the truth, we might conclude erroneously that PIE */t/ had simply remained unchanged in Swedish. Reversal is one type of **homoplasy**.

reversal of merger (also **unmerger**) The phenomenon in which the speakers of a language in which an earlier distinction between two segments has disappeared reintroduce the earlier distinction. By **Garde's principle** (sense 1), reversal of merger is theoretically impossible, but a number of apparent cases of it have been described in the literature, such as the reversal of the merger of the vowels of *mate* and *meat* in English. At least seven types of explanation have been advanced. (1) Speakers retained differing underlying representations in their heads for generations after the surface forms had fallen together (Halle 1962, a view no longer taken seriously). (2) The merger genuinely occurred, but just one of the merged segments had a distinctive phonological role in the language, and speakers were later able to distinguish instances of the merged result which bore this role from those which did not. This is the interpretation offered by Michelena (1957, 1977: 194–195) for the merger of /ʃ/ (resulting from the strengthening of /j/) with pre-existing /ʃ/ in the Gipuzkoan dialect of Basque, followed by a reversal in which /ʃ/ derived from earlier /j/ developed to /χ/ while original /ʃ/ did not. All instances of original /ʃ/, like all palatal consonants in Basque, had a clear 'expressive' function, serving only to form diminutives and hypocorisms. Instances of /ʃ/ derived from /j/ lacked this expressive function and hence could be separated out. (3) The merger took place in the prestige variety but not in other varieties, and a change in the prestige of the competing varieties shows up in the record as an apparent reversal, since only prestige varieties tend to be well recorded. This is the view famously presented by Weinreich *et al.* (1968). (4) The merger genuinely occurred, but only variably, and speakers retained both merged and unmerged pronunciations, even though they may have reported the merged pronunciation as the only possibility. This is the view defended by Milroy (1992: 154–160). (5) The merger never really occurred; instead, there was only a **near-merger** resulting in the usual failure of speakers to observe the objectively real contrast. This view is championed by Labov (1975, 1994: ch. 13) and by Faber *et al.* (1995, 1997). (6) The merger never really occurred; instead, an imperfect spelling system spelled different segments identically (L. Wright 1997). (7) The merger occurred for most (or even all) speakers, but a handful of conservative and influential speakers succeeded in reversing it by educational action (Jahr 1989 for Icelandic, Skautrup 1968 for Danish).

reversion A label occasionally applied to a development in which the effect of a regular phonological change is reversed by **analogical levelling**. For example, the **Second Palatalization** in Slavic produced alternations in a number of Old Russian verbs, as in *pomog-* 'help', infinitive *pomogti* but imperative *pomozi*; levelling has restored *pomogi* as the modern imperative.

Rhaeto-Romance A small branch of the **Romance** family spoken in eastern Switzerland and northeastern Italy, including *Romansh*, *Friulian* and *Ladin*. See Haiman and Benincà (1992).

Rhenish fan A famous map of the German-speaking region along the Rhine, compiled by Georg Wenker in 1876, and showing that the boundaries between High and Low German forms lay in different positions for different words (where a High German form has undergone the **Second Germanic Consonant Shift** and a Low German form has not). From north to south, the boundaries between competing forms are as follows (Low German form always first): *ik/ ich* 'I', *maken/machen* 'make', *dorp/dorf* 'village', *dat/das* 'that'. This map is often credited with having initiated **dialect geography**, and it has the further point that all of the several linguistic boundaries correlate with medieval political and ecclesiastical boundaries in the area. The map itself can be found in many textbooks.

rhizotic model A **model of linguistic descent** which, in its extreme form, denies that a language derives from a single ancestor and instead stresses the multiple sources, or 'roots', from which elements can be extracted and combined in order to produce a single linguistic system. Though the name was coined only by Moore (1994a, 1994b), the model itself has been advanced since the early twentieth century. Somewhat surprisingly, it has been applied most prominently to the **Indo-European** languages; all of C. C. Uhlenbeck, Nikolai Trubetzkoy and Antonio Tovar argued at times that the IE languages should not be seen as descending from PIE (whose existence they doubt) but as resulting from intense interactions among speakers of two or three unrelated languages or groups of languages. Miller (1980) has likewise suggested that Japanese emerged out of successive waves of Turkic, Mongolian and Tungusic invasions of Japan. The rhizotic model has a good deal in common with the **crystallization model**. See **portmanteau language**.

rhotacism Any phonological change in which some other segment turns into a rhotic consonant (an 'r-sound'). For example, in Pre-Latin, intervocalic /s/ changed first to [z] and then to /r/, producing in the classical language alternations like *flos* 'flower', genitive *floris* (from earlier **flosis*). In medieval Basque, intervocalic /l/ developed into /r/, so that, for example, the Latin word *gula* 'appetite', originally borrowed as **gula*, appears in modern Basque as *gura* 'desire'.

rhotic accent Any accent of English in which the historical /r/ is retained in all positions, so that *farther* remains distinct from *father* and *star* does not rhyme with *Shah*. Rhotic accents are typical of southwest England, Scotland, Ireland, parts of the Caribbean and most of North America. The property of a rhotic accent is *rhoticity*. Compare **non-rhotic accent**.

rhyming formation Any of various types of paired or reduplicated formations in which some kind of similarity in sound between the two elements appears to be important; this similarity need not be rhyme in the ordinary sense. English exhibits several types: (1) true rhymes, as in *hoity-toity, helter-skelter, hurdy-gurdy, pell-mell, wine and dine*; (2) simple alliteration, as in *go-getter, tattle-tale, gewgaw, rock 'n' roll, kit and caboodle*; (3) vowel mutation, as in *riff-raff, zigzag, flip-flop, flim-flam, tick-tock*. Compare **echo word**.

Rising Sonority, Law of Another term for the (Law of) **Open Syllables**.

ritualization A very general term used by Haiman (1994) for the routine repetition of linguistic patterns, resulting in the fixing of innovations in languages.

Rix's Law A type of systematic **anaptyxis** occurring in early Greek, by which the word–initial sequence **HRC-*, where *H* is any laryngeal, *R* is a syllabic resonant, and *C* is a consonant, developed into **HVRC-*, in which the inserted vowel was coloured normally by the preceding laryngeal, which then dropped normally. Thus, for example, PIE **H₁rgh-* yielded *érkhomai* 'come', **H₂rg-* yielded *argós* 'white', and **H₃nbh-* yielded *omphalós* 'navel'. The change was identified by Rix (1970) and named by Joseph (1975). See Collinge (1985: 236–237) for an account.

r/n **stem** See under **heteroclitic noun**.

Romance The group of languages descended from the spoken **Latin** of the late Roman Empire. They include **Portuguese**, *Galician*, **Spanish** (with its very distinctive offshoot *Judaeo-Spanish*, or *Ladino*), *Catalan*, *Occitan*, **French**, *Romansh*, *Ladin*, *Friulian*, **Italian**, *Sardinian*, *Romanian* (with its distinctive offshoots *Arumanian* and *Moldavian*), and the extinct **Dalmatian**; some would also include the various Romance-based **creoles**. See Posner (1996) for a historical summary, Elcock (1975) for a linguistic history, and Harris and Vincent (1997) for a survey of the modern languages. Iordan and Orr (1970) is a history of Romance linguistics. The standard (but dated) Romance etymological dictionary is Meyer-Lübke (1935).

Romania The area in which the **Romance** languages are spoken.

root 1. The minimal form of a lexical morpheme. Roots are important in IE studies; see **Indo-European root theory**. 2. Especially in **Austronesian** linguistics, a morph of constant form and meaning which recurs in a number of items in various languages for which no reconstruction can be assigned to the ancestral language, such as the final element of widespread **gilap* ~ **kilap* 'lustre, shine', Tagalog *kisláp* 'sparkle' and Malay *relap* 'glint, flash'. These things appear to be **phonaesthemes**. Blust (1988, 1990) argues that the frequency of such roots in Austronesian provides an opportunity for applying the **comparative method** to one language at a time.

root cognates (also **root etymology**, Ger *Wurzeletymologie*) Words or forms which are constructed upon **cognate** roots but at least some of which also contain additional morphological material which is not cognate. For example, English *head* and Spanish *cabeza* 'head' are both descended from the PIE root **kaput*, but the Spanish word contains additional material not historically present in the English one. Root cognates are the most familiar kind of **partial cognates**. Note: the term *root etymology* has often been used dismissively, to label a set of proposed cognates in which no material other than the putative root is accounted for, and which is therefore presumably suspect; the label *root cognates* has no such dismissive sense.

root extension (Ger *Wurzelerweiterung*) In PIE, any of several recurrent formatives which were seemingly suffixed to roots in word-formation for unknown purposes. Examples include the **-wo-* of **ker-wo-s* 'stag' (from **ker-* 'horn') and the **-sko-* of **prk-sko-* 'ask' (from **perk-* 'ask'). The reality of these extensions is not in doubt, though critics have complained that these things are invoked far too freely in proposing etymologies. See **Indo-European root theory**.

root noun (Ger *Wurzelnomen*) In IE languages, a noun to which inflectional endings are added directly to the root, with no intervening thematic vowel: an **athematic** noun. An example is Latin *rēx* 'king', which consists of the root *rēk-* and the case-ending *-s*; compare *portus* 'door', in which the case-ending is separated from the root *port-* by the thematic vowel *-u-* (historically *-o-*). Many root nouns are actually bases derived from verbal roots with reduced vowels, such as Greek *líps* 'stream, source', beside the verb *leíbō* 'pour'.

rounding Any phonological change in which a segment (usually a vowel) acquires lip-rounding which it formerly lacked. For example, Latin *demandare* 'ask' and *limaca* 'slug' have become *domandare* and *lumaca* in Italian, with rounding (and backing) of the first vowel in each case. The opposite is **unrounding**.

routinization Another term for **idiomatization**.

Rückschreibung The German for **backspelling**.

Rückverwandlung The German for **reversal**.

Rückwanderer A **loan word** which passes from language A to language B and then back to language A. For example, French *bœuf* was borrowed into English as *beef*; this word formed a compound *roast beef*, which has been borrowed back into French as *rosbif*.

ruki A phonological change occurring in early **Slavic**. PIE */s/ developed into /ş/, and then usually into /x/, after any of PIE */i u r k g gʰ/, except before a stop. The same occurred in **Indo-Iranian**. See **Pedersen's Law** (sense 1). See Andersen (1968).

rule addition A type of **rule change** in which a new rule is introduced into the grammar so that it applies after all previously existing rules; the most familiar type of rule change. An example is the rule deleting all word-final consonants which has been added to several Polynesian languages, producing interesting alternations in originally consonant-final stems. Compare **rule insertion**.

rule atrophy (also **rule fading**) The phenomenon in which a formerly productive phonological rule ceases to apply to new cases and instead becomes gradually eliminated from the language by other developments, often especially **analogical levelling**. The final result is **rule loss**.

rule borrowing 1. The diffusion of a linguistic rule across a language boundary. For example, several unrelated but neighbouring languages of Guatemala and southern Mexico have acquired a rule placing the word-stress on the vowel preceding the last consonant in a word. 2. A label often given to the consequences of the following state of affairs. Language A has a rule applying regularly to a number of items, producing alternations. Language B borrows so many items from language A that those alternations become prominent in B, and therefore the rule obtaining in A can now also be said to be present in B. An example is English **velar softening**, borrowed from French. Here the name is strictly a misnomer, since only items exhibiting the effect of the rule are borrowed, and not the rule itself.

rule change Any of various types of **phonological change** in which a rule is introduced, lost or modified, or in which the order of two rules changes. See King (1969), Kiparsky (1971) or Sommerstein (1977: ch. 10).

rule complication A type of **rule change** in which a rule becomes more complex than formerly. This is not usually regarded as a primary type of change, but only as the consequence of independent changes which have the effect of disturbing the operation of the original rule. See Bach and Harms (1972) for examples.

rule contraction A proposed label for the opposite of **rule simplification**, in which a rule comes to apply to fewer cases than formerly. Such changes appear to be rare at best.

rule expansion Another term for **rule simplification**.

rule extension Another term for **rule simplification**.

rule fading Another term for **rule atrophy**.

rule generalization Another term for **rule simplification**.

rule insertion A putative type of **rule change** in which a new rule is added to the grammar, not at the end of the existing rules, but at an earlier point, so that it has an effect upon the operation of later rules. There appear to be no certain cases of rule insertion, and many linguists would deny its existence. See King (1973). Compare **rule addition**.

rule interaction Another term for **rule ordering**.

rule inversion A type of **rule change** in which a rule is replaced by one operating in the opposite direction – that is, the original derived form is taken as underlying, and the original underlying form is derived by rule. For example, in medieval Basque, the segment /l/ uniformly changed to /r/ in intervocalic position but remained /l/ elsewhere, producing such alternations as *euskara* 'Basque language (< *euska-la), euskaldun* 'Basque-speaker'. However, the Latin word *sagmarius* 'pack horse' was borrowed into Basque as *zamari* 'horse'; this now forms derivatives like *zamaldun* 'horseman', showing that the original rule converting /l/ to /r/ between vowels has been inverted; /r/ is now taken as underlying, and the inverted rule converts /r/ to /l/ before a consonant. Rule inversion was first pointed out by Vennemann (1972).

rule loss A type of **rule change** in which a rule that was formerly present disappears from the language. For example, all southern varieties of German historically acquired a rule devoicing final obstruents. Standard German still has this rule, which is responsible for such alternations as *Bund* [bunt] 'league', genitive *Bundes* [bundəs]; compare *bunt* [bunt] 'mottled', genitive *buntes* [buntəs]. Many Swiss German and Yiddish varieties have lost the devoicing rule, producing [bund], [bundəs] 'league' but [bunt], [buntəs] 'mottled'; the former presence of the rule is shown by the continued devoicing in forms which do not alternate, such as *weg* [vek] 'away'. It is not certain that rule loss is distinct from **rule atrophy**. See Joseph (1983) for rule loss in syntax.

rule ordering (also **rule interaction**) The state of affairs in which several independent changes expressible as phonological rules and applying at different times in the history of a language interact so as to produce complex results which can only be understood by placing those changes in a particular historical order. Newman (1996) cites an example from Cantonese. Middle Chinese **a* is regularly lost in Cantonese by *nucleus deletion* when preceded by an onglide and followed by another segment, as in **miau > miu* 'ticket'. If there is no onglide, **a* undergoes *lengthening* to *a:*, as in **nai > na:i* 'ticket'. However, words in **-iai* appear to be exceptions to nucleus deletion, since they yield *-ai*, as in **niai > nai* 'mud'. Invoking an earlier rule of *palatal dissimilation*, by which **i* is lost in the configuration **-iai* would account for the non-application of nucleus deletion, but would also make the result subject to lengthening, wrongly predicting **na:i* 'mud'. The solution is to order the rules as follows: (1) lengthening, (2) palatal dissimilation, (3) nucleus deletion. This gives the right result in all cases, and presumably reflects the **relative chronology** of the changes in Cantonese.

rule pool A state of affairs in which a number of different phonological rules exist within some geographical area, with each local variety exhibiting some of those rules but not others, and possibly also with differences in ordering among rules shared among several localities.

rule reaffirmation (also **rule reapplication**) The phenomenon in which a phonological change which has gone to completion continues to apply to new cases at a later time; one kind of **drift** (sense 1). For example, after final devoicing had affected all German words, final-vowel loss created new word-final voiced obstruents in some dialects, and these too then underwent final devoicing. In other words, the rule remained active in the language and continued to be applied to new cases meeting its structural description.

rule reordering A type of **rule change** in which the order of two existing rules is reversed, thus changing the output. For example, some Bizkaian dialects of Basque have one rule which raises a mid vowel before a non-high vowel and a second rule which raises /a/ to /e/ before /a/. In varieties with the original ordering, original /ea/ becomes [ia], while original /aa/ becomes [ea]. Some varieties, however, have reordered the two rules, so that both original /ea/ and original /aa/ are realized as [ia]. See Kiparsky (1968).

rule simplification (also **rule extension, rule generalization, (rule) expansion**) A type of **rule change** in which, by the removal of some of the conditions on its operation, a rule comes to apply to a wider range of cases than formerly. For example, all varieties of English have lost word-final /b/ after a nasal, as in *climb* and *lamb*; most varieties have generalized this to the loss of word-final non-coronal voiced plosives (including /g/) after a nasal, as in *sing* and *long*; and some southern and black varieties of American English have generalized it further to the loss of all word-final voiced plosives (including /d/) after a nasal, as in /stæn/ for *stand* and /maɪn/ for *mind*. If the three versions of the rule are formalized, each version requires fewer feature specifications than the preceding one.

rule stagnation The state of affairs, particularly in **lexical diffusion**, in which an innovation is introduced into a speech variety in a few cases, spreads to further cases, and then ceases to spread further, leaving some relevant items unaffected.

Russian One of the world's major languages, the principal language of the Russian Federation, also widely spoken in the other former members of the USSR. A 1989 census reported nearly 165 million native speakers and about 70 million other speakers. Russian is an eastern **Slavic** language which grew up as the language of a series of powerful Slavic states beginning with Kievan Rus over a thousand years ago. The prestige of **Old Church Slavonic** greatly delayed the creation of an agreed literary standard form of the language, something not finally achieved until the beginning of the nineteenth century. Dialectal diversification is small, mostly north-south, and confined to rustic varieties. The southern and western varieties *Ukrainian* and *Belarussian* have diverged more substantially (especially the first) and are now regarded as distinct languages with their own standard forms. See Price (1998: 395–404).

S

Sabellian A label applied variously to certain **Italic** languages. For some, it denotes the entire Osco-Umbrian grouping; for others, it denotes only a smaller group consisting of **Aequian, Marrucinian, Marsian, Paelignian, Sabine, Vestinian** and **Volscian,** or whichever of these are regarded as Italic.

Sabine An extinct and virtually unrecorded language spoken northeast of Rome before the Roman conquest of Italy. No certain Sabine text survives, and Sabine is known only through a few words cited by Roman writers; it appears to have been **Italic.**

Salience, Principle of A putative principle, put forward by Lemle and Naro (1977), governing the effect of phonological change on inflectional morphology. It says this: the more prominent an inflectional marking is (that is, the more phonetic substance associated with it), the greater the tendency to retain the inflection in the face of sound changes tending to reduce it.

Salishan A large and diverse language family (about twenty-three languages) extending from British Columbia to central Oregon and inland to Montana and Idaho; its best-known member is *Bella Coola*. It is included in the **Mosan** hypothesis.

SALTATION

saltation A dramatic and discontinuous change in the phonetic quality of a segment, such as /u/ > /ɛ/. Lass (1997: 226227) examines some apparent instances of saltations in English vowels, such as Northumbrian /uːt/ but Derbyshire /ɛːt/ *out* and the Scots regional variation between /o/ and /e/ in words like *home*, and concludes that saltations rarely if ever occur, and that apparent saltations result either from a sequence of smaller changes or from borrowing. Compare **stepwise shift, superjump.**

Samoyed A group of about five languages spoken in northern Siberia and forming one of the two main branches of the **Uralic** family.

samprasāraṇa In PIE and some early IE languages, the change of a nonsyllabic resonant (in a full grade) to a syllabic resonant (in the zerograde), as in PIE **kleu-* ~ **klu-* 'hear', in which /u/ is non-syllabic in the e-grade but syllabic in the zero-grade, and in Sanskrit *prach* 'ask' but *prcchảti* 'he asks', with non-syllabic /r/ in the first but syllabic /r/ in the second. See **ablaut.**

sandhi Any of various phonological processes applying to sequences of segments either across morpheme boundaries (*internal sandhi*) or across word boundaries (*external sandhi*). An example of the first is **velar softening** in English; an example of the second is Sanskrit *saː* 'he' plus *uːvača* 'spoke' > *sovača* 'he spoke'.

Sanskrit The most important of the ancient **Indo-Aryan** languages, recorded in the first millennium BC and famously codified by the grammarian Pāṇini in the fifth or fourth century BC, in the form called *classical Sanskrit*, by which time it was already a somewhat archaic literary language. Sanskrit is rather conservative among IE languages, especially in its retention of the PIE **ablaut** and of the elaborate PIE case-system. It was the discovery of Sanskrit by European linguists in the late eighteenth century, and their realization that it was related to Greek and Latin, that led to the widespread recognition of the **Indo-European** family. Note: the still earlier **Vedic** has often been classified as a version of Sanskrit, *Vedic Sanskrit*, but specialists today generally prefer to restrict the name *Sanskrit* to the classical language and closely related varieties, and to regard Vedic as distinct. See Lazzeroni (1998) for an account, and compare **Prākrits.**

Sapir's principle Another term for the **age-area hypothesis.**

satem language Any branch of **Indo-European** in which certain PIE consonants (the supposed **first palatal series**) developed into palatals, and later usually into sibilants. These consonants remained distinct from the inherited PIE velars, which in the satem languages usually merged with the inherited labio-velars. The satem languages include **Indo-Iranian, Balto-Slavic, Armenian** and (with qualifications) **Albanian**. The name derives from the IE word for '100', which began with one of the relevant consonants: Avestan *satəm*, Sanskrit *śatám*, Old Church Slavonic *sŭto*, Lithuanian *šimtas*, and so on. Compare **centum language**, and see the remarks there.

Saussurean paradox The following problem: how can a language continue to function effectively as a structured system when it is in the middle of a number of changes? This paradox has only been resolved since the 1960s with the realization that **variation** is always part of the structure of a language, and that variation is the vehicle of change.

Saussure's Law The observation, put forward by Saussure (1894, 1896) with an attempted explanation, that in certain circumstances in Lithuanian the word–stress moves rightwards from a short or rising syllabic nucleus to a falling nucleus. See Collinge (1985: 149–152).

Šaxmatov's Law The statement, by Šaxmatov (1915), that, in certain Slavic languages, a word-accent originally on a short circumflex syllable moves leftwards. The proposal is very controversial; see Collinge (1985: 153–154) for discussion.

Sayhedic Another term for **Epigraphic South Arabian**.

sc. The abbreviation for Latin *scilicet* 'it is permitted to know', used to introduce an explanation of an obscure or unrecognizable term or to insert a missing word required for comprehension, most often in quotations, as in 'Chaucer's *queynte* (*sc.* 'cunt')', in 'the Aryan (*sc.* Indo-European) languages', or in 'the First Palatalization (*sc.* in Slavic)'.

Scaliger classification An early attempt at classifying the languages of Europe into families, published by the French scholar J. J. Scaliger in 1610. Scaliger classified languages exclusively by their word for 'God', and obtained eleven families. His 'major' families were more or less equivalent to Slavic, Germanic, Romance and Turkic; his 'minor' families to Greek, Albanian, Hungarian, Finnic, Goidelic, Brythonic and Basque. This was the most wide-ranging and successful of a number of similar classifications proposed in the medieval and early modern periods, but Scaliger made no attempt to look for further links. Compare the **Dante classification**.

schematization The removal from a semantically specific word or morpheme of a number of semantic features, leaving behind a kind of semantic 'skeleton' which can be applied much more broadly to anything possessing this skeleton. For example, English *head* has been schematized to 'thing on top', and hence its extension to cases like *head* (of a corporation).

schwa indogermanicum (also **schwa primum**) A vowel /ə/ formerly posited for PIE, to explain the frequent correspondence of Indo-Iranian /i/ with /a/ elsewhere, as in Sanskrit *pitar-* 'father' but Latin *pater*, and so on. Today this vowel is not usually recognized, since the introduction of **laryngeals** explains most such cases.

schwa secundum Another term for the **reduced grade**; see under **ablaut**.

Schwebeablaut (also **secondary ablaut**) In PIE, a case of apparent metathesis between vowel and resonant in a root, as in **ters- ~ *tres-* 'tremble' and **perk- ~ *prek-* 'ask, entreat'. It is not clear whether such alternations resulted from genuine metatheses or from other causes, such as the differential reduction of disyllabic forms like **ter-es-*. See Anttila (1969).

Schwundhypothese The hypothesis that all of the categories which are absent from **Anatolian** but present in all other branches of IE were simply lost from Anatolian, and that Anatolian is accordingly an innovating branch of IE. The opposing view is the *Herkunfthypothese*. See Luraghi (1998: 190–191).

Schwundstufe See under **ablaut**.

Scots The rather distinctive varieties of **English** spoken in the lowlands of Scotland, also called *Lallans*, and regarded by a few nationalistic Scots as a language distinct from English. Do not confuse Scots with the **Celtic** language *Scots Gaelic*.

Scottish vowel-length rule Another term for **Aitken's Law**.

Scythian The extinct and unrecorded Iranian language of a people who invaded much of eastern Europe during the first millennium BC.

search problem The problem of combing languages for possible **cognates**, particularly in the case in which the languages are not known to be related and the investigator is seeking evidence for a remote genetic link. The search problem is essentially mathematical in nature; it consists of finding statistical techniques for overcoming the background noise caused by the inevitable **chance resemblances** between languages. Work on the search problem is still in its infancy, but it has been stimulated by recent attempts at identifying remote genetic links. Two approaches are the **Monte Carlo test** and the **Oswalt shift test**. See also Bender (1969), Nichols (1995b), and see the **probabilistic approach**.

secondary Of a linguistic form, **innovating**: exhibiting the effects of a change which has not affected earlier or more conservative forms recorded elsewhere. The term is particularly applied to forms which have undergone **syntagmatic change**. For example, Basque *gau* 'night' plus the article *-a* yields *gaua* 'the night' in most varieties, but *gaba* in western varieties, by the conditioned change of /u/ to /b/ between low vowels; the form *gaba* is secondary. The opposite is **conservative** (sense 1).

secondary ablaut Another term for *Schwebeablaut*.

secondary endings One of the two sets of verbal agreement suffixes found in all the early IE languages and reconstructible for PIE. The secondary endings are found in the imperfect and aorist indicative, in the optative mood, and to some extent in the imperative. The secondary endings are shorter and older than the **primary endings**, which appear to be derived from them. See Beekes (1995: 232–234).

secondary recategorization The shift of an item from one category to another for specific purposes. For example, the English nouns *coffee*, *wine* and *intelligence* are uncountable in their primary senses, but they can be counted when recategorized in special senses: *two coffees* (measures), *Australian wines* (varieties), *an alien intelligence* (embodiment).

secondary source In philological work, a dictionary, handbook, textbook, monograph or other piece of scholarly work which is compiled by a specialist scholar from the evidence of the **primary sources** and which attempts to provide an organized presentation of some of the linguistic facts of the language under investigation. For example, for Old English, Henry Sweet's *Anglo-Saxon Primer* was long a major secondary source, since it was virtually the only book attempting to present an organized description of the facts of the language. Secondary sources, if well done, are extremely valuable to later generations of scholars, but all contain errors of fact and interpretation, and the philologists' favourite dictum is 'check the texts.'

secondary split See under **split**.

secondary transmission The conveying of phonological information about a dead language by means of loan words into and out of that language. For example, Greek <K> is regularly rendered in Latin spelling by <C>, and Latin <C> is regularly rendered as <K> in Greek and other languages, confirming that Latin <C> represented /k/.

Second Germanic Consonant Shift (also **High German Consonant Shift**) A series of rather dramatic changes in the nature of certain consonants which affected most southern varieties of **German** in the early centuries AD and which are responsible for the prominent differences in consonantism between southern ('High') German and northern ('Low') German. The changes were complex and variable, and not all varieties were affected equally. Oversimplifying somewhat, the changes were as follows. Voiceless plosives developed differently, according to position; here Position 1 means word-initially, after another consonant or when geminated, and Position 2 is elsewhere. See Table 7.

Standard High German exhibits most of these developments rather well, except that it does not reflect the change of /k/ to /kx/ and that the geminate fricatives have more recently been degeminated. In Table 8, English, which did not undergo the shift, represents the rest of the Germanic family.

The voiced plosives were devoiced:

$$/b/ > /p/ \quad /d/ > /t/ \quad /g/ > /k/$$

		Position 1	Position 2
/p/	>	/pf/	/ff/
/t/	>	/ts/	/ss/
/k/	>	/kx/	/xx/

Table 7

Position 1		Position 2	
English	**German**	**English**	**German**
plum	*Pflaume*	*open* [adj.]	*offen*
ten	*zehn* /tseːn/	*water*	*Wasser*
cold	*kalt*	*make*	*machen* /maxən/

Table 8

This change is not generally reflected in modern High German except for the coronal plosive, as shown in Table 9.

Finally, the dental fricative /θ/ changed to /d/, as shown in Table 10.

Some specialists prefer to reserve the label for the changes affecting the voiceless plosives only, regarding the others as unrelated changes. See Robinson (1992: 239–244) for a brief survey. Compare **First Germanic Consonant Shift**, and see also **bifurcational theory**.

Second Palatalization In common **Slavic**, the change of */k g x/ to palatals /c ɟ ç/, usually developing later to /ts z s/, before front vowels and before non-syllabic /u/ followed by a front vowel.

Second Slavic Vowel Shift In common **Slavic**, a change in the vowel system by which the earlier contrast between long and short vowels of similar quantity was reinterpreted as a contrast between tense /i y u ě a/ and lax /ĭ ŭ e o/.

English	**German**
daughter	*Tochter*
adder [ME *nadder*]	*Natter*
good	*gut*

Table 9

English	German
thick	*dick*
brother	*Bruder*
bath	*Bad*

Table 10

secretion [*rare*] The term used by Jespersen (1922) for the process of creating a **splinter** and forming words with it.

secret language A language, of whatever origin, known to and used by only a subsection of a speech community and used only for certain special purposes. See Muysken (1997b) for an account of Callahuaya, the secret language of Bolivian itinerant healers.

seeds-of-destruction paradox The name given by Lass (1987: 170) to the puzzle of how identical or nearly identical changes can occur independently in related but geographically separated languages, as in **drift** (sense 2).

segmentalization Another term for **unpacking**.

segmentation In historical linguistics, the practice of inserting (usually non-obvious) morpheme boundaries into a single linguistic form, either to elucidate the etymological structure of the form or to provide a morph which can be satisfactorily matched with a form in another language in **comparison**. All linguists tolerate a degree of segmentation, but some are far more generous than others. For example, according to the usual correspondences, we would expect the ancient Greek words for 'nine' and '100' to begin with /n/ and /k/, respectively; but, since the attested forms are *ennéa* and *hekatón*, respectively, we feel justified in segmenting the morphs *en-* and *he-* away, possibly as later accretions, since doing so leaves us with perfect matches with the other IE languages. However, invoking unconstrained and arbitrary segmentations is potentially very dangerous, since it leads rapidly to spurious cognates and etymologies. For example, Greenberg (1987) takes Proto-Algonquian *šenkihšin- 'lie down' and extracts the morph *šenk-, which he compares with forms meaning 'lie down' in other languages, but Goddard (1987: 656) points out that *šenk- in fact means 'flat', while 'lie' is *-hšin. Failure to recognize morpheme boundaries is likewise destructive, as when Greenberg (1987) compares Cakchiquel *paruwi* 'above' with Tunica *ʔaparu* 'heaven, cloud', but Campbell (1988: 606) points out that the Cakchiquel word is composed of *pa* 'in, on' plus *ru-* 'his/her' plus *-wiʔ* 'head', and is thus literally 'on his head'. See **false segmentation**.

segment borrowing The acquisition of a new phoneme by a language as a result of the **borrowing** of words containing it. For example, English /ʒ/ is entirely confined to loan words, either taken over intact (as in *rouge* and *Zhivago*) or acquired from the resolution of the non-native sequence /zj/ (as in *measure*).

selection 1. See under **language planning**. 2. See under **profligacy**.

Selian (also **Selonian**) An extinct and unrecorded **Baltic** language spoken until the sixteenth century in parts of Latvia and Lithuania.

semantic age In the work of Joan Bybee and her colleagues, such as Bybee *et al.* (1991), any one of the several semantic stages which can be distinguished during an instance of **grammaticalization**, such as the conversion of a 'want' verb into a future-tense marker.

semantic assimilation A term used by Schlesinger (1979: 317 *ff.*) to label instances of semantic broadening such as the extension of English *with* from an instrumental sense (as in *She wrote it with a pen*) to a manner sense (as in *She wrote it with enthusiasm*).

semantic change Any type of change in the meaning of a linguistic form, usually (though not invariably) excluding changes in the grammatical function of a grammatical morpheme (**remorphologization**). Semantic change is one of the most difficult types of change to identify principles for, though interesting progress has been made, for example the **Traugott progression**. There are, however, a number of familiar types of semantic change which have been named, including **broadening, narrowing, amelioration, pejoration, metaphor, metonymy, synecdoche, euphemism, referent change, semantic merger** and **semantic split**, among others.

semantic copying [*rare*] Another term for the creation of a **calque**.

semantic depletion, semantic fading Another term for **bleaching**.

semantic gain The addition to a linguistic form of semantic content which it formerly lacked. The term is most commonly used in **grammaticalization**. For example, the English *be going to* construction, which formerly expressed only directed motion, has been grammaticalized and has acquired the semantic value of 'intention', as in *I'm going to buy a car.*

semanticization The acquisition of new semantic value by a linguistic form, often especially as part of some kind of **reanalysis**. For example, English *while* formerly meant 'during', and still does in cases like *While I was in the bath, the phone rang.* However, it has also been semanticized to the concessive sense of 'although', as in *While I'd like to see the match, I can't spare the time.* Its German cognate *weil*, also originally 'during', has been semanticized to 'because' and lost its original sense entirely, a development that has not occurred in English, in spite of the potential offered by cases like *While this government is in power, we aren't going to have a decent school system.*

semantic merger 1. The loss of a formerly obligatory semantic distinction, as when Latin *albus* 'white' and *candidus* 'shining white' were replaced by French *blanc* 'white' (unmarked for shininess), or when English *actor* (male) and *actress* (female) are replaced by the invariant *actor*, unmarked for sex. The opposite is **semantic split**. 2. The term used by Kilroe (1994) for a change introducing homophony between two semantically distinct items, especially grammatical items. She cites the Latin prepositions *ad* 'to, at' and *ab* 'from', which merged in Old French as *à*, a single preposition with the functions of both of the Latin ones (and a third Latin preposition, *apud* 'near, by, in the presence of', later also merged with *à*).

semantic reconstruction The process of determining the original meaning of a linguistic form which can be securely reconstructed for an ancestral language. For example, Basque exhibits a sizeable number of compounds and derivatives which allow us securely to reconstruct an earlier noun **ortzi*, but the attested meanings of this form include all of 'sky', 'storm', 'thunder' and 'cloud', and there is a tiny amount of evidence suggesting that it might also have been the name of a pagan deity. The problem is to work out just what the word originally meant.

semantics control problem In **comparison**, the difficulty of deciding whether a possible cognate of suitable form has an acceptable semantic value to be treated as a cognate. For example, English *clean* and German *klein* 'small' are perfect phonological matches, but the semantic mismatch prohibits them from being treated as secure cognates without independent evidence (which is available in this case). Under PIE **leuk-* 'light, brightness', Watkins (1969) lists words meaning 'light', 'moon', 'purify', 'meadow', 'shine', 'flame, fire', 'lamp', 'rabies' and possibly 'lynx', and these are only the cognates retrievable from English. The critics of the various proposed **remote relationships** (such as **Amerind** and **Nostratic**) have often focused their fire on what they see as excessive semantic latitude in recognizing 'cognates', such as Greenberg's 1987 comparison involving the senses of 'feather', 'leaf', 'fly', 'short hair', 'wing', 'hair' and 'beard'. Clearly such semantic variation is not intrinsically out of the question; it is rather that uncontrolled semantics may enormously increase one's chances of finding spurious 'cognates', and hence of claiming a genetic link where none exists. The problem is fundamental and serious, and it is a major motivation for those who advocate **closed comparison**. See Wilkins (1996).

semantic shift (also **resemanticization**) A type of **semantic change** in which the meaning of a word changes so completely that nothing at all is covered by both the earlier and later meanings. Examples include the shift of English *bead* from 'prayer' to 'small ball' and *silly* from 'blessed' to 'foolish'.

semantic similarity The degree to which linguistic forms in different languages are similar in meaning. In **comparison**, the allowable degree of semantic similarity in seeking **cognates** is a thorny problem: see the **semantics control problem**, and see Wilkins (1996) and the references there.

semantic split The introduction of an obligatory semantic distinction which was formerly absent, as when Latin *avis* 'bird' (of any size) was replaced by Spanish *ave* 'big bird' and *pájaro* 'little bird'. The opposite is **semantic merger**.

semantic transparency Another term for **isomorphy**.

semantic weakening Another term for **bleaching**.

semi-creole A language which develops by a mixture of two processes: ordinary internal changes in an ancestral language, and extensive simplification resulting from contact, as in **creole**-formation. It is far from clear whether any such languages exist. A favourite, but controversial, example is Afrikaans; see Thomason and Kaufman (1988: 251–256). See **abrupt creolization**.

semi-learnèd word A word in a language which is in principle inherited from an ancestral language but which shows the effects of only some, and not all, of the regular phonological changes which have applied in the language. For example, Latin *rēgula(m)* should have yielded **reja* in Spanish by ordinary developments, and indeed does so in the sense of 'ploughshare', but the form meaning 'rule, ruler' is *regla*, in which the word has undergone the popular loss of the medial vowel but not the normal treatment of the cluster. Compare **learnèd word**.

semiotic fallacy The term applied by Lass (1990a and elsewhere) to the belief that every element in a language is meaningful or functional. Lass champions the view that every language always contains a measure of meaningless and functionless **junk** which is merely the dead residue of defunct systems. But see Bolinger (1977) or Vincent (1995) for contrary views.

semi-speaker 1. A person who has only a limited command of a language which is the traditional language of his/her community, often especially a language which is dying. Normally such a speaker is fluent in another language, the local prestige language. 2. A person who is fluent in no language at all. Bloomfield (1927) cites the case of White Thunder, a Menomini who spoke nothing but 'atrocious' Menomini and even worse English.

Semitic A large family of languages in the Near East and northern and eastern Africa, containing about twenty languages (some of them extinct), and forming one branch of the **Afro-Asiatic** family. The *eastern* branch consists only of the extinct **Akkadian**; the *southern* branch includes **Arabic**, the **Epigraphic South Arabian** languages, *Maltese*, and the numerous Semitic languages of Ethiopia, including *Amharic* and the classical language **Ge'ez**; the *northwestern* branch includes **Hebrew**, **Aramaic**, the extinct **Phoenician**, and a few others. (This traditional classification has recently been called into question, and other classifications have been put forward; see Versteegh 1997: 9–15 or Faber 1997.) Many Semitic languages were written down very early in the history of writing, and Semitic-speakers invented the first alphabet, though this lacked vowel letters. See Hetzron (1997) for a survey of the family.

sequential chain shift See under **chain shift**.

series A group of consonant phonemes in a language which agree in voicing and manner of articulation but differ in place of articulation. For example, PIE is commonly reconstructed with three series of plosives: voiceless */p t (k′) k kʷ/, voiced */b d (g′) g gʷ/, and voiced aspirated */bh dh (gh′) gh ghʷ/. Compare **order**.

seseo In **Spanish**, a type of pronunciation in which the fricatives /θ/ and /s/, distinguished in standard European Spanish, are merged, usually as /s/, thereby converting to homophones such pairs as *casa* /kasa/ 'house' and *caza* /kaθa/ 'hunting'. *Seseo* is typical of all American Spanish and of some southern varieties in Spain. In some places, the result of the merger is a strongly fronted dental variety of [s] perceptually resembling [θ]; this is called *ceceo*.

seṭ-**root** In Sanskrit, a root which exhibits a final -*i* in the normal grade but a final long resonant in the zero grade, such as *bhávi-*, *bhū-* 'be'. These derive from PIE roots ending in a laryngeal: in this case, **bhewH-*, **bhwH-*, with different treatment of the laryngeal in the two contexts. Compare *aniṭ*-root, and see **laryngeal base**.

sex-differentiation in language Systematic differences between the speech of men and women in a single community. In some cases, this can be quite large, involving different phonemes, different words or different grammatical forms.

shaftless arrow Either of the two symbols '<' and '>'. 1. One of these indicates the direction of a sound change or of an etymology. For example, the notation '/s/ > /h/' indicates that earlier /s/ has changed to /h/, while 'Lat *muliere(m)* > Sp *mujer*' indicates that Latin *muliere(m)* 'woman' has developed in Spanish into the form *mujer* 'woman, wife', and 'Sp *aguijada* < Lat **aquileāta*' indicates that Spanish *aguijada* 'goad' is directly descended from an unrecorded Latin **aquileāta* 'sharpened'. 2. A notation of the form '< OFr' attached to a word indicates that the word has been borrowed from another language – in this case, from Old French.

shallow family A **language family** whose members are rather closely related and whose common ancestor therefore probably dates back no more than a couple of thousand years. Compare **deep family**.

shared anomaly (also **shared aberrancy**) An irregular and highly distinctive characteristic common to two or more languages. For example, certain highly irregular English verbs and adjectives, such as *sing/sang/sung* and *good/better/best*, are shared with German, which has *singen/sang/gesungen* and *gut/besser/beste*. Such shared anomalies provide powerful evidence for a **genetic relationship** between the languages in question, since common inheritance from a single ancestor seems to be the only plausible explanation.

shared archaism (also **shared retention, symplesiomorphy**) A linguistic feature found in two or more genetically related languages which has been directly inherited from their common ancestor. An IE example is the class of **heteroclitic nouns**, found in Hittite, Greek, Latin and Indo-Iranian, and inherited from PIE, but not in the other IE languages, which have eliminated this class. Shared archaisms are of little use in **subgrouping**, since there is no reason to expect all the members of a branch to uniformly retain or lose an ancestral feature. Compare **shared innovation**.

shared innovation (also **synapomorphy**) A linguistic feature which is present in some languages of a family but absent in others and which cannot be reconstructed for their common ancestor. An IE example is the **First Germanic Consonant Shift**, which has applied in all the **Germanic** languages but in no other IE languages. Providing they are not so natural that they might readily occur independently several times (such as the palatalization of velars before front vowels or the devoicing of word-final obstruents), shared innovations are powerful evidence in **subgrouping**, and languages with shared innovations can in most cases be confidently assigned to a single branch of the family – indeed, this is precisely how subgrouping is commonly done. Compare **shared archaism**, and see **character**.

shared retention Another term for **shared archaism**.

sharpening Another term for **Holtzmann's Law**.

shift See **language shift**.

shift-induced interference The term used by Thomason and Kaufman (1988) for the case in which people shifting from their ancestral tongue to a different language carry features of their mother tongue into that second language, where they are picked up by other speakers and become usual in that second language. This is what happens in cases of **substrate** influence.

shift of markedness See **markedness shift** (sense 1).

shift test See **Oswalt shift test**.

shortening (often **correption** in classical philology) Any **phonological change** in which a formerly long segment becomes short. Shortening may be syntagmatic, as when Old English *cēpte*, *fīftig*, *twēntig*, *shēpherde*, *wīsdōm*, all with long vowels, gave rise to modern *kept*, *fifty*, *twenty*, *shepherd*, *wisdom*, all with short vowels, because of the following consonant clusters. Alternatively, it can be paradigmatic, as when all of the inherited long vowels of Greek were shortened, thus merging with their short counterparts. The opposite is **lengthening**.

Sibero-European The name given by Dolgopolsky (1964, 1965) to a putative language family embracing **Indo-European, Afro-Asiatic, Kartvelian, Uralic, Altaic** and **Eskimo-Aleut**. He later abandoned this name in favour of **Nostratic**, with a slightly different list of families.

sic The Latin for 'thus'. Enclosed in square brackets and following a quoted linguistic form or other quoted material, this indicates that the writer realizes that the quoted form or material is clearly erroneous, but is citing it as it occurs in the source.

Sicanian An extinct and virtually unrecorded language spoken in central Sicily in pre-Roman times. It was probably not Indo-European.

Sicel (also **Siculan**) The extinct and sparsely recorded language spoken in eastern Sicily in pre-Roman times. Little is known about it, but it appears to have been **Indo-European**.

Siebs's Law The (controversial) claim that PIE exhibited systematic word-initial alternations of the type illustrated by $*/sk^{(h)}-/ \sim */k^{(h)}-/ \sim */g-/$; this was proposed by Siebs (1904). See Collinge (1985: 155–158) for an account.

Sievers's Law Either of two statements, but especially the first. 1. (also **Sievers-Edgerton Law**) The statement that, in PIE and some early IE languages, the glides /y/ (= /j/) and /w/ must be realized as the vowels /i/ and /u/, respectively, when preceded by certain sequences. For example, the Sanskrit dative plural ending *-bhyas* must be read as *-bhias* or *-bhiyas* in the relevant circumstances. The law was put forward by Sievers (1878) and refined by Edgerton (1934, 1943). See **Lindemann's rule**, and see Collinge (1985: 159–174) for a critical account. 2. A proposed reduction of */gw/ to */w/ in certain conditions in Germanic, put forward by Sievers (1878: 149). See Collinge (1985: 175–178) for discussion.

siglum Especially in philological work, a conventional abbreviation for a major work in the field, such as *REW* for Meyer-Lübke's *Romanisches etymologisches Wörterbuch*.

signature A degree of inherited material in a language which is sufficient to allow linguists to assign it confidently to a **language family**. This signature may be conspicuous (as with shallow families like **Bantu** and **Mayan**), or it may be obscure enough that detailed scrutiny of the evidence is necessary to prove relatedness (as with deeper families like **Indo-European**), or it may be so faint and diffuse that the family is barely detectable at all (as with **Afro-Asiatic**).

simplicity Any of various criteria which may be invoked in evaluating a **reconstruction**. So far as the evidence permits, we prefer the reconstructed phoneme system to be as natural as possible, we prefer the posited sound changes to be as few and as natural as possible, and we prefer to posit a given innovation in a single branch of the family, rather than independently in multiple branches.

simplification 1. An impressionistic label applied to any of a variety of linguistic changes which, in some pretheoretical sense, appear to remove elements of complexity from a language; but see '**simplification brings complication**'. The opposite is **complication**. 2. In phonology, the reduction of a consonant cluster by the loss of one or more of its members, as in the reduction of English *sixths* /sɪksθs/ to /sɪks/. 3. The term used by Milroy (1992: 95–109 and elsewhere) for a particular property of some speech varieties. Milroy reports that the speech of closely-knit communities, above all in inner cities, is characterized by great phonological complexity; there is a large amount of low-level allophonic variation, and multiple phonetic and phonemic realizations are available for many words. However, the speech varieties of less closely knit communities, such as those in the suburbs, exhibit few of these phenomena; instead, allophonic variation is minimal, and a word typically has only one realization, even though the two types of accent are impressionistically very similar to outsiders. Milroy calls the suburban state of affairs *simplification*. 4. A label sometimes applied to the creation of a **pidgin**, which is always much simpler in structure than its source language(s), and also in **linguistic obsolescence**. The opposite is **elaboration** (sense 3).

'simplification brings complication' A dictum in language change: any change that simplifies one subsystem of a language is likely to complicate some other subsystem at the same time. For example, the Serbo-Croatian merger of /ɨ/ with /i/ simplified the phoneme system, but it also complicated the morphology; the formerly totally regular shift of /k g x/ to /c z s/ before /i/ was now opaque, since the shift did not occur before new instances of /i/ derived from earlier /ɨ/. The ancestor of Spanish had the four mid vowels /e ɛ o ɔ/, of which /ɛ ɔ/, but not /e o/, automatically diphthongized under stress; the following merger of /ɛ/ with /e/ and of /ɔ/ with /o/ simplified the vowel system, but complicated the morphology, since only some instances of the new /e o/ diphthongized under stress, in an unpredictable manner.

Many different terms have been applied to this phenomenon: *blindness principle, local optimization, local simplification, equilibrium principle, see-saw principle* and the engaging *Hydra's razor*, among others, but none has established itself.

simplification explanation of change Any proposal to account for language change by arguing that speakers tend constantly to make their languages 'simpler' in some way – for example, by making them more transparent, more regular or easier to pronounce. In fact, while it is easy to point to particular changes that resulted in some kind of simplification of some part of the language, it is equally easy to point to changes which have undeniably led to increased complexity. Moreover, as noted under **'simplification brings complication'**, a single change very often produces both greater simplicity and greater complexity at the same time. Certain types of simplification are nevertheless invoked in Chomskyan discussions of language change; see for example the **Lightfoot framework**.

simplification preference Another term for the principle of **archaic heterogeneity** (version 2).

Sinitic Another term for **Chinese**. Note, however, that a few linguists would place the isolated language **Bai** into Sinitic as a non-Chinese member, but this view is not generally accepted.

Sino-Caucasian A name given to an earlier version of **Dene-(Sino-) Caucasian** which excluded **Na-Dene**.

Sino-Tibetan A large language family of eastern Asia, usually divided into two branches, **Chinese** (or **Sinitic**) and **Tibeto-Burman**, but see **Karen**.

Siouan A family of fifteen or so languages of North America, mostly in the Great Plains; among the best known are *Dakota, Omaha, Kansa-Osage, Winnebago, Crow* and *Hidatsa*. The two *Catawban* languages of the Carolinas are linked to Siouan in a larger *Siouan-Catawban* family. See **Macro-Siouan**.

sister language Either of two (or more) languages which share a single common direct ancestor: languages which were earlier only distinct dialects of a single language. Sister languages are **coordinate languages**.

skewed correspondence The relation which holds between words or forms in related languages which appear to be **cognate** but which do not exhibit the regular **systematic correspondences**. This is a cover term intended to include any of several possible explanations: (1) at least one of the items has undergone irregular or sporadic changes; (2) the items are undetected **partial cognates**; (3) the regular correspondences are in fact more complex than we have so far realized; (4) the item has been borrowed into some of the languages involved. See **word-family**.

slang Informal and often ephemeral linguistic forms. Particular slang items may be used throughout a community or may be confined to particular social groups in which they serve as a badge of member-ship. Slang items may be coined for just about anything of interest to speakers, but are particularly frequent in certain semantic areas. An example of these is 'excellent', for which such slang terms as *groovy, fab, brill, tremendous, wicked, ace, spiffing, cool, far out, awesome, sweet,* *triff* and *def* have been used by some English-speakers in the twentieth century. Slang terms rarely endure, but *booze* 'alcoholic drinks' is an example of a slang term which has been in English for centuries, while *mob* is an example of a former slang term which has lost its slang status and become mainstream English. Compare **argot**.

slash The symbol '/'. 1. An alternative to the **swung dash** for listing variant forms. Sometimes only the relevant part of a form is repeated, as when Basque *esne* 'milk' is derived from **ez-* / **esende*, meaning from **ezende* or **esende*. 2. A symbol used to separate related forms illustrating variants of a single root or stem, as in Old Church Slavonic *mlěti* / *meljõ*, the infinitive and first-singular present of the verb 'grind, mill'. 3. A device used to represent the presence of a line break in an original inscription or manuscript when the text is printed in run-on fashion.

Slavic (also **Slavonic**) A major branch of the **Indo-European** language family. Its members are (eastern branch) **Russian**, *Belarusian*, *Ukrainian*, (southern branch) *Bulgarian*, *Macedonian*, *Serbo-Croatian*, *Slovenian*, (western branch) *Czech*, *Slovak*, *Upper* and *Lower Sorbian* (*Wendish*), *Polish* and *Kashubian*, plus the extinct *Polabian* and *Slovincian*. The earliest recorded Slavic language is **Old Church Slavonic** (*Old Bulgarian*), recorded in writing in the ninth and tenth centuries. Slavic is widely thought to be closely related to **Baltic** within a larger **Balto-Slavic** grouping. See Andersen (1998) for a historical survey, Carlton (1990) or Shevelov (1964) for a phonological history, Vaillant (1950–77) for a complete linguistic history, and Comrie and Corbett (1993) for a survey of the languages.

***s*-mobile** (also **mobile** *s*, **movable** *s*) In PIE, an /s/ which may optionally be attached to the beginning of a root without affecting the meaning: **leim-* ~ **sleim-* 'slime, mucus'; **teg-* ~ **steg-* 'cover'; **pek-* ~ **spek-* 'observe'. Its origin is unknown; it may possibly have been a nominal case-ending which became transferred to a following verb root by metanalysis.

smoothing Especially in **Germanic**, a type of **monophthongization** in which an off-glide is simply lost, as when Old English *ēa* and *ea* were reduced to *ē* and *e*, respectively. This is one type of **reduction** (sense 1). The opposite is **breaking**.

s.n. In **onomastics**, the equivalent of *s.v.*, but denoting a name, rather than a word, from Latin *sub nomine* 'under the name'.

social dialect (also **sociolect**) A distinctive variety of a language used by the members of a particular social group.

social explanation of change (also **sociolinguistic theory of change**) Any proposal to account for **language change** in terms of the social circumstances and behaviour of its speakers. Such approaches typically stress neither internal structural characteristics nor the communicative needs of speakers, but rather the desire of speakers to maintain and exhibit membership of particular social groups by speaking in an appropriate way. The social approach to language change was pioneered by William Labov in the 1960s and has been developed by Labov and others in the succeeding decades; it is now the most widely accepted interpretation of most kinds of language change. See Hock (1986: 646–661) for a summary of Labov's conclusions, see Milroy (1992) for a major (but distinctive) statement of this approach, see Milroy (1993) for a brief survey and see the **WLH model of language change**.

social history The history of the speakers of a language, one aspect of its **external history**. A social history describes the fortunes of those speakers, and examines the various social, cultural and political forces to which those speakers have been subjected and the consequences of these forces for the form, development, geographical distribution and status of the language. In recent years, the social history of language has become far more prominent than formerly, and social histories exist for a number of major languages. For English, see McCrum *et al.* (1992), Blake (1996) and Leith (1997), as well as Dillard (1992) for American English.

socially relevant innovation An innovation which is perceived as typical of a particular group of speakers, either by those who use it or by those who do not (or both). Those who do not use it may therefore make an **act of identity**, either accepting it or rejecting it because of its social significance.

social-network model A **model of linguistic descent** put forward by M. Ross (1997 and elsewhere). Ross begins by picturing a speech community as a social network of the kind recognized by some sociolinguists (see, for example, Milroy 1992), and he calls the speech of the community a *lectal linkage*. Depending on circumstances, the community and its speech may meet several different fates, and each interesting kind of development is a *speech-community event*. *Linkage breaking* occurs when the community splits into two or more distinct and isolated communities, and the linguistic consequence is *language fissure*, as recognized in the familiar **genetic model** of divergence. Ross regards this as rare, and proposes that a more normal event is *lectal differentiation*, in which the community spreads out geographically and forms subcommunities which are still linked with one another but less strongly than are people within a single subcommunity, so that innovations typically spread across only part of the whole community, as recognized in the **wave model**.

Ross also recognizes reverse processes. The re-establishment of previously broken links is *linkage rejoining*, and the linguistic consequence is *language fusion*, in which varieties that were developing separately again become versions of a single language within a single community.

social stratification The existence of systematic differences in the speech of people belonging to different social classes in a single community, when those classes can be ranked hierarchically. Often the differences are statistical in nature, with a given form becoming steadily more or less frequent as we move up the social scale.

socio-historical linguistics The application of the concepts, techniques and findings of sociolinguistics to the problems of historical linguistics. The idea is that the observed properties of contemporary speech communities, such as **variation**, the social significance of variants, and **social stratification** must also have been typical of earlier speech communities, and hence that what we can learn by studying **change in progress** today can be usefully applied in elucidating earlier language changes. See Romaine (1982).

sociolect Another term for **social dialect**.

sociolinguistic theory of change Another term for the **social explanation of change**.

softening A somewhat loose label variously applied to instances of **lenition** or of **palatalization**. The term is particularly applied to Germanic languages – for example, to the development in the history of English by which earlier */ki-/ and */gi-/, after probably being fronted to */ci-/ and */ɟi-/, were 'softened' to /tʃi-/ and /ji-/. See also **velar softening**.

soft mutation In Welsh, a **mutation** which changes /p t k/ to /b d g/, /b d g/ to /v ð ɣ (> Ø)/ and /m/ to /v/.

solidarity chain The name given by Hock (1986: 157–158) to a type of **chain shift** in which, instead of shifting into one another's positions, the shifting segments move 'parallel' in phonological space. Hock's example is an Illinois accent in which the widespread American fronting of [ʊw] to [ɨw] (as in 'boot') has apparently triggered the further frontings of [ʊ] to [ɨ] (in 'foot'), [ow] to [əw] (in 'go'), and [ʌ] to [ə] (in 'cut').

sonant (Ger *Sonant*) In PIE, another term for **resonant**.

sonant coefficient (Fr *coéfficient sonantique*) Saussure's original term for any PIE consonant which could be syllabic: a **resonant** or a **laryngeal**.

Songhai A language spoken along the bend of the Niger in west Africa. It has often been regarded as an isolate, though Greenberg (1963b) considers it a single coordinate branch of his **Nilo-Saharan** family.

Sorothaptic The name given to the unknown language of the pre-Celtic Bronze Age people of the Urnfield culture in the Iberian Peninsula. It is sometimes invoked as the source of problematic words in Ibero-Romance.

sound change The traditional term for **phonological change**.

sound correspondence Another term for **systematic correspondence**.

sound law (Ger *Lautgesetz*) (also **sound shift**, Ger *Lautverschiebung*) A traditional term for a **phonological change** which is perceived as being totally regular and exceptionless, as required by the **Neogrammarian Hypothesis**.

sound symbolism The coining or use of a linguistic item whose form bears some kind of direct (non-arbitrary) relation to its meaning.

Three important types are **onomatopoeia, ideophones** and **phonaesthemes**. Sound-symbolic formations must be used with caution in **comparison**, and some types are not available for comparison at all.

source For a linguistic form, a label applied broadly to any of the following: its **etymology**, an **etymon** of it, or (in the case of **borrowing**) the donor language.

South Caucasian Another term for **Kartvelian**.

Southern Shift A general type of **vowel shift** which has affected, or is currently affecting, most varieties of English spoken in the southern United States, in southern England, and in all Southern Hemisphere countries. High and mid vowels are fronted, while low vowels are backed and raised. See Labov (1994: 201–218) for an account. Compare the **Northern Cities Shift**.

South Lusitanian (also **Tartessian**) The name given to an extinct and unknown language recorded in some seventy inscriptions of uncertain date (possibly fourth to second centuries BC) in southern Portugal and Spain, in a script derived from Punic and Greek. We cannot read the inscriptions, but the view of most specialists is that the language recorded is neither Indo-European nor related to any other known language.

South Picene An extinct language, probably **Italic**, sparsely recorded between the Apennines and the Adriatic in Italy between the sixth and fourth centuries BC. Compare **North Picene**.

Spanish One of the world's major languages, the principal language of Spain and of nineteen countries in the Americas, also widely spoken in the USA and elsewhere. Spanish is a **Romance** language which developed out of the Latin spoken in the centre of the Iberian Peninsula. After the collapse of Roman power in the west, the Germanic-speaking Visigoths conquered most of Spain, but the Visigothic language had little effect upon Iberian Romance. Much more significant was the Muslim conquest of the southern three-quarters of the peninsula in the early eighth century. This event made Arabic the chief administrative and literary language of Muslim Spain, while the local Romance vernaculars in the Muslim region, called *Mozarabic*, enjoyed little prestige. Significantly, the remote northern parts of Spain remained free of Muslim rule, and, when these northern kingdoms launched the eventually successful Reconquest of Spain, it was their previously rustic varieties of Romance which were carried southwards with the advancing armies. Most important of all was Castile, a formerly dusty and backward interior province which finally succeeded in establishing its authority throughout most of the peninsula. Accordingly, it was the linguistically rather unusual *Castilian* dialect which became the prestige form of Spanish throughout the finally unified Kingdom of Spain, and Castilian is the basis of modern standard Spanish. In the last several centuries, Castilian has been steadily obliterating the numerous other dialects of Spanish, such as *Leonese*, *Asturian*, *Navarrese* and *Aragonese*, though it has failed to displace the substantially distinct Romance languages *Galician* (in the northwest) and *Catalan* (in the east), and only partly displaced the isolated language **Basque** in the north.

The Spanish conquest and settlement of much of the Americas in the sixteenth century and after introduced Spanish as the first language over a huge area of the New World. There Spanish has obliterated or reduced to insignificance any number of indigenous languages, though a number of local languages are still spoken by larger or smaller numbers of people, and *Guaraní* in Paraguay has achieved co-official status with Spanish. Also still important are the several varieties of **Quechuan** in the Andes, the **Mayan** languages in Guatemala and southern Mexico, and *Nahuatl* (the Aztec language) in central Mexico. Today there are notable differences among the several regional varieties of Spanish, with Argentine and Puerto Rican Spanish sometimes singled out as particularly divergent. Latin American migration to the USA has made Spanish a major language, sometimes locally dominant, in New York City, Florida, Texas, the southwest and California. See Price (1998: 451–460) for a summary, Penny (1991) for a history of Spanish, Lipski (1994) for American Spanish.

speaker-innovation In Milroy (1992: ch. 6), a linguistic act by a speaker which is potentially capable of affecting the structure of the language. Milroy distinguishes between a speaker-innovation and a linguistic *change*, since not every innovation leads to a change. He makes the point that scrutiny of speaker-innovations is crucial in understanding the **actuation problem**, since the familiar quantitative methods cannot be usefully applied until the innovation has won a significant degree of acceptance in the community, by which time it is too late.

From Trudgill (1986: *p.c.*) he cites the example of a labio-dental realization of /r/ in Norwich, noted rarely and sporadically by Trudgill in a 1968 survey and dismissed then as merely deviant, but found eighteen years later to be firmly embedded in the linguistic system in a way accessible to quantitative study. Milroy further notes that the realization of /t/ as [ʔ] has recently begun to appear very sporadically in Belfast English, chiefly among female adolescents, and surmises that this innovation may be a pointer to a forthcoming change.

speaker-oriented framework An approach to historical linguistics which takes the proper domain of investigation to be speakers, rather than languages. The proponents of this approach are now increasingly challenging the formerly unquestioned **language-oriented framework**. See, for example, Milroy (1992) and Durie and Ross (1996).

specialization 1. Any process in which a linguistic form comes to be used in a narrower range of functions than formerly. For example, the Basque verb **edun* 'have' was formerly a full lexical verb, and still is in the east, while in the west it has been specialized as a pure transitive auxiliary. 2. Especially in **grammaticalization**, any process in which one of several equivalent and competing forms is selected for a particular function to the exclusion of the others. For example, Old French reinforced the negative *ne* 'not' with a wide variety of items, but modern French retains only two of these: *pas*, originally 'step', for ordinary negation, and *point*, originally 'point', for emphatic negation. See Hopper and Traugott (1993: 113–116). 3. Another term for **narrowing**.

speech-community event See under the **social-network model**.

speech formula See under **entrenchment**.

speech island A language or group of related languages entirely surrounded by very different languages. Examples include the Munda, Dravidian and Burushaski islands surrounded by Indo-Aryan in the Indian subcontinent and the Uralic islands surrounded by Slavic in Russia. Most such islands are thought to be relics of languages that were once widespread but have been largely displaced by **intrusive languages** arriving more recently, but there are exceptions; the Uralic island Hungarian is itself intrusive into the surrounding IE languages.

spelling pronunciation A pronunciation which does not derive normally from an earlier pronunciation but which is instead based upon the spelling of the word. For example, many English-speakers have introduced a /t/ into *often* under the influence of the spelling (but not into *soften* or *fasten*); during the last century, the spelling of words like *missile*, *sterile* and *fertile* has induced speakers in England to pronounce the last syllable like *mile*; and all Britons now pronounce *herb* with an /h/ under the influence of the spelling.

spirantization (also **fricativization**) Any **phonological change** in which another segment (most often a plosive) is converted into a fricative. For example, PIE */p t k/ were changed in most circumstances in Proto-Germanic into the fricatives /f θ x/, as a part of the **First Germanic Consonant Shift**.

spirant mutation In Welsh, a **mutation** which changes /p t k/ to /f θ x/.

splinter The term used by Adams (1973) for a morph which is arbitrarily extracted from an existing word and used as an affix for coining new words. Examples include *-gate* ('scandal') from *Watergate* (as in *Irangate*), *-(o)gram* ('something delivered') from *telegram* (as in *kissogram*), and *para-* ('involving a parachute') from *parachute* (as in *paragliding*). Such formations might be called *splinter formations*, but the term is not in use.

split 1. (also **phonemic split, phonologization**) Any **phonological change** in which a single phoneme gives rise to two distinct phonemes. Two distinct types are recognized: *primary split* and *secondary split*. In primary split, one outcome of the split immediately merges with another existing phoneme, so that the total number of phonemes remains unchanged. For example, early Latin /s/ changed to [r] between vowels and merged there with the existing /r/, so that only the distribution of /s/ and /r/ changed. In secondary split, neither outcome of the split finds anything to merge with, and hence the total number of phonemes increases. For example, Old English /θ/ has split into two phonemes, /θ/ and /ð/, in modern English. Frequently, though not invariably, secondary split results from **loss of the conditioning environment**. The opposite is **merger**. Compare **unpacking**. 2. The breaking up of a single language into two or more **daughter languages**, as pictured in the **genetic model**. 3. Another term for **divergence** (sense 2). 4. The separation of function which occurs in **polygrammaticalization**. See also **lexical split** (both senses).

splitter An informal label for a linguist who is perceived as being reluctant to accept any but the most obvious genetic links between languages and who prefers to recognize a rather large number of rather small families. The opposite is **lumper**.

spoonerism The transposition of segments between the words of a phrase, as in *slow and sneet, our queer old dean, a blushing crow, The Lord is a shoving leopard*, and the classic if doubtless apocryphal *You have hissed all my mystery lectures and tasted the whole worm.*

sporadic change Any linguistic change, but especially a phonological change, which is not regular. The term is applied to several cases. First, it is applied to the creation of **allegro forms**. Second, it is applied to generally unpredictable but still comprehensible changes in individual words, like **metathesis, haplology** and **dissimilation**. Third, it is applied to cases in which a seemingly 'regular' change applies only to some forms but not to others; many such cases are instances of **lexical diffusion** which have not gone to completion. Fourth, it is applied to the creation of **expressive forms**. Finally, it is applied to irregular and sometimes more or less inexplicable changes affecting individual words; examples include the development of Basque *tipi* 'small' into western *tiki*, of Latin *cattu(m)* 'cat' into Spanish *gato* (with an unexpected voiced initial), and of Latin *meridianu(m)* 'of midday' into western Basque *biao* 'siesta', with irregular reductions. Mańczak (1996) argues that sporadic changes of this last kind tend to affect words of high discourse frequency.

Sprachbund The German for **linguistic area**.

Sprachelement In the older literature, a German term for *phoneme*.

Sprachfamilie The German for **language family**.

Sprachlaut Literally, the German for *speech sound*, but, in the older literature, more usually a term for *phoneme*.

Sprachstamm The German for **stock**.

spread of change See **implementation of change**.

spread zone In **population typology**, a geographical region which is occupied by a single language or family at any given time, with that one being eventually displaced by another, so that linguistic diversity does not tend to accumulate. An example is the grasslands of central Asia. Compare **accretion zone**.

Sprechsprache A language which exhibits a significant degree of individual, social and regional variation in phonology, grammar and lexicon, but not enough to prevent successful communication among its speakers; the ordinary state of a language.

Sprossvokal The German term for a vowel inserted by **anaptyxis**.

spurious form A non-existent linguistic form which has been reported or inferred in error. Campbell (1997a: 237–239) cites some examples of spurious forms which have crept into **comparisons** of various American languages, leading to false conclusions.

square brackets The notational convention '[ ]', with two uses. 1. It is used in a **reconstruction** to indicate that the bracketed segment or material is of doubtful, or variable, presence in the form. For example, a reconstruction **maN[i]gV* indicates that either **maNigV* or **maNgV* is possible. Note that some authors use **parentheses** instead, and would write **maN(i)gV*. 2. In a published version of an ancient text, an indication of a **lacuna** (gap) in the text. If the lacuna occurs at one end of a line, only one bracket is used. Any material appearing inside the brackets is a proposal made by the editor. If dots appear inside the brackets, they represent the number of missing characters (three dots means three characters missing); if the brackets are empty or filled by three dashes, the number of missing characters cannot be determined (some editors use three dots here). For example, a certain early Basque text contains a line published as follows: *Deus peretençia lur<r>ac dac[a]r og[* … Here a missing or illegible character has been read as <a> by the editor, while the end of the line is missing. (For the <r>, see **angle brackets** (sense 1).)

square-root sign The symbol '$\sqrt{}$', which indicates that what it precedes or encloses is a root, and not a free form, as in the Arabic $\sqrt{}$ktb 'write'.

stabilization The process in which a **pidgin** loses its original variety of expression and acquires a more or less fixed form.

stable-morphology hypothesis The conjecture that morphological patterns (the distinctions made and the positions in which morphological markers occur) are typically so stable in languages that common patterns can be taken as good evidence of a **genetic relationship** between languages even when there exists no phonological resemblance at all between lexical items or bound morphemes. This conjecture has often been enthusiastically advanced, but it is now known to be false. See Thomason (1980) and Thomason and Kaufman (1988) for examples both of rapid change in morphological patterns and of shared patterns arising entirely through contact, and see **metatypy**.

stable vocabulary Lexical items which are thought to undergo **lexical replacement** seldom or never, such as those in the **Dolgopolsky list**. It seems certain that no totally stable lexical items exist.

stadialism (also **stadial theory**) Any theory which holds that every language must pass through an identifiable series of stages, each characterized by particular structural characteristics. Once popular, such ideas are almost universally rejected today.

Stamm The German for **stock**.

Stammbaum The German for **family tree**.

Stammbaum **model** Another term for **genetic model**.

standardization The process of creating a **standard language**.

standard language A highly codified and usually elaborated variety of a language which is regarded by its speakers as the most appropriate (often the *only* appropriate) variety suitable for educated discourse. Standard languages have various origins. Standard English, French and Spanish largely developed out of the speech of politically preeminent regions. Standard Italian and German were mainly the creations of prominent literary figures. Standard Norwegian (of which there are two varieties), Finnish, Basque and Turkish were mainly constructed by conscious and deliberate **language planning** by governments or language academies. Standard Arabic is based upon the language of the Koran.

Stang's Law The statement, put forward by Stang (1957: 168–169), that, in common **Slavic**, an accent falling on a word-final syllable with a long vowel and a falling intonation shifts to the penult, usually with a concomitant shortening of the long vowel. See Collinge (1985: 179) for an account.

starred form Any linguistic form which is preceded by an **asterisk**, in any function of that marker, but most particularly to denote that the form is unattested and has been reconstructed by linguists.

static See under **accent in PIE**.

stem-incorporation Another term for **demorphologization**.

stemma A tree-like graph, particularly one depicting the proposed relationships among the several manuscript copies of a single text.

stemmatics The study of lineages. Stemmatics is important in several historical disciplines: in text philology, where it is called **stemmatology**, in historical linguistics, where it is called **comparative linguistics**, and in biology.

stemmatology The study of the various existing copies of an ancient document, which itself most often no longer exists. Stemmatologists are concerned to put the existing copies into relative chronological order and to determine which copies have been copied from which others; the result, if successful, may be a tree diagram showing how the original gave rise to multiple copies, each of which in turn gave rise to multiple copies, and scholars may be able thus to deduce the former existence of copies which have disappeared.

stepwise shift Any phonological change in the phonetic nature of a segment which proceeds by small increments from one natural segment-type to another, instead of by a saltation, or large jump. For example, the change of /k/ to zero proceeds stepwise when it follows the trajectory /k/ > /x/ > /h/ > Ø, but by **saltation** if /k/ > Ø, or even /k/ > /h/, is a single step. Stepwise shift appears to be the norm in language change, and Lass (1997: ch. 5) argues that *all* changes in segment-type must proceed in this manner. The hypothetical minimal/maximal degree of phonetic change permissible in a single step is occasionally called a **quantum**. See **universal category space**.

stimulus diffusion A type of social change in which an *idea* is transmitted from one society to another, without any transfer of material.
The term has most often been applied to cases in which the idea of
writing passed from one people to another, who proceeded to invent
their own writing system, independent of the system used by those
from whom they got the idea, but Thomason and Kaufman (1988:
194–199) discuss the possibility that some **pidgins** may have arisen
by stimulus diffusion. See **acculturation**.

stock (Ger *Stamm*, *Sprachstamm*) A linguistic **taxon**. Like all such
terms, this one has no agreed meaning. In the past, it commonly
meant the same as **family**. It has sometimes been used specifically to
denote a very large-scale grouping, often one which is speculative and
unestablished. Johanna Nichols has recently been using it to denote
the maximal lineage whose ancestral language can be substantially
reconstructed. By this criterion, **Indo-European** is a stock, and an
isolate like **Basque** is a stock by default, but **Afro-Asiatic** and
Niger-Congo are not stocks, even though they are secure families,
because we are at present unable to reconstruct their ancestral proto-
languages to any significant extent. Compare **quasi-stock**.

stock density In the work of Johanna Nichols, a measure of **genetic
density** based upon her definition of a **stock**.

stratum In the work of Johanna Nichols (e.g. 1994/95), a coherent
geographical region within which the existing language families tend
to share important structural characteristics. She interprets these
strata as representing the results of ancient population movements,
and hence of language movements.

Streitberg's Law A putative change in early PIE, put forward by
Streitberg (1893, 1894) in multiple versions. A familiar version says
this: if an unaccented syllable disappears, a preceding accented
syllable becomes long if previously short and circumflex if previously
long. See Collinge (1985: 181–182) for critical discussion.

strengthening Another term for **fortition**.

stress shift Any phonological change in which the position of a word-
stress is moved from one syllable to another within a word. A stress
shift may be highly systematic, affecting all words of a particular
class, or it may be sporadic, affecting only the occasional word.

stronger, law of the Another term for **Grammont's Law**.

strong verb In the Germanic languages, a verb which inflects by changing the vowel of the stem, like English *sing*, *sang*, *sung* or *drive*, *drove*, *driven*. Compare **weak verb**, and see **ablaut**.

Structural Compensation, Principle of A putative principle of language change, put forward by Labov (1994: 604). It says this: when the rate of deletion of a meaningful feature of a language increases, the frequency of features that redundantly carry this meaning will increase.

structural dialectology An approach to **dialectology**, most commonly to phonological variation, in which a single abstract underlying system (an *overall pattern*) is set up for a number of related dialects, and then the facts of each dialect are interpreted as identifiable variations on the overall pattern. The approach was pioneered by Weinreich (1954).

structural explanation of change Any proposal to account for **language change** in terms of the requirements of a linguistic system. Such approaches are most often proposed in connection with phonology; for example, it may be maintained that phoneme systems tend towards symmetry, so that **holes in the pattern** are filled while phonemes which 'spoil' the symmetry tend to be lost. A standard example is the English fricatives: Old English had only /f θ s ʃ x/, but the acquisition of /v/ and /ʒ/ in loans from French supposedly induced the introduction of /ð/ to partner /θ/, even though the functional load of the contrast is minimal, and /x/ supposedly disappeared because it had no voiced partner. The most prominent development of such ideas is Martinet (1955), but see King (1969) for a critique.

structural pool The term used by Nichols (1997b) to denote a regional group of languages which cannot be shown to be related but which share some highly distinctive and unusual feature or features. A classic instance is the click languages of Africa (excluding the Bantu click languages).

Stufe The German for *grade*; see under **ablaut**.

stump compound A word coined by combining arbitrary initial sequences of two or more words making up a phrase of identical meaning: English *sci-fi* 'science fiction' and *sitcom* 'situation comedy', German *Gestapo* (from *Geheime Staatspolizei* 'Secret State Police'), Russian *Sovnarkom* (from *Soviet Narodnyx Komissarov* 'Council of People's Commissars'). Compare **clipped form, blend**.

Sturtevant's Law The observation that Hittite orthography consistently distinguishes between single consonants (representing voiced plosives) and double consonants (representing voiceless stops). Edgar Sturtevant made this observation in 1932 and published his definitive account in Sturtevant and Hahn (1951: 58 *ff.*). See Szemerényi (1996: 56, fn. 8) for references to discussion of this in the literature.

Sturtevant's paradox The following statement, first put forward by Sturtevant (1917): phonological change is regular, but produces irregularity; analogical change is irregular, but produces regularity.

s.u. A variant of *s.v.*

subduction [*rare*] Another term for **grammaticalization**.

subfamily Another term for a **branch** of a **language family**.

subgrouping The problem of arranging the languages of a family into a **family tree**. This requires that we determine which languages are more closely related than others within the family – that is, which languages share a single common ancestor which is later in time than the common ancestor of the whole family. This is most often done by seeking **characters** which can be regarded as **shared innovations**, since, providing an innovation is not so natural and frequent that it might recur independently in different branches of the family, we prefer to assign an innovation to a single language somewhere in the tree, the language ancestral to all the later languages exhibiting it. However, since languages do not necessarily (or usually) split sharply and decisively, innovations may diffuse across linguistic boundaries which have already been introduced by earlier changes, thus greatly complicating the problem. For example, Iceland was settled from Norway, at a time when Norwegian had already begun to diverge from Danish and Swedish, and so Icelandic ought historically to form a subgroup with Norwegian, but in fact the continuing coexistence of Norwegian, Danish and Swedish has made them far more similar to one another today than any of them is to Icelandic. Recently some linguists have been exploring the **best-tree approach** to subgrouping. It should be noted that **shared archaisms** are of little use in subgrouping.

submerged feature A label famously applied by Sapir (1925: 492) to a curious grammatical pattern buried deep in the structure of a language but still detectable. Sapir's idea is that similar submerged features in two or more languages are good evidence for an ancient genetic link between them. His example is Choctaw la^nsa 'scar', mi^nsa 'scarred', versus Subtiaba *daša* 'grass', *maša* 'be green', suggesting residues of an ancient nominalizing prefix *l- common to both languages. The idea is a generalization of the notion of **shared anomalies**, but it has proved to be far too optimistic; for example, the apparent Choctaw–Subtiaba match is now known to be a mere coincidence, and there is no evidence to relate the two languages.

subphonemic change Another term for **phonetic change**.

subset principle A proposed principle of first-language acquisition. It says: a child assumes that a conceivable structure is impossible unless it hears direct positive evidence that it *is* possible. In other words, a child constructs the 'smallest' language that is compatible with the positive evidence so far encountered. Proposed by Baker (1979), this principle has sometimes been invoked in discussions of language change, but see van der Wurff (1995) for a critical discussion with references. Compare the **catapult mechanism**.

substrate (also **substratum**) With respect to a language which has moved into an area, an earlier language which was already being spoken in the area and which has had a detectable effect upon the newly arrived one, contributing some or all of vocabulary, phonological features and grammatical features. At the time of examination, the substrate language may already have died out, though not necessarily. For example, Vineis (1998) notes the presence in **Latin** of words taken from, or influenced by, other languages of Italy – Italic, Etruscan, Greek, Celtic, even Punic – as Latin spread out over the country: *lingua* 'tongue', *lacrima* 'tear', *Caesar* (a name), *casa* 'house', *cāseus* 'cheese', *olīva* 'olive', *vīnum* 'wine', *persōna* 'mask', *fenestra* 'window', *carrus* 'wagon', *ave* 'greetings!', and others. These other languages are thus substrates with respect to Latin. The term *substrate* is also applied to the linguistic features taken into the affected language from the substrate languages. Compare **adstrate**, **superstrate**.

substrate explanation of change The policy of attributing features of, or changes in, a language to **substrate** languages formerly spoken in the area. The reality of substrate languages is not in doubt, but many linguists have often abused the idea, attributing every problematic word or form, and every phonological or grammatical change, to the influence of a substrate language about which nothing whatever may be known. In fact, if we wish to make a case that feature F of language L results from the influence of substrate language S, we must provide good evidence for all of the following: (1) language S actually existed; (2) S and L coexisted in the same place for a length of time; (3) there is reason to suppose the existence of speakers who were bilingual in S and L, at least to some extent; (4) substrate S is known to have had a characteristic which, if carried into L, would account for the presence of feature F; (5) feature F appeared in L during the period of coexistence; (6) feature F cannot be regarded as the result of a change which is natural and frequent in languages; (7) feature F did not appear independently in varieties of L spoken where S was absent. In practice, overzealous proponents of substrate theory have often violated every one of these requirements. Changes are attributed to totally unknown and hypothetical substrates; they are attributed to substrates which are not known to have had any characteristic that would account for the changes in L, and even to substrates which are definitely known *not* to have had any such characteristic; changes are attributed to substrates which are known to have died out centuries before the change took place in L; perfectly natural and frequent changes are unnecessarily attributed to substrate influence; changes that occurred separately in several places are attributed to a substrate spoken in only one of them; and so on. Such misuse of substrate ideas is today generally condemned by linguists; it results from the naive perception that all, or virtually all, language change must result from external influences, while internal change is rare, a position now known to be quite false. See, for example, Trask (1997: 415–429) for a critique of the long-popular idea that Castilian Spanish originated as a Romance variety spoken by a Basque substrate.

substratum Another term for **substrate**.

succession With respect to a given geographical area, the sequence of languages or language families occupying that region over time.

Sumerian An ancient language of Mesopotamia (modern Iraq), recorded earlier than 3000 BC in a large number of cuneiform inscriptions. So far as we know, the Sumerians invented writing, and Sumerian was the first language ever written down. After the conquest of Sumer by the speakers of **Akkadian**, Sumerian eventually disappeared as a spoken language, though it continued to be used as a written languages for many more centuries. Sumerian is an **isolated language**.

sump Another term for **invasion zone**.

superjump A hypothetical type of **phonological change** in which the phonetic realization of a phoneme leaps discontinuously from one point to another in phonological space, passing over in the process another phoneme with which it does not merge – for example, a shift of /ɔ/ from [ɔ] to [u] in which an intervening /o/ ([o]) is unaffected. There seems to be little hard evidence for the reality of superjumps. The term was coined by Labov (1994: 147). Compare **saltation**.

superstrate (also **superstratum**) With respect to a given language, another and more prestigious language which is imposed upon the speakers of the first, usually by conquest or political absorption, and which exercises an identifiable effect upon that first language. For example, **French** is a superstrate with respect to the several **minority languages** of France, all of which have been influenced by French in one way or another. Compare **substrate, adstrate**.

suppletion The use of two or more historically distinct stems to provide the inflected forms of a single lexical item, or the historical process leading to this result. English examples include *person/people, good/better, go/went*, and the collapse of the three PIE stems **bheu-, *H₁es-* and **wes-* into the forms of the copula, as in *be, is, was*.

surd [*obsolete*] In early philological work, any voiceless consonant.

surname A personal name which is handed down within a family from one generation to the next. In Europe, surnames came into use in the Middle Ages and were at first confined to the upper echelons of society. Still today, Icelanders and Turkish Cypriots do not use surnames, relying on **patronymics** instead. Compare **by-name, given name**.

s.v. (also ***s.u.***) In an etymological entry referring to an **etymological dictionary**, an instruction to consult the word under discussion, or another cited word, in that dictionary for more information. For example, a discussion of Basque *asmatu* 'invent, think up' might derive it from Old Spanish *asmar* and then add '*DCELC s.v.*', meaning that the reader should consult a certain etymological dictionary of Spanish under the entry *asmar*, or it might instead add '*REW s.v. (ad)aestimare*', meaning that the reader should refer to a certain etymological dictionary of Romance under the entry *(ad)aestimare*. In **onomastics**, the equivalent is *s.n.* If more than one word is referred to, the abbreviation is *s.vv.* Latin *sub verbo* means 'under the word'.

svarabhakti Another term for **anaptyxis**.

svarita In Sanskrit, a label applied to a syllable immediately following the syllable bearing the main word-accent. See **anudātta, udātta**.

Swabian An extinct and unrecorded west **Germanic** language spoken by a people who occupied much of the Iberian Peninsula in the fifth and sixth centuries AD.

Swadesh word list Either of two lists of vocabulary, one of 100 words and the other of 200, both existing in several slightly different versions and both consisting of words supposedly belonging to the **basic vocabulary** of a language. The lists were originally drawn up by the American linguist Morris Swadesh for use in **lexicostatistics** and **glottochronology**, but they are sometimes used in various other types of comparative work. One or more versions of the list can be found in Gudschinsky (1956) and in several textbooks of historical linguistics, including Trask (1996: 408–409). Modified versions of the list have been prepared by specialists in particular regions (for example, James Matisoff's CALMSEA for Southeast Asia). See **Yakhontov's Principle**.

swamping The label applied by Lass (1990b) to the phenomenon in which the speech of a community containing individuals of several quite different backgrounds comes to resemble just one of those backgrounds. For example, South Africa, Australia and New Zealand were settled by English-speakers from southern, northern and western England, Wales, Scotland and Ireland, but in all three cases the result is a relatively homogeneous speech which is most similar to that of southeastern England.

swung dash (also **tilde**) The symbol '~', used to connect two or more **variants** of a linguistic form, as in Basque *eman* ~ *emon* 'give'. Some linguists use the **slash** instead: *eman* / *emon*. Compare **parentheses** (sense 1), **pipe**.

syllabication Another term for **syllabification**.

syllabic resonant In PIE, any **resonant** functioning as a syllabic nucleus, as often occurs in the zero-grade. For example, in the roots **perk-* 'ask' and **bhew-* 'be, grow', the zero-grade forms **prk-* and **bhu-* exhibit syllabic /r/ and /w/.

Syllabic Synharmonism, Law of In the **Slavic** languages, a prominent type of **drift** by which several independent assimilations conspire to convert individual syllables, and sometimes adjacent syllables, into sequences of segments with common 'tonality'. Among the processes involved are palatalization of velars before front vowels and fronting of back vowels after palatal consonants.

syllabification (also **syllabication**) Any change in which a formerly non-syllabic segment (most commonly a resonant) becomes syllabic. For example, the Slavic loss of the ultra-short vowels called **jers** caused previously non-syllabic liquids to become syllabic in some Slavic languages, as in the change of earlier *brŭzŭ* 'rapid' to Old Serbo-Croat *brz*, with syllabic /r/. The opposite is **desyllabification**.

symbolic reconstruction Another term for **algebraism**.

symmetry 1. A principle of **reconstruction**, by which a set of reconstructed phonemes should be as symmetric as possible while remaining consistent with the data. Compare **economy**. 2. The property of a phoneme system in which the phonetic features present are maximally utilized, so that both **holes in the pattern** and isolated segments are absent. Some versions of the **structural explanation of change** maintain that the drive to maintain or restore symmetry is a major factor in phonological change.

symplesiomorphy A technical term for **shared archaism**, borrowed by Lass (1997) from biological cladistics.

synaeresis (also **syneresis**) The combining of two adjacent vowels within a word into a single syllable, as in the usual pronunciations of *familiar* and *righteous*. Compare **crasis, synizesis, synaloepha**.

synaloepha The coalescence of two syllables into one across a word boundary by reduction or loss of the first vowel, as in *Th'Almighty*. Compare **crasis, synizesis, synaeresis**.

synapomorphy A technical term for **shared innovation**, borrowed by Lass (1997) from biological cladistics.

synchrony The absence of a time element in language; the examination of a language at any given moment in time (not necessarily the present), without reference to earlier or later stages of it. Compare **diachrony**.

syncope A **syntagmatic change** in which a (usually unstressed) vowel is lost between consonants in a polysyllabic word. Syncope is frequent in the history of the western Romance languages: Lat *manicam* > Sp *manga* 'sleeve'; Lat *septimana* > Sp *semana* 'week'; Lat *viridem* > Sp *verde* 'green'; Lat *temporanum* > Sp *temprano* 'early'; Lat *stabilem* > Sp *estable* 'steady'.

syncretism (also **neutralization**) Any linguistic change or changes by which originally distinct morphosyntactic forms come to be phono-logically identical, or the state of affairs resulting from such changes. For example, the **Ingvaeonic** ancestor of English distinguished three personal endings in the plural, as in **beram* 'we carry', **beraþ* 'you (plural) carry', **beranþ* 'they carry'; phonological change con-verted the third-plural form to *beraþ*, making it identical to the second-plural form, and this syncretized form was then extended by analogy to the first plural, producing the totally syncretized plural forms of Old English: *beraþ, beraþ, beraþ*. The opposite change is sometimes called **deneutralization**.

synecdoche The use of a part to denote the whole, or of the whole to denote a part, as when we use *hand* to mean 'employee' or 'crew member' or *Brazil* to denote the Brazilian national football team. Synecdoche is of some importance in semantic change, as when *redbreast* came to denote any of several bird species with red breasts, or as in the rather frequent semantic developments 'fingernail' > 'finger' > 'hand'. Compare **metonymy**.

syneresis See **synaeresis**.

synharmonism The spread of a phonetic feature from a single segment to the entire word containing it. For example, in some dialects of modern Aramaic, the former presence of a single velarized or pharyngeal consonant in a word has induced velarization of the entire word, leading to contrasts like unvelarized *ămra* 'she says' versus velarized *ămra* 'wool', from Middle Aramaic *āmrā* and *ʕamrā*, respectively. In these dialects, every word in the language is either velarized or unvelarized.

synizesis (rarely also **synecphonesis**) The fusion of two consecutive syllables into one by the coalescence of two adjacent vowels without the formation of a recognized diphthong. A common example is the development of the sequence /ia/ into /ja/, which is prominent in the histories of Greek and Spanish, among many other languages. Compare **crasis**, **synaeresis**, **synaloepha**.

syntactic blend 1. A 'compromise' syntactic construction which incorporates features of two other constructions with similar meanings. Hock (1986: 358) notes that the longstanding competition in German of preverbal and prepositional uses of certain elements, as in *Das Klavier ist nicht durchgegangen* 'The piano didn't go through' and *Das Klavier ist nicht durch die Türe gegangen* 'The piano didn't go through the door' has led to the frequent use of a blend, *Das Klavier ist nicht durch die Türe durchgegangen*, with *durch* 'through' occurring in both positions. 2. A syntactic formation, typically one in the middle of **grammaticalization**, to which either of two equally valid syntactic structures may be assigned.

syntactic borrowing The acquisition by a language of a novel syntactic construction by **contact** (see **language contact**). For example, both Basque and Turkish, which normally have preposed relative clauses lacking relative pronouns, have to some extent borrowed from their IE neighbours Spanish and Persian the typical IE type of relative clause, postposed and introduced by a pronoun or complementizer.

syntactic change Change in the syntactic patterns (sentence structures) of a language. Among the principal known pathways for such change are **syntacticization**, **reanalysis** (sense 2), **extension** (sense 4), **markedness shift** and **grammaticalization**. Some syntactic changes derive from contact: see **syntactic borrowing** and **meta-typy**. See also **word-order change**. See Trask (1996: ch. 6), Hock (1986: ch. 13), or Hock and Joseph (1996: ch. 6) for a textbook treatment, and see Harris and Campbell (1995) for a synthesis.

syntacticization The conversion of an optional discourse strategy into a syntactic structure, especially an obligatory one. For example, Mithun (1992) concludes that, in the Iroquoian languages, various discourse particles with meanings like 'so', 'then', 'next', 'moreover', 'besides' and 'also' have been syntacticized into coordinating conjunctions with the meaning 'and', in some cases completely and rigidly, in others only weakly and optionally. See Sankoff (1977) for some further examples.

syntactic reconstruction The **reconstruction** of the sentence structures of unrecorded languages. Since sentences, unlike words and morphemes, are not passed down from speaker to speaker, some linguists have queried whether syntactic reconstruction is possible. However, the literature now contains a number of striking and successful syntactic reconstructions; see Harris and Campbell (1995: ch. 12) for a survey.

syntagmatic change Any type of phonological change which has consequences for the sequence of sounds in particular words and forms: it changes the number of segments in the affected forms, or it changes their order, or it changes their phonetic nature. Among the very many named types of syntagmatic change are **epenthesis**, **loss** (sense 1), **unpacking, coalescence, metathesis, haplology**, and all of the ones in *-ization*, like **palatalization** and **nasalization**. Compare **paradigmatic change**.

syntagmatic compensation Any process which counteracts the natural tendency of phonological change to shorten words and other linguistic forms. See the examples under **phonogenesis**.

syntagmatic motivation for paradigmatic change A change in the paradigm of a lexical item resulting from its frequent collocation with another item having a different paradigm. Andersen (1980: 17) cites some dialects of Bulgarian in which the perfectly regular past tenses of the verb 'see' have been strongly assimilated to the uniquely irregular paradigm of 'go', apparently because of the high frequency of collocations like 'He went and saw it.'

synthetic compound In the early IE languages, a type of **compound** constructed from a nominal stem plus a following verbal root or base, as in Latin *fructifer* 'fruit-bearing', from *fructi-* 'fruit' and *fer-* 'bear'. These are frequent.

Syriac See under **Aramaic**.

systematic correspondence (also **recurrent correspondence, phonological correspondence, sound correspondence**) A general pattern of the following sort: whenever word W1 in language L1 contains sound S1 in a certain position, then a word W2 of the same or similar meaning in language L2 contains sound S2 in the same position. Table 11 illustrates such a correspondence; the languages are Sard(inian), It(alian), Rom(ansh), Fr(ench) and (European) Sp(anish).

These four words, and many others, illustrate the correspondences Sard /k-/ : It /tʃ-/ : Rom /ts-/ : Fr /s-/ : Sp /θ-/, all in word-initial position, and also incidentally illustrate some further correspondences which can be supported by further data, such as /-r-/ : /-r-/ : /-r-/ : /-r-/ : /-r-/ (in word-medial position) and /-u/ : /-o/ : zero : zero : /-o/ (in word-final position). Moreover, a sizeable number of other systematic correspondences in consonants and vowels, not illustrated here, can be found to link vocabulary items in all these languages, and in further languages besides. In general, the existence of widespread systematic correspondences in form between languages can only be explained by concluding that the languages descend from a common ancestor and are hence genetically related. (Exception: we must be careful to exclude **loan words**, since words borrowed from a single source may exhibit spurious correspondences.) This result depends crucially on the observation that phonological change is typically regular; that is, that a single sound in a given environment in the single ancestral language develops in the same way in every relevant word in each daughter language, though often differently in different daughter languages.

	Sard	*It*	*Rom*	*Fr*	*Sp*
'100'	kɛntu	tʃɛnto	tsjɛnt	sã	θjen
'sky'	kɛlu	tʃelo	tsil	sjɛl	θjelo
'stag'	kɛrbu	tʃɛrvo	tsɛrf	sɛr	θjerbo
'wax'	kɛra	tʃera	tsaira	sir	θera

Table 11

In our example, of course, these languages (and others) all belong to the **Romance** family, and are descended from **Proto-Romance** (spoken Latin). In Proto-Romance, all these words began with the same sound in the same environment; in fact, on phonetic and other grounds, we reconstruct an original */k-/ followed in each case by a front vowel. That */k-/ has remained unchanged in Sardinian, but in each other language it has undergone various regular phonological changes, leading to the same outcome for every word in each language.

In seeking **genetic relationships** and **cognates**, it is essential to identify such systematic correspondences, since mere miscellaneous resemblances are worthless. Indeed, systematic correspondences need not involve similarities at all: see the Muskogean example under **portmanteau reconstruction**. See **skewed correspondence**.

system collapse Any set of changes in phonology or grammar which collectively have the effect of dramatically reducing the number of sounds or grammatical markers present in the language. For example, the three (or more) series of plosives in PIE (of the types *p, *b, *bh) collapsed in Tocharian into a single series (of type p). The elaborate case-system of nouns in Latin collapsed and disappeared entirely in all the western Romance languages.

system congruency The degree to which a particular form fits naturally into the system of its language. Language change is more natural when it increases system congruency rather than the opposite, a fact often invoked in **reconstruction**. For example, Watkins (1969: 1496) notes that several IE languages require the earlier word for 'daughter-in-law' to be reconstructed as *$snus\acute{o}s$, while several others require *$snus\acute{a}:$. Since in PIE a feminine noun in -os is anomalous while one in -$a:$ is commonplace, we may reasonably surmise that the anomalous *$snus\acute{o}s$ is the original PIE form, and that *$snus\acute{a}:$ results from transfer of the word to the more usual feminine class in -$a:$, in order to increase system congruency. The reverse shift would be inexplicable.

system naturalness The degree to which a reconstructed linguistic system (especially a phonological system) conforms to the known facts about attested systems. For example, if the data allowed us to reconstruct an obstruent system as either */p t k b d g/ or */b d g f θ x/, we would normally prefer the first, since such systems are commonplace while the second type is rare to non-existent. This is one type of **typologically based reconstruction**.

system-oriented framework Another term for the **language-oriented framework**.

systole [*rare*] The **shortening** of a formerly long syllable. The opposite is **diastole**.

Szemerényi's Law An explanation for the long vowel in the final syllable of the nominative singular of certain PIE nouns, such as **mātēr* 'mother' and **k(u)wōn* 'dog', in which the long vowel is unexpected and seemingly unetymological. Szemerényi (1962: 13, 1970: 109, 1972: 142) interprets this long vowel as deriving from assimilation of an original nominative ending **-s* followed by length redistribution: **mātĕr-s* > **mātĕrr* > **mātēr*. See Collinge (1985: 237–238) for an account.

$$\boxed{\text{T}}$$

taboo The avoidance of a word or phrase, or its replacement by another, when the first is felt to be socially unacceptable – blasphemous, obscene, painful or whatever. Tabooed items may include terms pertaining to sex, excretion, death or parts of the body, names of divinities and religious figures, names of deceased persons, names of animals regarded as sacred or awe-inspiring, and indeed almost anything which a particular society comes to object to. English examples include or have included *pass away* for 'die', *make love* for 'copulate', *wee* for 'urinate', *white meat* for 'breast' (of poultry), and *bear* ('the brown one') for an animal whose original name has been completely lost. (These are **euphemisms**.) An arbitrary alteration in the form of an offensive word is a *taboo deformation* or **hlonipha**; examples are *sheesh* for 'shit', *gosh* for 'God' and *heck* for 'hell'. A striking recent case involves the name of *nuclear magnetic resonance* (NMR), a scientific and medical technique, which has now been replaced in medical use (only) by *magnetic resonance imaging* (MRI), because the word *nuclear* frightens people, as a result of collocations like *nuclear weapon. Taboo replacement* is the sudden and complete replacement of words by synonyms of different form, usually because of some connection with the name of a person who has died; this is widespread in Australia and known also in parts of North America.

tadpole-into-frog model The name given by Aitchison (1995) to the traditional view that language change consists of the conversion of one thing into another thing, such as the (gradual or sudden) replacement of one pronunciation by another. Recent work on language change has shown that this model is generally inadequate; see the **social explanation of change**. Compare **young-cuckoo model, multiple-birth model**.

Tai A sizeable language family of southeast Asia, with over forty languages and around 70 million speakers; best known are *Thai* and *Lao*. Counting languages is difficult, since much of the region consists of large and complex dialect continua. Attempts at linking Tai with other families in such groupings as **Tai-Kadai, Austro-Tai** and **Austric** have not won general support.

Tai-Kadai (also **Kam-Tai**) A proposed grouping of **Tai, Kadai** and **Kam-Sui**, put forward by Benedict (1942). The idea has won some support but is far from generally accepted. All these languages belong to the southeast Asian **linguistic area**, in which languages strongly resemble their neighbours without necessarily being related to them. See **Austro-Tai**.

tailfin interpretation A facetious label for the view that language change is largely or entirely a matter of fashion, like the length of hemlines or the introduction of tailfins for cars.

Tanoan A small language family (seven languages) of western North America; its best-known member is *Kiowa*. Tanoan is included in the **Aztec-Tanoan** hypothesis.

tantum The Latin adverb meaning 'only', used especially in historical linguistics for constructing labels for lexical items lacking the full range of forms normally displayed by their class, as in *plurale tantum* (a noun with only a plural form) and *activa tantum* (a verb with only an active voice).

tapping (also **flapping**) The conversion of intervocalic /t/ and /d/ to a tap (US 'flap'), as occurs in many varieties of English.

Tarde's Law The putative principle that most linguistic innovations originate among high-prestige social groups and spread from there into the speech of speakers of lower prestige – in other words, that

change from above is far more frequent than **change from below**. Proposed by Tarde (1890), this principle has been called into serious question by recent sociolinguistic work on language change, not least by the realization that there exist multiple and competing sources of linguistic prestige. See Collinge (1985: 255–256).

Tartessian Another term for **South Lusitanian**.

Tasmanian languages The extinct and poorly recorded languages of Tasmania. Almost nothing is known about them; they may or may not have been typical **Australian languages**. See **Indo–Pacific**.

tatpuruṣa In Sanskrit, a **compound** consisting of a final head modified by a preceding stem which stands in an unexpressed relation to the head, such as *paksa-dvāram* 'side door', from *dvāram* 'door' plus *paksa-*, stem of the word 'side', here representing an unexpressed locative relation: 'door at the side'. Such compounds are very frequent in Sanskrit; English equivalents are things like 'handmade', 'home-baked' and 'doorstop'.

taxon (plural **taxa**) (rarely also **clade**) A group of languages all of which are genetically more closely related to one another than any of them is to any other languages. In a **family tree** of the familiar type, each branch of the tree represents a single taxon, as does the entire tree. A taxon is identified by the presence of **shared innovations**, and determining the taxa within a family is **subgrouping**. Linguists use a variety of terms for labelling taxa of different sizes and time depths, but unfortunately there is no agreement as to how these terms should be defined. Above the obvious **dialect** and **language**, we find at least *group(ing)*, **branch**, **stock**, **family** and **phylum**, plus a variety of prefixes like *sub-*, *micro-*, *meso-*, *super-*, *hyper-* and **macro-**, with no great consistency of use. Note: strictly, a *taxon* is a pigeonhole within any kind of classification, while a *clade* is a taxon forming part of a tree, but the distinction is of little consequence in comparative linguistics.

taxonomy Another term for **genetic classification**.

tectal (also **guttural**) [*rare*] Especially in Indo-European studies, a cover term for any consonant which is palatal, velar or labio-velar.

Teeter's Law A facetious observation about the foibles of historical linguists. It says: in a given family, the language you know best always turns out to be the most archaic.

teknolalic word [*rare*] A **nursery word**.

teleological explanation of change Any proposal to account for **language change** which maintains that changes are typically motivated by the internal requirements of the linguistic system – that is, in some sense the system itself is 'striving' to attain some goal. Dismissed by most linguists, teleological accounts were to some extent favoured by the Prague School, who spoke of change as 'therapeutic' – that is, as occurring to 'repair' the 'damage' caused by earlier changes. Such interpretations have also been defended for phonological change by Roman Jakobson, who spoke of languages as attempting to maintain their 'equilibrium' in the face of disturbances, and by Roger Lass, who regards diachronic **conspiracies** as evidence of teleology; see, for example, Jakobson (1931) and Lass (1974, 1980) (Lass has more recently changed his views). Some have also pointed to cases of **independent parallel innovation** as evidence that languages are 'pre-programmed' to develop in certain directions. See **functionality of change**, **Darwinism**.

telescoping 1. A label occasionally applied to cases of word-formation like *glitterati* (from *glitter* + *literati*). 2. The collapse of a historical sequence of phonological changes into a single rule, often a purely morphological one.

temporal plausibility principle A principle invoked in addressing the **homeland problem**. It says this: the homeland should be identified at a time consistent with both the linguistic estimation of time depth and the evidence of any reconstructible cultural items of vocabulary. In the case of PIE, any date later than about 2500 BC is too late to account for the linguistic divergence observed in the first millennium BC, and any date earlier than the Neolithic is incompatible with the reconstructed cultural vocabulary of PIE.

tensing Any phonological change in which a lax vowel becomes tense, such as the change of lax /æ/ to tense /æ:/ in some American accents of English. The opposite is **laxing**.

tenuis [*obsolete*] Especially in the older IE philological literature, a term for a voiceless plosive, such as [p t k]. Sometimes, as in ancient Greek, the term denotes more specifically an unaspirated voiceless plosive. Compare **media, aspirata**.

test language (Ger *Testsprache*) In a language family, a language which retains a contrast which is reconstructed for the proto-language but which has been lost in other languages of the family. A test language provides direct confirmation of the existence of the contrast in the ancestral language.

Teutonic An obsolete term for the **Germanic** languages.

textual method The term used by Campanile (1998: 4) to denote an approach to **reconstruction** which depends heavily upon the reconstruction of culture. His example is the use of a word meaning 'wolf' in Old Irish, Germanic, Hittite and Vedic to denote a person estranged from the tribe or hostile to it. He therefore proposes that just such a usage can be reconstructed for PIE, even though the words for 'wolf' are different and non-cognate in all four languages. Compare the **lexicalist method**.

t-**glottalling** The phenomenon, occurring in many varieties of English, in which the phoneme /t/ is realized in certain positions as an oral-glottal plosive [ˀt] or (more particularly) as a glottal stop [ʔ].

thematic Of a lexical item in an inflecting language, inflected in such a way that a **thematic vowel** (a class vowel) is interposed between the root and any suffix. For example, Latin *am-* 'love', *mon-* 'warn' and *aud-* 'hear' take the infinitive suffix *-re* (from earlier **-se*) to form infinitives *am-ā-re*, *mon-ē-re* and *aud-ī-re*, respectively, with thematic vowels *-ā-*, *-ē-* and *-ī-*. Compare **athematic**.

thematic vowel In the older IE languages, a vowel which is always present after certain lexical stems and before any inflectional suffixes. Nouns, verbs and adjectives may exhibit such a thematic vowel, and each of these may be divided into several subclasses depending on which of the several thematic vowels is present, plus a further subclass in which no thematic vowel is present. Lexical items are characterized as **thematic** (having a thematic vowel) and **athematic** (having none); see those entries for examples.

Third Palatalization In common **Slavic**, a phonological change in which the velars /k g x/ were palatalized to /c ɟ ç/ (later mostly developing to /ts z s/) when preceded by a high front vowel and followed by a low back vowel. In spite of its name, this process seems to have been simultaneous with the **Second Palatalization**.

Third Slavic Vowel Shift (also **Fall of the Jers**) In common **Slavic**, the disappearance of the two weak vowels /ĭ ŭ/, called **jers**. In certain environments they were converted to /e o/ or to /ə/, according to language; elsewhere they disappeared, though /ĭ/ caused palatalization of a preceding consonant in all cases. Examples: Pre-Russian */dĭnĭ/ 'day' > Russian /dʲenʲ/; Pre-Russian */sŭnŭ/ 'sleep' > Russian /son/.

thorn cluster In PIE, any of various consonant clusters involving a dental plosive followed by a velar or palatal plosive. Such clusters were subject to complex developments in the daughter languages, often involving **metatheses**. For example, Sanskrit *ksám-*, Greek *khthó:n*, Tocharian A *tkam*, Hittite *tekan, takn-*, all 'earth', point to an original cluster $*d^hg^{wh}$- metathesized in the first two languages.

Thracian An extinct and poorly known **Indo-European** language of ancient Bulgaria and Romania. Its slightly distinct northern variety is sometimes distinguished as *Dacian*, in which case the label *Daco-Thracian* is applied to the whole complex. See Price (1998: 119–121), and see **Thraco-Phrygian**.

Thraco-Phrygian A posited grouping of the three IE languages **Thracian, Phrygian** and **Armenian**. This grouping is based upon anecdotal comments about the alleged similarity of the three languages in antiquity; it has no firm linguistic basis, and it is not generally accepted.

three-language problem The name given by Hoenigswald (1960: 144 *ff.*) to an idealized version of the **subgrouping** problem for the case of three languages.

three-witness principle Another term for **Meillet's principle**.

Thurneysen and Havet's Law The statement, put forward by Thurneysen (1887) and Havet (1885), that earlier */o(:)/ becomes /a(:)/ in Latin before /w/. It is widely accepted as essentially correct, with qualifications. See Collinge (1985: 193–195) for an account.

Thurneysen's Law A statement, put forward by Thurneysen (1898), designed to account for the puzzling voicing alternations in Gothic fricatives. Too long to state here, the law operates chiefly in terms of left-to-right dissimilations, with voiced consonants inducing following voiceless fricatives and voiceless consonants inducing following voiced fricatives. The law is controversial but widely accepted. See Collinge (1985: 183–191) for critical discussion with references.

Tibeto-Burman A large group of languages in southeast Asia, forming one of the two main branches of the **Sino-Tibetan** family; its two best-known members are *Tibetan* and *Burmese*. The sub-branching of this group is much debated, and some specialists would prefer to make the **Karen** group of languages coordinate with Tibeto-Burman in a larger *Tibeto-Karen* branch of Sino-Tibetan. See Ruhlen (1991: 143–148) for a survey of proposals.

tilde Another (but inappropriate) term for the **swung dash**.

time depth The length of time before the present at which some linguistic state of affairs existed or at which some linguistic event occurred. Most commonly, the term is applied to the estimated time when an ancestral language split into certain daughters. For example, the time depth of the Indo-European family is commonly estimated at around 6000 years, meaning that the ancestral language, PIE, began breaking up into distinct daughter languages around 6000 years ago (4000 BC).

time-depth problem The problem of ascertaining the maximum **time depth** at which **genetic relationships** can be securely identified, or sometimes the time depth at which **comparative reconstruction** can be performed. Due to the **fadeout effect**, it is certain that limits on these enterprises must exist, but specialists do not agree on any firm date or even on whether it makes any sense to try to estimate a time depth in absolute years. Many linguists would advocate a maximum time depth of 6000–8000 years, or at most 10,000 years, for one or both of these enterprises, but a few seemingly secure families, such as **Afro-Asiatic**, appear to be older than this, though reconstruction in these cases has not so far proved possible, and the proponents of **remote relationships**, such as **Nostratic**, are obliged to reject such cautious estimates. It should be noted that estimated time depths for particular language families found in the literature are in most cases little more than rough guesses based upon a gut feeling about how much time would have been required to produce the observed degree of divergence; only in a few cases, as with **Proto-Indo-European**, do we have any hard evidence on which to base our estimates. See Manaster Ramer (1999) for a critique.

tmesis Separation by other material of two linguistic elements which properly belong together, as in archaic English *what things soever* for *whatsoever things*. The earliest IE languages show a good deal of tmesis. For example, in early Old Irish, the preverb *imma-* 'about', which should properly be attached to a verb, is sometimes separated from that verb by other material, as in *imma- lanna -lig* 'which lies about lands', for expected *imma-lig lanna*.

Tobler–Mussafia Law The statement that, in the older Romance languages, a clitic (especially a pronoun) may not begin a clause. This observation was made by Tobler for Old French and by Mussafia for Old Italian; see Maiden (1995: 171–174) for a summary of the Italian case. This 'law' has been lost in all modern Romance languages except European Portuguese and some Italian dialects.

Tocharian (also **Tokharian**) A major branch of **Indo-European**, consisting of two languages, *Tocharian A* (*East Tocharian*, *Agnean*) and *Tocharian B* (*West Tocharian*, *Kuchean*), both extinct and both recorded in manuscripts dating from the second half of the first millennium AD in what is now the Xinjiang-Uyghur province of China (Chinese Turkestan). Tocharian is notable for the collapse of the PIE plosive system into a single series of plosives, for a total reorganization of the IE nominal morphology, and for a highly archaic verbal system. See Winter (1998) for a historical summary.

tone *sandhi* In a tone language, any change in the phonetic nature of a tone induced by the presence of an adjacent tone. For example, the Mandarin third tone (fall-rise) loses its fall when immediately followed by another third tone.

tonic Of a vowel or a syllable in a word, bearing the word-stress or word-accent. Compare **atonic**.

Tonkawa An **isolated language** formerly spoken in Texas, in an area of great linguistic complexity. Earlier and later attestations differ very substantially, possible because of rapid *taboo replacement* (see **taboo**).

No attempt at linking Tonkawa to anything else has yet found wide support.

tonogenesis Any process which leads to the introduction of tones into a language which formerly lacked them. For example, a southern dialect of Tlingit preserves the earlier contrast of /Vh Vʔ V:ʔ V:/, while other dialects have converted these into tonal contrasts (Krauss 1979).

tooth **problem** The problem in which obviously cognate forms in the several languages of a family appear to require different reconstructions in the ancestral language. The PIE word for 'tooth' is a classic example: Latin requires PIE *dent-*, Greek and most of Germanic require *dont-*, and Gothic requires *dn̥t-*. The Basque word for 'interval, space' is likewise problematic; some regional forms require a Pre-Basque *gune*, while others equally require *gunne*. Austronesian presents a sizeable number of these. Such cases are by no means rare, and it is possible that many of them represent evidence for **variation** in the ancestral language. Compare **doublet** (sense 2).

top-down reconstruction (also **inverted reconstruction**) A certain technique used in **comparative reconstruction**, as follows. Language family F contains a branch B, among other branches. There is a problem in reconstructing Proto-B, in that the data from B do not suffice to perform the reconstruction with confidence. However, the data from the other branches allow us to reconstruct with some confidence the position in Proto-F, and hence the reconstruction in Proto-F can be appealed to in order to work out what must have been the case in its daughter Proto-B. See Anttila (1989: 344–346) for some examples of this from Uralic and Indo-European. Compare **bottom-up reconstruction**.

toponym (also **place name**) In **onomastics**, the name of a feature of the landscape: the name of a town, a hill, a lake, or any other feature of the landscape, natural or man-made. The study of toponyms is *toponymy*.

total accountability principle A putative principle of **comparison**, advanced by Hamp (1998: 14), by which, in any comparison of linguistic forms between languages, all material must be expressly accounted for, and there must be no unanalysed residue. See **root cognates**.

total assimilation See under **assimilation**.

total distribution principle A principle sometimes invoked in addressing the **homeland problem**. It says this: a valid solution must account for the distribution of *all* the languages in the family.

total reduplication See under **reduplication**.

trade language Another term for a **lingua franca**, or sometimes also for a **pidgin** used in trading.

trajectory 1. (also **pathway**) In certain types of **phonological change**, the series of phonetic forms which a segment passes through over time. For example, Middle English /iː/ seems to have developed roughly as follows in Modern English: /iː/ > /əi/ > /ʌɪ/ > /aɪ/. 2. (also **pathway**) In **morphological change**, the series of stages through which a morpheme may pass; a familiar series is word > affix > phonological alternation > zero. 3. See **loan-word trajectory**. 4. In **linguistic geography**, the path followed by a language which spreads from one area to another.

transfer 1. Another term for **interference**. 2. The acquisition by a language of a linguistic feature which it formerly lacked as a result of contact with a neighbouring language. Lass (1997: 121–122) cites the example of Afrikaans. The Dutch ancestor of Afrikaans had the plosive system /p t k b d/, but Afrikaans has filled the gap by acquiring a phoneme /g/ as a result of extensive borrowing from several neighbouring languages. When documentary evidence is lacking, such transfer can obscure the historical development of a language. Transfer in this second sense is one type of **homoplasy**. 3. See under **merger**.

transferred sense A historically later meaning of a word which develops from an earlier meaning by some kind of **semantic change**, as when Basque *agor* developed from earlier 'barren, sterile' to 'dried up' (of a spring or well) and hence to 'dry'. The earlier sense does not necessarily disappear, though some linguists prefer to reserve *transferred sense* for cases in which the new meaning has no semantic features in common with the old one at all (**semantic shift**). The disappearance of an earlier sense in favour of a transferred sense is **fading** (sense 2). The careless use of transferred senses in **comparison** is one kind of **neglect of known history**. Compare **extended sense**.

transformation In historical linguistics, any particular instance of a **language change**, in which a linguistic form X is converted to, or replaced by, a different one Y. The term has nothing to do with *transformational grammar*.

transformation series (also **morphocline**) The chronological sequence of phonetic forms assumed by a segment in a language or a family over a time period in which one or more phonological changes affect it. An example is PIE */d/ > Proto-Germanic */t/ > High German /ts-/ (initially) and /-s-/ (medially).

transitional zone The geographical periphery of a language or language family, where it is in contact with neighbouring languages or families. It has been suggested that transitional zones may undergo external change from contact more readily than internal change, and that changes here are more likely to be complex and irregular than in **nuclear zones**.

transition area In **dialect geography**, with respect to a particular change, a region which lies between a **focal area** (in which the change is complete) and a **relic area** (in which it has never occurred at all), and within which the change has occurred only sporadically or less generally.

transition problem The problem of determining the routes by which languages change. See the **WLH model of language change**.

transmission The process by which a language is passed down, in a somewhat altered state, from one generation to the next. See **normally transmitted language, non-genetic language**.

transmission of change See **implementation of change**.

transparency Another term for **isomorphy**.

Transparency Principle 1. See under the **Lightfoot framework**. 2. See under **isomorphy**.

transphylic root A putative case of a root which occurs in several language families not known to be related. Such cases may result from ancient **borrowing**, but Blench (1997b) argues that some such cases may derive substantially from phonaesthetic factors.

Traugott progression A putative universal directionality in **semantic change**, put forward by Elizabeth Traugott (1982, 1989), by which the meaning of a word changes over time from an ordinary lexical ('propositional') meaning to a discourse-based ('textual') meaning and then to an 'expressive' function indicating the speaker's attitude. Schematically: Propositional > Textual > Expressive. These tendencies are illustrated by the semantic histories of English *but*, *while*, *after*, *apparently* and *probably*, among others.

tree See **family tree**.

tree model Another term for the **genetic model**.

triangulation Another term for **projection**.

Trisyllabic Laxing The historical process in English by which tense (long) vowels underwent laxing (shortening) whenever followed by two or more further syllables in the word. This process, followed by the **Great Vowel Shift**, is responsible for such modern alternations as *sane/sanity*, *serene/serenity*, *divine/divinity*, *profound/profundity* and *mode/modify*. It has, however, ceased to be productive; some or all speakers fail to apply it in *obese/obesity*, *pirate/piracy*, *grain/granary* and *code/codify*.

Trümmersprache A **dead language** which is only sparsely or incompletely recorded, such as Gothic or Runic Northwest Germanic.

truncation Another term for the **loss** (sense 1) of a segment, sometimes particularly of a vowel.

Tsimshian A group of closely related languages spoken in British Columbia and Alaska, variously counted as one to three distinct languages. It is included in the **Penutian** hypothesis.

Tungusic (also **Manchu-Tungus**) A language family of east Asia. It contains about sixteen languages, including the important *Evenki* (formerly *Tungus*) and the virtually extinct *Manchu*. Tungusic is included within the **Altaic** family by the supporters of that family.

Tupian (also **Tupi-Guaraní**) A family of over fifty languages spoken in Brazil and several neighbouring countries; best known are *Tupi* in northern Brazil and *Guaraní* in Paraguay. No broader genetic links are known.

Turkic A family of about thirty languages occupying much of central and western Asia and a small part of Europe; the best-known Turkic language is *Turkish*. Except for a few of the Turkic languages spoken in western China, which are more distantly related to the others, all the Turkic languages are very closely related, and they appear to be descended from the speech of an originally small group of Turks who burst out of central Asia in the medieval period and carved out a huge empire; in the process, Turkic languages have displaced and sometimes obliterated a number of other languages, many of them **Indo-European**, such as **Tocharian**. The earliest written texts in a Turkic language are the eighth-century Orkhon inscriptions. Turkic forms one branch of the controversial **Altaic** family. See Johanson and Csató (1998) for a survey of the family and its history and prehistory.

type-identifying criteria Typological criteria for classifying languages, such as basic word order and the presence or absence of ergativity, vowel harmony, tones, gender systems and non-configurationality. It has been recognized at least since Meillet (1958: 90) that such criteria are worthless for establishing genetic relationships between languages. Compare **individual-identifying criteria**.

typological change See **typological shift**.

typological distance The degree of typological (structural) difference between two languages, especially neighbouring languages.

typological harmony The degree to which a given language exhibits a set of structural features which are consistent with those features we expect to see together, according to a particular system of typological classification. The term is most often used in connection with the famous word-order typology of Greenberg (1963a). It is sometimes suggested that a language which is low in typological harmony may be in the middle of a **typological shift**.

typological isogloss A line on a map which broadly separates neighbouring regions characterized by significant typological differences, regardless of any genetic boundaries which may or may not be present. For example, such an isogloss can be drawn across east Asia to separate monosyllabic tone languages from polysyllabic non-tone languages, and this cuts across both the Sino-Tibetan and the Austro-Asiatic families.

typologically based reconstruction An approach to **reconstruction,** or a particular reconstruction, which depends heavily upon appeals to **typology.** The general idea is that nothing should be reconstructed which is significantly different from what is observed in attested languages; this is sometimes called the *typological plausibility principle*, and it represents an explicit appeal to the **Uniformitarian Principle.** A classic example is the **glottalic theory of PIE.** See Comrie (1993).

typological shift (also **typological change**) Any substantial change in the typological characteristics of a language, such as from isolating to agglutinating, or from agglutinating to inflecting, or a **word-order change** from Verb-Object to Object-Verb (or vice versa), with corresponding changes in the various linguistic features associated with each type.

typology The classification of languages according to their structural characteristics, and not according to their ancestry. Typological similarities are not considered to be indicative of genetic relatedness.

udātta In Sanskrit, the label applied to the syllable bearing the main word-accent in a word. Compare **anudātta, svarita.**

Ugaritic An extinct northwest **Semitic** language recorded in a number of inscriptions in western Syria between the fifteenth and thirteenth centuries BC, in a unique cuneiform alphabet. See Pardee (1997).

Ugric One of the two major sub-branches of the **Finno-Ugric** branch of the **Uralic** family, including *Hungarian* and the two **Ob-Ugric** languages.

Umbrian An extinct **Italic** language, very sparsely recorded in east-central Italy about 350–50 BC, closely related to **Oscan** in a **Sabellian** grouping.

Umgangssprache The German for 'colloquial speech'. In historical linguistics, the term denotes the often unrecorded colloquial speech which coexists with a formal and codified written language.

umlaut (also **vowel mutation, metaphony**) Any of various types of
anticipatory vowel **assimilation** occurring in the Germanic languages. The general pattern is this: a vowel (short or long) undergoes
partial assimilation (**fronting, backing, lowering** or **rounding**) to
a vowel or a glide in the following syllable. Umlaut is visible in all the
Germanic languages except **Gothic**, but the details vary considerably from language to language. Three main types of umlaut may be
distinguished, as follows. (1) *i-umlaut*: [u] is fronted to [y], [o] is
fronted to [œ] or [ø], and [ɑ] is fronted to [æ], [ɛ] or [e], when the
following syllable contains [i] or [j]. (2) *a-umlaut*: [i] is lowered to [e],
and [u] is lowered to [o], when the next syllable contains [ɑ] (or
sometimes another low vowel). (3) *u-umlaut*: [i] is rounded to [y], [e]
is rounded to [ø], and [ɑ] is rounded to [ɔ], when the next syllable
contains [u] or [w].

Even in the earliest-recorded languages, the action of umlaut is
often obscured by **analogical levelling** of the alternations introduced by it, by loss or modification of the conditioning environment,
and by the failure of scribes always to distinguish umlauted vowels
from their non-umlauted counterparts.

Old English illustrates *i*-umlaut very well. Proto-Germanic **muː-
siz* 'mice', **foːtiz* 'feet' and **satjan* 'set' appear in OE as *myːs*, *føːt*
and *settan*, respectively; later unrounding of the front rounded
vowels, followed by the **Great Vowel Shift**, produced the modern
umlauting plurals *mice* and *feet* (singulars *mouse* and *foot*) and the
causative *set* of *sit*. Certain diphthongs are also affected by *i*-umlaut,
but we do not illustrate these here.

In OE, we also find *a*-umlaut, as in *cnotta* 'knot', from earlier
*knutta (compare the related verb *cnyttan* 'tie in knots, knit' from the
earlier **knutjan*, with *i*-umlaut), in *cossa* '(a) kiss', from **kussa*
(compare the related verb *cyssan* 'kiss', from **kussjan*, with *i*-umlaut;
the modern noun *kiss* is taken from the verb), and in *gold* 'gold' (from
*golda, from **gulda*; compare the related verb *gyldan* 'gild, cover in
gold', from **guldjan*).

OE does not exhibit simple *u*-umlaut, but Old Norse does. Note
ON *hɔnd* 'hand' next to Gothic *handus*, OHG *hand*; ON *syngva* 'sing'
next to Gothic *siggwan*, OHG OE *singan*; ON *allr* 'all', neuter dative
singular *ɔllu*; ON *jɔrð* 'earth' (from **jarðu*), genitive singular
jarðar.

In place of simple *u*-umlaut, OE exhibits a distinctive type of
umlaut called *back mutation* (*back umlaut, velar umlaut*). Here only
certain short vowels are affected: short [i] and [e] are converted to a
diphthong, variously written as <io> or <eo>, and short [æ] is

converted to a diphthong written <ea>, when the following syllable contains a back vowel [u] or [o], or rarely [ɑ]. This process is sporadic, and it affects some dialects of OE more than others. Examples with original /i/: *heora* 'their', *wreoton* 'they wrote', *leomu* 'limbs', but *gifu* 'gift'. Examples with original /e/: *meotudes* 'God's', *heofon* 'heaven', but *regol* 'rule', *sprecan* 'speak'. West Saxon shows no back umlaut of [æ], because [æ] itself was backed to [ɑ] by a separate change. (Examples from Lass 1994: 52.)

The earlier view that umlaut arose as allophonic variation in Proto-Germanic is now generally rejected in favour of the view that it arose independently in the several Germanic languages. See Robinson (1992) or Voyles (1992) for a survey of umlaut in the ancient Germanic languages, and compare **ablaut**.

The term *umlaut* is applied both to the historical change and to the resulting alternations.

unattested form A linguistic form, in a language, which is nowhere recorded but which has been reconstructed or posited by linguists. Such a form is always preceded by an **asterisk**. Compare **attested form**.

unconditioned change A **phonological change** which applies to every single instance of a segment, without exception. An example is the change of Proto-Polynesian */s/ to Hawaiian /h/, which affected every single instance of */s/. The opposite is **conditioned change**.

unconditioned merger See under **merger**.

underdot In an **edition** of a text, a dot placed under a character to indicate that the character is damaged or obscure in the original, and hence that the reading is uncertain.

unheeded-contradiction principle The principle that an instance of **grammaticalization** may be seen to have gone to completion when the grammaticalized item can occur in a context in which its lexical source is semantically inappropriate. For example, the Egyptian Arabic verb *ʔâm* 'get up', which remains in lexical use, has been grammaticalized as an auxiliary expressing inchoative action, and it can be used in sentences like *ʔom-t nim-t* 'I fell asleep', in which no semantic notion of getting up is conceivable. The term was coined by Hagège (1993: 224–225). Compare the **proof-by-anachrony principle**.

unidirectionality The property of a type of linguistic change which frequently happens in one direction but not in the reverse direction. The term is most often encountered in studies of **grammaticalization,** in which unidirectionality appears to be the norm: words of concrete meaning develop abstract meanings (but not the reverse); lexical items become grammatical markers (but not the reverse); and so on. Such observations constitute one kind of **diachronic universal,** and the statement that such changes are unidirectional is called the *unidirectionality hypothesis* or the *unidirectionality principle.* Possible counterexamples are represented by apparent instances of such phenomena as **degrammaticalization** and **deaffixization.** See Hopper and Traugott (1993: ch. 5) for an account of unidirectionality and possible counterexamples. Unidirectionality is also observed in phonological change: for example, the developments /s/ > /h/ > Ø are commonplace, but reverse developments are vanishingly rare. Bichakjian (1988, 1997) argues for a different kind of unidirectionality; he maintains that languages universally tend to change in such a way as to make the features acquired early by children more prominent, and those acquired later by children less prominent. This view finds little support at present.

Uniformitarian Principle A fundamental principle of science, which may be informally stated as follows: the same physical laws apply everywhere, all the time, whether we are looking or not. Historical linguistics has its own version of this: ancient languages were not different from modern ones. This was the chief contribution of the **Neogrammarians.** Lass (1997: 28) puts it like this: no linguistic state of affairs can have been the case only in the past. Labov (1972: 161) puts it like this: the same mechanisms which operated to produce the large-scale changes of the past may be observed operating in the current changes taking place around us. This principle prevents us from positing or reconstructing states of affairs in ancient languages which are not known to exist in modern languages, and it militates against such ideas as **stadialism** and **Darwinism.** It also places some limits on our ability to reconstruct. For example, **internal reconstruction** commonly derives alternations from the effect of phonological changes upon an earlier absence of alternations; this appears to lead to the conclusion that every language has an ancestor which lacked alternations, but such a conclusion is prohibited by the Uniformitarian Principle. See Christy (1983). See also the **Uniform Probabilities Principle.**

uniformity in language The absence of **variation** in language. Uniformity is commonly regarded by non-linguists as normal, or at least as proper, and it is also the basis of a great deal of linguistic theorizing, ranging from Saussure's introduction of structuralism through Meillet's famous dictum that a language is a system where *tout se tient* to the abstract idealizations of Chomsky and his followers. Nevertheless, it has become clear since the 1960s that variation is the norm in languages, and that uniformity is at best a sometimes convenient abstraction and at worst a serious distortion of reality.

Uniform Probabilities Principle A putative constraint on historical linguistics, proposed by Lass (1997: 29): the global (cross-linguistic) likelihood of any linguistic state of affairs has always been roughly the same as it is now. This is debatable. For example, since object-initial languages are rare today, the principle requires that they have always been rare, but many linguists would be happy to accept that their current rarity may be no more than a historical accident resulting from the spread of a few non–object-initial languages.

unique correspondence In the case of two or more languages or varieties which are generally linked by a number of **systematic correspondences**, a correspondence which appears only in a single word. For example, in Basque, whose regional dialects exhibit several systematic correspondences, the verb meaning 'say' is *esan* in the western dialects but *erran* in the eastern ones, and the unique correspondence /s/ : /rr/ occurs in no other word than this one, which possibly reflects a Pre-Basque **esran*, with the unique cluster */sr/. Watkins (1990: 297) cites the unique correspondence of Greek /s-/ and Vedic /ty-/ in Greek *sébomai* 'feel awe, venerate' and the related causative *sobéō* 'scare away, shoo' and Vedic *tyájati* 'leaves'; these derive from a PIE root **tyeg^w-* 'retreat in awe', with a unique initial cluster **ty-*, and the Greek verb-stem represents the sole instance of the apparently regular Greek development **ty- > s-*.

uniqueness principle See under **isomorphy**.

univerbation Any linguistic change in which two (or more) independent words are fused into a single word. The term is most commonly used in connection with **morphologization**. A simple example is the development of Latin phrases like *clara mente* 'with a clear mind' into Romance adverbs like Spanish *claramente*, French *clairement* 'clearly'. Andersen (1987: 28–33) cites the example of the modern Polish preterite, in which what was originally a periphrastic construction with a copula and a past participle has fused into a single verb-form.

universal Ideally, a statement which is true for all natural languages without exception, and which may therefore constitute part of the definition of a human language. More broadly, and more usually, a statement which is true of the overwhelming majority of known languages, and to which exceptions are at best very rare. Any **reconstruction** which violates a seemingly well-founded universal is therefore deeply suspect. See **diachronic universal**.

universal category space A theoretical and multidimensional 'space' within which are located all possible segment-types. Many types of **phonological change** can be viewed as movements within this space. See **stepwise shift**.

universal tendency Any instance of a putative principle holding that languages tend universally to change in certain directions and not in others. Familiar examples include the observations that intervocalic consonants undergo **lenition** rather than **fortition** and that word-final obstruents undergo **devoicing** rather than **voicing**. A more ambitious example is Humboldt's Universal (see under **isomorphy**).

Unmarking Principle A putative principle of phonological change applying to **chain shifts**, proposed by Labov (1994: 288–291). It says this: in chain shifts, elements of the marked system become unmarked. For example, nasalized vowels may become oral vowels, but not normally the other way round.

unmerger [*rare*] Another term for **reversal of merger**.

unnatural change (also **abnormal change**) A linguistic change which is both rare and hard to imagine a motivation or pathway for. Blust (1990: 245–248) notes a number of unnatural phonological changes in Austronesian languages, including */t/ > /k/ (in a sizeable number of geographically scattered languages, including Hawaiian), */-b-/ > /-k-/ in several languages of Borneo, */l/ > /ŋg/ in Rennellese, and */w/ > /c-/, /-nc-/ in Sundanese (where /c/ is a coronal affricate). Campbell (1997a: 113) reports that several Athabaskan languages have changed */ts/ to one of /kʷ/, /p/ or /f/, and some have also changed */t/ to /k/. Crowley (1997: 56) cites from certain Pacific and Papuan languages the unconditioned shifts

*/t/ > /w/, */d/ > /ŋ/ and */l/ > /ŋ/, each of which appears incomprehensible, but argues that such a change typically represents only the beginning and end of a series of changes, each of which is itself natural. The opposite is **natural change**.

unpacking (also **segmentalization, linearization**) A **syntagmatic change** in which a single segment develops into a sequence of two segments, each of which retains some phonetic features of the original segment. Two examples are the development of a historical palatal nasal /ɲ/ into /in/ in some varieties of Basque (hence /baino/ 'than' for earlier /baɲo/) and into /nj/ in some varieties of French (hence /minjõ/ 'cute' for standard /miɲõ/). An instance of unpacking after another earlier change may produce a result that looks like **metathesis** but is not. For example, Pre-Basque *arrani* 'fish' yields *arrain* in many modern varieties, but no metathesis has occurred; instead, the categorical loss of intervocalic */n/ left behind **nasalization** of the adjoining vowels, and hence *arrãĩ*, and the nasalization was then reinterpreted as (unpacked into) a *following* /n/, producing the result. The opposite is **coalescence**. Compare **split**.

unrounding A phonological change in which lip-rounding is lost from a segment (usually a vowel). An example is the change of Attic Greek [y] and [y:] into [i] and [i:] in later Greek. The opposite is **rounding**.

Upper Exit Principle A putative principle of phonological change applying to high tense vowels in **chain shifts**, proposed by Labov (1994: 281–284). It says this: in chain shifts, the first of two high moras may change peripherality, and the second may become non-peripheral. This principle is designed to account for changes like [i:] > [əɪ] in the English **Great Vowel Shift**. Compare **Mid Exit Principle, Lower Exit Principle**.

Ural-Altaic A putative macro-family including **Uralic** and **Altaic**. This proposal was put forward in the nineteenth century on typological grounds: both families have SOV order, agglutinating and overwhelmingly suffixing morphology, and vowel harmony. Today probably no one accepts Ural-Altaic as a valid grouping, but note that both the **Nostratic** and the **Eurasiatic** hypotheses attempt to integrate Uralic and Altaic within larger groupings.

Uralic A large language family occupying much of northern Europe and Siberia and also a sizeable area of central Europe. The Uralic family is divided into two branches: the small **Samoyed** branch and the much larger **Finno-Ugric** branch. Except for Samoyed, which was added later, the existence and the structure of the Uralic family were largely worked out in the eighteenth century, and in 1799 Sámuel Gyarmathi published a decisive reconstruction of the family. Uralic was thus the first major language family to be definitively established. On the basis of their similar personal pronouns, Uralic has often been suspected of being related to **Indo-European**, and it is always included in the **Nostratic** hypothesis. See Abondolo (1998) for a survey, and see **Uralic-Yukaghir, Ural-Altaic**.

Uralic-Yukaghir A putative language family including **Uralic** and **Yukaghir**. Vigorously defended in places (such as Collinder 1965 and Harms 1977), the idea has won some support but is not generally accepted.

Urartian An extinct language recorded in eastern Anatolia about 850–600 BC in a cuneiform script. The language was closely related to the earlier **Hurrian** but is not directly descended from it. It otherwise appears to have no relatives, though some linguists suspect a link with **Nakh-Dagestan**.

urban dialect A **dialect** which is typical of an urban area. Early dialectologists were inclined to think that only rural areas preserved 'pure' dialects, while urban speech was merely 'corruptions' of standard speech and unworthy of study. Thanks to the investigations of the sociolinguists, we now know that this is not so. First, urban speech is invariably **vernacular** in form, and cannot be regarded as derived from standard varieties. Second, there is a great deal of evidence that most linguistic changes originate in urban communities and then spread slowly out over adjoining rural areas, so that rural dialects, far from being 'pure', are often no more than versions of the urban speech of several generations ago.

Urheimat The German for **homeland**.

Ursprache 1. The German for **proto-language**. 2. A label formerly used for the hypothetical ancestral language of all humankind, *Proto-World* (see **Proto-World hypothesis**), sometimes especially by those who fancifully believed that this language was still spoken unchanged in some favoured corner of the world.

Uto-Aztecan A major language family of North America, extending from the Great Basin to Central America, and containing over thirty languages, some of them extinct. Among its best-known members are *Nahuatl* (the language of the Aztecs), *Hopi, Comanche, Northern* and *Southern Paiute, Pima-Papago, Tübatulabal, Luiseño, Tarahumara, Huichol* and *Pipil*. Uto-Aztecan is one of the largest American families in terms of number of languages and number of speakers, and one of the most geographically extended; it also seems to have an unusually great time depth (perhaps 5000 years). Uto-Aztecan is included in the **Aztec-Tanoan** hypothesis.

uvularization Any phonological change in which a non-uvular consonant is converted into a uvular one, such as the change of a coronal [r] into a uvular [ʁ] in some varieties of French, Occitan, Basque, Breton, Italian, German, Dutch, Danish and Norwegian.

$$\boxed{V}$$

v. 1. The abbreviation for 'see' (Latin *vide*), used to instruct the reader to consult a named source for further information, as in 'The history of the Balto-Slavic word-accent is complex; *v.* Collinge (1985).' See *q.v.* and compare *cf.* 2. The abbreviation for 'it is empty' (Latin *vacat*), used in an **edition** of an inscription to indicate the presence of an empty space at this point.

Vandalic The extinct and unrecorded east **Germanic** language of the Vandals, who invaded Spain, Africa and other areas in the fifth century AD before finally disappearing.

van Wijk's Law A process in common **Slavic** by which a CR cluster was reduced to a single consonant with concomitant lengthening of the following vowel. The law was stated by van Wijk (1916); see Collinge (1985: 197–198) for an account.

variable A point in a linguistic system in a single speech community at which two or more **variants** are available. Typically, any given speaker sometimes uses one variant and sometimes another, with a comparative frequency which depends on any of a number of possible social factors like age, sex, social class and degree of formality. An example in most English-speaking communities is the variation between velar /ŋ/ and coronal /n/ in forms like *going*. A variable is conventionally represented by some convenient symbol enclosed in **parentheses** – in this case, (ng). See **indicator, marker**.

variable rule A rule-like statement which expresses a process which occurs only variably in the speech of some group and which is favoured or disfavoured by identifiable linguistic factors but which is typically neither categorical nor impossible in all or most contexts. Here is a typical variable rule:

$$t, d \rightarrow <\text{Ø}> / [+ \text{cons}] <-\#>^{\beta} \_ \#\# <-\text{syll}>^{\alpha}$$

This says that /t/ and /d/ are variably deleted when preceded by a consonant and followed by a word boundary; deletion is favoured by the absence of a morpheme boundary immediately before the segment to be deleted and by the absence of a following vowel, with the second factor (α) being more important than the first (β).

Variable rules were introduced by Labov (1969) and developed by Labov and others, notably by Cedergren and Sankoff (1974), who developed the VARBRUL computer program for calculating, from a database, the propensity of a rule to apply and the weighting of each factor.

variant Any one of two or more different forms in which a single word or other linguistic item exists in the same language at the same time. For example, the Basque word for 'birch' exists as both *burki* and *urki*; the Basque word for 'wine' exhibits the variants *ardao*, *ardo*, *arno* and *ardũ*; the PIE root meaning 'cover' apparently had the variants **teg-* and **steg-*. The term is also applied to each of the several realizations of a linguistic form, or set of linguistic forms, available within a single linguistic **variable**. Compare **alternation**.

variant reading In philological work, one of two or more significantly different linguistic forms occurring at the same point in different versions of the same document, or of different interpretations suggested by scholars for a single puzzling form. See *lectio difficilior*.

variation The existence of competing linguistic forms within a single speech community or language. The linguists of the past often tended to regard a language as essentially homogeneous and invariant at any point in time, and they accordingly interpreted language change as a more or less abrupt shift from one steady state to another. In this view, variation was regarded as peripheral at best and as a nuisance at worst. However, since the pioneering work of the socio-linguists in the 1960s, we have come to realize that variation is the *normal* state of a language, and that the absence of variation would be pathological. The key point is that much of this variation is highly structured, though much of this structure only shows up statistically, and very often the choice among variants has clear social significance. Almost all contemporary work on language change recognizes the central role of variation; variation is seen as the vehicle of change, providing an elegant resolution to the **Saussurean paradox**.

variational stasis A state of affairs in which a pattern of variation in a language remains stable for generations or centuries. Romaine (1982) cites the case of relative-clause formation in Scottish English, which has maintained the same distribution of variant forms unaltered since the sixteenth century.

Vasiljev and Dolobko, Law of Another term for **Dolobko's Law**.

Vedic The earliest recorded **Indo-Aryan** language, and one of the earliest **Indo-European** languages to be recorded. Vedic is the language of the Vedas, the earliest-known Hindu hymns; the first records of it go back at least to 1000 BC and possibly to the middle of the second millennium BC. Once regarded as a distinctive early version of **Sanskrit**, Vedic today is usually classified as a distinct language; in any case, Vedic is not the direct ancestor of Sanskrit, since it exhibits a few innovations not found in Sanskrit. Vedic is remarkably conservative, and it retains some conspicuous features of PIE, particularly in the verbal system, not found in Sanskrit. The Vedic texts are not uniform; they exhibit a significant amount of both regional and stylistic variation. Vedic is not the direct ancestor of the **Prākrits**, though it is generally more similar to them than is Sanskrit. See Lazzeroni (1998).

velarization Any phonological change in which a segment acquires a velar quality which it formerly lacked.

velar softening The phenomenon in English by which velar /k/ and /g/ are palatalized respectively to /s/ (or /ʃ/) and /dʒ/ before certain suffixes beginning with front vowels or glides, as in *electric/electricity* and *analogous/analogy*. This palatalization is not native in

English; it occurred in early Romance and has been imported from French. It is commonly extended also to words of Latin and even Greek origin, in which it is not historically appropriate, as in *classic/classicist* and *pedagogue/pedagogy*. Velar softening is now effectively a morphological marker of the Latino-Romance portion of the English vocabulary.

vel sim. Attached to a hypothetical linguistic form or to a **gloss**, an abbreviation for Latin *vel simile* 'or something similar'. This indicates that the writer is not quite sure of the exact form or meaning.

Vendryes' Law An accent shift affecting the Attic dialects of Greek (only), first noted by Vendryes (1929: 263). In a polysyllabic word, a circumflex accent on the penult changed to an acute accent on the antepenult, providing the antepenult was light (contained only one mora). See Collinge (1985: 199–202).

Venetic An extinct and sparsely recorded language of northeastern Italy. It is certainly **Indo-European**, but its affinities are debated; it was formerly attached to **Illyrian**, but today it is usually seen as most closely related to **Italic** and possibly even as a member of that group.

vernacular Ordinary everyday speech, the kind of speech used by speakers when they are not being observed and are not self-conscious. This is usually the central object of linguistic investigation, but examination of the vernacular is complicated by the existence of the *observer's paradox*, by which people tend to modify their speech self-consciously when they know they are being observed.

vernacularization In a particular speech community, a noticeable shift away from the forms typical of educated standard speech towards forms which are stigmatized or absent in standard speech. This has recently been observed, for example, among black speakers of English in certain communities in Britain and in the USA.

Verner's Law A major development in the consonants of Proto-Germanic, uncovered by Karl Verner (1876). The problem addressed by Verner was a set of Germanic forms which appeared to be exceptions to the **First Germanic Consonant Shift (Grimm's Law)**. Specifically, PIE */p t k/, instead of developing as usual into Germanic /f θ x/, develop into voiced plosives /b d g/. For example, the inherited /p t k/ of Greek *hypér* 'over', *patér* 'father' and *hekyrá* 'mother-in-law' are matched by /b d g/ in Old High German *ubar*, Old English *fæder*, and Old High German *swigur*. There appeared to be no possible conditioning environment for this anomalous development in Germanic. However, upon examining the forms in Sanskrit and Greek, which largely preserve the PIE accent, Verner realized that a conditioning factor existed in the form of that very PIE accent: whenever the consonant in question was either word-initial or immediately preceded by the PIE accent, it developed regularly according to Grimm's Law, but, whenever these conditions were not met, the other change regularly applied instead. Clearly both consonant shifts occurred at a time when early Proto-Germanic still preserved the PIE accent; after the shifts, Germanic shifted the word-accent to initial position in all cases, destroying the evidence for the conditioning environment within Germanic itself, so that only a comparison with accentually conservative languages like Greek and Sanskrit could reveal what had happened.

Verner's formulation immediately accounted for the previously mysterious Germanic alternations helplessly dubbed **grammatical change**. Compare the Sanskrit verb *vártate* 'turn' and its Old English cognate *weorþan* 'become', in four cognate forms, as in Table 12 (*þ* represents /θ/).

Verner's Law succeeded in removing all remaining exceptions to Grimm's Law, and its success provided the immediate inspiration for the **Neogrammarian Hypothesis**. See Collinge (1985: 203–216) for an account with references.

Verschärfung Another term for **Holtzmann's Law**.

vertical bilingualism A noteworthy distribution of languages in mountainous regions. In all cases reported in modern times, the people living at a given altitude are bilingual in the language of the people below them (if any), but not in the language of the people above them. Nichols (1997b: 373) interprets this as evidence that lowland languages tend to spread uphill during times (as in recent centuries) when global cooling makes high-altitude living precarious, and

Sanskrit	*vártate*	*vavárta*	*vavrtimá*	*vavrtāná*
Old English	*weorþan*	*wearþ*	*wurdon*	*worden*

Table 12

argues that, when the global climate is warmer, it works the other way round, with highland languages spreading into the lowlands.

Vestinian An extinct language, very sparsely recorded in east-central Italy about 250–100 BC, and often classed as **Italic**.

vide infra (abbreviated *v. infra*) The Latin for 'see below', which advises the reader that further information on the current topic will be provided later in the same work.

vide supra (abbreviated *v. supra*) The Latin for 'see above', which advises the reader that further information on the current topic was provided earlier in the same work.

v. infra See *vide infra*.

visarga A word-final /h/ in Sanskrit, generally deriving from PIE */s/, and frequent in inflections, as in the nominative singular form of certain noun-classes. For example, Sanskrit *aśvaḥ* 'horse' corresponds to Latin *equus* and Greek *hippós*. The name is also given to the symbol :, used to represent the sound in the most familiar Sanskrit orthography.

vocalization The conversion of another segment to a vowel. For example, PIE syllabic */m/ and */n/ were converted to /a/ in Greek and Indo-Iranian, and PIE */y/ [j] was converted to /i/ in Latin, as in PIE **alyos* (two syllables) > Latin *alius* 'other' (three syllables).

voicing Any phonological change in which a formerly voiceless segment becomes voiced. For example, Latin intervocalic /p t k/ have been voiced to /b d g/ in Spanish: Latin *cūpa(m)* 'vat', *catēna(m)* 'chain', *sēcūru(m)* 'sure' become Spanish *cuba*, *cadena*, *seguro*. The opposite is **devoicing**.

voicing crossover A phonological change in which a historically voiced consonant becomes voiceless while its historically voiceless counterpart becomes voiced. This occurs sporadically in some Austronesian languages, in which the historical */k/ and */g/ sometimes give rise to /g/ and /k/, respectively. This is one type of **flip-flop rule**.

Vollstufe See under **ablaut**.

Volscian An extinct language very sparsely recorded just south of Rome in the third century BC, sometimes classed as **Italic**.

Voltaic Another term for **Gur**.

Votic An extinct **Fennic** language formerly spoken in scattered villages in northeastern Estonia and adjoining areas of Russia. Its speakers were deported by the Nazis in 1940 and apparently none survive today.

vowel gradation Another term for **ablaut**.

vowel mutation Another term for **umlaut**.

vowel shift Any development in which several vowels in a language change their phonetic values significantly within a fairly short period. The **Great Vowel Shift** of English is a famous example. See **chain shift**.

vṛddhi See under **ablaut**.

v. supra See *vide supra*.

Wackernagel's Law 1. The statement, put forward by Wackernagel (1892), that, in early Indo-European, enclitics occupied the second position in a sentence, the position now called *Wackernagel's position*. Often this statement is generalized to assert that clitics tend universally to occur in second position. See Collinge (1985: 217–219) for a critical discussion with references. 2. The observation, credited to Wackernagel (1889), that in Greek and in other early IE languages, hiatus across morpheme boundaries is avoided by elision of the first vowel and lengthening of the second, as in Greek *strato-* 'army' plus *agós* 'leader' yielding *stratāgós* ~ *stratēgos* 'general'. See Collinge (1985: 238–239).

Wakashan A small language family (six languages) of the Pacific Northwest of North America; its best-known members are *Nootka* and *Kwakiutl*. It is included in the **Mosan** hypothesis.

Wanderwort A word which has been borrowed from language to language to language, across a significant geographical area. Names of metals, artefacts, foodstuffs and animals often exhibit this kind of behaviour. Typical examples are the Chinese words for 'tea', roughly *te* and *cha*, the names of *copper* and *tobacco*, the words *tomato*, *potato* and *lemon*, and possibly certain words for 'dog' and 'cat'. Bauer (1992, 1993/94) suggests that words for 'soap' and 'wheel' may be further examples.

Waterloo, Law of A famous analogy proposed by Edgar Sturtevant, who compared the historical 'sound law' *All instances of intervocalic /s/ changed to /r/ in early Latin* to the statement *All Prussians over six feet tall were killed at the battle of Waterloo*. The point of the analogy is that changes like rhotacism are historical events which happen at one point in time and are not repeated throughout the subsequent history of the language. See Anttila (1989: 59–60) for an account.

Watkins's Law The observation that, when the verbal morphology of a language is analogically reorganized, it is the third-singular form which serves as the model for re-creating the other forms. Just such reorganizations have occurred in Persian, Polish and Celtic, among others. The statement was made by Watkins (1962: 93–96).

wave model (also **wave theory**, Ger *Wellentheorie*) **A model of linguistic descent** put forward by J. Schmidt (1872). This model compares language changes to the ripples produced by tossing pebbles into a pond. A single change originates at some geographical point and proceeds to spread out over time over some smaller or larger area, before dissipating and spreading no further. Eventually, therefore, an originally rather homogeneous language breaks up into a complex **dialect continuum**, with each local variety having been reached by some changes but not by others. Like the **genetic model**, the wave model focuses on **divergence**, but, unlike the genetic model, it does not see change as converting an original language into several well-defined daughters. The wave model is highly consistent with the findings of **dialect geography**.

weakening Another term for **lenition**.

weak-ties theory of change A theory of **language change** developed by Milroy and Milroy (1985b) and Milroy (1992). Their idea is that a society characterized by strong ties between individuals will exhibit little language change and little tendency towards regional differentiation, while a society characterized by weak ties will exhibit rapid and conspicuous change and prominent regional differentiation. The principal cases adduced are Icelandic (strong ties) and English (weak ties), though the authors briefly consider other cases.

weak verb In the Germanic languages, a verb which inflects by adding a coronal suffix, like English *love*, *loved*, *loved* or *spend*, *spent*, *spent*. Compare **strong verb**.

Wellentheorie The German for **wave model**.

West Atlantic One of the major branches of the **Niger-Congo** family, containing about sixty languages spoken at the western edge of Africa. Among its best-known members are *Fula*, *Wolof* and *Temne*.

Wheeler's Law A putative shift of the word-accent in early Greek from the final mora to the penultimate mora when the preceding syllable was heavy, intended to account for variations in accent placement like /skoliós/ but /ple:síos/ and /trisí/ but /andrási/. First noted by Wheeler (1885), the law has many exceptions and is controversial. See Collinge (1985: 221–223) for an account with references.

whole-segment process Any phonological change in which an entire segment is introduced, lost, or moved to another location. Examples are **epenthesis**, **loss** (sense 1) and **metathesis**.

Whorf's Law The change of Proto-Uto-Aztecan */t/ to the affricate /tl/ before */a/ (and possibly elsewhere) in Nahuatl. The process was identified by Whorf (1937) and named by Manaster Ramer (1996c), who proposes some modifications.

widening Another term for **broadening**.

wide-scope comparison The term used by Manaster Ramer and Hitchcock (1996) for a type of comparison in which the investigator searches for *any* apparent matches in form and meaning which may exist in the languages being examined. Compare **narrow-scope comparison**.

Winter's Law A putative change in early **Balto-Slavic**, by which a short vowel with other than acute accent was lengthened when followed by one of the PIE mediae */b d g/. First proposed by Winter (1978), this interpretation is very controversial; see Collinge (1985: 225–227) for a critical discussion with references.

witness 1. In **reconstruction**, an attested linguistic form which is adduced as a **comparandum** and which supports the reconstruction proposed. 2. In **etymology** and **onomastics**, an attested linguistic form which provides support for a proposed etymology.

WLH model of language change The sociolinguistic model of **language change** put forward by Weinreich *et al.* (1968). The authors argue that an adequate theory of language change must successfully address five problems: the **constraints problem**, the **transition problem**, the **embedding problem**, the **evaluation problem** and the **actuation problem**. For an update and a literature review, see Labov (1982).

word-family The term used in Sino-Tibetan linguistics for a group of two or more words (usually within a single language) which are clearly of common origin but among which the historical details are obscure. See **skewed correspondence**.

word-formation The process of creating new lexical items by means other than **borrowing**. There are very many ways of coining new words. Among the most frequent are *compounding* (see **compound**) and **derivation** (*affixation*); others include **conversion**, *clipping* (see **clipped form**), *blending* (see **blend**), reanalysis (sense 1), **back-formation**, **acronyms**, **initialisms** and **word-manufacture**.

word-manufacture (also **invention**) The process of creating a new lexical item out of thin air. This is particularly common with trade names, such as *Teflon* and *Kodak*, but other examples exist, such as *blurb*, *quark* and *googol*. Some such formations may have a vague source, such as *gas*, derived from an arbitrary deformation of Greek *khaos* 'chaos', and Basque *idatzi* 'write', based on an archaic verb *iraatsi* 'carve'.

word-order change Change in the ordinary word-order patterns of a language, such as the change from Subject-Object-Verb (SOV) order in Latin to SVO or VSO order in its Romance descendants. Such change may result from internal developments like **markedness shift** or from *contact* with a language with a different word order (see **language-contact**). It is reported that American Sign Language has changed from SOV to SVO in the last century.

Wörter und Sachen An approach to **etymology** and **philology** which stresses the need to integrate linguistic work with ethnographic work on the history of culture. The applicability of the label overlaps with that of **linguistic palaeontology**, but the term is most obviously appropriate for cases in which cultural information is invoked in order to explain seemingly surprising semantic developments. For example, the development of *money* from Latin *monēta* 'who adminishes' can only be understood by realizing that an important Roman mint was located in the temple of Juno, whose epithet was *Monēta*; the word *southpaw* 'left-handed person' can only be understood by realizing that it originated in the game of baseball, in which the pitcher always has the south on his left. The unified study of language change and culture was championed by Jacob Grimm, and the *Wörter und Sachen* movement has been maximally prominent in Germany; a journal of this name was regularly published there until about 1940.

written evidence Evidence of language change derived from written records, sometimes particularly from comparison of written records of a single language at different times. Such evidence must be treated with caution, especially since writing systems tend to be conservative and hence may fail to indicate changes which have occurred in speech until much later, or even at all. Moreover, written texts tend to record only locally prestigious varieties of language and speech, and may silently exclude a great proportion of the real linguistic position.

written language 1. A language which is regularly written in a conventional writing system. 2. The written form of a language, as opposed to its spoken form, which may be substantially different.

Wurzelerweiterung The German for **root extension**.

Wurzeletymologie The German for **root etymology** (see **root cognates**).

Wurzelnomen The German for **root noun**.

x 1. When preposed in superscript to a reconstructed form, this symbol indicates that the reconstruction is erroneous. 2. A rare alternative to the **asterisk** (senses 2, 3).

Yakhontov's Principle A certain putative principle of **lexical replacement**. Sergei Yakhontov, in unpublished work, divides a slightly modified version of the 100-word **Swadesh word list** into a group of thirty-five words and one of sixty-five words, and then draws the following conclusion: if two languages are genetically related, the percentage of cognates within the thirty-five-word list must be higher than the percentage of cognates within the sixty-five-word list. For a presentation, see Starostin (1991: 59).

Yassic An extinct **Iranian** language, known only from a fifteenth-century word list found in Hungary; it was apparently the language of the Iranians who invaded Hungary in the thirteenth century.

Yatvingian An extinct and unrecorded **Baltic** language spoken along the Polish-Lithuanian border until perhaps the seventeenth century.

yeismo In Spanish, the merger as some kind of non-lateral palatal segment of the two consonants which in standard European Spanish are distinguished as /ʎ/ and /j/, and hence the merger of such pairs as *mallo* 'mallet' and *mayo* 'May'. Yeismo is widespread in southern Spain and in the Americas; the phonetic realization of the merged sound varies widely.

Yeniseian A small language family of Siberia. Its only surviving member is *Ket*, though several other members were recorded before they died out: *Yug*, *Kott*, *Arin*, *Pumpokol* and *Assan*.

yer Another spelling of **jer**.

'Yesterday's syntax is today's morphology' A slogan adopted by those who embrace (at least part of) the **linguistic cycle hypothesis**. It expresses the view that most morphological markers derive from the reduction of syntactic structures. This view was advanced by Givón (1971), but it has been criticized - for example, by Comrie (1980b).

Yokutsan A family of a dozen or more languages formerly spoken in and near the San Joaquin Valley of California. It is included in the **Penutian** hypothesis.

young-cuckoo model A particular model of **language change**. In this model, a newer form Y arises and coexists for a while with an older form X, with Y eventually ousting X from the language. A good deal of sociolinguistic work on language change is based upon this model. The term is introduced by Aitchison (1995). Compare **multiple-birth model, tadpole-into-frog model**.

Yuchi An **isolated language** formerly spoken in Georgia but now spoken in Oklahoma. No attempt at finding relatives for it has won acceptance.

Yukaghir A language spoken by several hundred people in northeastern Siberia. Its two close relatives, *Chuvantsy* and *Omok*, are extinct, and Yukaghir has been widely considered an isolated language, but see **Uralic-Yukaghir**.

Yukian A family of four extinct languages in northern California, including *Yuki* and *Wappo*. No broader genetic links are known, though several proposals exist.

Yuman A family of about a dozen languages spoken along the western end of the US-Mexican border; it includes *Yavapai*, *Havasupai*, *Mojave* and *Diegueño*. The extinct *Cochimí* was clearly related to Yuman in a larger *Cochimí-Yuman* family. No broader links are known, though one is suspected with **Pomoan**.

Zemgalian An extinct and unrecorded **Baltic** language once spoken in parts of Latvia and Lithuania.

Zend [*obsolete*] A former term for **Avestan**.

zero-derivation Another term for **conversion**.

zero grade See under **ablaut**.

zetacism The change of another sound into /z/, usually excluding simple **voicing** of /s/ to /z/. For example, some specialists believe that an inherited */r/ developed into /z/ in certain Turkic languages. Compare **rhotacism**.

Zipf's principles Two putative principles advanced by George Zipf, the first in 1929, the second in 1936. 1. A segment will remain phonologically stable so long as it remains within its range of acceptable frequency of incidence, but, if it becomes either too frequent or too rare, it is susceptible to phonological change. 2. A segment of very high frequency tends to become phonologically simple (unmarked). This second is one version of the **economy-of-effort principle**. See Collinge (1985: 256–258) for a survey with references.

zoomorphic model (also **pastoralist model**) The creation of spatial terms from names of body parts of animals, rather than from human beings, as when *back* and *head* are used to denote *on* and *front*, respectively. Compare **anthropomorphic model**.

Zuni An **isolated language** spoken in New Mexico. No attempt at finding relatives for it has won acceptance.

References

Abondolo, Daniel (ed.). 1998. *The Uralic Languages*. London: Routledge.

Adams, Valerie. 1973. *An Introduction to Modern English Word-Formation*. London: Longman.

Adelaar, Willem F. H. 1989. Review of Greenberg (1987). *Lingua* 78: 249–255.

Agud, Manuel and Antonio Tovar. 1988–. *Diccionario etimológico vasco*. Donostia/San Sebastián: Anejos del Seminario de Filología Vasca 'Julio de Urquijo'. Published in fascicles.

Aitchison, Jean. 1980. Review of Lightfoot (1979). *Linguistics* 18: 137–146.

——— 1995. 'Tadpoles, cuckoos, and multiple births: language contact and models of change'. In Fisiak (1995), pp. 1–13.

Aitken, A. J. 1981. 'The Scottish vowel-length rule'. In M. Benskin and M. L. Samuels (eds), *So Many people longages and tongs (for Angus McIntosh)*, pp. 131–157, Edinburgh: Middle English Dialect Project.

Ajello, Roberto. 1998. 'Armenian'. In Giacalone Ramat and Ramat (1998), pp. 197–227.

Algeo, John and Thomas Pyles. 1993. *The Origins and Development of the English Language*, 4th edn. Fort Worth, TX: Harcourt.

Andersen, Henning. 1968. 'IE *s after i, u, r, k in Baltic and Slavic'. *Acta Linguistica Hafniensia* 11: 171-190.

——— 1973. 'Abductive and deductive change'. *Language* 49: 765–793.

——— 1980. 'Morphological change'. In Fisiak (1980), pp. 1–50.

——— 1987. 'From auxiliary to desinence'. In Martin B. Harris and Paolo Ramat (eds), *Historical Development of Auxiliaries*, pp. 21–51, Berlin: Mouton de Gruyter.

——— 1988. 'Centre and periphery: adoption, diffusion and spread'. In J. Fisiak (ed.), *Historical Dialectology*, pp. 39–85, Berlin: Mouton de Gruyter.

——— 1998. 'Slavic'. In Giacalone Ramat and Ramat (1998), pp. 415–453.

Anderson, John M. and Charles Jones (eds). 1974. *Historical Linguistics*, 2 vols. Amsterdam: North Holland.

Anderson, Stephen R. 1988. 'Morphological change'. In Newmeyer (1988), vol. I, pp. 324–362.

Anttila, Raimo. 1969. *PIE Schwebeablaut*. Berkeley/Los Angeles: University of California.

———— 1977. *Analogy*. The Hague: Mouton.

———— 1989. *An Introduction to Historical and Comparative Linguistics*, 2nd edn. Amsterdam: John Benjamins.

Asher, R. E. and J. M. Y. Simpson (eds). 1994. *Encyclopedia of Language and Linguistics*, 10 vols. Oxford: Pergamon.

Bach, Emmon and Robert T. Harms. 1972. 'How do languages get crazy rules?' In Stockwell and Macaulay (1972), pp. 1–21.

Bailey, Charles-James N. 1996. *Essays on Time-Based Linguistic Analysis*. Oxford: Clarendon Press.

Baker, Carl L. 1979. 'Syntactic theory and the projection problem'. *Linguistic Inquiry* 10: 533–581.

Bakker, Peter. 1997. *A Language of Our Own: The Genesis of Michif, the Mixed Cree-French Language of the Canadian Métis*. Oxford: Oxford University Press.

Bakker, Peter and Maarten Mous (eds). 1994. *Mixed Languages*. Amsterdam: Institute for Functional Research into Language and Language Use.

Bakker, Peter and Robert A. Papen. 1997. 'Michif: a mixed language based on Cree and French'. In Thomason (1997a), pp. 295–363.

Baldi, Philip. 1983. *An Introduction to the Indo-European Languages*. Carbondale, IL: Southern Illinois University Press.

———— (ed.). 1990. *Linguistic Change and Reconstruction Methodology*. Berlin: Mouton de Gruyter.

Baldi, Philip and Ronald N. Werth (eds). 1978. *Readings in Historical Phonology: Chapters in the Theory of Sound Change*. University Park, PA: Pennsylvania State University Press.

Ball, Martin J. and Glyn E. Jones (eds). 1993. *The Celtic Languages*. London: Routledge.

Barber, Charles. 1993. *The English Language: A Historical Introduction*. Cambridge: Cambridge University Press.

Bartholomae, Christian. 1883. *Handbuch der altiranischen Dialekte*. Leipzig: Breitkopf & Härtel. Reprinted (1968), Wiesbaden: Sandig.

Bàrtoli, Matteo. 1930. 'Ancora una deviazione del greco all'ossitonia asio-europea'. *Rivista di filologia e di istruzione classica* 58: 24–29.

Bateman, Richard, Ives Goddard, Richard O'Grady, V. A. Funk, Rich Mooi, W. John Kress and Peter Cannell. 1990. 'Speaking of forked tongues: the feasibility of reconciling human phylogeny and the history of language'. *Current Anthropology* 31: 1–183.

Bauer, Robert S. 1992. '**SOAP* rings the globe'. *Linguistics of the Tibeto-Burman Area* 15(1): 125–137.

———— 1993/94. 'Global etymology of **KOLO* "wheel"'. *Dhumbadji!* 1(3): 3–17.

Baxter, William H. 1995. '"A stronger affinity . . . than could have been produced by accident": a probabilistic comparison of Old Chinese and Tibeto-Burman'. In W. S.-Y. Wang (ed.), *The Ancestry of the Chinese Language*, pp. 1–39, Berkeley: *Journal of Chinese Linguistics* Monograph Series, no. 8.

—— 1998. 'Response to Oswalt and Ringe'. In Salmons and Joseph (1998), pp. 217–236.

Baxter, William H. and Alexis Manaster Ramer. 1996. Review of Ringe (1992). *Diachronica* 13: 371–384.

Beade, P. 1974. 'Diffusion, generalization and the High German shift'. In Anderson and Jones (1974), vol. I, pp. 61–70.

Beekes, Robert S. P. 1995. *Comparative Indo-European Linguistics*. Amsterdam: John Benjamins.

Behaghel, Otto. 1932. *Deutsche Syntax IV.* Heidelberg: Winter.

Bellwood, Peter. 1997. 'Prehistoric cultural explanations for widespread linguistic families'. In McConvell and Evans (1997), pp. 123–134.

Bender, Marvin L. 1969. 'Chance CVC correspondences in unrelated languages'. *Language* 45: 519–531.

Bendor-Samuels, John and Rhonda L. Hartell (eds). 1989. *The Niger-Congo Languages*. Lanham, MD: University Press of America.

Benedict, Paul K. 1942. 'Thai, Kadai, and Indonesian: a new alignment in southeastern Asia'. *American Anthropologist* 44: 576–601.

—— 1975. *Austro-Thai: Language and Culture*. New Haven, CN: Yale University Press.

Bennett, Paul. 1979. 'Observations on the Transparency Principle'. *Linguistics* 17: 843–861.

Benveniste, Émile. 1935. *Origines de la formation des noms en indo-européen*. Paris: Adrien-Maisonneuve.

—— 1968. 'Mutations of linguistic categories'. In Lehmann and Malkiel (1968), pp. 83–94.

Bergin, Osborn J. 1938. 'On the syntax of the verb in Old Irish'. *Ériu* 12: 197–214.

Bever, T. G. and D. T. Langendoen. 1971. 'A dynamic model of the evolution of language'. *Linguistic Inquiry* 2: 433–460.

—— 1972. 'The interaction of speech perception and grammatical structure in the evolution of language'. In Stockwell and Macaulay (1972), pp. 32–95.

Bichakjian, Bernard H. 1988. *Evolution in Language*. Ann Arbor, MI: Karoma.

—— 1997. 'Evolution and the biological correlates of linguistic features'. In Blench and Spriggs (1997), pp. 31–42.

Bickerton, Derek. 1981. *Roots of Language*. Ann Arbor, MI: Karoma.

—— 1984. 'The language bioprogram hypothesis'. *Behavioral and Brain Sciences* 7: 173–221.

—— 1988. 'Creole languages and the bioprogram'. In Newmeyer (1988), vol. II, pp. 268–284.

Blake, N. F. 1996. *A History of the English Language*. London: Macmillan.

Blansitt, Edward L. 1988. 'Datives and allatives'. In Michael Hammond, Edith Moravcsik and Jessica Wirth (eds), *Studies in Syntactic Typology*, pp. 173–191, Amsterdam: John Benjamins.

Blench, Roger M. 1995. 'Is Niger-Congo simply a branch of Nilo-Saharan?' In R. Nicolai and F. Rottland (eds), *Proceedings: Fifth Nilo-Saharan Linguistics Colloquium, Nice, 1992*, pp. 83–130, Cologne: Rudiger Köppe.

———— 1997a. 'General introduction'. In Blench and Spriggs (1997), pp. 1–17.

———— 1997b. 'Crabs, turtles and frogs: linguistic keys to early African subsistence systems'. In Blench and Spriggs (1997), pp. 166–183.

Blench, Roger and Matthew Spriggs (eds). 1997. *Archaeology and Language I: Theoretical and Methodological Orientations*. London: Routledge.

Bloomfield, Leonard. 1927. 'Literate and illiterate speech'. *American Speech* 2 (10): 432–439. Reprinted in Charles F. Hockett (ed.) (1970), *A Leonard Bloomfield Anthology*, pp. 147–156, Bloomington, IN: University of Indiana Press.

Blust, Robert. 1970. 'Proto-Austronesian addenda'. *Oceanic Linguistics* 9 (2): 104–162.

———— 1980. 'Austronesian etymologies'. *Oceanic Linguistics* 19: 1–181.

———— 1988. 'Beyond the morpheme: Austronesian root theory and related matters'. In Richard McGinn (ed.), *Studies in Austronesian Linguistics*, pp. 3–90, Columbus, OH: Ohio University Monographs in International Studies, Southeast Asia Series, no. 76.

———— 1990. 'Summary report: linguistic change and reconstruction methodology in the Austronesian language family'. In Baldi (1990), pp. 133–153.

———— 1996. 'The Neogrammarian Hypothesis and pandemic irregularity'. In Durie and Ross (1996), pp. 135–156.

Bolinger, Dwight. 1977. *Meaning and Form*. London: Longman.

Bomhard, Allan R. 1990. 'A survey of the comparative phonology of the so-called "Nostratic" languages'. In Baldi (1990), pp. 331–358.

———— 1996. *Indo-European and the Nostratic Hypothesis*. Charleston, SC: Signum.

Bomhard, Allan R. and John C. Kerns. 1994. *The Nostratic Macrofamily: A Study in Distant Linguistic Relationship*. Berlin: Mouton de Gruyter.

Bonfante, Giulio and Larissa Bonfante. 1983. *The Etruscan Language: An Introduction*. Manchester: Manchester University Press.

Breivik, Leiv Egil and Ernst Håkon Jahr (eds). 1989. *Language Change: Contributions to the Study of Its Causes*. Berlin: Mouton de Gruyter.

Breton, Roland J.-L. 1991. *Geolinguistics: Language Dynamics and Ethnolinguistic Geography*, tr. Harold F. Schiffman. Ottawa: University of Ottawa Press.

Bright, William (ed.) 1992. *International Encyclopedia of Linguistics*, 4 vols. Oxford: Oxford University Press.

Brown, C. H. 1979. 'A theory of lexical change (with examples from folk biology, human anatomical partonomy and other domains)'. *Anthropological Linguistics* 21: 257–276.

Brown, C. H. and Stanley R. Witkowski. 1983. 'Polysemy, lexical change, and cultural importance'. *Man* 18: 72–89.

Brugmann, Karl. 1876. 'Zur Geschichte der stammabstufenden Declinationen'. *Studien zur griechische und lateinische Grammatik* 9: 361–406.

───── 1879. 'Zur Geschichte der Nominalsuffixe -as-, -jas- und -vas-'. *Zeitschrift für vergleichende Sprachforschung auf dem Gebiete der indogermanischen Sprachen* 24: 1–99.

Brugmann, Karl and Berthold Delbrück. 1886–1900. *Grundriss der vergleichenden Grammatik der indogermanischen Sprachen*, 5 vols. Strasburg: Trübner.

Buccelati, Giorgio. 1997. 'Akkadian'. In Hetzron (1997), pp. 69–99.

Bugge, E. Sophus. 1874. 'Altitalische Studien'. *Zeitschrift für vergleichende Sprachforschung auf dem Gebiete der indogermanischen Sprachen* 22: 388–466.

───── 1887. 'Etymologische Studien über germanische Lautverschiebung'. *Beiträge zur Geschichte der deutschen Sprache und Literatur* 12: 399–430.

Bybee, Joan and Dan I. Slobin. 1982. 'Why small children cannot change language on their own: suggestions from the English past tense'. In Anders Ahlqvist (ed.), *Papers from the 5th International Conference on Historical Linguistics*, pp. 29-37, Amsterdam: John Benjamins.

Bybee, Joan L., William Pagliuca and Revere D. Perkins. 1991. 'Back to the future'. In Traugott and Heine (1991), vol. II, pp. 17–58.

Bybee, Joan, Revere Perkins and William Pagliuca. 1994. *The Evolution of Grammar*. Chicago, IL: University of Chicago Press.

Caland, Wilhelm. 1892. 'Beiträge zur Kenntniss des Avesta, no. 19'. *Zeitschrift für vergleichende Sprachforschung auf dem Gebiete der indogermanischen Sprachen* 31: 266–268.

───── 1893. 'Beiträge zur Kenntniss des Avesta, no. 26'. *Zeitschrift für vergleichende Sprachforschung auf dem Gebiete der indogermanischen Sprachen* 32: 592.

Caldwell, Robert. 1856. *A Comparative Grammar of the Dravidian or South-Indian Family of Languages*. London. Reprinted (1976), Madras: University of Madras Press.

Callaghan, Catherine. 1980. 'An "Indo-European" type paradigm in Proto Eastern Miwok'. In Katheryn Klar, Margaret Langdon and Shirley Silver (eds), *American Indian and Indoeuropean Studies: Papers in Honor of Madison S. Beeler*, pp. 31–41, The Hague: Mouton.

Camara, J. Mattoso, Jr. 1972. *The Portuguese Language*, tr. Anthony J. Naro. Chicago, IL: University of Chicago Press.

Campanile, Enrico. 1998. 'The Indo-Europeans: origins and culture'. In Giacalone Ramat and Ramat (1998), pp. 1–24.

Campbell, Lyle. 1976. 'Language contact and sound change'. In William Christie (ed.), *Current Progress in Historical Linguistics*, pp. 181–194. Amsterdam: North Holland.

───── 1988. Review of Greenberg (1987). *Language* 64: 591–615.

───── 1991. 'Some grammaticalization changes in Estonian and their implications'. In Traugott and Heine (1991), vol. I, pp. 285–299.

───── 1996. 'On sound change and challenges to regularity'. In Durie and Ross (1996), pp. 72–89.

───── 1997a. *American Indian Languages: The Historical Linguistics of Native America*. Oxford: Oxford University Press.

———— 1997b. 'Amerind personal pronouns: a second opinion'. *Language* 73: 339–351.

———— 1998. *Historical Linguistics*. Edinburgh: Edinburgh University Press.

Campbell, Lyle and Marianne Mithun (eds). 1979. *The Languages of Native America: Historical and Comparative Assessment*. Austin, TX: University of Texas Press.

Carlton, Terence R. 1990. *Introduction to the Phonological History of the Slavic Languages*. Columbus, OH: Slavica.

Cavalli-Sforza, Luigi Luca. 1991. 'Genes, people and languages'. *Scientific American* 265 (5) (November), 72–78.

Cavalli-Sforza, Luigi Luca, Eric Minch and J. L. Mountain. 1992. 'Coevolution of genes and languages revisited'. *Proceedings of the National Academy of Sciences of the USA* 89: 5620–5624.

Cavalli-Sforza, Luigi Luca, Alberto Piazza, Paolo Menozzi and Joanna Mountain. 1988. 'Reconstruction of human evolution: bringing together genetic, archaeological, and linguistic data'. *Proceedings of the National Academy of Sciences of the USA* 85: 6002–6006.

Cedergren, Henrietta and David Sankoff. 1974. 'Variable rules: performance as a statistical reflection of competence'. *Language* 50: 333–355.

Chambers, J. K. and Peter Trudgill. 1998. *Dialectology*, 2nd edn. Cambridge: Cambridge University Press.

Chen, Matthew and William Wang. 1975. 'Sound change: implementation and actuation'. *Language* 51: 255–281.

Chew, J. J. 1976. 'Standard Japanese and the Harara dialect: a case of linguistic convergence'. *Journal of the Association of Teachers of Japanese* 11 (2/3).

———— 1981. 'The relation between Japanese, Korean, and the Altaic languages: in what sense genetic?' *Bulletin of the Institute of Linguistic Sciences* (Kyoto Sangyo University) 2 (4): 7–38.

Chomsky, Noam and Morris Halle. 1968. *The Sound Pattern of English*. New York: Harper and Row.

Christie, William M., Jr. 1982. 'Locative, possessive and existential in Swahili'. *Foundations of Language* 6: 166–177.

Christy, C. 1983. *Uniformitarianism in Linguistics*. Amsterdam: John Benjamins.

Clackson, James. 1994. *The Linguistic Relation Between Armenian and Greek*. Oxford: Blackwell/Philological Society.

Clark, Cecily. 1991. 'Towards a reassessment of "Anglo-Norman influence on English place-names"'. In P. Sture Ureland and George Broderick (eds), *Language Contact in the British Isles: Proceedings of the Eighth International Symposium on Language Contact in Europe, Douglas, Isle of Man, 1988*, pp. 275–295, Tübingen: Niemeyer. Reprinted in Peter Jackson (ed.) (1995), *Words, Names and History: Selected Writings of Cecily Clark*, pp. 144–155, Cambridge: D. S. Brewer.

Claudi, Ulrike. 1994. 'Word order change as category change: the Mande case'. In Pagliuca (1994), pp. 191–231.

Claudi, Ulrike and Bernd Heine. 1986. 'On the metaphorical basis of grammar'. *Studies in Language* 10 (2): 297–335.

Coates, Richard. 1994. 'Morphophonemics'. In Asher and Simpson (1994), vol. 5, pp. 2602–2612.

Collinder, Björn. 1965. *An Introduction to the Uralic Languages*. Berkeley, CA: University of California Press.

Collinge, N. E. 1985. *The Laws of Indo-European*. Amsterdam: John Benjamins.

Comrie, Bernard. 1980a. 'The order of case and possessive suffixes in Uralic languages: an approach to the comparative-historical problem'. *Lingua Posnaniensis* 23: 81–86.

———— 1980b. 'Morphology and word order reconstruction: problems and prospects'. In Fisiak (1980), pp. 83–96.

———— 1993. 'Typology and reconstruction'. In Jones (1993), pp. 74–97.

———— 1998. 'The Indo-European linguistic family: genetic and typological perspectives'. In Giacalone Ramat and Ramat (1998), pp. 74–97.

Comrie, Bernard and Greville G. Corbett (eds). 1993. *The Slavonic Languages*. London: Routledge.

Corominas, Juan and José A. Pascual. 1980. *Diccionario crítico etimológico castellano e hispánico*, 6 vols. Madrid: Gredos.

Craig, Colette. 1991. 'Ways to go in Rama: a case study in polygrammaticalization'. In Traugott and Heine (1991), vol. II, pp. 455–492.

Crowley, Terry. 1997. *An Introduction to Historical Linguistics*, 3rd edn. Oxford: Oxford University Press.

Crystal, David. 1997. *The Cambridge Encyclopedia of Language*, 2nd edn. Cambridge: Cambridge University Press.

Dahl, Östen. 1979. 'Typology of sentence negation'. *Linguistics* 17: 79–106.

Daniels, Peter T. and William Bright (eds). 1996. *The World's Writing Systems*. Oxford: Oxford University Press.

Décsy, Gyula. 1983. *Global Linguistic Connections*. Bloomington, IN: Eurolingua.

Demiraj, Shaban. 1998. 'Albanian'. In Giacalone Ramat and Ramat (1998), pp. 480–501.

Denison, David. 1992. 'Counterfactual *may have*'. In Gerritsen and Stein (1992), pp. 229–256.

———— 1993. *English Historical Syntax*. London: Longman.

Devoto, Giacomo. 1978. *The Languages of Italy*, tr. V. Louise Katainen. Chicago, IL: University of Chicago Press.

Dillard, James L. 1992. *A History of American English*. London: Longman.

Dimmendaal, Gerrit J. 1992. 'Nilo-Saharan languages'. In Bright (1992), vol. 3, pp. 100–104.

Disterheft, Dorothy. 1990. 'The role of adaptive rules in language change'. *Diachronica* 7: 181–198.

Dixon, R. M. W. 1980. *The Languages of Australia*. Cambridge: Cambridge University Press.

———— 1997. *The Rise and Fall of Languages*. Cambridge: Cambridge University Press.

Dixon, Roland B. and Alfred L. Kroeber. 1913. 'New linguistic families in California'. *American Anthropologist* 15: 647–655.

Dolgopolsky, Aharon. 1964. 'Gipoteza drevnejšego rodstva jazykovyx semei severnoj Evrazii s verojatnostnoj točki zrenija'. *Voprosy jazykoznanija* 2: 53–63. English translation, 'A probabilistic hypothesis concerning the oldest relationships among the language families in northern Eurasia', in Vitalij V. Shevoroshkin and Thomas L. Markey (eds) (1986), *Typology, Relationship and Time: A Collection of Papers on Language Change and Relationship by Soviet Linguists*, pp. 27–50, Ann Arbor, MI: Karoma.

——— 1965. 'Metody rekonstrukcii obščindoevropejskogo jazyka i sibiroevropejskaja gipoteza'. *Ètimologija* 1964: 259–270.

——— 1998. *The Nostratic Macrofamily and Linguistic Palaeontology*. Cambridge: McDonald Institute for Archaeological Research.

Dolobko, M. G. 1927. 'Nóč'-nočés', ósen'-osenés', zimá-zimús', léto-létos''. *Slavia* 5: 678–717.

Donegan, Patricia J. and David Stampe. 1979. 'The study of natural phonology'. In Daniel Dinnsen (ed.), *Current Approaches to Phonological Theory*, pp. 126–173, Bloomington, IN: Indiana University Press.

Dorian, Nancy C. (ed.) 1989. *Investigating Obsolescence: Studies in Language Contraction and Death*. Cambridge: Cambridge University Press.

Dorsey, James Owen. 1885. 'On the comparative phonology of four Siouan languages'. *Smithsonian Institution Annual Report for 1883*, pp. 919–929. Washington: Government Printing Office.

Durie, Mark and Malcolm Ross (eds). 1996. *The Comparative Method Reviewed*. Oxford: Oxford University Press.

Dybo, Vladimir A. 1962. 'O rekonstrukcii udarenija v praslavjanskom glagole'. *Voprosy slavjanskogo jazykoznanija* 6: 3–27.

Dyen, Isidore. 1956. 'Language distribution and migration theory'. *Language* 32: 611–626.

——— 1965. 'A lexicostatistical classification of the Austronesian languages'. *International Journal of American Linguistics, Memoir* 19 (vol. 31, no. 1).

Ebeling, Carl L. 1963. 'Questions of relative chronology in Common Slavic and Russian phonology'. In [no ed.], *Dutch Contributions to the Fifth International Congress of Slavicists*, pp. 27–42, The Hague: Mouton.

Ebert, Robert Peter. 1992. 'Internal and external factors in syntactic change in an historical speech community'. In Gerritsen and Stein (1992), pp. 201–228.

Edgerton, F. 1934. 'Sievers' law and Indo-European weak grade vocalism'. *Language* 10: 235–265.

——— 1943. 'The Indo-European semivowels'. *Language* 19: 83–124.

Ehret, Chris. 1995. *Reconstructing Proto-Afro-Asiatic (Proto Afrasian): Vowels, Tone, Consonants, and Vocabulary*. Berkeley, CA: University of California Press.

Elcock, W. D. 1975. *The Romance Languages*, revised by John N. Green. London: Faber and Faber.

Embleton, Sheila. 1986. *Statistics in Historical Linguistics*. Bochum: Brockmeyer.

——— 1991. 'Mathematical methods of genetic classification'. In Lamb and Mitchell (1991), pp. 365–388.

——— 1992. 'Historical linguistics: mathematical concepts'. In Bright (1992), vol. 2, pp. 131–135.

Endzelin, I. M. 1922. *Lettische Grammatik*. Riga: Gulbis; Heidelberg: Winter.

——— 1948. *Baltu valodu skanas un formas*. Riga: Latvijas valsts izdevniectba.

Ernout, A. and Antoine Meillet. 1959. *Dictionnaire étymologique de la langue latine: histoire des mots*, 4th edn., J. André (ed.). Paris: Klincksieck.

Ewert, Alfred. 1933. *The French Language*. London: Faber and Faber.

Faber, Alice. 1997. 'Genetic subgrouping of the Semitic languages'. In Hetzron (1997), pp. 3–15.

Faber, Alice, Marianna Di Paolo and Catherine T. Best. 1995. 'The peripatetic history of Middle English *ɛ*'. Unpublished paper, Haskins Laboratories, Yale University.

——— 1997. 'Perceiving the unperceivable: the acquisition of near-merged forms'. Unpublished paper, Haskins Laboratories, Yale University.

Ferguson, Charles. 1959. 'Diglossia'. *Word* 15: 325–340. Reprinted in Pier Paolo Giglioli (ed.) (1972), *Language and Social Context*, pp. 232–251, London: Penguin.

Fischer, Wolfdietrich. 1997. 'Classical Arabic'. In Hetzron (1997), pp. 187–219.

Fisiak, Jacek (ed.). 1980. *Historical Morphology*. The Hague: Mouton.

——— (ed.). 1990. *Historical Linguistics and Philology*. Berlin: Mouton de Gruyter.

——— (ed.). 1995. *Linguistic Change under Contact Conditions*. Berlin: Mouton de Gruyter.

Foley, James. 1977. *Foundations of Theoretical Phonology*. Cambridge: Cambridge University Press.

Foley, William. 1986. *The Papuan Languages of New Guinea*. Cambridge: Cambridge University Press.

Fortunatov, F. F. 1880. 'Zur vergleichenden Betonungslehre des lituslavischen Sprachen'. *Archiv für slavische Philologie* 4: 575–589.

——— 1881. 'L + Dental im Altindischen'. *Beiträge zur Kunde der indogermanischen Sprachen* 6: 215–220.

Fourquet, Jean. 1976. 'Spuren eines vorindogermanischen Wechsels Tenuis/ Aspirata'. *Sprachwissenschaft* 1: 108–114.

Fox, Anthony. 1995. *Linguistic Reconstruction*. Oxford: Oxford University Press.

Francis, W. N. 1983. *Dialectology: An Introduction*. London: Longman.

Freeborn, Dennis. 1992. *From Old English to Standard English*. London: Macmillan.

Friedrich, Johannes. 1952. *Hethitisches Wörterbuch*. Heidelberg: Winter.

——— 1960. *Hethitisches Elementarbuch*, vol. I. Heidelberg: Winter.

Fries, Charles C. and Kenneth L. Pike. 1949. 'Coexistent phonemic systems'. *Language* 25: 29–50.

Gamkrelidze, Thomas V. and Vjačeslav V. Ivanov. 1973. 'Sprachtypologie und die Rekonstruktion der gemeinindg. Verschlüsse'. *Phonetica* 27: 150–156.

———— 1995. *Indo-European and the Indo-Europeans*, 2 vols. Berlin: Mouton de Gruyter.

Garde, Paul. 1961. 'Réflexions sur les différences phonétiques entre les langues slaves'. *Word* 17: 34–62.

———— 1976. *L'histoire de l'accentuation slave*, 2 vols. Paris: Institut d'Études Slaves.

Georgiev, Vladimir. 1965. 'Problèmes phonématiques du slave commun'. *Revue des Études Slaves* 44: 7–17.

Gerritsen, Marinel and Dieter Stein (eds). 1992. *Internal and External Factors in Syntactic Change*. Berlin: Mouton de Gruyter.

Giacalone Ramat, Anna and Paolo Ramat (eds). 1998. *The Indo-European Languages*. London: Routledge.

Givón, Talmy. 1971. 'Historical syntax and synchronic morphology: an archaeologist's field trip'. *Chicago Linguistic Society Papers* 7: 394–415.

———— 1977. 'The drift from VSO to SVO in biblical Hebrew: the pragmatics of tense-aspect'. In Li (1977), pp. 181–254.

———— 1991. 'Isomorphism in the grammatical code: cognitive and biological considerations'. *Studies in Language* 15 (1): 85–114.

Goddard, Ives. 1987. Review of Greenberg (1987). *Current Anthropology* 28: 656–657.

Gordon, Cyrus H. 1997. 'Amorite and Eblaite'. In Hetzron (1997), pp. 100–113.

Grace, George W. 1981. 'Indirect inheritance and the aberrant Austronesian languages'. In J. Hollyman and A. Pawley (eds), *Studies in Pacific Languages and Cultures*, pp. 255–267, Auckland: Linguistic Society of New Zealand.

———— 1990. 'The "aberrant" (vs "exemplary") Melanesian languages'. In Baldi (1990), pp. 155–173.

———— 1996. 'Regularity of change in what?' In Durie and Ross (1996), pp. 157–179.

Graddol, David, Dick Leith and Joan Swann. 1996. *English: History, Diversity and Change*. London: Routledge/Open University.

Gragg, Gene. 1997. 'Ge'ez (Ethiopic)'. In Hetzron (1997), pp. 242–260.

Grammont, Maurice. 1933. *Traité de phonétique*. Paris: Delagrave.

Grassmann, Hermann. 1863. 'Über die Aspiration und ihr gleichzeitiges Vorhandensein im An- und Auslaute der Wurzeln'. *Zeitschrift für vergleichende Sprachforschung auf dem Gebiete der indogermanischen Sprachen* 12: 81–138. Partial English translation in W. P. Lehmann (1967: 109–131).

Greenberg, Joseph. 1960. 'The general classification of Central and South American languages'. In Anthony F. C. Wallace (ed.), *Men and Cultures: Selected Papers of the Fifth International Congress of the Anthropological and Ethnological Sciences*, pp. 791–794, Philadelphia, PA: University of Pennsylvania Press.

———— 1963a. 'Some universals of grammar with particular reference to the order of meaningful elements'. In Joseph H. Greenberg (ed.), *Universals of Language*, pp. 73–113, Cambridge, MA: MIT Press.

———— 1963b. *The Languages of Africa*. Bloomington, IN: University of Indiana Press.

———— 1971. 'The Indo-Pacific hypothesis'. In Thomas A. Sebeok (ed.), *Current Trends in Linguistics*, vol. 8: *Linguistics in Oceania*, pp. 807–871, The Hague: Mouton.

———— 1978. 'How does a language acquire gender markers?' In Greenberg *et al.* (1978), vol. 3, pp. 47–82.

———— 1987. *Language in the Americas*. Stanford, CA: Stanford University Press.

———— 1989. 'Classification of American Indian languages: a reply to Campbell'. *Language* 65: 107–114.

———— 1991. 'The last stages of grammatical elements: contractive and expansive desemanticization'. In Traugott and Heine (1991), vol. I, pp. 301–314.

Greenberg, Joseph H., Charles Ferguson and Edith Moravcsik (eds). 1978. *Universals of Human Language*, 4 vols. Stanford, CA: Stanford University Press.

Greenberg, Joseph H. and Merritt Ruhlen. 1992. 'Linguistic origins of native Americans'. *Scientific American* 267 (5) (November), pp. 60–65.

Greenberg, Joseph H., Christy G. Turner II and Stephen L. Zegura. 1986. 'The settlement of the Americas: a comparison of the linguistic, dental and genetic evidence'. *Current Anthropology* 27: 477–497.

Greenberg, Joseph H., Wallace Chafe, Regna Darnell, Ives Goddard, Victor Golla, Dell Hymes, Richard A. Rogers and J. David Sapir. 1987. Presentation and review of Greenberg (1987). *Current Anthropology* 28: 647–667.

Gregerson, Edgar A. 1972. 'Kongo-Saharan'. *Journal of African Languages* 11: 69–89.

Grimes, Barbara F. (ed.) 1992. *Ethnologue: Languages of the World*, 12th edn. Dallas, TX: Summer Institute of Linguistics.

Grimm, Jacob. 1822. *Deutsche Grammatik*, vol I (of four, published 1822–37), 2nd edn. Göttingen: Dieterich.

Gudschinsky, Sarah C. 1956. 'The ABC's of lexicostatistics (glottochronology)'. *Word* 12: 175–220.

Gumperz, John and Robert Wilson. 1971. 'Convergence and creolization: a case from the Indo-Aryan/Dravidian border in India'. In Dell Hymes (ed.), *Pidginization and Creolization of Languages*, pp. 151–167, Cambridge: Cambridge University Press.

Gyarmathi, Sámuel. 1799. *Affinitas linguae Hungaricae cum linguis fennicae originis grammatice demonstrata*. Göttingen. Reprinted (1968), Bloomington, IN: University of Indiana Press.

Haas, Mary R. 1968. *The Prehistory of Languages*. The Hague: Mouton.

Hagège, Claude. 1990. *The Dialogic Species: A Linguistic Contribution to the Social Sciences*, tr. Sharon L. Shelby. New York: Columbia University Press.

———— 1993. *The Language Builder*. Amsterdam: John Benjamins.

Haiman, John. 1994. 'Ritualization and the development of language'. In Pagliuca (1994), pp. 3–28.

Haiman, John and Paola Benincà. 1992. *The Rhaeto-Romance Languages*. London: Routledge.

Halle, Morris. 1962. 'Phonology in generative grammar'. *Word* 18: 54–72. Reprinted in Jerry A. Fodor and Jerrold J. Katz (eds), *The Structure of Language: Readings in the Philosophy of Language*, pp. 334–352, Englewood Cliffs, NJ: Prentice-Hall.

Hamp, Eric P. 1974. 'The Mac Neill-O'Brien law'. *Ériu* 25: 172–180.

——— 1998. 'Some draft principles for classification'. In Salmons and Joseph (1998), pp. 13–15.

Harms, Robert T. 1977. 'The Uralic-Yukaghir focus system: a problem in remote genetic relations'. In Paul J. Hopper (ed.), *Studies in Descriptive and Historical Linguistics*, pp. 301–316, Amsterdam: John Benjamins.

Harris, Alice C. and Lyle Campbell. 1995. *Historical Syntax in Cross-linguistic Perspective*. Cambridge: Cambridge University Press.

Harris, Martin. 1978. *The Evolution of French Syntax: A Comparative Approach*. London: Longman.

Harris, Martin and Nigel Vincent (eds). 1997. *Romance Languages*. London: Routledge.

Hartmann, H. 1936. *Studien über die Betonung der Adjektiva im Russischen. Veröffentlichungen des Slavistischen Instituts*, University of Berlin, 16. Max Vasmer (ed.). Leipzig: Harrassowitz.

Haspelmath, Martin. 1993. 'The diachronic externalization of inflection'. *Linguistics* 31: 279–309.

Havet, Louis. 1885. 'Mélanges latins'. *Mémoires de la Société de Linguistique de Paris* 6: 11–39.

Heath, Jeffrey. 1978. *Linguistic Diffusion in Arnhem Land*. Canberra: Australian Institute of Aboriginal Studies.

——— 1994. Review of Nichols (1992). *Anthropological Linguistics* 36: 92–96.

Hegedűs, Irén. 1997. 'Principles for palaeolinguistic reconstruction'. In Blench and Spriggs (1997), pp. 65–73.

Heine, Bernd. 1989. 'Adpositions in African languages'. *Linguistique Africaine* 2: 77–127.

Heine, Bernd, Ulrike Claudi and Friederike Hünnemeyer. 1991a. *Grammaticalization: A Conceptual Framework*. Chicago, IL: University of Chicago Press.

——— 1991b. 'From cognition to grammar evidence from African languages'. In Traugott and Heine (1991), vol. 1, pp. 149–187.

Heine, Bernd and Mechthild Reh. 1984. *Grammaticalization and Reanalysis in African Languages*. Hamburg: Helmut Buske.

Hetzron, Robert. 1990. 'Dialectal variation in Proto-Afroasiatic'. In Baldi (1990), pp. 577–597.

——— (ed.). 1997. *The Semitic Languages*. London: Routledge.

Hirt, Herman. 1895. *Der indogermanische Akzent: Ein Handbuch*. Strasbourg: Trübner.

——— 1904. 'Zur Entstehung der griechischen Betonung'. *Indogermanische Forschungen* 16: 71–92.

Hjelmslev, Louis. 1932. *Études baltiques*. Copenhagen: Levin & Munksgaard.

Hock, Hans Henrich. 1986. *Principles of Historical Linguistics*. Berlin: Mouton de Gruyter.

Hock, Hans Henrich and Brian D. Joseph. 1996. *Language History, Language Change and Language Relationship: An Introduction to Historical and Comparative Linguistics*. Berlin: Mouton de Gruyter.

Hockett, Charles F. 1958. *A Course in Modern Linguistics*. New York: Macmillan.

Hodge, Carleton T. 1998. 'The implications of Lislakh for Nostratic'. In Salmons and Joseph (1998), pp. 237–256.

Hoenigswald, Henry M. 1960. *Language Change and Linguistic Reconstruction*. Chicago, IL: University of Chicago Press.

―――― 1998. 'Greek'. In Giacalone Ramat and Ramat (1998), pp. 228–260.

Hoffman, Karl. 1967. *Der Injunctiv im Veda*. Heidelberg: Winter.

Holm, John. 1988/89. *Pidgins and Creoles*, 2 vols. Cambridge: Cambridge University Press.

Holtzmann, Adolf. 1835. Review of H. F. Massman, *Skeireins*. *Heidelberger Jahrbücher der Literatur* 28: 854–863.

Hopper, Paul J. 1973. 'Glottalized and murmured occlusives in IE'. *Glossa* 7: 141–166.

―――― 1979a. 'Aspect and foregrounding in discourse'. In Talmy Givón (ed.), *Discourse and Syntax: Syntax and Semantics* 12, pp. 213–241, New York: Academic Press.

―――― 1979b. 'Some observations on the typology of focus and aspect in narrative language'. *Studies in Language* 3 (1): 37–64.

―――― 1982. 'Aspect between discourse and grammar'. In P. J. Hopper (ed.), *Tense-Aspect: Between Semantics and Pragmatics*, pp. 3–18, Amsterdam: John Benjamins.

―――― 1987. 'Emergent grammar'. *Papers from the 13th Meeting of the Berkeley Linguistics Society*, pp. 139–157.

―――― 1990. 'Where do words come from?' In William Croft, Keith Denning and Suzanne Kemmer (eds), *Studies in Typology and Diachrony (for Joseph Greenberg)*, pp. 151–160, Amsterdam: John Benjamins.

―――― 1994. 'Phonogenesis'. In Pagliuca (1994), pp. 29–45.

Hopper, Paul J. and Elizabeth Closs Traugott. 1993. *Grammaticalization*. Cambridge: Cambridge University Press.

Horrocks, Geoffrey. 1997. *Greek: A History of the Language and Its Speakers*. London: Longman.

Hymes, Dell H. 1983. 'Lexicostatistics and glottochronology in the nineteenth century (with notes towards a general history)'. In D. H. Hymes (ed.), *Essays in the History of Linguistic Anthropology*, pp. 59–113, Amsterdam: John Benjamins.

Illič-Svityč, V. M. 1979. *Nominal Accentuation in Baltic and Slavic*, tr. R. Leed and R. Feldstein. Cambridge, MA: MIT Press.

Iordan, Iorgu and John Orr. 1970. *An Introduction to Romance Linguistics: Its Schools and Its Scholars*, revised by Rebecca Posner. Oxford: Basil Blackwell.

Jablonski, Nina G. and Leslie C. Aiello (eds). 1998. *The Origin and Diversification of Language*. San Francisco, CA: Memoirs of the California Academy of Sciences, no. 24.

Jahr, Ernst Håkon. 1989. 'Language planning and language change'. In Breivik and Jahr (1989), pp. 99–113. Reprinted in Peter Trudgill and Jenny Cheshire (eds) (1998), *The Sociolinguistics Reader*, vol. 1: *Multilingualism and Variation*, pp. 263–275, London: Arnold.

Jakobson, Roman. 1931. 'Prinzipien der historischen Phonologie'. *Travaux du Cercle Linguistique de Prague* 4: 247–267. Reprinted in R. Jakobson (1962), *Selected Writings*, vol. 1, pp. 202–220, The Hague: Mouton. French translation appended to N. S. Trubetzkoy (1949), *Principes de phonologie*, Paris: C. Klincksieck. English translation 'Principles of historical phonology' in Baldi and Werth (1978), pp. 103–120.

Jespersen, Otto. 1909–49. *A Modern English Grammar on Historical Principles*. Copenhagen: Munksgaard.

——— 1917. *Negation in English and Other Languages*. Copenhagen: Videnskabernes Selskab.

——— 1922. *Language: Its Nature, Development and Origin*. London: George Allen and Unwin.

Johanson, Lars and Éva Csató (eds). 1998. *The Turkic Languages*. London: Routledge.

Jones, Charles (ed.) 1993. *Historical Linguistics: Problems and Perspectives*. London: Longman.

Joseph, Brian D. 1975. 'Laryngeal before i/u in Greek; the role of morphology in diachronic change'. *Proceedings of the 11th Regional Meeting of the Chicago Linguistic Society*, pp. 319–328.

——— 1983. *The Synchrony and Diachrony of the Balkan Infinitive*. Cambridge: Cambridge University Press.

Joseph, Brian D. and Richard D. Janda. 1988. 'The how and why of diachronic morphologization and de-morphologization'. In M. Hammond and M. Noonan (eds), *Theoretical Morphology*, pp. 193–210, Orlando, FL: Academic Press.

Kaiser, Mark and Vitaly Shevoroshkin. 1988. 'Nostratic'. *Annual Review of Anthropology* 17: 309–329.

Kaufman, Stephen A. 1997. 'Aramaic'. In Hetzron (1997), pp. 114–130.

Kaufman, Terrence. 1990. 'Language history in South America: what we know and how to know more'. In Doris L. Payne (ed.), *Amazonian Linguistics: Studies in Lowland South American Languages*, pp. 13–73, Austin, TX: University of Texas Press.

——— 1994. 'The native languages of South America'. In Christopher Moseley and R. E. Asher (eds), *Atlas of the World's Languages*, pp. 46–76, London: Routledge.

Keller, R. E. 1978. *The German Language*. London: Faber and Faber.

Keller, Rudi. 1990. *On Language Change: The Invisible Hand in Language*. London: Routledge.

Kilroe, Patricia. 1994. 'The grammaticalization of French *à*'. In Pagliuca (1994), pp. 49–61.

King, Robert D. 1967. 'Functional load and sound change'. *Language* 43: 831–852.

—————— 1969a. *Historical Linguistics and Generative Grammar*. Englewood Cliffs, NJ: Prentice-Hall.

—————— 1969b. 'Push-chains and drag-chains'. *Glossa* 3: 3-21.

—————— 1973. 'Rule insertion'. *Language* 49: 551-578.

Kiparsky, Paul. 1968. 'Linguistic universals and linguistic change'. In Emmon Bach and Robert T. Harms (eds), *Universals in Linguistic Theory*, pp. 171–202, New York: Holt.

—————— 1971. 'Historical linguistics'. In W. O. Dingwall (ed.), *A Survey of Linguistic Science*. College Park, MD: University of Maryland.

—————— 1988. 'Phonological change'. In Newmeyer (1988), vol. I, pp. 363–415.

Kitson, P. R. 1996. 'British and European river-names'. *Transactions of the Philological Society* 94 (2): 73–118.

Klein, Ernest. 1971. *A Comprehensive Etymological Dictionary of the English Language*. Amsterdam: Elsevier.

Koch, Harold. 1996. 'Reconstruction in morphology'. In Durie and Ross (1996), pp. 218–263.

Kogan, Leonid E. and Andrey V. Korotayev. 1997. 'Sayhadic (epigraphic South Arabian)'. In Hetzron (1997), pp. 220–241.

König, Ekkehard and Johann van der Auwera (eds). 1994. *The Germanic Languages*. London: Routledge.

Kortland, Frederik H. H. 1974. 'Old Prussian accentuation'. *Zeitschrift für vergleichende Sprachforschung auf dem Gebiete der indogermanischen Sprachen* 88: 299–306.

Kovács, F. 1961. 'A propos d'une loi sémantique'. *Acta Linguistica Academiae Scientarum Hungaricae* 11: 405–411.

Krahe, Hans. 1962. *Die Struktur der alteuropäischen Hydronomie*. Wiesbaden: F. Steiner.

Krauss, Michael. 1979. 'Na-Dene and Eskimo-Aleut'. In Campbell and Mithun (1979), pp. 803–901.

Kronasser, Heinz. 1952. *Handbuch der Semasiologie*. Heidelberg: Winter.

Kuryłowicz, Jerzy. 1927. 'ə indo-européen et *h* hittite'. In *Symbolae grammaticae in honorem Ioannis Rozwadowski*, vol. I, pp. 95–104, Kraków: Gebethner & Wolff.

—————— 1947. 'La nature des procès dits analogiques'. *Acta Linguistica* 5: 121–138. Reprinted in Eric P. Hamp, Fred W. Householder and Robert Austerlitz (eds) (1966), *Readings in Linguistics II*, pp. 158–174, Chicago, IL: University of Chicago Press.

Labov, William. 1963. 'The Social motivation of a sound change'. *Word* 19: 273–309. Reprinted in Labov (1972), pp. 1-42.

—————— 1969. 'Contraction, deletion and inherent variability in the English copula'. *Language* 45: 715–762.

────── 1972. *Sociolinguistic Patterns*. Philadelphia, PA: University of Pennsylvania Press.

────── 1975. 'On the use of the present to explain the past'. In L. Heilmann (ed.), *Proceedings of the 11th International Congress of Linguists*, pp. 825–851, Bologna: Il Muligno.

────── 1982. 'Building on empirical foundations'. In W. P. Lehmann and Y. Malkiel (eds), *Perspectives on Historical Linguistics*, pp. 17-92, Amsterdam: John Benjamins.

────── 1994. *Principles of Linguistic Change*, vol. I: *Internal Factors*. Oxford: Blackwell.

Labov, William, Mark Karen and Corey Miller. 1991. 'Near-mergers and the suspension of phonemic contrast'. *Language Variation and Change* 3: 33–74.

Labov, William, Malcah Yeager and Richard Steiner. 1972. *A Quantitative Study of Sound Change in Progress*. Philadelphia, PA: US Regional Survey.

Lachmann, Karl. 1850. *Lucretius: De rerum natura*. Reprinted (1979), New York: Garland.

Lamb, Sydney M. 1959. 'Some proposals for linguistic taxonomy'. *Anthropological Linguistics* 1 (2): 33–49.

Lamb, Sydney M. and E. Douglas Mitchell (eds). 1991. *Sprung from Some Common Source: Investigations into the Prehistory of Languages*. Stanford, CA: Stanford University Press.

Langacker, Ronald W. 1977. 'Syntactic reanalysis'. In Li (1977), pp. 57–139.

────── 1991. *Concept, Image and Symbol: The Cognitive Basis of Grammar*. Berlin: Mouton de Gruyter.

Langdon, Margaret. 1990. 'Morphosyntax and problems of reconstruction in Yuman and Hokan'. In Baldi (1990), pp. 57–72.

Lass, Roger. 1974. 'Linguistic orthogenesis? Scots vowel length and the English length conspiracy'. In Anderson and Jones (1974), pp. 311–343.

────── 1976. *English Phonology and Phonological Theory: Synchronic and Diachronic Studies*. Cambridge: Cambridge University Press.

────── 1978. 'Mapping constraints in phonological reconstruction: on climbing down trees without falling out of them'. In Jacek Fisiak (ed.), *Recent Developments in Morphological Theory*, pp. 245–286, The Hague: Mouton.

────── 1980. *On Explaining Language Change*. Cambridge: Cambridge University Press.

────── 1984. *Phonology: An Introduction to Basic Concepts*. Cambridge: Cambridge University Press.

────── 1987. 'Language, speakers, history and drift'. In Willem Koopman, Frederike van der Leek, Olga Fischer and Roger Eaton (eds), *Explanation and Linguistic Change*, pp. 151–176, Amsterdam: John Benjamins.

────── 1990a. 'How to do things with junk: exaptation in language evolution'. *Journal of Linguistics* 26: 79–102.

────── 1990b. 'Where do extraterritorial Englishes come from? Dialect input and recodification in transported Englishes'. In S. Adamson, V. Law, N.

Vincent and S. Wright (eds), *Papers from the Fifth International Conference on English Historical Linguistics*, pp. 245–280, Amsterdam: John Benjamins.

———— 1993. 'How real(ist) are reconstructions?' In Jones (1993), pp. 156–189.

———— 1994. *Old English: A Historical Linguistic Companion*. Cambridge: Cambridge University Press.

———— 1997. *Historical Linguistics and Language Change*. Cambridge: Cambridge University Press.

Latham, R. G. 1851. *The Germania of Tacitus, with Ethnological Dissertations and Notes*. London: Taylor, Walton & Maberly.

———— 1862. *Elements of Comparative Philology*. London: Walton & Maberly.

Lazzeroni, Romano. 1998. 'Sanskrit'. In Giacalone Ramat and Ramat (1998), pp. 98–124.

Leer, Jeff. 1990. 'Tlingit: a portmanteau language family?' In Baldi (1990), pp. 73–98.

Lees, Robert B. 1953. 'The basis of glottochronology'. *Language* 29: 113–127.

Lehmann, Christian. 1982. *Thoughts on Grammaticalization: A Programmatic Sketch.*, vol. 1. Cologne: Universität zu Köln Institut für Sprachwissenschaft.

———— 1985. 'Grammaticalization: synchronic variation and diachronic change'. *Lingua e Stile* 20 (3): 303–318.

———— 1991. 'Grammaticalization and related changes in contemporary German'. In Traugott and Heine (1991), vol. II, pp. 493–535.

Lehmann, Winfred P. 1952. *Proto-Indo-European Phonology*. Austin, TX: University of Texas Press and Linguistic Society of America.

———— (ed.). 1967. *A Reader in Nineteenth-Century Historical Indo-European Linguistics*. Bloomington, IN: University of Indiana Press.

———— 1974. *Proto-Indo-European Syntax*. Austin, TX: University of Texas Press.

———— 1992. *Historical Linguistics*, 3rd edn. London: Routledge.

———— 1993. *Theoretical Bases of Indo-European Linguistics*. London: Routledge.

Lehmann, Winfred P. and Yakov Malkiel (eds). 1968. *Directions for Historical Linguistics*. Austin, TX: University of Texas Press.

Leith, Dick. 1997. *A Social History of English*, 2nd edn. London: Routledge.

Lemle, Miriam and Anthony Naro. 1977. *Competências básicas do português*. Rio de Janeiro: MOBRAL.

Le Page, Robert B. 1993. 'Conflicts of metaphors in the discussion of language and race'. In Ernst Håkon Jahr (ed.), *Language Conflict and Language Planning*, pp. 143–164, Berlin: Mouton de Gruyter.

Le Page, Robert B. and A. Tabouret-Keller. 1985. *Acts of Identity: Creole-Based Approaches to Language and Ethnicity*. Cambridge: Cambridge University Press.

Leskien, August. 1881. 'Die Quantitätsverhältnisse im Auslaut des Litauischen'. *Archiv für slavische Philologie* 5: 188–190.

Li, Charles N. (ed.) 1977. *Mechanisms of Syntactic Change*. Austin, TX: University of Texas Press.

Lichtenberk, Frantisek. 1991. 'On the gradualness of grammaticalization'. In Traugott and Heine (1991), vol. I, pp. 37–80.

Lightfoot, David W. 1979. *Principles of Diachronic Syntax*. Cambridge: Cambridge University Press.

———— 1981. 'Explaining syntactic change'. In Norbert Hornstein and David Lightfoot (eds), *Explanation in Linguistics: The Logical Problem of Language Acquisition*, pp. 209–240, London: Longman.

———— 1988. 'Syntactic change'. In Newmeyer (1988), vol. I, pp. 303–323.

———— 1998. *The Development of Language: Acquisition, Change and Evolution*. Oxford: Blackwell.

Lindemann, Frederik Otto. 1987. *Introduction to the 'Laryngeal Theory'*. Oslo: Norwegian University Press/Institute for Comparative Research in Human Culture.

Lipski, John M. 1994. *Latin American Spanish*. London: Longman.

Locke, John L. 1983. *Phonological Acquisition and Change*. New York: Academic Press.

Lockwood, W. B. 1965. *An Informal History of the German Language*. Cambridge: W. Heffer.

———— 1969. *Indo-European Philology*. London: Hutchinson.

———— 1972. *A Panorama of Indo-European Languages*. London: Hutchinson.

Lodge, R. Anthony. 1993. *French: From Dialect to Standard*. London: Routledge.

Loprieno, Antonio. 1995. *Ancient Egyptian: A Linguistic Introduction*. Cambridge: Cambridge University Press.

Luraghi, Silvia. 1998. 'The Anatolian languages'. In Giacalone Ramat and Ramat (1998), pp. 169–196.

MacAulay, Donald (ed.). 1993. *The Celtic Languages*. Cambridge: Cambridge University Press.

Mac Neill, John. 1908/09. 'Notes on the distribution, history, grammar, and import of the Irish Ogham inscriptions'. *Proceedings of the Royal Irish Academy* 27, section C, pp. 329–370.

Maher, Julianne. 1985. *Contact Linguistics: The Language Enclave Phenomenon*. Unpublished New York University PhD dissertation.

Maiden, Martin. 1995. *A Linguistic History of Italian*. London: Longman.

Mallory, J. P. 1973. 'A short history of the Indo-European problem'. *Journal of Indo-European Studies* 1: 21–65.

———— 1989. *In Search of the Indo-Europeans: Language, Archaeology and Myth*. London: Thames & Hudson.

———— 1997. 'The homelands of the Indo-Europeans'. In Blench and Spriggs (1997), pp. 93–121.

Manaster Ramer, Alexis. 1992. 'Tubatulabal "man" and the subclassification of Uto-Aztecan'. *California Linguistic Notes* 23: 30–31.

———— 1993a. 'On Illič-Svityč's Nostratic theory'. *Studies in Language* 17: 205–250.

———— 1993b. '"One" and "only"'. *California Linguistic Notes* 24: 4.

———— 1996a. 'Sapir's classifications: Coahuiltecan'. *Anthropological Linguistics* 38: 1–38.

———— 1996b. 'Sapir's classifications: Nadene'. *Anthropological Linguistics* 38: 1–38.

———— 1996c. 'On Whorf's law and related questions of Aztec phonology and etymology'. *International Journal of American Linguistics* 62: 176–187.

———— 1999. 'On the uses and abuses of mathematics in linguistics'. In C. Martin-Vide (ed.), *Issues from Mathematical Linguistics: A Workshop*, pp. 70–130, Amsterdam: John Benjamins.

Manaster Ramer, Alexis, Karen Adams, Karen Baertsch and Peter Michalove. 1998. 'Exploring the Nostratic hypothesis'. In Salmons and Joseph (1998), pp. 61–84.

Manaster Ramer, Alexis and Christopher Hitchcock. 1996. 'Glass houses'. *Anthropological Linguistics* 38: 601–619.

Mańczak, Witold. 1958. 'Tendances générales des changements analogiques'. *Lingua* 7: 298–325, 387–420.

———— 1996. 'Irregular sound change due to frequency in compounded words'. *Kwartalnik Neofilologiczny* 43: 207–215.

Mannheim, Bruce. 1986. '[Comentario sobre] Willem Adelaar, "la relación quechua-aru: perspectivas para la separación del léxico"'. *Revista Andina* 4: 413–418.

Marchese, Lynell. 1984. 'Exbraciation in the Kru-language family'. In Jacek Fisiak (ed.), *Historical Syntax*, pp. 249–270, Berlin: Mouton.

Markey, Thomas L. 1990. 'The development of standard language (koine) and dialect: language split and dialect merger'. In Polomé (1990a), pp. 455–469.

Martinet, André. 1953. 'Remarques sur le consonantisme sémitique'. *Bulletin de la Société Linguistique de Paris* 49: 67–78.

———— 1955. *Économie des changements phonétiques*. Bern: A. Francke.

Matisoff, James A. 1973. *The Grammar of Lahu*. Berkeley: University of California Press.

———— 1990. 'On megalocomparison'. [Review of Greenberg 1987]. *Language* 66: 106–120.

———— 1991. 'Areal and universal dimensions of grammatization in Lahu'. In Traugott and Heine (1991), vol. II, pp. 383–453.

McAlpin, David W. 1974. 'Toward Proto-Elamo-Dravidian'. *Language* 50: 89–101.

———— 1975. 'Elamite and Dravidian: further evidence of relationship'. *Current Anthropology* 16: 105–115.

———— 1981. *Proto-Elamo-Dravidian: The Evidence and Its Implications*. Philadelphia: American Philosophical Society.

McConvell, Patrick and Nicholas Evans (eds). 1997. *Archaeology and Linguistics: Aboriginal Australia in Global Perspective*. Melbourne: Oxford University Press.

McCrum, Robert, William Cran and Robert MacNeil. 1992. *The Story of English*, 2nd edn. London: Faber and Faber/BBC Books.

McMahon, April M. S. 1994. *Understanding Language Change*. Cambridge: Cambridge University Press.

Meillet, Antoine. 1902. 'O nekotoryx anomalijax udarenija v slavjanskix imenax'. *Russkii Filologičeskii Vestnik* 48: 193–200.

——— 1912. 'L'évolution des formes grammaticales'. *Scientia* 12, no. 26, 6. Reprinted in Meillet (1958), pp. 130–148.

——— 1958. *Linguistique historique et linguistique générale*. Paris: Société Linguistique de Paris.

Meinhof, Carl. 1932. *Introduction to the Phonology of the Bantu Languages*. Berlin: Reimer.

Meyer-Lübke, W. 1935. *Romanisches etymologisches Wörterbuch*, 3rd edn. Heidelberg: Carl Winter.

Michalove, Peter, Ralf-Stefan Georg and Alexis Manaster Ramer. 1998. 'Current issues in linguistic taxonomy'. *Annual Review of Anthropology* 27: 451–472.

Michelena, Luis. 1957. 'Las antiguas consonantes vascas'. In *Miscelánea homenaje a André Martinet*, vol. I, pp. 113–157, La Laguna. Reprinted in L. Michelena (1988), Joseba A. Lakarra (ed.), *Sobre historia de la lengua vasca*, vol. I, pp. 166–189, Donostia/San Sebastián: Anejos del Anuario del Seminario de Filología Vasca 'Julio de Urquijo'.

——— 1977. *Fonética histórica vasca*, 2nd edn. San Sebastián: Publicaciones del Seminario de Filología Vasca 'Julio de Urquijo'.

Migliorini, Bruno. 1984. *The Italian Language*, revised by T. Gwynfor Griffith. London: Faber and Faber.

Miller, Roy Andrew. 1980. *The Origins of the Japanese Language*. Seattle: University of Washington Press.

Milroy, James. 1983. 'On the sociolinguistic history of /h/-dropping in English'. In M. Davenport, E. Hansen and H.-F. Nielsen (eds), *Current Topics in English Historical Linguistics*, pp. 37–53, Odense: University of Odense Press.

——— 1992. *Linguistic Variation and Change*. Oxford: Blackwell.

——— 1993. 'On the social origins of language change'. In Jones (1993), pp. 215–236.

Milroy, James and Lesley Milroy. 1985a. *Authority in Language*. London: Routledge and Kegan Paul.

——— 1985b. 'Linguistic change, social network and speaker innovation'. *Journal of Linguistics* 21: 339–384.

Miner, Kenneth. 1979. 'Dorsey's Law in Winnebago-Chiwere and Winnebago accent'. *International Journal of American Linguistics* 45: 25–33.

Mithun, Marianne. 1992. 'External triggers and internal guidance in syntactic development: coordinating conjunctions'. In Gerritsen and Stein (1992), pp. 89–129.

Moore, J. H. 1994a. 'Ethnogenetic theory'. *Research and Exploration* 10: 10–23.

——— 1994b. 'Putting anthropology back together again: the ethnogenetic critique of cladistic theory'. *American Anthropologist* 96: 925–948.

Moravcsik, Edith. 1978. 'Language contact'. In Greenberg *et al.* (1978), vol. 1, pp. 93–123.

Muysken, Pieter. 1997a. 'Media Lengua'. In Thomason (1997a), pp. 365–426.

———— 1997b. 'Callahuaya'. In Thomason (1997a), pp. 427–447.

Nash, David. 1997. 'Comparative flora terminology of the central Northern Territory'. In McConvell and Evans (1997), pp. 187–206.

Newman, John. 1996. 'Footnotes to a history of Cantonese: accounting for the phonological irregularities'. In Durie and Ross (1996), pp. 90–111.

Newmeyer, Frederick J. (ed.). 1988. *Linguistics: The Cambridge Survey*, 4 vols. Cambridge: Cambridge University Press.

Nichols, Johanna. 1988. 'On alienable and inalienable possession'. In W. Shipley (ed.), *In Honor of Mary Haas: From the Haas Festival Conference on Native American Linguistics*, pp. 557–609, Berlin: Mouton de Gruyter.

———— 1990. 'Linguistic diversity and the first settlement of the New World'. *Language* 66: 475–521.

———— 1992. *Linguistic Diversity in Space and Time*. Chicago, IL: University of Chicago Press.

———— 1993. 'Ergativity and linguistic geography'. *Australian Journal of Linguistics* 13: 39–89.

———— 1994/95. 'The spread of language around the Pacific rim'. *Evolutionary Anthropology* 3: 206–215.

———— 1995a. 'Diachronically stable structural features'. In Henning Andersen (ed.), *Historical Linguistics 1993. Papers from the Eleventh International Conference on Historical Linguistics*, pp. 337–357, Amsterdam: John Benjamins.

———— 1995b. 'Shaped by some common contingency: genetic and historical markers'. Unpublished paper, University of California at Berkeley.

———— 1996. 'The comparative method as heuristic'. In Durie and Ross (1996), pp. 39–71.

———— 1997a. 'The epicentre of the Indo-European linguistic spread'. In Blench and Spriggs (1997), pp. 122–148.

———— 1997b. 'Modeling ancient population structures and movement in linguistics'. *Annual Review of Anthropology* 26: 359–384.

———— 1997c. 'Sprung from two common sources: Sahul as a linguistic area'. In McConvell and Evans (1997), pp. 135–168.

———— 1997d. 'Of needles and haystacks: searches and heuristics in comparative method'. Unpublished paper; under review.

———— 1997e. 'The geography of language origins'. *Proceedings of the 22nd Annual Meeting of the Berkeley Linguistic Society*, pp. 267–278.

———— 1998. 'The origin and dispersal of languages: linguistic evidence'. In Jablonski and Aiello (1998), pp. 127170.

Nichols, Johanna and David A. Peterson. 1996. 'The Amerind personal pronouns'. *Language* 72: 336–371.

———— 1998. 'Amerind personal pronouns: a reply to Campbell'. *Language* 74: 605–614.

Nichols, Johanna and Alan Timberlake. 1991. 'Grammaticalization as retextualization'. In Traugott and Heine (1991), vol. I, pp. 129–146.

Nieminen, Eino V. K. 1922. *Der urindogermanische Ausgang -āi des Nominativ-Akkusativ Pluralis des Neutrums im Baltischen.* Helsinki: Academia Scientarum Fennica.

Norman, Jerry. 1988. *Chinese.* Cambridge: Cambridge University Press.

O'Grady, Richard T., Ives Goddard, Richard M. Bateman, William A. DiMichele, V. A. Funk, W. John Kress, Rich Mooi and Peter F. Cannell. 1989. 'Genes and tongues'. *Science* 243: 1651.

Ohala, John J. 1981. 'The listener as a source of sound change'. In C. S. Masek, R. A. Hendrick and M. F. Miller (eds), *Papers from the Parasession on Language and Behavior*, pp. 178–203, Chicago, IL: Chicago Linguistic Society.

——— 1987. 'Explanation in phonology: opinions and examples'. In Wolfgang Dressler, H. C. Luschützky, O. E. Pfeiffer and J. Rennison (eds), *Phonologica 1984*, pp. 215–225, Cambridge: Cambridge University Press.

——— 1989. 'Sound change is drawn from a pool of synchronic variation'. In Breivik and Jahr (1989), pp. 173–198.

——— 1993. 'The phonetics of sound change'. In Jones (1993), pp. 237–278.

Onions, C. T. (ed.). 1966. *The Oxford Dictionary of English Etymology.* Oxford: Clarendon.

Orel, V. and O. Stolbova. 1995. *Hamito-Semitic Etymological Dictionary.* Leiden: Brill.

Osthoff, Hermann. 1879. 'Kleine Beiträge zur Declinationslehre der indogermanischen Sprachen II'. In K. Brugmann and H. Osthoff (eds), *Morphologische Untersuchungen auf dem Gebiete der indogermanischen Sprachen*, vol. 2, pp. 1–47, Leipzig: Hirzel.

——— 1881. Review of G. Mayer, *Griechische Grammatik. Philologische Rundschau* 1, cols. 1593 *ff.*

——— 1884. *Zur Geschichte des Perfects im Indogermanischen.* Strasbourg: Trübner.

Oswalt, Robert L. 1991. 'A method for assessing distant linguistic relationships'. In Lamb and Mitchell (1991), pp. 389–404.

——— 1998. 'A probabilistic evaluation of North Eurasiatic Nostratic'. In Salmons and Joseph (1998), pp. 199–216.

Pagliuca, William (ed.). 1994. *Perspectives on Grammaticalization.* Amsterdam: John Benjamins.

Paolillo, John C. 1994. 'The co-development of finiteness and focus in Sinhala'. In Pagliuca (1994), pp. 151–170.

Pardee, Dennis. 1997. 'Ugaritic'. In Hetzron (1997), pp. 131–144.

Partridge, Eric. 1958. *Origins: An Etymological Dictionary of Modern English.* London: Routledge and Kegan Paul.

Paul, Hermann. 1920. *Prinzipien der Sprachgeschichte*, 5th edn. Tübingen: Max Miemeyer. (1st edn. 1880.) English translation of 2nd edn. (1886) by H. A. Strong (1891), *Principles of the History of Language*, London. Extract 'On sound change' in Baldi and Werth (1978), pp. 3–22.

Pedersen, Holger. 1895. 'Das indogermanische *s* im Slavischen'. *Indogermanische Forschungen* 5: 33–87.

———— 1903. 'Türkische Lautgesetze'. *Zeitschrift der deutschen morgenländischen Gesellschaft* 57: 535–561.

———— 1933. *Études lituaniennes*. Copenhagen: Levin & Munksgaard.

Penny, Ralph. 1991. *A History of the Spanish Language*. Cambridge: Cambridge University Press.

Plank, Frans. 1984. 'The modals story retold'. *Studies in Language* 8: 305–364.

Pokorny, Julius. 1959/69. *Indogermanisches Etymologisches Wörterbuch*, 2 vols. Bern: Francke.

Polivanov, E. D. 1928. 'Faktory fonetičeskoj evoljucii jazyka kak trudovogo processa'. *Inst. Jaz. i Lit. Ross. Assoc. naučno-issledovatel'skix institutov obščestvennyx nauk* 3: 20–42.

Polomé, Edgar C. (ed.). 1990a. *Research Guide on Language Change*. Berlin: Mouton de Gruyter.

———— 1990b. 'Etymology'. In Polomé (1990a), pp. 415–440.

Poppe, Nicholas. 1960. *Vergleichende Grammatik der altaischen Sprachen*, vol. I: *Vergleichende Lautlehre*. Wiesbaden: Harrasowitz.

———— 1965. *Introduction to Altaic Linguistics*. Wiesbaden: Harrasowitz.

Posner, Rebecca. 1996. *The Romance Languages*. Cambridge: Cambridge University Press.

Price, Glanville. 1971. *The French Language: Present and Past*. London: Arnold.

———— (ed.). 1998. *Encyclopedia of the Languages of Europe*. Oxford: Blackwell.

Prokosch, Eduard. 1939. *A Comparative Germanic Grammar*. Baltimore, ML: Linguistic Society of America.

Ramat, Paolo. 1998. 'The Germanic Languages'. In Giacalone Ramat and Ramat (1998), pp. 380–414.

Ramsey, S. Robert. 1987. *The Languages of China*. Princeton, NJ: Princeton University Press.

Randall, Janet H. 1990. 'Catapults and pendulums: the mechanics of language acquisition'. *Linguistics* 28: 1381–1406.

Rask, Rasmus K. 1818. *Undersøgelse om det gamle Nordiske eller Islandske Sprogs Oprindelse*. Copenhagen: Gyldendalske.

Renfrew, Colin. 1987. *Archaeology and Language: the Puzzle of Indo-European Origins*. London: Jonathan Cape.

———— 1989. 'The origins of Indo-European languages'. *Scientific American* 261 (4) (October), pp. 82–90.

———— 1991. 'Before Babel: speculations on the origin of linguistic diversity'. *Cambridge Archaeological Journal* 1 (1): 3–23.

———— 1992a. 'Archaeology, genetics and linguistic diversity'. *Man* 27: 445–478.

———— 1992b. 'World languages and human dispersals: a minimalist view'. In John A. Hall and I. C. Jarvie (eds), *Transition to Modernity: Essays on Power, Wealth and Belief*, pp. 11–68, Cambridge: Cambridge University Press.

———— 1994. 'World linguistic diversity'. *Scientific American* 270 (1) (January), pp. 104–110.

———— 1995. 'Language families as evidence of human dispersals'. In Sidney Brenner and Kazuro Hanihara (eds), *The Origin and Past of Modern Humans as Viewed from DNA*, pp. 285–306, Singapore: World Scientific.

———— 1997. 'World linguistic diversity and farming dispersals'. In Blench and Spriggs (1997), pp. 82–90.

———— 1998. 'The origins of world linguistic diversity: an archaeological perspective'. In Jablonski and Aiello (1998), pp. 171–192.

Renfrew, Colin, David W. Anthony, Bernard Wailes, P. Baldi, Graeme Barker, Robert Coleman, Marija Gimbutas, Evžen Neustepný, Andrew Sherratt. 1988. Presentation and review of Renfrew (1987). *Current Anthropology* 29: 437–468.

Ringe, Donald. 1992. *On Calculating the Factor of Chance in Language Comparison*. Philadelphia, PA: American Philosophical Society (= *Transactions of the American Philosophical Society* 82: 1–110).

———— 1995a. ' "Nostratic" and the factor of chance'. *Diachronica* 12: 55–74.

———— 1995b. 'The "Mana" languages and the three-language problem'. *Oceanic Linguistics* 34: 99–122.

———— 1996. 'The mathematics of "Amerind" '. *Diachronica* 13: 135–154.

———— 1998. 'Probabilistic evidence for Indo-Uralic'. In Salmons and Joseph (1998), pp. 153–197.

———— forthcoming. 'How hard is it to match CVC-roots?' Unpublished paper, under review.

Rix, Helmut. 1970. 'Anlautender Laryngal vor Liquida oder Nasalis Sonans im griechischen'. *Münchener Studien zur Sprachwissenschaft* 27: 79–110.

Robinson, Orrin W. 1992. *Old English and Its Closest Relatives*. London: Routledge.

Romaine, Suzanne. 1982. *Sociohistorical Linguistics*. Cambridge: Cambridge University Press.

———— 1988. *Pidgin and Creole Languages*. London: Longman.

Ross, Malcolm D. 1996. 'Contact-induced change and the comparative method: cases from Papua New Guinea'. In Durie and Ross (1996), pp. 180–217.

———— 1997. 'Speech networks and kinds of speech-community event'. In Blench and Spriggs (1997), pp. 209–261.

Ross, Philip E. 1991. 'Hard words'. *Scientific American* 264 (4) (April), pp. 70–79.

Ruhlen, Merritt. 1991. *A Guide to the World's Languages*, vol. 1: *Classification*, 2nd edn. London: Edward Arnold.

———— 1994. *On the Origin of Languages: Studies in Linguistic Taxonomy*. Stanford, CA: Stanford University Press.

Russell, Paul. 1995. *An Introduction to the Celtic Languages*. London: Longman.

Salmons, Joseph C. 1992. 'A look at the data for a global etymology: *tik* "finger"'. In Garry W. Davis and Gregory K. Iversen (eds), *Explanation in Historical Linguistics*, pp. 207–228, Amsterdam: John Benjamins.

Salmons, Joseph C. and Brian D. Joseph (eds). 1998. *Nostratic: Sifting the Evidence*. Amsterdam: John Benjamins.

Sankoff, Gillian. 1977. 'Variability and explanation in language and culture: cliticization in New Guinea Tok Pisin'. In M. Saville-Troike (ed.), *Linguistics and Anthropology*, pp. 59–73, Washington: Georgetown University Press.

Sapir, Edward. 1913. 'Wiyot and Yurok, Algonkin languages of California'. *American Anthropologist* 15: 617–646.

——— 1915. 'The Na-Dene languages, a preliminary report'. *American Anthropologist* 17: 534–558.

——— 1916. *Time Perspective in Aboriginal American Culture: A Study in Method*. Canada Department of Mines, Geological Survey, Memoir no. 90, Anthropological Series no. 13. Ottawa: Government Printing Bureau. Reprinted in David G. Mandelbaum (ed.) (1949), *Selected Writings of Edward Sapir*, pp. 389–467, Berkeley, CA: University of California Press.

——— 1921a. *Language: An Introduction to the Study of Speech*. New York: Harcourt, Brace and World.

——— 1921b. 'A bird's-eye view of American languages north of Mexico'. *Science* 54: 408.

——— 1925. 'The Hokan affinity of Subtiaba in Nicaragua'. *American Anthropologist* 27: 402–435, 491–527.

——— 1929. 'Central and North American Indian languages'. In *Encyclopedia Britannica*, 14th edn., 5: 138–141.

Saussure, Ferdinand de. 1879. *Mémoire sur le système primitif des voyelles dans les langues indo-européennes*. Leipzig: Teubner.

——— 1894. 'À propos de l'accentuation lituanienne'. *Mémoires de la Société de Linguistique de Paris* 8: 425–446.

——— 1896. 'Accentuation lituanienne'. *Indogermanische Forschungen Anzeiger* 6: 157–166.

——— 1916. *Cours de linguistique générale*. Reprinted (1972), Paris: Payot.

Šaxmatov, A. A. 1915. 'Očerk drevnekšego perioda istorii russkogo jazyka'. In V. Jagič (ed.), *Encyklopedija slovjanskoj filologii* 2.7, Petrograd. Reprinted (1967), The Hague: Mouton.

Scaliger, J. J. 1610. 'Matricum vero inter se nulla cognatio est, neque in verbis neque in analogia'. *Diatriba de Europaeorum linguis. Opscula varia*, Paris, pp. 119–122.

Schindler, Jochem. 1974. 'Fragen zum paradigmatischen Ausgleich'. *Die Sprache* 20: 1–9.

——— 1975. 'Zum Ablaut der neutralen s-Stämme des Indogermanischen'. In Helmut Rix (ed.), *Flexion und Wortbildung*, pp. 259–267, Wiesbaden: Reichert.

Schleicher, August. 1871. *Compendium der vergleichenden Grammatik der indogermanischen Sprachen*. Weimar: Hermann Böhlau.

Schlesinger, I. M. 1979. 'Cognitive structures and semantic deep structures: the case of the instrumental'. *Journal of Linguistics* 15: 307–324.

Schmalstieg, William R. 1998. 'The Baltic languages'. In Giacalone Ramat and Ramat (1998), pp. 454–479.

Schmid, Wolfgang P. 1987. ' "Indo-European" — "Old European" (on the reexamination of two linguistic terms)'. In Susan Nacev Skomal and Edgar C. Polomé (eds), *Proto-Indo-European: The Archaeology of a Linguistic Problem. Studies in Honor of Marija Gimbutas*, pp. 322–338, Washington, DC: Institute for the Study of Man.

Schmidt, Johannes. 1872. *Die Verwandtschaftsverhältnisse der indogermanischen Sprachen*. Weimar: Hermann Böhlau.

Schmidt, Wilhelm. 1906. *Die Mon-Khmer-Völker, ein Bindgelied zwischen Volkern Zentralasiens und Austronesiens*. Braunschweig: Vieweg.

Schuh, Russell G. 1990. 'Re-employment of grammatical morphemes in Chadic: implications for language history'. In Baldi (1990), pp. 599–618.

Sebba, Mark. 1997. *Contact Languages: Pidgins and Creoles*. London: Macmillan.

Segert, Stanislav. 1997. 'Phoenician and the eastern Canaanite languages'. In Hetzron (1997), pp. 174–186.

Shevelov, George Y. 1964. *A Prehistory of Slavic: The Historical Phonology of Common Slavic*. Heidelberg: Carl Winter.

Shevoroshkin, Vitaly (ed.). 1991. *Dene-Sino-Caucasian Languages*. Bochum: Brockmeyer.

Shevoroshkin, Vitaly and Alexis Manaster Ramer. 1991. 'Some recent work on the remote relations of languages'. In Lamb and Mitchell (1991), pp. 178–199.

Shnirelman, Victor. 1997. 'Linguoarchaeology: goals, advances and limits'. In Blench and Spriggs (1997), pp. 158–165.

Siebs, Theodor. 1904. 'Anlautstudien'. *Zeitschrift für vergleichende Sprach-forschung auf dem Gebiete der indogermanischen Sprachen* 37: 277–324.

Sievers, Eduard. 1878. 'Zur accent- und lautlehre der germanischen Sprachen, II & III'. *Beiträge zur Geschichte der deutschen Sprache und Literatur* 5: 63–163.

Silvestri, Domenico. 1998. 'The Italic languages'. In Giacalone Ramat and Ramat (1998), pp. 322–344.

Sim, R. J. 1994. 'Nilo-Saharan languages'. In Asher and Simpson (1994), vol. 5, pp. 2804–2808.

Sims-Williams, Nicholas. 1998. 'The Iranian languages'. In Giacalone Ramat and Ramat (1998), pp. 125–153.

Sims-Williams, Patrick. 1998. 'The Celtic languages'. In Giacalone Ramat and Ramat (1998), pp. 345–379.

Skautrup, Peter. 1968. *Det danske sprogs historie*, vol. 4. Copenhagen: Fra J. P. Jacobsen til Johs. V. Jensen.

Smith, Jeremy. 1996. *An Historical Study of English*. London: Routledge.

Smith, Neil and Ianthi-Maria Tsimpli. 1995. *The Mind of a Savant*. Oxford: Blackwell.

Sommerstein, Alan H. 1977. *Modern Phonology*. London: Edward Arnold.

Southworth, Franklin C. 1964. 'Family-tree diagrams'. *Language* 40: 557–565.

Specht, Franz. 1947. *Der Ursprung der indogermanischen Deklination*. Göttingen: Vandenhoek and Ruprecht.

Stampe, David. 1969. 'The acquisition of phonetic representation'. *Papers from the Fifth Regional Meeting of the Chicago Linguistic Society*, pp. 443–454.

Stang, Christian S. 1957. *Slavonic Accentuation*. Oslo: Aschehoug.

Starostin, Sergei. 1991. *Altaiskaya problema i proiskhozhdenie yaponskogo yazyka*. Moscow: Nauka.

Steever, Sanford B. (ed.). 1997. *Dravidian Languages*. London: Routledge.

Steiner, Richard C. 1997. 'Ancient Hebrew'. In Hetzron (1997), pp. 145–173.

Stockwell, Robert P. and Ronald K. S. Macaulay (eds). 1972. *Linguistic Change and Generative Theory*. Bloomington, IN: University of Indiana Press.

Streitberg, Wilhelm. 1893. 'Ein Ablautproblem der Ursprache'. *Transactions of the American Philological Association* 14: 29–49.

——— 1894. 'Die Entstehung der Dehnstufe'. *Indogermanische Forschungen* 3: 305–416.

Sturtevant, Edgar H. 1917. *Linguistic Change*. Chicago, IL: University of Chicago Press.

——— 1962. 'The Indo-Hittite hypothesis'. *Language* 38: 105–110.

Sturtevant, Edgar H. and E. Adelaide Hahn. 1951. *A Comparative Grammar of the Hittite Language*, vol. I, 2nd edn. New Haven, CO: Yale University Press.

Swadesh, Morris. 1950. 'Salish internal relationships'. *International Journal of American Linguistics* 16: 157–167.

——— 1951. 'Diffusional cumulation and archaic residue as historical explanations'. *Southwestern Journal of Anthropology* 7: 1–21. Revised version, 'Glottochronology', reprinted in Morton H. Fries (ed.), (1959), *Readings in Anthropology*, pp. 199–218, New York: Thomas Crowell. Second edn. 1968. Further revised version, 'Glottochronology', reprinted in Dell Hymes (ed.) (1964), *Language in Culture and Society*, pp. 624–635, New York: Harper & Row.

——— 1952. 'Lexicostatistic dating of prehistoric ethnic contacts'. *Proceedings of the American Philosophical Society* 96: 453–462.

——— 1954. 'Perspectives and problems of Amerindian comparative linguistics'. *Word* 10: 306–332.

——— 1971. *The Origin and Diversification of Language*, Joel Sherzer (ed). London: Routledge.

Sweetser, E. 1990. *From Etymology to Pragmatics: Metaphorical and Cultural Aspects of Semantic Structure*. Cambridge: Cambridge University Press.

Szemerényi, Oswald J. L. 1962. *Trends and Tasks in Comparative Philology*. London: University College.

——— 1970. *Einführung in die vergleichende Sprachwissenschaft*. Darmstadt: Wissenschaftliche Buchgesellschaft.

——— 1972. 'Comparative linguistics'. In T. A. Sebeok (ed.), *Current Trends in Linguistics*, vol. 9, pp. 119–195. The Hague: Mouton.

——— 1973. 'La théorie des laryngales de Saussure à Kuryłowicz et à Benveniste. Essai de réévaluation'. *Bulletin de la Société de Linguistique de Paris* 68: 1–25. Reprinted in O. Szemerényi (1987), *Scripta Minora: Selected Papers in Indo-European, Greek and Latin*, P. Considine and J. T. Hooker (eds), pp. 191–215, Innsbruck: Institut für Sprachwissenschaft der Universität Innsbruck.

—— 1996. *Introduction to Indo-European Comparative Linguistics*. Oxford: Oxford University Press.

Tarde, Gabriel de. 1890. *Les lois de l'imitation: étude sociologique*. Paris: Baillère.

Thomason, Sarah Grey. 1980. 'Morphological instability, with and without language contact'. In Fisiak (1980), pp. 359–372.

—— (ed.). 1997a. *Contact Languages: A Wider Perspective*. Amsterdam: John Benjamins.

—— 1997b. 'Mednyj Aleut'. In Thomason (1997a), pp. 449–468.

—— 1997c. 'Ma'a (Mbugu)'. In Thomason (1997a), pp. 469–487.

Thomason, Sarah Grey and Terrence Kaufman. 1988. *Language Contact, Creolization, and Genetic Linguistics*. Berkeley, CA: University of California Press.

Thurneysen, Rudolf. 1887. 'Lateinischer Lautwendel'. *Zeitschrift für vergleichende Sprachforschung auf dem Gebiete der indogermanischen Sprachen* 28: 154–162.

—— 1898. 'Spirantenwechsel im Gotischen'. *Indogermanische Forschungen* 8: 208–214.

Thurston, W. R. 1989. 'How exoteric languages build a lexicon: esoterogeny in West New Britain'. In R. Harlow and R. Hooper (eds), *VICAL 1, Oceanic Languages: Papers from the Fifth International Conference on Austronesian Linguistics*, pp. 555–579, Auckland: Linguistic Society of New Zealand.

Timberlake, Alan. 1977. 'Reanalysis and actualization in syntactic change'. In Li (1977), pp. 141–177.

Tolomei, Claudio. 1535. *Il Cesano*. Vinegia: G. Giolito de Ferrari.

Trask, R. L. 1990. 'The -*n* class of verbs in Basque'. *Transactions of the Philological Society* 88 (1): 111–128.

—— 1996. *Historical Linguistics*. London: Arnold.

—— 1997. *The History of Basque*. London: Routledge.

Traugott, Elizabeth Closs. 1972. *The History of English Syntax*. New York: Holt, Rinehart, Winston.

—— 1982. 'From propositional to textual and expressive meanings: some semantic-pragmatic aspects of grammaticalization'. In W. P. Lehmann and Y. Malkiel (eds) (1982), *Perspectives on Historical Linguistics*, pp. 245–271, Amsterdam: John Benjamins.

—— 1989. 'On the rise of epistemic meanings in English: an example of objectification in semantic change'. *Language* 65: 31–55.

Traugott, Elizabeth Closs and Bernd Heine (eds). 1991. *Approaches to Grammaticalization*, 2 vols. Amsterdam: John Benjamins.

Trudgill, Peter. 1986. *Dialects in Contact*. Oxford: Blackwell.

Trudgill, Peter and Nina Foxcroft. 1978. 'On the sociolinguistics of vocalic mergers: transfer and approximation in East Anglia'. In P. Trudgill (ed.), *Sociolinguistic Patterns in British English*, pp. 69–79, London: Edward Arnold.

Uspenskij, B. A. 1965. *Strukturnaja tipologija jazykov*. Moscow: Nauka.

Vaillant, André. 1950–77. *Grammaire comparée des langues slaves*, 5 vols. Lyon: IAC; Paris: Klincksieck.

van der Wurff, Wim. 1995. 'Language contact and syntactic change: some formal linguistic diagnostics'. In Fisiak (1995), pp. 383–420.

van Marle, Jaap and Caroline Smits. 1989. 'Morphological erosion in American Dutch'. In Norbert Boretzky *et al.* (eds), *Vielfalt der Kontakte*, pp. 37–65, Bochum: Brockmeyer.

van Wijk, Nicolaas. 1916. 'Zur sekundären steigenden Intonation im Slavischen, vornehmlich in ursprünglich kurzen Silben'. *Archiv für slavische Philologie* 36: 346–348, 368–374.

Vendryes, Joseph. 1929. *Traité d'accentuation grecque*. Paris: Klincksieck.

Vennemann, Theo. 1972. 'Rule inversion'. *Lingua* 29: 209–242.

——— 1974. 'Restructuring'. *Lingua* 33: 137–156.

——— 1984. 'Hochgermanisch und Niedergermanisch: die Verzweigungstheorie der germanisch-deutschen Lautverschiebungen'. *Beiträge zur Geschichte der deutschen Sprache* 111: 355–368.

——— (ed.). 1985. *The New Sound of Indo-European: Essays in Phonological Reconstruction*. Berlin: Mouton de Gruyter.

——— 1988. 'Systems and changes in early Germanic phonology: a search for hidden identities'. In Daniel G. Calder and T. Craig Christy (eds), *Germania: Comparative Studies in the Old Germanic Languages and Literatures*, pp. 45–65, Wolfeboro, NH: Brewer.

——— 1994. 'Linguistic reconstruction in the context of prehistory'. *Transactions of the Philological Society* 92 (2): 215–284.

Verner, Karl. 1876. 'Eine Ausnahme der ersten Lautverschiebung'. *Zeitschrift für vergleichende Sprachforschung auf dem Gebiete der indogermanischen Sprachen* 23: 97–130.

Versteegh, Kees. 1997. *The Arabic Language*. Edinburgh: Edinburgh University Press.

Vincent, Nigel. 1995. 'Exaptation and grammaticalization'. In Henning Andersen (ed.), *Historical Linguistics 1993*, pp. 443-448, Amsterdam: John Benjamins.

Vineis, Edoardo. 1998. 'Latin'. In Giacalone Ramat and Ramat (1998), pp. 261–321.

Visser, F. Th. 1963–73. *An Historical Syntax of the English Language*, 4 vols. Leiden: E. J. Brill.

Voyles, Joseph B. 1992. *Early Germanic Grammar: Pre-, Proto-, and Post-Germanic Languages*. San Diego, CA: Academic Press.

Wackernagel, Jacob. 1889. 'Das Dehnungsgesetz der griechischen Komposita'. *Programm zur Rektoratsfeier der Universität Basel*, pp. 1–65. Reprinted in J. Wackernagel (1955), *Kleine Schriften*, vol. II, pp. 897–961, Göttingen: Vandenhoek & Ruprecht.

——— 1892. 'Über ein Gesetz der indo-germanischen Wortstellung'. *Indogermanische Forschungen* 1: 333–436.

Wang, William S.-Y. 1969. 'Competing sound changes as a cause of residue'. *Language* 45: 9–34.

——— 1994. 'Glottochronology, lexicostatistics, and other numerical methods'. In Asher and Simpson (1994), vol. 3, pp. 1445–1450.

Wang, William S.-Y. and Chinfa Lien. 1993. 'Bidirectional diffusion in sound change'. In Jones (1993), pp. 345–400.

Warner, Anthony. 1983. Review of Lightfoot (1979). *Journal of Linguistics* 19: 187–209.

Warnow, Tandy, Donald Ringe and Ann Taylor. 1995. *Reconstructing the Evolutionary History of Natural Languages*. Institute for Research in Cognitive Science, IRCS Report 95–16. Philadelphia, PA: University of Pennsylvania.

Watkins, Calvert. 1962. *Indo-European Origins of the Celtic Verb*, vol. 1: *The Sigmatic Aorist*. Dublin: Institute of Advanced Studies.

——— 1969. 'Indo-European and the Indo-Europeans'. Appendix to *The American Heritage Dictionary of the English Language*, pp. 1496–1550, Boston: American Heritage/Houghton Mifflin.

——— 1990. 'Etymologies, equations, and comparanda: types and values, and criteria for judgement'. In Baldi (1990), pp. 289–303.

——— 1998. 'Proto-Indo-European: comparison and reconstruction'. In Giacalone Ramat and Ramat (1998), pp. 25–73.

Weinreich, Uriel. 1953. *Languages in Contact: Findings and Problems*. The Hague: Mouton.

——— 1954. 'Is a structural dialectology possible?' *Word* 10: 388–400.

——— 1958. 'On the compatibility of genetic relationship and convergent development'. *Word* 14: 374–379.

Weinreich, Uriel, William Labov and Marvin I. Herzog. 1968. 'Empirical foundations for a theory of language change'. In Lehmann and Malkiel (1968), pp. 95–195.

Wells, C. J. 1985. *German: A Linguistic History to 1945*. Oxford: Clarendon Press.

Wells, John. 1982. *Accents of English*, 3 vols. Cambridge: Cambridge University Press.

Wenker, Georg. 1876. *Deutscher Sprachatlas*, vol. 1. Marburg: Elwert.

Wheeler, Benjamin I. 1885. *Der griechische Nominalaccent*. Dissertation, University of Strasbourg.

Whorf, Benjamin Lee. 1937. 'The origin of Aztec tl'. *American Anthropologist* 39: 265–274.

Whorf, Benjamin Lee and George Trager. 1937. 'The relationship of Uto-Aztecan and Tanoan'. *American Anthropologist* 39: 609–624.

Wilkins, David. 1996. 'Natural tendencies of semantic change and the search for cognates'. In Durie and Ross (1996), pp. 264–304.

Winter, Werner. 1978. 'The distribution of short and long vowels in stems of the type Lith. *ésti* : *vèsti* : *mèsti* and OCS *jasti* : *vesti* : *mesti* in Baltic and Slavic languages'. In Jacek Fisiak (ed.), *Recent Developments in Historical Phonology*, pp. 431–446, The Hague: Mouton.

———— 1998. 'Tocharian'. In Giacalone Ramat and Ramat (1998), pp. 154–168.

Witkowski, S. R. and C. H. Brown. 1985. 'Climate, clothing and body-part nomenclature'. *Ethnology* 24: 197–214.

Wolff, Hans. 1950–51. 'Comparative Siouan: parts I–IV'. *International Journal of American Linguistics* 16: 61–66; 113–121; 168–178; 17: 197–204.

Wright, Joseph. 1910. *Grammar of the Gothic Language.* Oxford: Clarendon Press.

Wright, Laura. 1997. 'More on the history of "shit" and "shut"'. *Studia Anglica Posnaniensia* 32: 3–16.

Wright, Robert. 1991. 'Quest for the mother tongue'. *Atlantic Monthly* (April), pp. 39–68.

Wright, Roger. 1982. *Late Latin and Early Romance in Spain and Carolingian France.* Liverpool: Francis Cairns.

Wurm, Stephen A. 1982. *The Papuan Languages of New Guinea.* Tübingen: Gunter Narr.

Zipf, George K. 1929. 'Relative frequency as a determinant of phonetic change'. *Harvard Studies in Classical Philology* 40: 1–95.

———— 1936. *The Psycho-Biology of Language: An Introduction to Dynamic Phonology.* London: Routledge.

Flagler College Library
P.O. Box 1027
St. Augustine, FL 32085